Reading STREET

Program Authors

Peter Afflerbach

Camille Blachowicz

Candy Dawson Boyd

Elena Izquierdo

Connie Juel

Edward Kame'enui

Donald Leu

Jeanne Paratore

Sam Sebesta

Deborah Simmons

Alfred Tatum

Sharon Vaughn

Susan Watts Taffe

Karen Kring Wixson

PEARSON

Glenview, Illinois • Boston, Massachusetts
Chandler, Arizona • Upper Saddle River, New Jersey

We dedicate Reading Street to
Peter Jovanovich.

His wisdom, courage,
and passion for education
are an inspiration to us all.

This work is protected by the United States copyright laws and is
provided *solely for the use of teachers and administrators* in teaching
courses and assessing student learning in their classes and schools.
Dissemination or sale of any part of this work (including the World
Wide Web) will destroy the integrity of the work and is *not* permitted.

Accelerated Reader

ISBN-13: 978-0-328-46995-6
ISBN-10:   0-328-46995-5

Copyright © 2011 Pearson Education, Inc. or its affiliate(s).

1 2 3 4 5 6 7 8 9 10   13 12 11 10 09

Any Path, Any Pace

Reading STREET

CALLE de la Lectura

"Welcome to Reading Street! Bienvenidos too."

PEARSON

PEARSON

SCOTT FORESMAN

Find Your Place on Reading Street!

Who said so?

The Leading Researchers,

Program Authors

Peter Afflerbach, Ph.D.
Professor
Department of Curriculum
and Instruction
University of Maryland
at College Park

Camille L. Z. Blachowicz, Ph.D.
Professor of Education
National-Louis University

Candy Dawson Boyd, Ph.D.
Professor
School of Education
Saint Mary's College of California

Elena Izquierdo, Ph.D.
Associate Professor
University of Texas at El Paso

Connie Juel, Ph.D.
Professor of Education
School of Education
Stanford University

Edward J. Kame'enui, Ph.D.
*Dean-Knight Professor of
Education and Director*
Institute for the Development of
Educational Achievement and
the Center on Teaching and Learning
College of Education
University of Oregon

Donald J. Leu, Ph.D.
*John and Maria Neag Endowed
Chair in Literacy and Technology
Director, The New Literacies
Research Lab*
University of Connecticut

Jeanne R. Paratore, Ed.D.
Associate Professor of Education
Department of Literacy and
Language Development
Boston University

P. David Pearson, Ph.D.
Professor and Dean
Graduate School of Education
University of California, Berkeley

Sam L. Sebesta, Ed.D.
Professor Emeritus
College of Education
University of Washington, Seattle

Deborah Simmons, Ph.D.
Professor
College of Education and
Human Development
Texas A&M University

Alfred W. Tatum, Ph.D.
*Associate Professor and Director
of the UIC Reading Clinic*
University of Illinois at Chicago

Sharon Vaughn, Ph.D.
*H. E. Hartfelder/Southland
Corporation Regents Professor
Director, Meadows Center for
Preventing Educational Risk*
University of Texas

Susan Watts Taffe, Ph.D.
Associate Professor in Literacy
Division of Teacher Education
University of Cincinnati

Karen Kring Wixson, Ph.D.
Professor of Education
University of Michigan

Consulting Authors

Jeff Anderson, M.Ed.
Author and Consultant
San Antonio, Texas

Jim Cummins, Ph.D.
Professor
Department of Curriculum,
Teaching and Learning
University of Toronto

Lily Wong Fillmore, Ph.D.
Professor Emerita
Graduate School of Education
University of California, Berkeley

Georgia Earnest García, Ph.D.
Professor
Language and Literacy Division
Department of Curriculum
and Instruction
University of Illinois at
Urbana-Champaign

George A. González, Ph.D.
Professor (Retired)
School of Education
University of Texas-Pan American,
Edinburg

Valerie Ooka Pang, Ph.D.
Professor
School of Teacher Education
San Diego State University

Sally M. Reis, Ph.D.
*Board of Trustees Distinguished
Professor*
Department of Educational
Psychology
University of Connecticut

Jon Scieszka, M.F.A.
*Children's Book Author
Founder of GUYS READ
Named First National Ambassador
for Young People's Literature 2008*

Grant Wiggins, Ed.D.
Educational Consultant
Authentic Education
Concept Development

Lee Wright, M.Ed.
Pearland, Texas

Practitioners, and Authors.

Consultant

Sharroky Hollie, Ph.D.
Assistant Professor
California State University
Dominguez Hills

Teacher Reviewers

Dr. Bettyann Brugger
*Educational Support Coordinator—
Reading Office*
Milwaukee Public Schools
Milwaukee, WI

Kathleen Burke
K–12 Reading Coordinator
Peoria Public Schools, Peoria, IL

Darci Burns, M.S.Ed.
University of Oregon

Bridget Cantrell
District Intervention Specialist
Blackburn Elementary School
Independence, Missouri

**Tahira DuPree Chase,
M.A., M.S.Ed.**
*Administrator of Elementary
English Language Arts*
Mount Vernon City School District
Mount Vernon, NY

Michele Conner
Director, Elementary Education
Aiken County School District
Aiken, SC

Georgia Coulombe
*K–6 Regional Trainer/
Literacy Specialist*
Regional Center for Training and
Learning (RCTL), Reno, NV

Kelly Dalmas
Third Grade Teacher
Avery's Creek Elementary, Arden, NC

Seely Dillard
First Grade Teacher
Laurel Hill Primary School
Mt. Pleasant, South Carolina

Jodi Dodds-Kinner
Director of Elementary Reading
Chicago Public Schools, Chicago, IL

Dr. Ann Wild Evenson
District Instructional Coach
Osseo Area Schools, Maple Grove, MN

Stephanie Fascitelli
Principal
Apache Elementary, Albuquerque
Public Schools, Albuquerque, NM

Alice Franklin
*Elementary Coordinator, Language
Arts & Reading*
Spokane Public Schools, Spokane, WA

Laureen Fromberg
Assistant Principal
PS 100 Queens, NY

Kimberly Gibson
First Grade Teacher
Edgar B. Davis Community School
Brockton, Massachusetts

Kristen Gray
Lead Teacher
A.T. Allen Elementary School
Concord, NC

Mary Ellen Hazen
State Pre-K Teacher
Rockford Public Schools #205
Rockford, Illinois

Patrick M. Johnson
Elementary Instructional Director
Seattle Public Schools, Seattle, WA

Theresa Jaramillo Jones
Principal
Highland Elementary School
Las Cruces, NM

Sophie Kowzun
*Program Supervisor, Reading/
Language Arts, PreK-5*
Montgomery County Public Schools
Rockville, MD

David W. Matthews
Sixth Grade Teacher
Easton Area Middle School
Easton, Pennsylvania

Ana Nuncio
Editor and Independent Publisher
Salem, MA

Joseph Peila
Principal
Chappell Elementary School
Chicago, Illinois

Ivana Reimer
Literacy Coordinator
PS 100 Queens, NY

Sally Riley
Curriculum Coordinator
Rochester Public Schools
Rochester, NH

Dyan M. Smiley
*English Language Arts Program
Director, Grades K-5*
Boston Public Schools, Literacy
Department, Boston, Massachusetts

Michael J. Swiatowiec
Lead Literacy Teacher
Graham Elementary School
Chicago, Illinois

Dr. Helen Taylor
Director of Reading/English Education
Portsmouth City Public Schools
Portsmouth, VA

Carol Thompson
Teaching and Learning Coach
Independence School District
Independence, MO

Erinn Zeitlin
Kindergarten Teacher
Carderock Springs Elementary School
Bethesda, Maryland

Any Path, Any Pace

UNIT R

My World

In this Teacher's Edition Unit R, Volume 2

WEEK 4 · The Big Top

WEEK 5 · School Day

WEEK 6 · Farmers Market

In the First Stop on Reading Street

- **Dear First Grade Teacher**
- **Research into Practice**
- **Guide to Reading Street**
- **Assessment on Reading Street**
- **Customize Writing on Reading Street**
- **Differentiated Instruction on Reading Street**

- **ELL on Reading Street**
- **Customize Literacy on Reading Street**
- **Digital Products on Reading Street**
- **Teacher Resources for Grade 1**
- **Index**

 GO Digital!

See It!

- **Big Question Video**
- **Concept Talk Video**
- **Interactive Sound-Spelling Cards**
- **Envision It! Animations**
- **Sing with Me Animations**

Hear It!

- **Sing with Me Animations**
- **eSelections**
- **Grammar Jammer**
- **eReaders**
- **Leveled Reader Database**

Do It!

- **Vocabulary Activities**
- **Online Journal**
- **Story Sort**
- **21st Century Skills Activities**
- **Online Assessment**
- **Letter Tile Drag and Drop**

UNIT R

My World

Volume 1

Volume 2

UNIT 1

Animals, Tame and Wild

Volume 1

Volume 2

UNIT 2

Communities

Volume 1

WEEK 1 • **A Big Fish for Max** Animal Fantasy 12a–43l

At Home Literary Nonfiction

Differentiated Instruction SI OL A ELL .... DI•1–DI•21

WEEK 2 • **The Farmer in the Hat** Realistic Fiction 44a–77l

Helping Hands at 4-H Expository Text

Differentiated Instruction SI OL A ELL .... DI•22–DI•42

WEEK 3 • **Who Works Here?** Expository Text 78a–103l

Neighborhood Map Procedural Text

Differentiated Instruction SI OL A ELL .... DI•43–DI•63

Volume 2

WEEK 4 • **The Big Circle** Fiction 104a–137l

We Are Safe Together Literary Nonfiction

Differentiated Instruction SI OL A ELL .... DI•64–DI•84

WEEK 5 • **Life in the Forest** Expository Text 138a–169l

A Mangrove Forest Magazine Article

Differentiated Instruction SI OL A ELL .... DI•85–DI•105

WEEK 6 • **Honey Bees** Expository Text........................170a–201n

Poetry Collection Poetry

Differentiated Instruction SI OL A ELL .... DI•106–DI•126

Customized Writing ....CW•1–CW•20
Customize Literacy..CL•1–CL•47
Let's Learn Amazing Words ....OV•1–OV•3

UNIT 3

Changes

Volume 1

WEEK 1 · A Place to Play Realistic Fiction....................12a–43l
My Neighborhood, Then and Now Autobiography
Differentiated Instruction SI OL A ELL ....DI•1–DI•21

WEEK 2 · Ruby in Her Own Time
Animal Fantasy...44a–83l
The Ugly Duckling Fairy Tale
Differentiated Instruction SI OL A ELL ....DI•22–DI•42

WEEK 3 · The Class Pet Expository Text........................84a–117l
Belling the Cat Fable
Differentiated Instruction SI OL A ELL ....DI•43–DI•63

Volume 2

WEEK 4 · Frog and Toad Together
Animal Fantasy...118a–149l
Growing Plants How-to Article
Differentiated Instruction SI OL A ELL ....DI•64–DI•84

WEEK 5 · I'm a Caterpillar Literary Nonfiction.........150a–181l
My Computer 21st Century Skills
Differentiated Instruction SI OL A ELL ....DI•85–DI•105

WEEK 6 · Where Are My Animal Friends? Drama............182a–217n
Poetry Collection Poetry
Differentiated Instruction SI OL A ELL ....DI•106–DI•126

UNIT 4

Treasures

Key
- **SI** Strategic Intervention
- **OL** On-Level
- **A** Advanced
- **ELL** ELL

Volume 1

Volume 2

UNIT 5

Great Ideas

Volume 1

Volume 2

Skills Overview

Key	
T	Tested Skill
	Target Skill

	WEEK 1 	WEEK 2 
	Sam Realistic Fiction pp. 18–27	**Snap!** Realistic Fiction pp. 44–53
	Rip Van Winkle Folk Tale pp. 32–33	**Families** Photo Essay pp. 58–59

Get Ready to Read

	WEEK 1	WEEK 2
Question of the Week	What is around us at home?	Who is in our family?
Amazing Words	*furniture, tidy, unwind, cozy, middle, straw, yawn*	*adult, childhood, depend, portrait, gallery, entertain, scurry*
Phonemic Awareness	Match Initial Phonemes Isolate Phonemes Blend Onset and Rime	Match Initial and Final Phonemes Isolate Initial, Medial, and Final Phonemes Identify Words that Rhyme and Don't Rhyme
Phonics	**T** Consonants *m, s, t* **T** Vowel: Short *a*	**T** Consonants *c, p, n* **T** Vowel: Short *a*

Read and Comprehend

	WEEK 1	WEEK 2
Comprehension	**T** **Skill** Character **Strategy** Questioning Review **Skill** Setting	**T** **Skill** Setting **Strategy** Predict and Set Purpose Review **Skill** Character
High-Frequency Words	**T** *I, see, a, green*	**T** *we, like, the, one*
Vocabulary	Sort Nouns	Descriptive Words
Fluency	Oral Rereading	Oral Rereading

Language Arts

	WEEK 1	WEEK 2
Writing	Nouns in Sentences Trait: Word Choice	Nouns in Sentences Trait: Word Choice
Conventions	**T** Nouns: People, Animals, and Things	**T** Nouns: Places
Speaking/Listening	Listen Attentively	Speak in Front of Others
Research Skills	Parts of a Book	Parts of a Book

The Big Question
What is all around me?

WEEK 3	WEEK 4	WEEK 5	WEEK 6
Tip and Tam Realistic Fiction pp. 70–79 **Yards** Photo Essay pp. 84–85	**The Big Top** Realistic Fiction pp. 96–105 **Around the Block** Procedural Text pp. 110–111	**School Day** Realistic Fiction pp. 122–131 **How Do You Get to School?** Photo Essay pp. 136–137	**Farmers Market** Realistic Fiction pp. 148–157 **The Maid and the Milk Pail** Fable pp. 162–163
What is outside our door?	What can we do with our neighborhood friends?	What is around us at school?	What can we see around our neighborhood?
active, lawn, pavement, newspaper, puddle, banner, overflowing, patio	*amusing, neighbor, introduce, corner, trouble, deliver, porch, squirrel*	*classmate, education, polite, principal, recess, science, complicated, success, applaud*	*bargain, browse, bustling, library, fact, cost, customer, scale*
Isolate Initial, Medial, and Final Phonemes Blend and Segment Phonemes Count Phonemes	Isolate Initial, Medial, and Final Phonemes Blend Onset and Rime Blend and Segment Phonemes	Blend and Segment Phonemes Distinguish Words that Rhyme and Don't Rhyme Identify Syllables	Isolate Initial, Medial, and Final Phonemes Blend and Segment Phonemes Identify Syllables
T Consonants *b, g, f* T Vowel: Short *i*	T Consonants *d, l, h* T Vowel: Short *o*	T Consonants *r, w, j, k* T Vowel: Short *e*	T Consonants *v, y, z, qu* T Vowel: Short *u*
Skill Plot **Strategy** Story Structure Review **Skill** Setting	**Skill** Realism and Fantasy **Strategy** Questioning Review **Skill** Plot	**Skill** Plot **Strategy** Monitor and Clarify Review **Skill** Realism and Fantasy	**Skill** Realism and Fantasy **Strategy** Background Knowledge Review **Skill** Setting
T *look, do, you, was, yellow*	T *they, have, two, that, are*	T *is, he, three, with, to*	T *where, go, here, for, me*
Sort Nouns and Verbs	Sort Descriptive Words	Use Descriptive Words	Sort Nouns
Oral Rereading	Oral Rereading	Oral Rereading	Oral Rereading
Verbs in Sentences Trait: Word Choice	Simple Sentences Trait: Sentences	Sentences with Adjectives Trait: Word Choice	Sentences with Nouns, Verbs, and Adjectives Trait: Sentences
T Verbs	T Simple Sentences	T Adjectives	T Sentences
Participate in a Discussion	Share Ideas	Follow Instructions	Share Information and Ideas
Signs	Maps	Calendar	Library/Media Center

UNIT R

Monitor Progess
Make Data-Driven Decisions

Data Management
- Assess
- Diagnose
- Prescribe
- Disaggregate

Classroom Management
- Monitor Progress
- Group
- Differentiate Instruction
- Inform Parents

Don't Wait Until Friday

SUCCESS PREDICTORS	WEEK 1	WEEK 2	WEEK 3	WEEK 4
Word Reading / **Phonics**	T Consonants *m, s, t* T Vowels: Short *a*	T Consonants *c, p, n* T Vowels: Short *a*	T Consonants *b, g, f* T Vowels: Short *i*	T Consonants *d, l, h* T Vowels: Short *o*
WCPM / **Fluency**	Oral Rereading	Oral Rereading	Oral Rereading	Oral Rereading
Vocabulary / **High-Frequency Words**	T I T see T a T green	T we T like T the T one	T look T do T you T was T yellow	T they T have T two T that T are
Vocabulary / **Oral Vocabulary/ Concept Development** (assessed informally)	furniture tidy unwind cozy middle straw yawn	adult childhood depend portrait gallery entertain scurry	active lawn pavement newspaper puddle banner overflowing patio	amusing neighbor introduce corner trouble deliver porch squirrel
Retelling / **Text Comprehension**	T **Skill** Character **Strategy** Questioning	T **Skill** Setting **Strategy** Predict and Set Purpose	T **Skill** Plot **Strategy** Story Structure	T **Skill** Realism and Fantasy **Strategy** Questioning

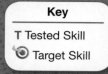

Key

T Tested Skill

Target Skill

WEEK 5	WEEK 6
T Consonants *r, w, j, k* T Vowels: Short *e*	T Consonants *v, y, z, qu* T Vowels: Short *u*
Oral Rereading	Oral Rereading
T is T he T three T with T to	T where T go T here T for T me
classmate education polite principal recess science complicated success applaud	bargain browse bustling library fact cost customer scale
T **Skill** Plot **Strategy** Monitor and Clarify	T **Skill** Realism and Fantasy **Strategy** Background Knowledge

Online Classroom

Manage Data

- Assign the Unit R Benchmark Test for students to take online.

- Online Assessment records results and generates reports by school, grade, classroom, or student.

- Use reports to disaggregate and aggregate Unit R skills and standards data to monitor progress.

- Based on class lists created to support the categories important for AYP (gender, ethnicity, migrant education, English proficiency, disabilities, economic status), reports let you track adequate yearly progress every six weeks.

Group

- Use results from Unit R Benchmark Tests taken online through Online Assessment to measure whether students have mastered the English-Language Arts Content Standards taught in this unit.

- Reports in Online Assessment suggest whether students need Extra Support or Intervention.

Individualized Instruction

- Tests are correlated to Unit R tested skills and standards so that prescriptions for individual teaching and learning plans can be created.

- Individualized prescriptions target instruction and accelerate student progress toward learning outcome goals.

- Prescriptions include remediation activities and resources to reteach Unit R skills and standards.

UNIT R

Assessment and Grouping
for Data-Driven Instruction

4-Step Plan for Assessment
1 Diagnose and Differentiate
2 Monitor Progress
3 Assess and Regroup
4 Summative Assessment

STEP 1 Diagnose and Differentiate

Baseline Group Test

Diagnose

To make initial grouping decisions, use the Baseline Group Test or another initial placement test. Depending on children's ability levels, you may have more than one of each group.

Differentiate

If... student performance is **SI** **then...** use the regular instruction and the daily **Strategic Intervention** small group lessons.

If... student performance is **OL** **then...** use the regular instruction for and the daily **On-Level** small group lessons.

If... student performance is **A** **then...** use the regular instruction and the daily **Advanced** learners small group lessons.

Small Group Time

SI Strategic Intervention

- Daily small group lessons provide more intensive instruction, more scaffolding, more practice, and more opportunities to respond.
- Reteach lesson in the *First Stop on Reading Street* provide additional instructional opportunities with target skills.
- Leveled readers build background and practice target skills and vocabulary.

OL On-Level

- Explicit instructional routines teach core skills and strategies.
- Daily On-Level lessons provide more practice and more opportunities to respond.
- Independent activities provide practice for core skills and extension and enrichment options.
- Leveled reader provides additional reading and practice core skills and vocabulary.

A Advanced

- Daily Advanced lessons provide instruction for accelerated learning.
- Leveled reader provides additional reading tied to lesson concepts.

Additional Differentiated Learning Options

Reading Street Intervention Kit
- Focused intervention lessons on the five critical areas of reading: phonemic awareness, phonics, vocabulary, comprehension, and fluency.

My Sidewalks on Reading Street
- Intensive intervention for struggling readers.

STEP 2 Monitor Progress

Use these tools during lesson teaching to **monitor student progress.**

- **Skill and Strategy** instruction during reading.
- **Don't Wait Until Friday** boxes to check word reading, retelling, fluency, and oral vocabulary.
- **Weekly Assessment** on Day 5 checks phonics and fluency.
- **Reader's and Writer's Notebook** pages at point of use.
- **Weekly Tests** assess target skills for the week.
- **Fresh Reads** for Fluency and Comprehension.

Weekly Tests

Fresh Reads for Fluency and Comprehension

STEP 3 Assess and Regroup

Use these tools during lesson teaching assess and regroup.

- **Weekly Assessments** Record results of weekly assessments in retelling, phonics, and fluency to track student progress.
- **Unit Benchmark Test** Administer this test to check mastery of unit skills.
- **Regroup** We recommend the first regrouping to be at the end of Unit 1. Use weekly assessment information and Unit Benchmark Test performance to inform regrouping decisions. Then regroup at the end of each subsequent unit.

First Stop on Reading Street Assessment Chart

Group
Baseline ———→ Regroup ———→ Regroup ———→ Regroup ———→ Regroup ———→ End of Year
Group Test   Units R and 1   Unit 3   Unit 4   Unit 5

| Unit R Weeks 1–6 | Unit 1 Weeks 7–12 | Unit 2 Weeks 13–18 | Unit 3 Weeks 19–24 | Unit 4 Week 25–30 | Unit 5 Weeks 31–36 |

Outside assessments, such as DRA, TPRI, and DIBELS, may recommend regrouping at other times during the year.

STEP 4 Summative Assessment

Use these tools after lesson teaching to assess students.

- **Unit Benchmark Tests** Use to measure a student's mastery of each unit's skills.
- **End-of-Year Benchmark Test** Use to measure a student's mastery of program skills covered in all six units.

Unit and End of Year Benchmark Tests

Understanding By Design

Grant Wiggins, Ed. D.
Reading Street Author

"Big ideas are the building material of understandings. They can be thought of as the meaningful patterns that enable one to connect the dots of otherwise fragmented knowledge."

My World

Reading Street Online

www.ReadingStreet.com
• Big Question Video
• eSelections
• Envision It! Animations
• Story Sort

What is all around me?

UNIT **R**

Small Group Time
Flexible Pacing Plans

Small Group Time

Sometimes you have holidays, programs, assemblies, or other interruptions to the school week. This plan can help you make Small Group Time decisions if you have less time during the week.

Key
SI Strategic Intervention
OL On-Level
A Advanced
ELL ELL

A **OL** **SI**

5 Day Plan
DAY 1
- Phonemic Awareness
- Phonics
- Reading Practice

DAY 2
- Phonemic Awareness
- Phonics
- Reading Practice

DAY 3
- Phonics
- Leveled Reader

DAY 4
- High-Frequency Words
- Reading Practice

DAY 5
- Phonics
- Comprehension

4 Day Plan
DAY 1
- Phonemic Awareness
- Phonics
- Reading Practice

DAY 2
- High-Frequency Words
- Leveled Reader

DAY 3
- Phonics
- Leveled Reader

DAY 4
- High-Frequency Words
- Reading Practice

3 Day Plan
DAY 1
- Phonemic Awareness
- Phonics
- Reading Practice

DAY 2
- Phonics
- Leveled Reader

DAY 3
- High-Frequency Words
- Reading Practice

ELL

5 Day Plan
DAY 1
- Concepts
- Comprehension
- Phonemic Awareness/ Phonics

DAY 2
- Concepts and Oral Vocabulary
- Phonemic Awareness/ Phonics
- Spelling

DAY 3
- Concepts
- Vocabulary
- Comprehension

DAY 4
- Concepts
- Vocabulary
- ELL/ELD Readers

DAY 5
- Concepts
- Conventions
- Editing and Revising

4 Day Plan
DAY 1
- Concepts
- Comprehension
- Phonemic Awareness/ Phonics

DAY 2
- Concepts
- Vocabulary
- Comprehension

DAY 3
- Concepts
- Vocabulary
- ELL/ELD Readers

DAY 4
- Concepts
- Conventions
- Editing and Revising

3 Day Plan
DAY 1
- Concepts
- Comprehension
- Phonemic Awareness/ Phonics

DAY 2
- Concepts
- Vocabulary
- Comprehension

DAY 3
- Concepts
- Vocabulary
- ELL/ELD Readers

This Week's ELL Overview

ELL Handbook

- Maximize Literacy and Cognitive Engagement
- Research Into Practice
- Full Weekly Support for Every Selection

The Big Top
- Multi-Lingual Summaries in Five Languages
- Selection-Specific Vocabulary Word Cards
- Frontloading/Reteaching for Comprehension Skill Lessons
- ELD and ELL Reader Study Guides

- Transfer Activities
- Professional Development

Daily Leveled ELL Notes

ELL notes appear throughout this week's instruction and ELL Support is on the DI pages of your Teacher's Edition. The following is a sample of an ELL note from this week.

English Language Learners

Beginning After reading, lead children through a picture walk through *On Top*. Have children tell what Tom or Dot is doing in each picture.

Intermediate After reading, have children make up a sentence about one of the characters: Tom, Dot, or Mom. Monitor children's pronunciation.

Advanced After reading, draw a T-chart with the headings: *Names with o* and *Words with o.* Have children write the short *o* names and words from the story in the appropriate column. Then have them select four to use in sentences.

Advanced High After reading, organize children into pairs. Have partners discuss the characters and the main idea of the story, using the short *o* names and words from the story in their discussion.

ELL by Strand

The ELL lessons on this week's Support for English Language Learners pages are organized by strand. They offer additional scaffolding for the core curriculum. Leveled support notes on these pages address the different proficiency levels in your class. See pages DI•75–DI•84.

ELL Guy
Dr. Jim Cummins

The Three Pillars of ELL Instruction

ELL Strands	Activate Prior Knowledge	Access Content	Extend Language
Vocabulary p. DI•79	Preteach	Teach/Model	Practice
Reading Comprehension p. DI•80	Preteach	Reteach/Practice	Leveled Practice Activities
Phonics, Spelling, and Word Analysis pp. DI•76–DI•77	Preteach	Listen and Write	Leveled Practice Activities
Listening Comprehension p. DI•78	Prepare for the Read Aloud	First Listening	Second Listening
Conventions and Writing pp. DI•83–DI•84	Preteach	Leveled Practice Activities	Leveled Practice Activities; Leveled Writing Activities
Concept Development p. DI•75	Activate Prior Knowledge	Develop Concepts	Review Concepts and Connect to Writing

This Week's Practice Stations Overview

Six Weekly Practice Stations with Leveled Activities can be found at the beginning of each week of instruction. For this week's Practice Stations, see pp. 88h–88i.

Small Group • Teacher-led

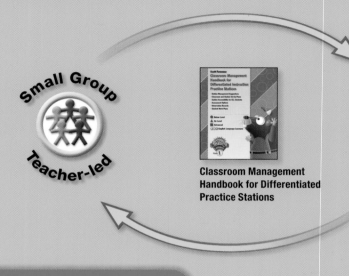

Classroom Management Handbook for Differentiated Practice Stations

Practice Stations

Daily Leveled Center Activities

- ● Below
- ▲ On-Level
- ■ Advanced
- **E L L**

Practice Stations Flip Charts

	Listen Up!	Word Work	Words to Know	Let's Write!	Read for Meaning	Get Fluent
Objectives	• Identify things with sounds /b/, /g/, /f/, and /i/. • Distinguish between initial and final /b/, /g/, and /f/.	• Identify words with the sounds of *b, g, f,* and *i/i/.* • Pronounce and spell words with *b, g, f,* and *i/i/.*	• Identify high-frequency words *look, do, you, was, yellow.* • Spell high-frequency words *look, do, you, was, yellow.*	• Write sentences with verbs that show action.	• Identify the plot of a story. • Identify the problem in a plot. • Identify the solution to the problem.	• Develop fluency by listening and following along with familiar texts.
Materials	• *Listen Up!* Flip Chart Activity R4 • Picture Cards	• *Word Work* Flip Chart Activity R4 • ELL Poster • Letter Tiles • Picture Cards	• *Words to Know* Flip Chart Activity R4 • Word Cards • paper and pencils • Letter Tiles	• *Let's Write!* Flip Chart Activity R4 • Picture Cards of animals • paper • pencils	• *Read for Meaning* Flip Chart Activity R4 • Student Edition Unit R • paper • pencils • crayons	• AudioText CD for *The Big Top* and "Around the Block" • Student Edition • CD player

This Week on Reading Street!

Question of the Week
What can we do with our neighborhood friends?

My World

Daily Plan

Don't Wait Until Friday

Whole Group
- Consonants *d, l, h*
- Short *o: o*
- Vocabulary

MONITOR PROGRESS	Success Predictor			
Day 1 Check Word Reading	Day 2 Check Word Reading	Day 3 Check Word Reading Check High-Frequency Words	Day 4 Check Word Reading: Check Retelling	Day 5 Check Oral Vocabulary: Check Phonemic Awareness

Small Group

Teacher-Led
- Reading Support
- Skill Support

Practice Stations

Independent Activities

Customize Literacy More support for a Balanced Literacy approach, see CL•1–CL•47.

Customize Writing More support for a customized writing approach, see pp. CW•11–CW•20.

Whole Group
- Writing: Simple Sentences
- Conventions: Simple Sentences

Assessment
- Weekly Tests
- Day 5 Assessment
- Fresh Reads

You Are Here! Unit R Week 4

This Week's Reading Selections

Main Selection Genre: Realistic Fiction

Paired Selection

Decodable Practice Readers

Concept Literacy Reader

ELL and ELD Readers

Resources on Reading Street!

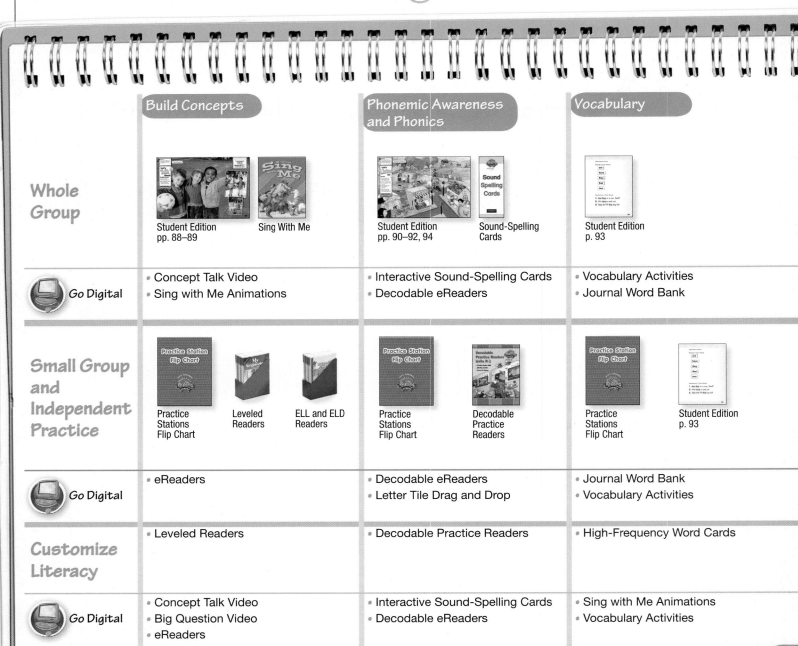

	Build Concepts	**Phonemic Awareness and Phonics**	**Vocabulary**
Whole Group	Student Edition pp. 88–89 — Sing With Me	Student Edition pp. 90–92, 94 — Sound-Spelling Cards	Student Edition p. 93
Go Digital	• Concept Talk Video • Sing with Me Animations	• Interactive Sound-Spelling Cards • Decodable eReaders	• Vocabulary Activities • Journal Word Bank
Small Group and Independent Practice	Practice Stations Flip Chart — Leveled Readers — ELL and ELD Readers	Practice Stations Flip Chart — Decodable Practice Readers	Practice Stations Flip Chart — Student Edition p. 93
Go Digital	• eReaders	• Decodable eReaders • Letter Tile Drag and Drop	• Journal Word Bank • Vocabulary Activities
Customize Literacy	• Leveled Readers	• Decodable Practice Readers	• High-Frequency Word Cards
Go Digital	• Concept Talk Video • Big Question Video • eReaders	• Interactive Sound-Spelling Cards • Decodable eReaders	• Sing with Me Animations • Vocabulary Activities

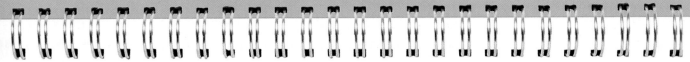

 Question of the Week
What can we do with our neighborhood friends?

Week 4

Comprehension

Student Edition
pp. 96–107

- Envision It! Animations
- eSelections

Practice
Stations
Flip Chart

Leveled
Readers

ELL and ELD
Readers

- eReaders

- Envision It! Skills and Strategies
  Handbooks
- Leveled Readers

- Envision It! Animations
- eReaders

Conventions and Writing

Student Edition
pp. 108–109

- Grammar Jammer
- Online Journal

Practice
Stations
Flip Chart

Reader's and
Writer's Notebook

- Grammar Jammer
- Online Journal

- Reader's and Writer's Notebook

- Grammar Jammer
- Online Journal

You Are Here! Unit R Week 4

My 5-Day Planner for Reading Street!

SUCCESS PREDICTOR — Don't Wait Until Friday

	Check Word Reading **Day 1** pages 88j–91i	**Check Word Reading** **Day 2** pages 92a–93e
Get Ready to Read	**Concept Talk,** 88j–89 **Oral Vocabulary,** 89a–89b *amusing, introduce, neighbor* **Phonemic Awareness,** 90–91 Match Initial, Medial, and Final Phonemes **Phonics,** 91a–91c ◉ Consonant *d* /d/	**Concept Talk,** 92a–92b **Oral Vocabulary,** 92b *corner, trouble* **Print Awareness,** 92c Identify Information **Phonemic Awareness,** 92d Isolate Initial, Medial, and Final Phonemes **Phonics,** 92e–92 ◉ Consonant *l, ll* /l/
Read and Comprehend	**Listening Comprehension,** 91d–91e ◉ Realism and Fantasy	**Comprehension,** 93a ◉ Realism and Fantasy **Vocabulary,** 93a Sort Descriptive Words **High-Frequency Words,** 93 Introduce *are, have, that, they, two*
Language Arts	**Conventions,** 91f Simple Sentences **Handwriting,** 91g Letter *D* and *d*; Proper Letter Size **Writing,** 91h Simple Sentences **Listening and Speaking,** 91i Share Information and Ideas	**Conventions,** 93b Simple Sentences **Handwriting,** 93c Letter *L* and *l*; Proper Body/Paper Position **Writing,** 93d Simple Sentences **Listening and Speaking,** 93e Give Directions

You Are Here! Unit R Week 4

Check Word Reading: Check High-Frequency Words	Check Word Reading: Check Retelling	Check Oral Vocabulary: Check Phonemic Awareness
Day 3 pages 94a–94l	**Day 4** pages 94m–109c	**Day 5** pages 110a–113e
Concept Talk, 94a–94b **Oral Vocabulary,** 94b *deliver* **Print Awareness,** 94c Sequence Letters **Phonological Awareness,** 94d Rhyming Words **Phonics,** 94e–94g ◉ Consonant *h* /h/	**Concept Talk,** 94m–94n **Oral Vocabulary,** 94n *porch, squirrel* **Print Awareness,** 94o Sequence Letters **Phonemic Awareness,** 94p Segment and Blend Phonemes **Phonics,** 94q–94 ◉ Short *o: o* **READ Decodable Practice Reader** R4A, 95a–95b	**Concept Wrap Up,** 110a `Review` **Oral Vocabulary,** 110b **Print Awareness,** 110c Sequence Letters **Phonological Awareness,** 110d Blend Onsets and Rimes `Review` **Fluent Word Reading,** 110e `Review` **Phonics,** 110f ◉ *d* /d/, *l, ll* /l/, *h* /h/; Short *o: o* `Review` **High-Frequency Words,** 110f **READ Decodable Practice Reader** R4B, 110g–110h
High-Frequency Words, 94h Practice *are, have, that, they, two*	**Literary Text,** 95c Realistic Fiction **High-Frequency Words,** 95 Build Fluency *are, have, that, they, two* **Build Background,** 96a **READ Main Selection,** 96b–107a *The Big Top*	**Social Studies in Reading,** 110i **READ Paired Selection,** 110–111 "Around the Block" **Listening and Speaking,** 112–113 Give Instructions **Vocabulary,** 113a Sort Words **Handwriting,** 113a Letter Size **Assessment,** 113b–113c Monitor Progress
Conventions, 94i Simple Sentences **Handwriting,** 94j Letter *H* and *h*; Self-Evaluation **Writing,** 94k Simple Sentences **Listening and Speaking,** 94l Give Directions	**Conventions,** 108–109 Simple Sentences **Writing,** 109a Simple Sentences **Research,** 109b Maps **Handwriting,** 109c Letter *O* and *o*; Letter Size	`Review` **Conventions,** 113d Simple Sentences **Writing,** 113d Simple Sentences **Wrap Up Your Week,** 113e Question of the Week What can we do with our neighborhood friends?

Week 4

Grouping Options for Differentiated Instruction
Turn the page for the small group time lesson plan.

Planning Small Group Time on Reading Street!

SMALL GROUP TIME RESOURCES

Look for this Small Group Time box each day to help meet the individual needs of all your children. Differentiated Instruction lessons appear on the DI pages at the end of each week.

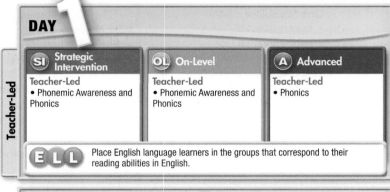

DAY 1

Teacher-Led

SI Strategic Intervention	**OL** On-Level	**A** Advanced
Teacher-Led	Teacher-Led	Teacher-Led
• Phonemic Awareness and Phonics	• Phonemic Awareness and Phonics	• Phonics

ELL Place English language learners in the groups that correspond to their reading abilities in English.

Practice Stations
• Listen Up
• Word Work

Independent Activities
• Reader's and Writer's Notebook
• Concept Talk Video

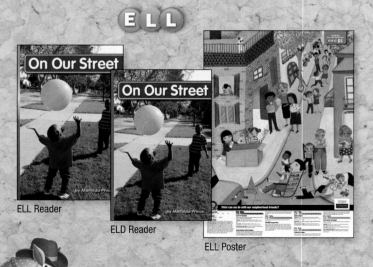

On Our Street

On Our Street

ELL Reader

ELD Reader

ELL Poster

Day 1

SI Strategic Intervention	**Phonemic Awareness and Phonics,** DI•64
OL On-Level	**Phonemic Awareness and Phonics,** DI•69
A Advanced	**Phonics,** DI•72
ELL English Language Learners	DI•75–DI•84 **Concepts and Oral Vocabulary Listening (Read Aloud)**

You Are Here! Unit R Week 4

Reading Street
Intervention Kit

Reading Street
Practice Stations Kit

What can we do with our neighborhood friends?

SI Strategic Intervention

Concept Literacy Reader

Decodable
Practice Readers
Units R-1
- Practice phonics skills
- Blending practice
- Reread for fluency

Decodable Practice Readers

OL On-Level

Concept Literacy Reader

A Advanced

My Friends
By Katherine Anthony

Concept Literacy
Reader

Hat Day on Lot Hill

Advanced Selection

Small Group Weekly Plan

Day 2	Day 3	Day 4	Day 5
Phonemic Awareness and Phonics, DI•65	**Phonemic Awareness and Phonics,** DI•66 **Read Concept Literacy Leveled Reader,** DI•66	**Phonemic Awareness and Phonics,** DI•67 **Read Decodable Practice Reader** R4A, DI•67	**High-Frequency Words,** DI•68 **Read Decodable Practice Reader** R4B, DI•68
Phonics and High-Frequency Words, DI•69	**Read Concept Literacy Leveled Reader,** DI•70	**Conventions,** DI•71	**Phonics Review,** DI•71
Phonics and Comprehension, DI•72	**Read Concept Literacy Leveled Reader,** DI•73	**Comprehension,** DI•74	**Comprehension,** DI•74
DI•75–DI•84 Concepts Vocabulary Phonics and Spelling Conventions	DI•75–DI•84 Concepts Vocabulary Comprehension Skill Main Selection	DI•75–DI•84 Concepts Vocabulary ELL/ELD Readers ELL Workshop	DI•75–DI•84 Concepts Vocabulary Simple Sentences

Practice Stations for Everyone on Reading Street!

Listen Up!
Match sounds and pictures.

Objectives
- Identify things with sounds /b/, /g/, /f/, and /i/.
- Distinguish between initial and final /b/, /g/, and /f/.

Materials
- *Listen Up!* Flip Chart Activity R4
- Picture Cards

Differentiated Activities

⬤ Find Picture Cards with things that start or end like the first sound in *bat.* Then find things that start or end with the first sounds in *go, fan,* and *in.*

▲ Find Picture Cards with things that start or end like the first sound in *bat.* Then find things that start or end with the first sounds in *go, fan,* and *in.* Find things in the room that begin with these sounds.

◼ Find Picture Cards with things that begin or end with the first sounds in *bat, go, fan,* and *in.* Sort them into piles for beginning sounds and ending sounds.

Technology
- Interactive Sound-Spelling Cards

Word Work
Identify the sounds of *b, g, f,* and *i/i/.*

Objectives
- Identify words with the sounds of *b, g, f,* and *i/i/.*
- Pronounce and spell words with *b, g, f,* and *i/i/.*

Materials
- *Word Work* Flip Chart Activity R4
- ELL Poster
- Letter Tiles
- Picture Cards

Have children look at the Picture Cards and the ELL Poster for ideas.

Differentiated Activities

⬤ Find Picture Cards that show things with *b, g, f,* and short *i.* Quietly say each word. Match one of more of the Letter Tiles to each Picture Card that shows a word with the sound of the letter.

▲ Find Picture Cards or objects with *b, g, f,* and short *i.* Quietly say each word. Then use Letter Tiles *b, g, f, i, m, s, t, p, n,* and *a* to spell two words. Say each word.

◼ Find Picture Cards or objects with *b, g, f,* and short *i.* Quietly say each word. Then use Letter Tiles *b, g, f, i, m, s, t, p, n,* and *a* to spell five words. Say each word.

Technology
- Interactive Sound Spelling Cards

Words To Know
Practice high-frequency words.

Objectives
- Identify high-frequency words *look, do, you, was,* and *yellow.*
- Spell high-frequency words *look, do, you, was,* and *yellow.*

Materials
- *Words to Know* Flip Chart Activity R4
- Word Cards
- paper and pencils
- Letter Tiles

Differentiated Activities

⬤ Look at the Word Cards for *look, do, you, was,* and *yellow.* Match Letter Tiles to the letters on the cards. Say each word quietly.

▲ Look at the Word Cards for *look, do, you, was,* and *yellow.* Copy the words on your paper. Say each word quietly.

◼ Look at the Word Cards for *we, the, like, one, look, yellow, do, you,* and *was.* Write two sentences using these words.

Technology
- Online Tested Vocabulary Activities

You Are Here!
Unit R
Week 4

Use this week's materials from the Reading Street Practice Stations Kit to organize this week's stations.

Let's Write!
Use verbs in writing.

Objective
• Write sentences with verbs that show action.

Materials
• *Let's Write!* Flip Chart Activity R4
• Picture Cards of animals
• paper
• pencils

Differentiated Activities

● Think of a verb that shows an action that you like to do. Write a sentence using the verb.

▲ Choose a Picture Card of an animal. Write one sentence that tells about an action that the animal does.

■ Choose three Picture Cards of animals. Write a sentence for each one explaining how that animal moves.

Technology
• Online Journals

Read For Meaning
Identify the plot of a story.

Objectives
• Identify the plot of a story.
• Identify the problem in a plot.
• Identify the solution to the problem.

Materials
• *Read for Meaning* Flip Chart Activity
• Student Edition Unit R
• paper
• pencils
• crayons

Differentiated Activities

A **plot** is what happens in a story. A plot often sets up a problem and builds to a solution.

● Reread *Tip and Tam.* Identify the plot in the story. Draw a picture that shows the problem.

▲ Reread *Tip and Tam.* Think about the story's plot. Write a sentence that explains the problem. Draw a picture to go with your sentence.

■ Reread *Tip and Tam.* Think about the plot of the story. Write a sentence that explains the problem. Then write a sentence that identifies its solution.

Technology
• Online Student Edition

Get Fluent
Listen to fluent reading.

Objective
• Develop fluency by listening and following along with familiar texts.

Materials
• AudioText CD for *The Big Top* and "Around the Block"
• Student Edition
• CD player

Activity

Open your book to the selection *The Big Top.* Track the print as you listen to the AudioText CD. Notice how the reader says the words on each page. Then listen to "Around the Block."

Technology
• Online Main Selection and Paired Selection eText

Week 4

Objectives
- Introduce concepts: neighborhoods and friends.
- Share information and ideas about the concept.

Today at a Glance

Oral Vocabulary
amusing, neighbor, introduce

Phonemic Awareness
Isolate Initial, Medial, Final Phonemes

Phonics
◉ Consonant *d* /d/

Comprehension
◉ Realism and Fantasy

Conventions
Simple Sentences

Handwriting
Letter *D* and *d*/Proper Letter Size

Writing
Simple Sentences

Listening and Speaking
Share Ideas

Concept Talk

Question of the Week

❓ **What can we do with our neighborhood friends?**

Introduce the concept

To build concepts and to focus children's attention, tell them that this week they will talk, sing, read, and write about neighborhoods and friends. Write the Question of the Week, and track the print as you read it.

ROUTINE | **Activate Prior Knowledge** | **Team Talk**

1. **Think** Have children think for a minute about neighborhoods and friends.
2. **Pair** Have pairs of children discuss the question.
3. **Share** Have children share information and their ideas with the group. Remind them to ask questions to clarify information. Guide discussion and encourage elaboration with prompts such as:
   - Who do you like to spend time with in your neighborhood?

Routines Flip Chart

Anchored Talk

Develop oral language

Have children turn to pages 88–89 in their Student Editions. Read the title and look at the photos. Use these questions to guide discussion and create the "What can we do with neighborhood friends?" concept map.

- Look at the picture of the boys. What is one boy holding? (a soccer ball) Soccer is a game, so I'll write *play a game* in a box below the question "What can we do with our neighborhood friends?"
- Look at the girl and the boy. What are they doing? (taking a walk) Let's write go for a *walk* in another box under the question.
- Look at the smallest picture. What are the two girls doing? (swinging) I'll write *swing* in another box.

Oral Vocabulary

Objectives
• Listen closely to speakers and ask questions to help you better understand the topic. • Share information and ideas about the topic. Speak at the correct pace.

Let's Talk About

Neighborhoods
● Share information about neighborhoods.
● Share ideas about what we can do with our neighborhood friends.

READING STREET ONLINE
CONCEPT TALK VIDEO
www.ReadingStreet.com

You've learned **0 2 2** Amazing Words so far this year!

88   89

Student Edition pp. 88–89

Amazing Words

You've learned **0 2 2** words so far
You'll learn **0 0 8** words this week!

amusing	trouble
neighbor	deliver
introduce	porch
corner	squirrel

Writing on Demand

Develop Writing Fluency
Ask children to write about what they know about friends. Have them write for two to three minutes. Children should write as much as they can. Tell them to try to do their best writing. You may want to discuss what children wrote during writing conferences.

Connect to reading

Explain to children that this week, they will read a story about two neighborhood friends, Pam and Dot. Add that children will learn about some of the things that Pam and Dot do together. In the story, Pam and Dot play some games together. Look at that—playing a game is already on our concept map!

What can we do with our neighborhood friends?
- play a game
- go for a walk
- swing

ELL English Language Learners

Listening Comprehension
English learners will benefit from additional visual support to understand the key terms in the concept map. Use the pictures on pp. 88–89 to scaffold understanding. For example, when talking about going for a walk, point to the picture of the girl and the boy walking together.

ELL Support Additional ELL support and modified instruction is provided in the *ELL Handbook* and in the ELL Support lessons on pp. DI•75–DI•84.

ELL Preteach Concepts Use the Day 1 instruction on ELL Poster R4 to assess and build background knowledge, develop concepts, and build oral vocabulary.

ELL Poster R4

Objectives
- Build oral vocabulary.
- Discuss the concept to develop oral language.
- Share information and ideas about the concept.

Oral Vocabulary
Amazing Words

Introduce Amazing Words

Display p. R4 of the *Sing with Me* Big Book. Tell children they are going to sing a song about a boy who moves into a new neighborhood Ask children to listen for the Amazing Words *amusing*, *introduce*, and *neighbor* as you sing. Sing the song again and have children join you.

 Sing with Me Big Book Audio

New Neighbor

May I introduce our new neighbor?
He just moved in next door today.
He is friendly and kind and amusing,
And always so ready to play.

Come on over.
We can share snacks and a game or two.
Come on over.
And do things that good neighbors do.

Sing with Me Big Book
p. R4

Teach Amazing Words

Amazing Words · Oral Vocabulary Routine

1 Introduce the Word Relate the word *amusing* to the song: The new boy in the neighborhood is *amusing*. Supply a child-friendly definition: *Amusing* means "funny" and "entertaining." Have children say the word.

2 Demonstrate Provide examples to show meaning: I laughed at the movie because it was *amusing*. Juan told an *amusing* joke. It's *amusing* to watch a puppy try to carry a big stick.

3 Apply Have children demonstrate their understanding: Tell me something *amusing* that you have seen in the last few days.

See p. OV•1 to teach *introduce* and *neighbor*.

Routines Flip Chart

Check understanding of Amazing Words

Have children look at the pictures on pp. 88–89.

How are the children in the pictures like your neighbors? Use the word neighbor in your answer. (Possible response: My neighbors are boys and girls who spend time together.)

What amusing things might the girls on the swings be talking about? Use the word amusing. (Possible response: Maybe they are telling each other amusing jokes or funny stories.)

How would you introduce yourself to one of these children if you moved into their neighborhood? Use the word introduce. (Possible response: I would introduce myself by saying "Hello! My name is _____.")

Apply Amazing Words

Have children demonstrate their understanding of the Amazing Words by completing these sentences orally.

It is **amusing** to _____.

I'd like to **introduce** you to _____.

My **neighbor** lives _____.

Corrective feedback

If...children have difficulty using the Amazing Words, **then...**remind them of the definitions and provide opportunities for children to use the words in sentences

Preteach Academic Vocabulary

Write the following on the board:

- realism and fantasy
- realistic fiction
- simple sentences

Have children share what they know about this week's Academic Vocabulary. Use children's responses to assess their prior knowledge. Preteach the Academic Vocabulary by providing a child-friendly description, explanation, or example that clarifies the meaning of each term. Then ask children to restate the meaning of the Academic Vocabulary in their own words.

 Amazing Words

amusing	trouble
introduce	deliver
neighbor	porch
corner	squirrel

Differentiated Instruction

SI Strategic Intervention

Act It Out To reinforce the meaning of *introduce*, have children act out introducing each other to you or to a friend. Have them use the sentence frame "I'd like to introduce you to my friend_____."

 ELL

English Language Learners

Choose the Word If children are reluctant to form sentences in English, you can check their understanding of the Amazing Words by offering them a choice of two possible words for each definition. For example, say "My word means *a person who lives near me*. Is the word *neighbor* or *amusing*?"

Objectives

- Isolate initial, medial, and final phonemes.
- Match initial, medial, and final phonemes.
- Associate consonant d with the sound /d/.
- Recognize and name the letters Dd.
- Write the letters Dd.

Skills Trace

◉ **Consonant d/d/**

Introduce **URW4D1**

Practice **URW4D4; URW4D5**

Reteach/Review **URW4D2; URW4D3; URW4D4; URW4D5**

Assess/Test **Weekly Test URW4**

Benchmark Test UR

Student Edition pp. 90–91

Phonemic Awareness
Match Initial, Medial, and Final Phonemes

Introduce
Read together the first bulleted point on pages 94–95 of the Student Edition. I see some kids with a *dog*. *Dog* starts with the /d/ sound. Touch the dog's *head*. *Head* ends with the sound /d/. I see some dolls at a table. It looks like they are *ready* for a picnic. The word *ready* has the sound /d/ in the middle.

Model
Listen to the first sound of *dog*: /d/. Listen to the last sound of *head*: /d/. Listen to the middle sound of *ready*: /d/. Continue modeling with *doll, child,* and *body.*

Guide practice
Guide children as they practice saying words from the picture: *dog, doll, door, head, child, odd, ready, body.*

Corrective feedback
If... children make an error,
then... model by saying the sound again, along with a word that begins or ends with the sound, and have them repeat the sound and the word.

Phonics
 Consonant *d* /d/

Hear

Today you will learn how to spell the sound /d/. Listen: /d/, /d/, /d/. When you say /d/, the tip of your tongue touches above your top teeth. Say /d/ and feel the tip of your tongue touch above your top teeth. Touch your throat and say /d/. Your voice box is on when you say /d/. Watch and listen as children produce the sound. Say /d/ with me: /d/, /d/, /d/.

Say

Display Sound-Spelling Card 5. This is a picture of a *dime*. Say it with me: *dime*. The first sound in *dime* is /d/. Listen: /d/, *dime*. Say it with me: /d/, *dime*. What is the first sound in *dime*?

See

Point to *d*. This is *d*. The sound /d/ is usually spelled *d*. *Dime* begins with /d/. *Dime* begins with the letter *d*. Have children say /d/ several times as you point to *d*.

Read ABC Rhyme Time

Display ABC Rhyme Time, p. 9. Point to the letters *Dd* at the top of the page. The name for both these letters is *d*. Point to *D*. This is an upper-case *D*. Point to *d*. This is a lower-case *d*. Point to each letter again and ask: What is the name of this letter?

This rhyme is called "Damselfly Dance." Explain that a damselfly is a small insect with four wings. Read the rhyme aloud, tracking the print with your finger. Then read it again. Point to examples of upper- and lower-case *d*'s as you read each word aloud.

Write

Now I will show you how to write upper-case *D* and lower-case *d*. Write *D*. Watch as I trace upper-case *D* with my finger. Follow the stroke instructions pictured. Now you write upper-case *D*. Repeat for lower-case *d*.

D'Nealian™   Ball and Stick

Dd

d

Sound-Spelling Card 5

ABC Rhyme Time p. 9

Professional Development

Letter *d* and Sound /d/ The letter *d* and the sound /d/ do not always go together. In some words with final *-ed,* such as *baked* and *tipped,* the *d* is pronounced /t/. In informal talk, the letters *t* or *tt* in words such as *metal* and *cutting* are sometimes pronounced as if they were /d/.

Spelling Pattern

/d/d The sound /d/ is usually spelled *d.*

Differentiated Instruction

SI Strategic Intervention

Distinguish b and d Children frequently confuse lower-case *b* and lower-case *d*. Help children by pointing out how the two letters are formed differently: *b* starting at the top and *d* starting in the middle. Have children trace the letters on sandpaper to help them distinguish the two more easily.

E L L

English Language Learners
Pronounce Words with Final *d* Speakers of Spanish and some other languages are used to words that end in vowels, so they may delete or replace final *d* and other final consonants in words such as *red, slid,* and *blend.* Provide extra practice with word pairs such as *may/maid* and *my/mind.*

Objectives
- Blend, read, and spell words with consonant *d* /d/.
- Associate the consonant *d* with the sound /d/.
- Write the letters *Dd*.
- Recognize and name the letters *Dd*.

Phonics—Teach/Model
 Consonant *d* /d/

ROUTINE **Blending Strategy** **Team Talk**

① **Connect** Connect consonant *d* to the sound /d/. Write *d*. This is *d*. The sound for *d* is /d/. Say the sound with me: /d/, /d/, /d/. When you see the letter *d*, what sound will you say?

② **Model** Model how to blend *dig*. Write *d*. What is the sound for this letter? Say the sound with me: /d/. Write *i*. Say this sound with me: /i/. Write *g*. Say this sound with me: /g/. Listen as I blend all the sounds together: /d/ /i/ /g/, *dig*. Blend the sounds with me: /d/ /i/ /g/, *dig*. Now blend the sounds without me.

③ **Guide Practice** Continue the process in Step 2 with the word *sad*. We are going to blend another word. First we say the sounds, then we blend the sounds to read the word. This time, the sound /d/ is at the end of the word. **For corrective feedback, model blending the sounds to read the word. Then have children blend the sounds and read it with you. Repeat with the words *big*, *did*, *bag*, *bid*, and *dad*.**

④ **Review** What do you know about reading words that begin or end with the letter *d*? The sound for *d* is /d/.

Routines Flip Chart

Spell Words Now we are going to spell words with the sound /d/ spelled *d*. The first word we will spell is *dip*. What sounds do you hear in *dip*? (/d/ /i/ /p/) What is the letter for /d/? Let's all write *d*. What is the letter for /i/? Write *i*. What is the letter for /p/? Write *p*. **Have children confirm their spellings by comparing them with what you have written. Continue the practice with *mad*.**

On their own Use the *Reader's and Writer's Notebook* p. 61 for additional practice with consonant *d* /d/.

Reader's and Writer's
Notebook, p. 61

Phonics
Identify Lower-Case and Upper-Case Letters

Guide Practice

Write a lower-case *d* and point to it. What letter is this? (lower-case *d*) Write an upper-case *D* and point to it. What letter is this? (upper-case *D*) Write a series of upper- and lower-case *d's*. Point to each and have children identify each as upper-case *D* or lower-case *d*.

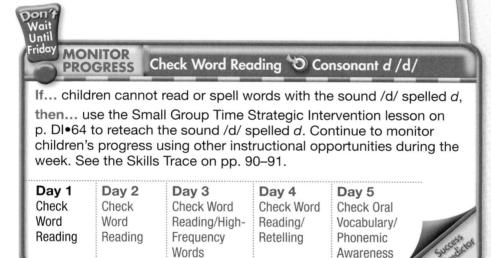

Don't Wait Until Friday

MONITOR PROGRESS Check Word Reading ⟳ Consonant *d* /d/

If... children cannot read or spell words with the sound /d/ spelled *d*,

then... use the Small Group Time Strategic Intervention lesson on p. DI•64 to reteach the sound /d/ spelled *d*. Continue to monitor children's progress using other instructional opportunities during the week. See the Skills Trace on pp. 90–91.

Day 1	Day 2	Day 3	Day 4	Day 5
Check Word Reading	Check Word Reading	Check Word Reading/High-Frequency Words	Check Word Reading/Retelling	Check Oral Vocabulary/Phonemic Awareness

Success Predictor

Small Group Time

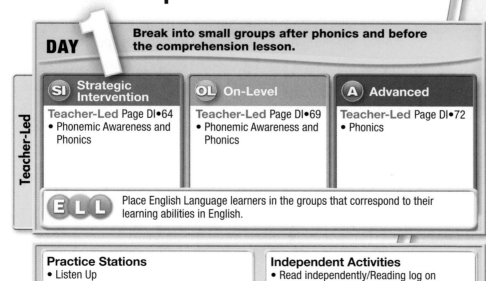

DAY 1

Break into small groups after phonics and before the comprehension lesson.

Teacher-Led

SI Strategic Intervention	**OL** On-Level	**A** Advanced
Teacher-Led Page DI•64 • Phonemic Awareness and Phonics	Teacher-Led Page DI•69 • Phonemic Awareness and Phonics	Teacher-Led Page DI•72 • Phonics

ELL Place English Language learners in the groups that correspond to their learning abilities in English.

Practice Stations
• Listen Up
• Word Work

Independent Activities
• Read independently/Reading log on *Reader's and Writer's Notebook* p. RR1
• Concept Talk Video

Differentiated Instruction

A **Advanced**

Initial and Final *d* Have children work in pairs. Give each pair a 3-column chart with the columns labeled *Words beginning with /d/*, *Words ending with /d/*, and *Words beginning and ending with /d/*. Have pairs generate and list words for each column, using their best spelling. You can also have children use a two-circle Venn diagram, with the circles for *Words beginning with /d/* and *Words ending with /d/*, if you think children are ready for this type of organizer.

English Language Learners
Rhyming Words Help children generate a list of words that rhyme with *red,* such as *head, sled, bed,* and *said.* Have children define the words they know, or provide child-friendly definitions. Then help children use these words in sentences, such as *I like* red *cars* or *My eyes are in my* head.

Objectives
○ Recognize the difference between realism and fantasy in narrative text.

Skills Trace

◎ **Realism and Fantasy**
Introduce/Teach URW4D1; URW6D1
Practice URW4D2; URW4D3; URW4D4; URW6D2; URW6D3; URW6D4
Reteach/Review URW4D5; URW6D5; U1W3D2
Assess/Test Weekly Tests URW4; URW6 Benchmark Tests UR

Listening Comprehension
🔊 Realism and Fantasy

Introduce
Envision It!

There are two kinds of fictional stories. **Realistic fiction** tells about something that could happen in real life. A **fantasy** is a story about something that could never happen in real life. Good readers look for clues that tell them whether a story is a realistic one or a fantasy.

Student Edition EI•2–EI•3

Have children turn to pp. E1•2–E1•3 in their Student Editions. These pictures show examples of realism and fantasy. Ask:

- Which picture shows something realistic? (the picture of the girl reading the book)
- Which picture shows a fantasy? How can you tell? (the picture of the bear family; bears don't wear clothes or eat at a table)

Model
Today we will read a story about two neighbors who organize a picnic. Read "A Neighborhood Picnic" and model how to distinguish realism from fantasy.

 Think Aloud I know this story is a fantasy because it is about things that could never happen. Real pigs and hens can't talk and don't live in homes with furniture. These clues help tell me this story is a fantasy.

Guide practice
Have children name other clues that tell this story is a fantasy. (Possible response: Patty Pig and Jenny Hen live in houses in a neighborhood.) Can this happen in real life? (no) Can Patty Pig and Jenny Hen really have a picnic? Why? (No, because animals can't talk or cook in real life.)

Reader's and Writer's Notebook p. 62

On their own
Use *Reader's and Writer's Notebook* p. 62.

Read Aloud

A Neighborhood Picnic

Patty Pig and her next-door neighbor, Jenny Hen, read the sign on the tree: "Come to a neighborhood picnic on Saturday at Duck Lake. Bring good food to share with your neighbors. There will be games and races."

"I'm going to bring a big fruit salad," said Jenny Hen, fluttering her feathers. "What about you, Patty?"

"I'm going to bring lots of tasty sandwiches," said Patty Pig. "I can't wait until Saturday! It will be fun to see all our friends."

However, when Saturday came, it was raining so hard that a picnic at Duck Lake was impossible. Patty thought and thought about what to do. Then she had a brilliant idea. She called Jenny to tell her. "I know how we can still have our picnic!" said Patty excitedly.

"How?" asked Jenny Hen. "It's pouring outside!"

"We can have an indoor picnic in our home—yours and mine!" said Patty. "We'll move our furniture against the walls and make a covered passage between your house and mine so people can walk back and forth."

"You're a genius!" said Jenny. "Let's call our neighbors and spread the news."

By noon, their furniture was pushed against the walls. Then Patty and Jenny made a covered path between their homes by tying umbrellas together. Soon the neighbors began to arrive with their food and blankets.

Since there were a few animals that were new to the neighborhood, Patty wanted to welcome them. "I'd like to introduce myself," she said. "My name is Patty and that is my dear friend, Jenny, on the porch next door. Welcome to our first neighborhood indoor picnic!"

The picnic turned out to be a huge success. Although there were no races, the animals sang songs, told amusing jokes, and shared stories. In fact, everyone had such a wonderful time that they decided to have other indoor picnics during rainy or cold weather!

Academic Vocabulary

fantasy a made-up story that could never really happen

realistic fiction a made-up story that could happen in real life

Objectives
- Identify and produce a simple sentence.
- Use proper letter size when writing.
- Write the letters *Dd*

Conventions
Simple Sentences

Model

Remind children that a **sentence** is a group of words that tells a complete idea. It begins with a capital letter and often ends with a period. *A boy rides a bike* is a sentence.

Display Grammar Transparency R4. Read the definition aloud. Model reading the sentence and identifying the noun and verb in the example. Point out capitalization and end punctuation in the sentence. Then read the directions and model number 1.

- I see a bear sleeping in the picture. I also see the words *bear* and *sleeps*. I know that *bear* is a noun and *sleeps* is a verb, so I can use these words to make a sentence.
- I will use the noun *bear* and the verb *sleeps* to make the sentence *The bear sleeps.* I begin my sentence with a capital letter and end it with a period.

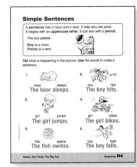

Grammar Transparency R4

Guide practice

Continue with items 2–6, having children use the words to make a sentence.

Connect to oral language

Have the class complete these sentence frames orally to tell a complete idea.

1. The trucks _____.

2. _____ walk.

On their own

Team Talk Pair children and ask them to identify the noun and verb in each sentence. Then have them discuss what belongs at the beginning and end of each sentence.

Handwriting
Letter *D* and *d*;
Proper Letter Size

Model letter formation

Display upper- and lower-case letters: *Dd.* Use the stroke instructions pictured below to model proper letter formation.

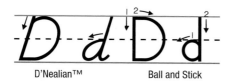

D'Nealian™   Ball and Stick

Model proper letter size

Remind children that to make sure people can read what we write, we must write letters the correct size. The letters cannot be too small or too large. Model how the lines on the paper can help determine letter size. Say: When I write upper-case *D*, I start at the top line. When I write lower-case *d,* I start at the top line for the straight part of the letter, but I use the middle line for the round part of the letter. Repeat this action several times. Then write the letters *Dd* on the board to model correct letter size.

Guide practice

Write the following words on the board: *dip, Dad, did, dig, mad*.

Team Talk Have children work together in pairs to identify the letters *Dd*. Then have them copy the words on lined paper. Remind them to use proper letter size.

On their own

Use the *Reader's and Writer's Notebook* p. 63

Reader's and Writer's Notebook p. 63

Objectives
- Produce a simple sentence.
- Write a simple sentence that states a complete idea.
- Share ideas about a topic.

Writing—Sentences

Connect to conventions

Review sentences: a **sentence** is a group of words that tells a complete idea. Explain that it begins with a capital letter and often ends with a period. We can write sentences to show we know how to state a complete idea that makes sense.

Model

Write the following complete and incomplete sentences: *The bus stops. The bus.* Read the sentences aloud. Only one of these groups of words tells a complete idea. The complete sentence is *The bus stops*. It tells *what the idea is about and what that thing does.* Circle this sentence.

Guide practice

Let's think of other sentences that tell what you might see as you come to school. As children give examples, write their sentences on the board and have them identify whether the sentences are complete. Then write these sentence frames and read them aloud.

> The _____ plays.
>
> The cars _____.

Model completing the first sentence frame. This first sentence says that something plays. I know that *plays* is a verb. What do I see that plays when I come to school? I know that a boy can play. Sometimes I see a boy play when I come to school. I will write *boy* in the blank to complete the sentence: *The boy plays.* Have children suggest words to complete the second sentence, guiding them to choose a verb that names an action.

Shared writing

Have children create new sentences. As they suggest sentences, write their suggestions on the board. Make sure that each sentence is complete. Invite other children to identify the nouns and verbs in the sentences.

On their own

Some children may be ready to write on their own. Write several more sentence frames on the board, each with a blank for a noun or a verb. Have children use nouns or verbs from the sentences on the board to complete the sentence on their own. Children may also write new sentences, if they can. Have children circle the noun and underline the verb in each sentence.

Listening and Speaking
Share Information About Trustworthiness

Introduce trustworthiness

Explain that being *trustworthy* is about doing what is right. When we are trustworthy, others know they can count on us.

- A trustworthy person tells the truth.
- A trustworthy person doesn't cheat or steal.
- A trustworthy person keeps promises.
- A trustworthy person does the right thing, even when it is hard.

Model

Think Aloud I will share information about being trustworthy. When you *trust* people, you count on them to do what they say they will. If you are *trustworthy,* that means that people can trust you.

Guide practice

Discuss trustworthiness with children. Have them share their ideas. Remind children to follow the rules for speaking and listening.

On their own

Have pairs of children take turns listening to and speaking about trust. Have them share information about who they trust and why.

Wrap Up Your Day

✔ **Consonants Dd /d/** Write *Dad* and *did.* Point to the *d*'s as you say the words. Have children repeat them after you.

✔ **Build Concepts** Monitor children's use of oral vocabulary as they respond. To develop the concept of Neighborhoods, ask children what neighbors do when it rains the day of their picnic.

✔ **Homework** Send home this week's Family Times Newsletter from the *Let's Practice It!* pp. 13–14 on the *Teacher Resource DVD ROM.*

Let's Practice It!
TR DVD • 13–14

Preview DAY 2

Tell children that tomorrow they will listen to a story about a first grader's first day at school.

Objectives
- Discuss the concept to develop oral language.
- Build oral vocabulary.

Today at a Glance

Oral Vocabulary
corner, trouble

Print Awareness
Identify Information

Phonemic Awareness
Isolate Initial, Medial, and Final Phonemes

Phonics and Spelling
◉ Consonant *l, ll /l/*

Comprehension
◉ Realism and Fantasy

Vocabulary
Sort Words

High-Frequency Words
are, have, that, they, two

Conventions
Simple Sentences

Handwriting
Letters L and l; Proper Body and Paper Position

Writing
Simple Sentences

Listening and Speaking
Give Oral Instructions

Concept Talk

Question of the Week

What can we do with our neighborhood friends?

Build concepts

To reinforce concepts and to focus children's attention, have children sing "New Neighbor" from the *Sing with Me* Big Book. When did the new neighbor move in? (today) Does the singer want to be friends with the new neighbor? How do you know? (yes; the neighbor is described as kind and amusing, and the singer invites him over to play)

 Sing with Me Big Book Audio

Introduce Amazing Words

Display the Big Book, *First Grade, Here I Come!* Read the title and identify the author. Explain that in the story, the author uses the word *corner* to describe a place in a first grade classroom. Have children listen to the story to find out what the main character does in first grade.

Big Book

ELL **Reinforce Vocabulary** Use the Day 2 instruction on ELL Poster R4 to discussion the lesson concept.

ELL Poster R4

Oral Vocabulary
Amazing Words

Teach Amazing Words

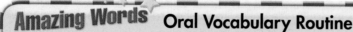
Amazing Words — Oral Vocabulary Routine

1. Introduce the Word Relate the word *corner* to the book. Henry's classroom has a science *corner.* Supply a child-friendly definition: A *corner* is the place where two walls meet or where two streets come together. Have children say the word.

2. Demonstrate Provide examples to show meaning. We can put crayons and paper in one *corner* of the room to make an art *corner.* Let's walk to the *corner* of the block. Sometimes people put their beds in one *corner* of their bedrooms.

3. Apply Have children demonstrate their understanding. Ask: Where is a *corner* in our classroom?

See p. OV • 1 to teach *trouble.*

Routines Flip Chart

Anchored Talk

Discuss things we can do with our neighborhood friends.

Add to the concept map

Display the concept map you began on Day 1. Explain that the class will now add to it. Review the information on the map. What else have you learned that you can do with your neighborhood friends?

- Recall the song "New Neighbor." What are the singer and the new neighbor going to do when the neighbor comes over? (share snacks and play games) We already have *play games* on our map. Let's add *share snacks.*

- Let's remember the Read Aloud story "Neighborhood Picnic." What do Patty Pig, Jenny Hen, and their neighbors do? (have an indoor picnic) Add *have a picnic* to the map. What do they do at the picnic besides eat? (sing songs, tell amusing jokes, share stories) Let's add those to our map too.

Amazing Words

amusing	trouble
introduce	deliver
neighbor	porch
corner	squirrel

Differentiated Instruction

SI Strategic Intervention

Pronunciation If children pronounce the sound /r/ with a vowel-like quality, they may have difficulty with the formal pronunciation of *corner*. Say the word slowly, stressing the sound /ôr/ in the first syllable, and have children repeat it several times.

English Language Learners
Two-Syllable Words Speakers of monosyllabic languages such as Hmong, Khmer, and Cantonese may pronounce two-syllable words such as *corner* and *trouble* as two separate words. Have children practice saying two-syllable words.

Print Awareness
Identify Information

Teach

The covers of books tell us some important information such as the name of the book. We use a special word to tell about the name of a book. That word is the *Title*. Book covers also tell the name of the *author*. The author is the person who writes the book. The title is the *name* of the book. The *author* is the person who wrote the book. Then there's the person who made the pictures. We call that person—the *illustrator*. The title, the author, and the illustrator. Those are three pieces of information we can learn from the cover of a book.

Model

Display the cover of a book children have read before. Be sure the cover lists the author and the illustrator, and gives the book's title in large letters. I'm going to look at this book cover to find the title, the author, and the—what? **Allow children to fill in the word** *illustrator.* It can be tricky to tell which words are the title and which tell the names of the author and the illustrator. Here's a clue. The title is usually written in very big letters. The title sometimes has a lot of words, too, and the title is often at the top of the cover. **Indicate the title on the cover. Then indicate the names of the author and the illustrator.** Book covers often say the word *by* next to the author's name. **Write the word** *by* **on the board and read it aloud with children.** Book covers often say *illustrated by* or *pictures by* when they give the name of the illustrator. **Note that sometimes the author and illustrator may be the same person.**

Guide practice

Display another book which lists the author and illustrator on the cover. Have children tell a partner which words they think form the title of the book. Repeat with author and illustrator.

On their own

Use *Reader's and Writer's Notebook* p. 64.

Reader's and Writer's Notebook, p. 64

Phonemic Awareness
Isolate Initial, Medial, and Final Phonemes

Model isolating sounds

Have children look at the picture on pages 90–91 in their Student Editions. I see some things that start with the sound /l/. Something has fallen from the trees. What? (leaves) I also see a *lake.* The first sound in *leaves* and *lake* is /l/. I also see something that ends with the sound /l/: a *doll.* The last sound in *doll* is /l/. Look for a boy who is using some money. The things he is buying cost several *dollars.* The sound /l/ is in the middle of the word *dollars.*

Student Edition pp. 90–91

Model matching phonemes

Listen to the first sound of *lake:* /l/. Say the sound with me: /l/. Listen to the last sound of *doll:* /l/. Say the sound with me: /l/. Continue modeling with *leaves* and *hill.*

Guide practice

Now we're going to listen to the first sound of some words. Say *la-la-la!* if the sound you hear is /l/. Don't say anything if it is not /l/. Say the words: *light, near, line, lap, lock, run.*

Now we're going to listen to the ending sound of some words. Give me a thumbs up if the sound you hear is /l/. Give me a thumbs down if it is not /l/. Say the words: *big, bill, fall, cap, pole, well.*

Corrective Feedback

If... children make an error,
then... model again the sound in isolation, along with a word that begins or ends with the sound and have them repeat the sound and the word.

On their own

Have children look at the picture and name more items that begin or end with the sound /l/ or have /l/ in the middle.

Differentiated Instruction

SI Strategic Intervention
Beginning and Ending Sounds
If children have trouble distinguishing beginning and ending sounds, have them say words slowly, raising their hands when they start saying it and lower their hands again when they stop saying it. For instance, for the word *lamb,* hands go up on /llll/ and come down on /mmmm/; when they say *mill,* the reverse is true.

Academic Vocabulary

phoneme The smallest part of spoken language that makes a difference in the meaning of words.

ELL

English Language Learners
Nouns To develop and practice vocabulary, have children open their books to the picture on pages 90–91. Tell children that they will play a game. Say *I see a tree* and have children find a picture of a tree. The next child then says *I see a tree and a* _____ and points to the object he or she names. Go around in a circle until you have a chain of 4–6 items; then begin again.

Objectives

- Associate the spellings *l, ll* with the sound /l/.
- Write the letters *Ll*.
- Blend, read, and spell words with *l* and *ll*.
- Recognize and name the letters *Ll*.

Phonics
 Consonant *l, ll* /l/

Hear
Today you will learn how to spell the sound /l/. Listen: /l/, /l/, /l/. When you say /l/, the tip of your tongue touches above your top teeth and stays there. Say /l/ and feel the tip of your tongue touch above your top teeth and stay there. **Watch and listen as children produce the sound.** Say /l/ with me: /l/, /l/, /l/.

Say
Display Sound-Spelling Card 14. This is a picture of a *ladder*. Say it with me: *ladder*. The first sound in *ladder* is /l/. Listen: /l/, *ladder*. Say it with me: /l/, *ladder*. What is the first sound in *ladder*?

See
Point to *l*. This is *l*. The sound /l/ is usually spelled *l*. *Ladder* begins with sound /l/. *Ladder* begins with the letter *l*. **Have children say sound /l/ several times as you point to *l*.**

Write the word *fill*. Point to *ll*. This is *ll*. The sound /l/ can be spelled *ll* at the end of a word. Listen to sound /l/ at the end of the word *fill*. *Fill* ends with sound /l/. It ends with the letters *ll*. **Have children say sound /l/ several times as you point to *ll*.**

Sound-Spelling Card 14

Read ABC Rhyme Time
Display ABC Rhyme Time, p. 17. Point to the letters Ll at the top of the page. The name for both of these letters is *l*. Point to L. This is an upper-case L. Point to l. This is a lower-case *l*. Point to each letter again and ask: What is the name of this letter?

This rhyme is called "Lollipops." Read the rhyme aloud, tracking the print with your finger. Then read it again. Point to examples of upper- and lower-case *l*'s as you read each word aloud.

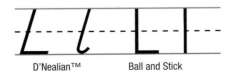

Lollipops
Look!
Lime and lemon lollipops
Are falling from the sky.
They're landing on the lovely lawns
Like leaves as we pass by.

ABC Rhyme Time p. 17

Write
Now I will show you how to write upper-case *L* and lower-case *l*. Write *L*. Watch as I trace upper-case *L* with my finger. Follow the stroke instructions pictured. Now you write upper-case *L*. Repeat for lower-case *l*.

D'Nealian™   Ball and Stick

Phonics—Teach/Model
↻ Consonant *l*, *ll* /l/

ROUTINE **Blending Strategy**

1 **Connect** Connect consonant *l* to the sound /l/. Write *l*. This is *l*. The sound for *l* is /l/. Say the sound with me: /l/, /l/, /l/. When you see the letter *l*, what sound will you say?

2 **Model** Model how to blend *lap*. Write *l*. What is the sound for this letter? Say the sound with me: /l/. Write *a*. Say this sound with me: /a/. Write *p*. Say this sound with me: /p/. Listen as I blend all the sounds together: /l/ /a/ /p/, *lap*. Blend the sounds with me: /l/ /a/ /p/, *lap*. Now blend the sounds without me.

3 **Guide Practice** Continue the routine in Step 2 with the words that follow. Remember, first we say the sounds. Then we blend the sounds to read the word.

| lid | lad | gill | gal | bill |

For corrective feedback, model blending the sounds to read the word. Then have children blend the sounds and read the word with you.

4 **Review** What do you know about reading words that begin or end with the letter *l* or end with the letters *ll*? (The sound for *l* and *ll* is /l/.)

Routines Flip Chart

Spell words Now we are going to spell words with the sound /l/ spelled *l* or *ll*. The first word we will spell is *lip*. What sounds do you hear in *lip*? (/l/ /i/ /p/) What is the letter for /l/ at the beginning of a word? Let's write *l*. What is the letter for /i/? Write *i*. What is the letter for /p/? Write *p*. Have children confirm their spellings by comparing them with what you have written. Continue practice with *lid, lap, mill,* and *pill*. Ask what letters change and what letters stay the same when you change *lip* to *lid*.

On their own Use the *Reader's and Writer's Notebook* p. 65 for additional practice with consonant *l*, *ll* /l/.

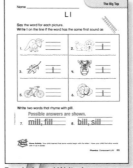

Reader's and Writer's Notebook p. 65

Differentiated Instruction

SI **Strategic Intervention**

Sound /l/ The sound /l/ is one of the harder sounds for young children to pronounce correctly. If children sometimes pronounce /l/ as /w/, /y/, or some other sound, have them say /l/ several times while looking in a mirror to see the position of their tongues and lips. Check to make sure they are saying the sound properly.

Spelling Pattern

/l/ *l*, *ll* The sound /l/ is usually spelled *l*, but at the end of a word it can often be spelled *ll*.

 ELL

English Language Learners

Words with Letters *ll* In Latin American Spanish, the letter combination *ll* does not refer to the sound /l/ but rather to the sound /y/. Children who can already read and write some Spanish may need extra practice spelling and saying words such as *bill, fill,* and *mill*.

Objectives
- ○ Associate the spellings *l* and *ll* with the sound /l/.
- ○ Associate the letter *d* with the sound /d/.
- • Write the letters *Ll.*
- • Blend, read, and spell words with *d, l,* and *ll.*
- • Recognize and name the letters *Ll.*

Phonics
Identify Lower-Case and Upper-Case Letters

Guide Practice

Write a lower-case *l* and point to it. What letter is this? (lower-case *l*) Write an upper-case *L* and point to it. What letter is this? (upper-case *L*) Write a series of upper- and lower-case *l's*. Point to each and have children identify each as upper-case *L* or lower-case *L*.

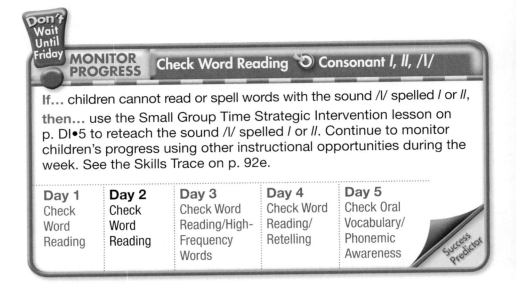

Don't Wait Until Friday

MONITOR PROGRESS Check Word Reading ↺ Consonant *l, ll,* /l/

If… children cannot read or spell words with the sound /l/ spelled *l* or *ll*,

then… use the Small Group Time Strategic Intervention lesson on p. DI•5 to reteach the sound /l/ spelled *l* or *ll*. Continue to monitor children's progress using other instructional opportunities during the week. See the Skills Trace on p. 92e.

Day 1	Day 2	Day 3	Day 4	Day 5
Check Word Reading	**Check Word Reading**	Check Word Reading/High-Frequency Words	Check Word Reading/Retelling	Check Oral Vocabulary/Phonemic Awareness

Success Predictor

Small Group Time

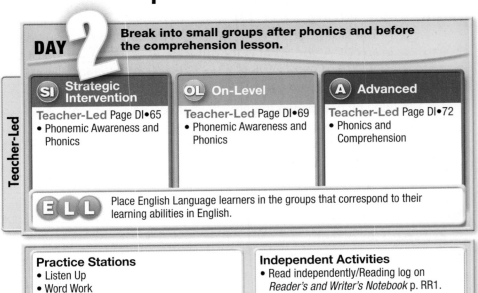

DAY 2 Break into small groups after phonics and before the comprehension lesson.

Teacher-Led

SI Strategic Intervention
Teacher-Led Page DI•65
- Phonemic Awareness and Phonics

OL On-Level
Teacher-Led Page DI•69
- Phonemic Awareness and Phonics

A Advanced
Teacher-Led Page DI•72
- Phonics and Comprehension

ELL Place English Language learners in the groups that correspond to their learning abilities in English.

Practice Stations
- Listen Up
- Word Work

Independent Activities
- Read independently/Reading log on *Reader's and Writer's Notebook* p. RR1.

Phonics—Build Fluency
Consonants d /d/, l, ll /l/

Model

Envision It!

Have children turn to page 92 in their Student Editions. Look at the pictures on this page. I see a picture of a *dime* and a picture of a *ladder*. When I say *dime*, I begin with the sound /d/. The /d/ sound is spelled with a *d*. When I say *ladder*, I begin with the sound /l/. The /l/ sound is spelled with an *l* at the beginning of a word. Sometimes it is spelled with an *ll* at the end of a word.

Guide practice

For each word in "Words I Can Blend," ask for the sound of each letter. Make sure that children identify the correct sound for *d*, *l*, or *ll*. Then have children blend the whole word.

Corrective feedback

If... children have difficulty blending a word,
then... model blending the word, and then ask children to blend it with you.

Objectives
- Decode words with consonants.
- Identify and read at least 100 words from a list of words that you use often.

Envision It! | Sounds to Know

dime

d

ladder

l

READING STREET ONLINE
SOUND-SPELLING CARDS
www.ReadingStreet.com

Phonics

Consonants d, l

Words I Can Blend

D	a	d
s	a	d
d	i	d
f	i	l	l
l	i	d

92

Student Edition p. 92

Differentiated Instruction

A Advanced

Extend Blending Provide children who can segment and blend all the words correctly with more challenging words such as: *dust, digs, dolly, damp, bride, grand, lady, leaves, lemon, stroll, until,* and *spelled.*

Spelling Patterns

/d/ Spelled *d* The sound /d/ is usually spelled *d.*

/l/ Spelled *l, ll* The sound /l/ is usually spelled *l,* but can also be spelled *ll* at the end of a word.

Objectives

○ Review the difference between realism and fantasy in narrative text.

• Identify and sort descriptive words.

• Read high-frequency words

Skills Trace

◎ **Realism and Fantasy**

Introduce/Teach URW4D1; URW6D1

Practice URW4D2; URW4D3; URW4D4; URW6D2; URW6D3; URW6D4

Reteach/Review URW4D5; URW6D5; U1W3D2

Assess/Test Weekly Tests URW4; URW6

Benchmark Test UR

Comprehension
↻ Realism and Fantasy

Review realism and fantasy

Remember, there are two kinds of stories—realistic stories that could happen and fantasies that could never happen. Good readers look for clues in words and pictures that tell them whether a story could really happen.

Guide practice

Reread the story "**A Neighborhood Picnic**" aloud. Have children listen for clues to tell them whether the story is realistic fiction or fantasy. Write children's answers to the questions below.

• What are some things that Patty Pig and Jenny Hen do in the story that show it is a fantasy? (Possible response: They talk, read a sign, call their neighbors, and tie umbrellas together.)

• Why do these things show the story is a fantasy? (Animals cannot do any of these things in real life.)

On their own

Have children discuss the clues in *Tip and Tam* and decide whether the story is realistic fiction or a fantasy. Then have children draw a picture from the story that shows why it is realistic fiction or fantasy.

Vocabulary
Sort Descriptive Words

Discuss descriptive words

Explain to children that descriptive words help us tell about something. Discuss how some descriptive words refer to the senses—touch, taste, smell, hearing, sight. Use the example: *I feel the scratchy sandpaper.*

Model

Create the following chart on the board and list the words: soft, shiny, loud, sweet. Sort *soft* under the sense *touch* and explain.

Touch	Taste	Smell	Hear	See
soft				

Guide practice

Have children sort the remaining words on the list as you fill in the chart on the board. Ask children which category was not filled in (smell). Ask them to think of a word to sort under this category.

On their own

Team Talk Have children work in pairs to identify other descriptive words and sort them in the chart. Have them share their words with the class.

High-Frequency Words

Introduce

ROUTINE
Nondecodable Words

1. **Say and Spell** Look at p. 93. Some words we have to learn by remembering the letters rather than saying the sounds. We will say and spell the words to help learn them.

2. **Identify Letters** Point to the first word. This word is *are*. The letters in *are* are a-r-e, *are*. Say and spell the word with me. **Say the word. Then point to each letter as you spell the word. Then say the word again. Have children repeat.**

3. **Demonstrate Meaning** Tell me a sentence using the word *are*. Repeat this routine with the other Words I Can Read.

Routines Flip Chart

Read words in isolation — Have children read the words on p. 93 aloud. Add the words to the Word Wall.

Read words in context — Have children read the sentences aloud. Have them identify this week's High-Frequency Words in the sentences.

On their own — Use *Reader's and Writer's Notebook* p. 70.

Reader's and Writer's Notebook, p. 70

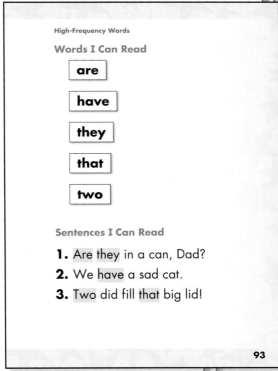

High-Frequency Words

Words I Can Read

| are |

| have |

| they |

| that |

| two |

Sentences I Can Read

1. Are they in a can, Dad?
2. We have a sad cat.
3. Two did fill that big lid!

93

Student Edition p. 93

 Strategic Intervention

Realism and Fantasy Make sure children understand the concepts of realism and fantasy. Have children think about the dog and cat in the story, *Tip and Tam*. Ask them to state something Tip and Tam could do in real life. Then ask them to think about something Tip and Tam would not do in real life, such as talk or drive a car. Use other examples to continue the discussion.

Objectives
- Identify and produce a simple sentence.
- Use proper body and paper position when writing.
- Write *Ll*.

Conventions
Simple Sentences

Model simple sentences

Write the following sentence on the board: *The cat runs*. Point to each word as you read it. Ask children what the sentence begins and ends with (a capital letter and a period). A sentence is a group of words that tells a complete idea. It includes a noun and a verb. What is the noun in this sentence? (cat) What is the verb? (runs)

Guide practice

Write the following sentences on the board. Read them aloud and have the children repeat after you. Have children identify the noun and verb in each sentence. Ask children why they are sentences. (They are complete ideas and include a noun and a verb.)

1. The dog barks.   (dog, barks)
2. A frog hops.   (frog, hops)
3. Some bugs glow.   (bugs, glow)

Connect to oral language

Have the class complete these sentence frames orally using nouns and verbs.

1. _____ digs.
2. Dad can _____.

On their own

Use *Reader's and Writer's Notebook* p. 66.

Reader's and Writer's Notebook, p. 66

Handwriting
Letter *L* and *l*;
Proper Body and Paper Position

Model letter formation

Display upper- and lower-case letters: *Ll*. Use the stroke instructions pictured below to model proper letter formation.

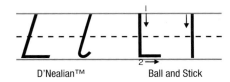

D'Nealian™   Ball and Stick

Model proper body and paper position

Remind children that when we write, it is important to sit and position the paper the correct way. When I write, I sit up straight and keep both feet on the floor. I keep my arms relaxed on the table or desk in front of me. If I am right-handed, I position the paper I am writing on so that it slants from the left at the top to the right at the bottom. If I am left-handed, I position it so that the paper slants from the right at the top to the left at the bottom. **Show correct body and paper positioning for children to follow.**

Guide practice

Write the following words on the board: *Lit, Lad, pill, fill, lap.*

Team Talk Have children work together in pairs to identify the letters *Ll*. Then have them copy the words on lined paper. Remind them to use proper body and paper positions while writing.

On their own

Use the *Reader's and Writer's Notebook* p. 67.

Reader's and Writer's Notebook, p. 67

Left-Handed Paper Positioning
Left-handed children may tend to slant their paper from left to right because they see right-handed children doing so. Monitor left-handed children closely and reposition from right to left as needed.

Daily Fix-It

3. do you see Mom
   <u>D</u>o you see Mom<u>?</u>
4. i hav the green bag
   <u>I</u> hav<u>e</u> the green bag<u>.</u>

Discuss the Daily Fix-It with children. Review sentence capitalization and punctuation, capitalization of *I*, and spelling.

 ELL

English Language Learners
The Terms *Left* and *Right* Help children understand the terms *left* and *right* by having them put their left and right hands in front of them with thumbs pointing out. The hand that makes the shape of an "L" is the left hand.

Objectives
- Produce a simple sentence.
- Write a simple sentence that states a complete idea.
- Give directions.

Writing—Sentences

Model

Have children recall the Read Aloud, "A Neighborhood Picnic." Patty Pig and Jenny Hen have an indoor picnic. Let's write a sentence about what they do to get ready for the picnic. Write the sentence below. Read the sentence and explain that it is a complete idea.

> **They call friends.**

Guide practice

Write more sentences about the picnic. Then read the sentences. Have children tell *whom* the idea is about and what those animals are doing.

> **The friends drag furniture.**
>
> **The friends tell stories.**
>
> **The friends tell jokes.**

Connect to phonics

Reread the sentences with children and have them point to the words with /d/ spelled *d* and /l/ spelled *l* or *ll*.

Shared writing

Rewrite the first sentence with a blank replacing the words *drag furniture*. Have children suggest different words to complete the sentence. Remind them to think of things that happen at the picnic and to create a sentence with a complete idea. Write children's suggestions on the board.

On their own

Some children may be ready to write on their own. Write another sentence frame on the board about the picnic. Have children complete the sentence on their own. Children may also write new sentences, if they can. Have children circle the nouns and underline the verbs in their sentences. Then have them read their sentences aloud.

Listening and Speaking
Give Directions

Teach giving directions

Explain that **directions** tell how to do or make something. It is important to speak clearly and to give directions in order. The **order** of things is the way that one thing follows another.

- Speak clearly.
- Give directions in order.

Model

 Think Aloud I will give you directions for wrapping a birthday gift. Listen to each step of the directions. First you must cut the wrapping paper so that there is enough for the gift. Then you must neatly fold the paper around the gift and tape it.

Guide practice

Have children give directions for other activities, such as making a birthday card or setting a table. Work with children to ensure they speak clearly and give the directions in order.

On their own

Have pairs of children take turns giving directions to do something simple, such as brushing your teeth, so that a partner can pantomime the action. Remind children to follow the rules for speaking and listening that they established in Week 1.

Wrap Up Your Day

- ✔ **Consonants Ll /l/** Write the letters *L* and *l*. Have children identify the letters. Write *Lad* and *lit*. Point to the *L* in *Lad* and the *l* in *lit* as you say the words aloud. Have children repeat them after you.

- ✔ **Build Concepts** Monitor children's use of oral vocabulary as they respond. Recall the Big Book, *First Grade, Here I Come!* Have children describe the new things and people that Henry was introduced to on his first day of first grade?

Differentiated Instruction

 Advanced
Give Directions Have pairs of children take turns giving directions that have three or four steps, rather than two. Remind them to give the directions in the order the listener must perform the steps.

Academic Vocabulary

directions how to do something or make something

order the way one thing follows another; sequence

English Language Learners
Act Out Directions Model acting out each step as you give directions. Have children repeat your actions. Then have them give the same directions to a partner.

Preview DAY 3

Tell children that tomorrow they will hear again about Henry's first day in first grade.

Objectives

- Build oral vocabulary.
- Identify details in text.
- Share information and ideas about the concept.

Today at a Glance

Oral Vocabulary
deliver

Print Awareness
Sequence Letters

Phonological Awareness
Rhyme words

Phonics
⊙ Consonant *h* /h/

High-Frequency Words
are, have, that, they, two

Conventions
Simple Sentences

Handwriting
Letters *H* and *h*/Self-Evaluation

Writing
Simple Sentences

Listening and Speaking
Give Oral Instructions

Concept Talk

 Question of the Week

What can we do with our neighborhood friends?

Build concepts

To reinforce concepts and to focus children's attention, have children sing "New Neighbor" from the *Sing with Me* Big Book. What kinds of games do you think the singer will play with the new neighbor? Why? (Possible Responses: board games, soccer, video games; these games are fun)

🔘 Sing with Me Big Book Audio

Monitor listening comprehension

Display the Big Book, *First Grade, Here I Come!* Tell children to listen to the story to learn how Henry felt about his first day of school. Then read the book aloud.

- How did Henry feel about first grade? (At first he didn't like it because it was different from kindergarten. Then he told his mother about everything he did, and he decided he liked it after all.)

Big Book

ELL **Expand Vocabulary** Use the Day 3 instruction on ELL Poster R4 to help children expand vocabulary.

ELL Poster R4

Go Digital!   Sing with Me Animations   Concept Talk Video

Whole Group

Oral Vocabulary
Amazing Words

Teach Amazing Words

 **Amazing Words**   Oral Vocabulary Routine

1 Introduce the Word Relate the word *deliver* to the book. Henry's teacher asked him to go to the principal's office to *deliver* a note. Supply a child-friendly definition: When you *deliver* something, you bring it from one person or place to another. Have children say the word.

2 Demonstrate Provide examples to show meaning. Letter carriers *deliver* the mail. That truck driver will *deliver* the package right to your door. Please *deliver* this message to your parents.

3 Apply Have children demonstrate their understanding. Which can someone *deliver* to your home: a pizza or a park?

Routines Flip Chart

Anchored Talk

Add to the concept map

Use this question to discuss what we can do with our neighborhood friends as you add to the concept map.

• Recall the Big Book, *First Grade, Here I Come!* What is Henry doing at the beginning of the story? (getting off the bus after school) That's right. He's getting off the bus with other children from his neighborhood. They go to school together. Let's add *go to school* to our map of things we can do with our neighborhood friends.

Amazing Words

amusing	trouble
introduce	deliver
neighbor	porch
corner	squirrel

Differentiated Instruction

A Advanced

Amazing Words Briefly review the Amazing Words introduced thus far during the week. Have children choose three of the words and draw a picture that shows all three in some way. For example, a picture might show a *neighbor* sitting in a *corner* while a cat is having *trouble* catching a mouse. Have children share their pictures and descriptions with a partner.

 ELL

English Language Learners
Pronunciation Children from various language backgrounds may pronounce the short /i/ in *deliver* as a long e. You can help children by having them say the word *live* (to rhyme with *give*). Then have them expand *live* into *liver* and finally *deliver*.

Objectives
- Understand that the letters of the alphabet are arranged in a sequence.
- Sequence the letters of the alphabet from *a* through *g.*
- Rhyme words.

Print Awareness
Sequence Letters

Introduce
Let's remember how to put letters in order. Today, we'll just use the letters that go from *a* to *g.* That's seven letters in all. These seven letters are the first seven letters of the alphabet.

Model
Place seven large sticky notes in a row across the board, or use tape or magnets to attach seven index cards in the same way. Touch the card or sticky note on the left. The first letter of the alphabet goes over here. That letter is *a.* Write *a* on the card and read the letter with children.

Touch the second card. Guess what goes here—the second letter of the alphabet. When I write the letters in order, the first letter is *a* and the second letter is *b.* Write *b* on the second card. Touch the two cards in order, first *a* and then *b.* The first letter is *a.* The second letter is *b.* Repeat, having children name the letters with you.

Continue in this way through the seventh letter, *g.* Remind children that they have studied all these letters, except *e,* since they began first grade. Touch all the letters in turn. The first seven letters of the alphabet, in order, are *a, b, c, d, e, f, g.* Say the letters again with children; then sing them to the tune of the first line of the Alphabet Song.

Guide practice
Now mix the letters up. Tell children that you are going to put them back in the correct order. I remember that the first letter is *a.* Here is *a.* I'll put it here, on the left, so it can be at the front of the line. What's next? I'll sing it—*a, b.* Okay, the next letter is *b.* This letter is *b.* I know it isn't *d* because when I write *b,* I start at the top, not with the curve. I'll put *b* next to *a.* Continue until the letters are once again in order from *a* to *g.*

On their own
Use *Reader's and Writer's Notebook* p. 68.

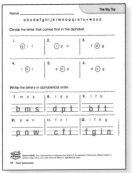

Reader's and Writer's
Notebook p. 68

Phonological Awareness
Rhyming Words

Model producing rhyming words

Have children look at the picture on pages 94–95 in their Student Editions. Today we are going to use this picture to help us produce rhyming words. Remember that **rhyming words** are words that end with the same sounds. The directions tell us to find three words that rhyme with *hop*. So, I need to find three words that end with the sound /op/. When I look at the picture, I see a *mop*, a sign that says *Stop*, and a *shop*. A *shop* is another name for a store. *Mop, stop,* and *shop* rhyme with *hop,* because these words all end with the sounds /o/, /p/, /op/. Listen: *hop, mop, stop, shop.* I also see a *tree. Tree* does not rhyme with *hop.* It does not end with the same sounds.

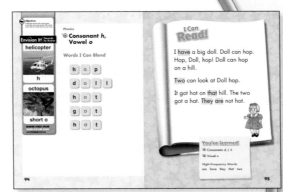

Student Edition pp. 94–95

Guide practice

Guide children to use the picture to produce words that rhyme with *log* (*dog* or *jog*) and *got* (*dot*). Then ask children to determine which of the following word pairs rhyme: *rod/nod* (yes); *lock/sock* (yes); *rob/rock* (no); *Tom/Mom* (yes); *top/tap* (no).

On their own

Have children produce words that rhyme with the following words.

pop	**hot**	**block**	**Todd**
rack	**pin**	**cap**	**rim**

Team Talk Have children create pairs of rhyming words with a partner. Provide prompts if needed, such as *What rhymes with the word* cob?

Differentiated Instruction

SI Strategic Intervention

Left-to-Right Progression If children try to arrange the letters of the alphabet backwards—that is, from *g* to *a* rather than from *a* to *g*—have children practice drawing lines from left to right across a page to internalize the proper direction. For further reinforcement, have children draw arrows pointing to the right on index cards or sticky notes. Have these children place the arrows on their desks to remind them which way we read.

Academic Vocabulary

rhyming words words that end with the same sound or sounds

ELL

English Language Learners
Word Meanings English language learners may not know the meanings of some of the words used in the rhyming activities. Have them share definitions they already know, helping them describe the meanings through language and gestures, and offer child-friendly definitions of less familiar words. For *rob*, for example, say *When you rob someone, you take a thing that belongs to them.*

Objectives
○ Associate the consonant *h* with the sound /h/.
• Write the letters *Hh*.
• Blend, read, and spell words with *h*.
• Recognize and name the letters *Hh*.

Phonics
↻ Consonant *h* /h/

Hear   Today you will learn how to spell the sound /h/. Listen: /h/, /h/, /h/. When you say /h/, some air comes out of your mouth. Put your hand in front of your mouth. Say /h/ and feel the air coming out of your mouth. Watch and listen as children produce the sound. Say /h/ with me: /h/, /h/, /h/.

Say   Display Sound-Spelling Card 10. This is a picture of a *helicopter*. Say it with me: *helicopter*. The first sound in *helicopter* is /h/. Listen: /h/, *helicopter*. Say it with me: /h/, *helicopter*. What is the first sound in *helicopter*?

See   Point to *h*. This is *h*. The sound /h/ is usually spelled *h*. *Helicopter* begins with /h/. *Helicopter* begins with the letter *h*. Have children say /h/ several times as you point to *h*.

Sound-Spelling Card 10

Read ABC Rhyme Time   Display ABC Rhyme Time, p. 13. Point to the letters *Hh* at the top of the page. The name for both of these letters is *h*. Point to *H*. This is an upper-case *H*. Point to *h*. This is a lower-case *h*. Point to each letter again and ask: What is the name of this letter?

This rhyme is about a hamster who is hiding somewhere in a house. Read the rhyme aloud, tracking the print with your finger. Then read it again. Point to examples of upper- and lower-case *h*'s as you read each word aloud.

Hamster in My House

ABC Rhyme Time p. 13

Write   Now I will show you how to write upper-case *H* and lower-case *h*. Write *H*. Watch as I trace capital *H* with my finger. Follow the stroke instructions pictured. Now you write upper-case *H*. Repeat for lower-case *h*.

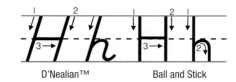

D'Nealian™   Ball and Stick

Phonics—Teach/Model
◉ Consonant *h* /h/

ROUTINE **Blending Strategy**

1 **Connect** Connect consonant *h* to the sound /h/. Write *h*. This is *h*. What is the sound for *h*? The sound for *h* is /h/. Say the sound with me: /h/, /h/, /h/. When you see *h*, what sound will you say?

2 **Model** Model how to blend *hat*. Write *h*. What is the sound for this letter? Say the sound with me: /h/. Write *a*. Say this sound with me: /a/. Write *t*. Say this sound with me: /t/. Listen as I blend all the sounds together: /h/ /a/ /t/, hat. Blend the sounds with me: /h/ /a/ /t/, *hat*. Now blend the sounds without me.

3 **Guide Practice** Continue the routine in Step 2 with the words that follow. Remember, first we say the sounds. Then we blend the sounds to read the word.

hill	had	hip	him	ham	hid	lid	dip	lad

For corrective feedback, model blending the sounds to read the word. Then have children blend the sounds and read the word with you.

4 **Review** What do you know about reading words that begin with the letter *h*? The sound for *h* is /h/.

Routines Flip Chart

Spell Now we are going to spell words with the sound /h/ spelled *h*. The first word we will spell is *hit*. What sounds do you hear in *hit*? (/h/ /i/ /t/) What is the letter for /h/? Let's all write *h*. What is the letter for /i/? Write *i*. What is the letter for /t/? Write *t*. Have children confirm their spellings by comparing them with what you have written. Continue practice with *ham, had, hip,* and *hill.* Ask children how the spellings of *hip* and *hill* are alike and different.

On their own Use the *Reader's and Writer's Notebook* p. 69 for additional practice with /h/ spelled *h*.

Reader's and Writer's Notebook, p. 69

Objectives
• Recognize and name the letters *Hh*.
• Distinguish upper- and lower-case letters.
• Practice high-frequency words.

Phonics
Identify Lower-Case and Upper-Case Letters

Guide practice

Write a lower-case *h* and point to it. What letter is this? (lower-case *h*) Write an upper-case *H* and point to it. What letter is this? (upper-case *H*) Write a series of upper- and lower-case *h*'s. Point to each and have children identify each as upper-case *H* or lower-case *H*.

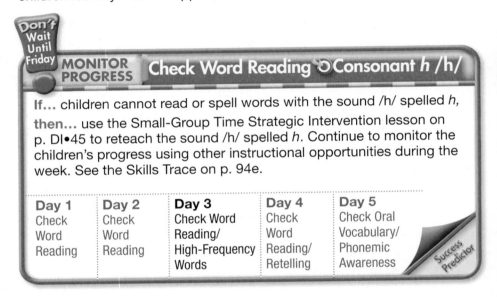

Don't Wait Until Friday

MONITOR PROGRESS | **Check Word Reading ↻ Consonant *h* /h/**

If... children cannot read or spell words with the sound /h/ spelled *h*,

then... use the Small-Group Time Strategic Intervention lesson on p. DI•45 to reteach the sound /h/ spelled *h*. Continue to monitor the children's progress using other instructional opportunities during the week. See the Skills Trace on p. 94e.

Day 1	**Day 2**	**Day 3**	**Day 4**	**Day 5**
Check Word Reading	Check Word Reading	Check Word Reading/ High-Frequency Words	Check Word Reading/ Retelling	Check Oral Vocabulary/ Phonemic Awareness

Success Predictor

Small Group Time

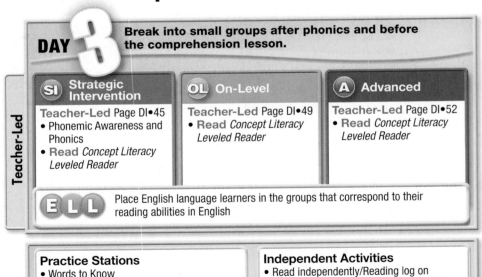

DAY 3 Break into small groups after phonics and before the comprehension lesson.

Teacher-Led

SI Strategic Intervention
Teacher-Led Page DI•45
• Phonemic Awareness and Phonics
• Read *Concept Literacy Leveled Reader*

OL On-Level
Teacher-Led Page DI•49
• Read *Concept Literacy Leveled Reader*

A Advanced
Teacher-Led Page DI•52
• Read *Concept Literacy Leveled Reader*

ELL Place English language learners in the groups that correspond to their reading abilities in English

Practice Stations
• Words to Know

Independent Activities
• Read independently/Reading log on *Reader's and Writer's Notebook* p. RR1.

Objectives

- Identify and produce a simple sentence.
- Use self-evaluation when writing.
- Write *Hh*.

Conventions
Simple Sentences

Review Simple Sentences

Remind children that a sentence is a group of words that tells a complete idea. It includes a noun and a verb. A sentence begins with a capital letter and often ends with a period.

Guide practice

Write this sentence on the board and read it aloud.

A leaf fell.

What is the noun in this sentence? (leaf) What is the verb? (fell)

Team Talk Have pairs of children create their own sentences by replacing the noun, verb, or both in the sentence above.

Connect to oral language

Have children complete these sentence frames orally using nouns and verbs.

1. The pot _____.
2. _____ hid a hat.
3. Sam can _____.

On their own

Use *Reader's and Writer's Notebook* p. 71.

Reader's and Writer's Notebook, p. 71

Handwriting
Letter *H* and *h*; Self-Evaluation

Model letter formation

Display upper- and lower-case letters: *Hh*. Use the stroke instructions pictured below to model proper letter formation.

D'Nealian™   Ball and Stick

Model self-evaluation

Explain that when we write a word, we should look back at our writing to see if we did a good job. We should ask ourselves: Do the letters look the way they are supposed to look? Did I use the correct upper-case and lower-case letters and write them from left to right on the page? Did I use correct spacing between letters? Remind children to completely erase any mistakes they find before rewriting.

Guide practice

Write the following sentence with obvious errors in capitalization and letter spacing.

The fat cat can nap.

Read the sentence aloud as you track the words. Have children find the errors in the sentence.

Team Talk Have children work in pairs to rewrite the sentence correctly and evaluate their work.

On their own

Use the *Reader's and Writer's Notebook* p. 72.

Reader's and Writer's Notebook, p. 72

Differentiated Instruction

SI **Strategic Intervention**

Ask Questions If children have difficulty evaluating the sentence, ask them the same questions you presented in the model. Then ask the children to consider any other errors that you might not have mentioned.

Daily Fix-It

5. Thut dol is yellow.

That doll is yellow.

6. the cat is yello.

The cat is yellow.

Discuss the Daily Fix-It corrections with children. Review sentence capitalization and spelling.

Objectives
- Produce a simple sentence.
- Write a simple sentence that states a complete idea.
- Give directions.

Writing — Sentences

Model

Have children recall the Big Book, *First Grade, Here I Come!* Yesterday and today we heard a story about Henry's first day in first grade. Let's write a sentence that tells what Henry does. Write the sentence below.

> **He meets a friend.**

Read the sentence and explain that it tells a complete idea.

Guide practice

Write more sentences about Henry's first day at school. Then read the sentences and have children identify the nouns and verbs.

> **Henry holds a note.**
>
> **The mouse sees the library.**

Connect to phonics

Reread the sentences with children and have them point to the words with /h/ spelled *h*.

Shared writing

Write the following sentence frame on the board: *Henry _____.* Have children complete the sentence. Tell children to think about the different things Henry does in the story. Use children's suggestions to complete the sentence.

On their own

Some children may be ready to write on their own. Write the following sentence frame on the board: *Henry _____.* Have children complete the sentence on their own. Children may also write new sentences, if they can. Have children circle the noun and underline the verb in the sentence. Then have them read their sentence aloud.

Listening and Speaking
Give Directions

Review Giving directions

Have children recall what they know about giving directions. Directions tell how to do or make something. It is important to give directions in the order in which they should be done. Review what to do when giving directions.

- Speak clearly.
- Give directions in order.

Model

 Think Aloud I will give you directions for making a sandwich. First get two slices of bread. Think about what you'd like to have in your sandwich. I like ham and cheese, so I'll have that. Next put a slice of ham and a slice of cheese between the slices of bread.

Guide practice

Have children give directions for making other snacks, such as cheese and crackers. Work with children to ensure they speak clearly and give the directions in order.

On their own

Have pairs of children take turns giving directions to do or make something simple. Remind children to follow the rules for speaking and listening that they established in Week 1. Have them take turns following the instructions while their partner observes.

Wrap Up Your Day

✔ **Consonants Hh /h/** Write *Hid and hat.* Point to the *H* in *Hid* and the *h* in *hat* as you say the words aloud. Have children repeat them after you.

✔ **High-Frequency Words** Point to the words *they, have, two, that,* and *are* on the Word Wall. Have children read each word and use it in a sentence.

✔ **Build Concepts** Monitor children's use of oral vocabulary as they respond. Recall the Big Book, *First Grade, Here I Come!* Have children explain if Henry has trouble making new friends in his neighborhood school.

Differentiated Instruction

 Strategic Intervention

Discuss Order If children have difficulty giving directions in order, have them practice talking about the order in which they do something every day, such as washing their hands. Guide children to understand that describing things in the correct order is important when giving directions.

English Language Learners
Create Sentences If children cannot create sentences on their own, try performing an action and having children describe it in a sentence. For example, hop up and down or run in place. Ask *What am I doing?*

Preview DAY 4

Tell children that tomorrow they will read about two friends and a cat in *The Big Top.*

Objectives

- Discuss the concept of friends and neighborhoods to develop oral language.
- Build oral vocabulary.
- Identify details in text.

Today at a Glance

Oral Vocabulary
porch, squirrel

Print Awareness
Sequence Letters

Phonemic Awareness
Blend and segment phonemes

Phonics
◉ Short *o: o*

Genre
Realistic Fiction

High-Frequency Words
Review

Comprehension
◉ Realism and Fantasy
◉ Questioning

Writing and Conventions
Simple Sentences

Research
Maps

Handwriting
Letter *O* and *o;* Letter Size

Concept Talk

 Question of the Week

What can we do with our neighborhood friends?

Build concepts

To reinforce concepts and to focus children's attention, have children sing "New Neighbor" from the *Sing with Me* Big Book. The song says that the new neighbor is kind. How do you know if somebody is kind? (they care about you, they treat you with respect)

 Sing with Me Big Book Audio

Monitor listening comprehension

Recall that children have sung a song about a new neighbor and have heard a story about Henry meeting a new friend at school. Explain that today, you will read a story about a girl who meets a new neighbor. Read the selection.

"My Puppy Sings the Blues"

ELL Produce Oral Language Use the Day 4 instruction on ELL Poster R4 to extend and enrich language.

ELL Poster R4

Oral Vocabulary
Amazing Words

Teach Amazing Words

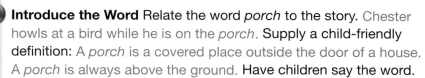

Amazing Words **Oral Vocabulary Routine**

① **Introduce the Word** Relate the word *porch* to the story. Chester howls at a bird while he is on the *porch*. Supply a child-friendly definition: A *porch* is a covered place outside the door of a house. A *porch* is always above the ground. Have children say the word.

② **Demonstrate** Provide examples to show meaning. We like to sit on our back *porch*. The ball rolled under the *porch*. I have to sweep the front *porch*.

③ **Apply** Have children demonstrate their understanding. Tell me some things you could do on a *porch*. Then tell me some things you could <u>not</u> do on a *porch*.

See p. OV•4 to teach *squirrel*.

Routines Flip Chart

Anchored Talk

Add to the concept map

Use these questions to discuss what children can do with their neighborhood friends as you add to the concept map.

- In the story "My Puppy Sings the Blues," what are Autumn and Laura doing when they meet each other? (walking their dogs) I'll add that to our concept map.

- We've learned a lot about neighborhood friends so far. Think about the song we've learned, the stories we've heard, and the pictures we've seen. Can you think of somebody who helped a neighborhood friend? (possible answer: the animals in "A Neighborhood Picnic" helped each other by bringing food for everyone) Let's add *help each other* to our concept map.

Amazing Words

amusing	trouble
introduce	deliver
neighbor	porch
corner	squirrel

Differentiated Instruction

SI **Strategic Intervention**

Increase Comprehension To help focus children's attention on the details and main ideas of the Read Aloud Anthology story, help children set a purpose for listening. For this story, you might ask children to listen to learn how Autumn's dog helps her make a new friend.

English Language Learners
Pronunciation Spanish, Hmong, Vietnamese, and many other languages do not have initial *s*-blends. Children from these language backgrounds may add a short *e* sound at the beginning of *squirrel,* or may insert a vowel between the *s* and the *qu*. To give children extra practice with pronunciation, have them say /sss/ and then /kw/ several times. Gradually have them move the sounds together to form the blend /skw/.

Objectives

- Understand that the letters of the alphabet are arranged in a sequence.
- Sequence the letters of the alphabet from a through p.
- Segment and blend phonemes.

Print Awareness
Sequence Letters

Review

Yesterday, we took the letters from *a* to *g* and put them in order. Say the letters with me: *a, b, c, d, e, f, g.* Now let's say them again, one person at a time. **Say *a* and then point to six children in turn, having each name the next letter in the sequence until you reach *g*.** We're going to study the next nine letters of the alphabet and put them in order, too.

Model

Write the letters *h, i, j, k, l, m, n, o, p* on the board and read them slowly from left to right, touching each in turn. Point out that *h* is the letter immediately after *g.* Read the letters once more, this time with children. Pay particular attention to *j, k,* and *o* as they have not yet been formally covered in this unit. Then have children close their eyes briefly. While their eyes are closed, erase the letter *n.* Have children open their eyes and look at the board.

Think Aloud
I erased one of the letters. I wonder which one it is? Let me see—I know I wrote the letters in order from *h* to *p*. So I can start at *h* and say the letters in order until I come to a letter that's missing. **Help me say the letters as I move from left to right. Move your hand slowly from left to right under the letters, naming them as you go.** I start with *h.* I see the letter *i,* which comes after *h.* I have *h, i, j, k, l, m, n*—wait a minute, there isn't any *n.* The letter *n* should be here, but it isn't. It's missing. I'll write it here and check from the beginning: *h, i, j, k, l, m, n, o, p.* I erased the letter *n.*

Guide practice

Repeat the modeling activity above, erasing the letter *m* while children's eyes are closed. Have children tell you the correct steps to determine the missing letter. Repeat two more times, erasing first *j* and then *p.*

On their own

Use *Reader's and Writer's Notebook* p. 73.

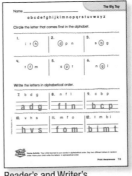

Reader's and Writer's Notebook p. 73

Phonemic Awareness
Blend and Segment Phonemes

Model

We just read about a dog named Chester. What does Chester do when he howls? **(points his head up high)** Listen to the sounds in *head*: /h/ /e/ /d/. Listen as I blend the sounds to say the word *head*: /h/ /e/ /d/, *head.* Say it with me: /h/ /e/ /d/, *head.* **Repeat with the word *dog*.**

Guide practice

Now we're going to blend sounds to say other words. Listen to the sounds in *hop*: /h/ /o/ /p/. Say the sounds with me: /h/ /o/ /p/. Now let's blend the sounds: /h/ /o/ /p/, *hop.* **Continue with the following words. Say the sounds in each word with the children and then blend the sounds to say the word.**

/l/ /o/ /t/, lot	**/d/ /o/ /l/**, doll	**/h/ /e/ /n/**, hen
/t/ /o/ /d/, Todd	**/f/ /i/ /l/**, fill	**/h/ /o/ /t/**, hot

Corrective feedback

If children make an error, model the correct response. Return to the word later in the practice.

On their own

Continue with the following words. Have children say the sounds in each word and then blend the sounds to say the word.

/d/ /i/ /d/, did	**/l/ /o/ /k/**, lock	**/h/ /i/ /p/**, hip
/r/ /e/ /d/, red	**/h/ /i/ /l/**, hill	**/n/ /o/ /d/**, nod

Objectives

- ○ Associate the letter *o* with the sound /o/.
- Write the letters *Oo*.
- Blend, read, and spell words with *o*.
- Recognize and name the letters *Oo*.

Skills Trace

◉ **Short *o*: *o***
Introduce URW4D4
Practice URW4D4; URW4D5
Reteach/Review URW4D5; URW5D1; URW5D2; URW5D3
Assess/Test Weekly Test URW4
Benchmark Test UR

Phonics
🎯 Short *o*: *o*

Hear

Today you will learn how to spell the sound /o/. Listen: /o/, /o/, /o/. When you say /o/, your mouth is open and your jaw drops. Put your hand under your chin and say /o/. Could you feel that your mouth opened and your jaw dropped? Say /o/ again. **Watch and listen as children produce the sound.** Say /o/ with me: /o/, /o/, /o/.

Say

Display Sound-Spelling Card 17. This is a picture of an *octopus*. Say it with me: *octopus*. The first sound in *octopus* is /o/. Listen: /o/, *octopus*. Say it with me: /o/, *octopus*. What is the first sound in *octopus*?

See

Point to *o*. This is *o*. The sound /o/ is usually spelled *o*. *Octopus* begins with /o/. *Octopus* begins with the letter *o*. **Have children say /o/ several times as you point to *o*.**

Sound-Spelling
Card 17

Read ABC Rhyme Time

Display ABC Rhyme Time, p. 20. Point to the letters *Oo* at the top of the page. The name for both of these letters is *o*. Point to *O*. This is an upper-case *O*. Point to *o*. This is a lower-case *o*. **Point to each letter again and ask: What is the name of this letter?**

This rhyme is about an odd otter. The word *odd* means *strange*. An *otter* is an animal that swims well. *Ottawa* is the name of a city in Canada. All those words begin with /o/. They begin with *o*. **Read the rhyme aloud, tracking the print with your finger. Then read it again. Point to examples of upper- and lower-case *o*'s as you read each word aloud.**

ABC Rhyme Time p. 20

Write

Now I will show you how to write upper-case *O* and lower-case *o*. Write *O*. Watch as I trace upper-case *O* with my finger. **Follow the stroke instructions pictured.** Now you write upper-case *O*. Repeat for lower-case *o*.

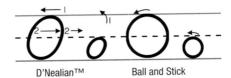

D'Nealian™   Ball and Stick

 **Interactive Sound-Spelling Cards**

Phonics—Teach/Model
↺ Short o: o

ROUTINE Blending Strategy

① **Connect** Connect o to the sound /o/. Write o. This is o. The sound for o is /o/. Say the sound with me: /o/, /o/, /o/. When you see the letter o, what sound will you say?

② **Model** Model how to blend *dot*. Write d. What is the sound for this letter? Say the sound with me: /d/. Write o. Say this sound with me: /o/. Write t. Say this sound with me: /t/. Listen as I blend all the sounds together: /d/ /o/ /t/, *dot*. Blend the sounds with me: /d/ /o/ /t/, *dot*. Now blend the sounds without me.

③ **Guide Practice** Continue the routine in Step 2 with the words that follow. Remember, first we say the sounds. Then we blend the sounds to read the word.

dot	hop	lock	hot	lot	mom	dock

For corrective feedback, model blending the sounds to read the word. Then have children blend the sounds and read the word with you.

④ **Review** What do you know about reading words that begin with the letter o or have o in the middle? (The sound for o is /o/.)

Routines Flip Chart

Spell words Now we are going to spell words with the sound /o/ spelled o. The first word we will spell is *nod*. What sounds do you hear in *nod*? (/n/ /o/ /d/) What is the letter for sound /n/? Let's all write n. What is the letter for /o/? Write o. What is the letter for sound /d/? Write d. Have children confirm their spellings by comparing them with what you have written. Continue practice with *got, hop, not*, and *top*. Ask what word you get if you change the t in *top* to m. (mop)

On their own Use the *Reader's and Writer's Notebook* p. 74 for additional practice with short vowel o.

Reader's and Writer's Notebook p. 74

Differentiated Instruction

SI **Strategic Intervention**
Sound /o/ To help children associate the sound /o/ with the letter o, have children pretend to be detectives. Give them magnifying glasses or have them make pretend ones out of cardboard. Point out that the circular part of the magnifying glass is shaped like o. Then have them move through the room "discovering" important clues through the magnifying glass while saying *Ah!* in a dramatic voice.

Spelling Pattern
/o/o The sound /o/ is usually spelled o at the beginning or in the middle of a word.

ELL
English Language Learners
Pronounce Words with Sound /o/ Speakers of Japanese, Urdu, Vietnamese, and other languages may struggle to distinguish short o from short a. If children cannot pronounce sound /o/ correctly, have them practice saying and reading word pairs such as *pat/pot, Dan/Don, map/mop*, and *sack/sock*.

Objectives

- ○ Associate consonant *h* with the sound /h/.
- ○ Associate vowel *o* with the sound /o/.
- • Write the letters *Oo*.
- • Blend, read, and spell words with *h* or *o*.
- • Recognize and name the letters *Oo*.

Phonics
Identify Lower-Case and Upper-Case Letters

Guide Practice

Write a lower-case *o* and point to it. What letter is this? (lower-case *o*)

Write an upper-case *O* and point to it. What letter is this? (upper-case *O*)

Write a series of upper- and lower-case *o's*. Point to each and have children identify each as upper-case *O* or lower-case *o*.

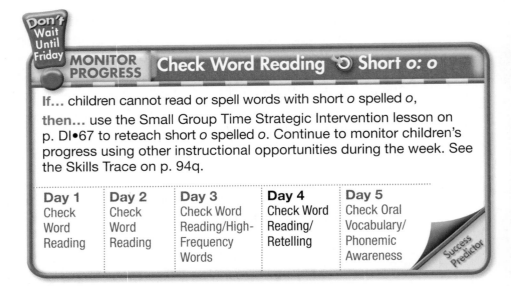

Don't Wait Until Friday

MONITOR PROGRESS | **Check Word Reading ⟳ Short *o*: *o***

If... children cannot read or spell words with short *o* spelled *o*,

then... use the Small Group Time Strategic Intervention lesson on p. DI•67 to reteach short *o* spelled *o*. Continue to monitor children's progress using other instructional opportunities during the week. See the Skills Trace on p. 94q.

Day 1	**Day 2**	**Day 3**	**Day 4**	**Day 5**
Check Word Reading	Check Word Reading	Check Word Reading/High-Frequency Words	Check Word Reading/Retelling	Check Oral Vocabulary/Phonemic Awareness

Success Predictor

Small Group Time

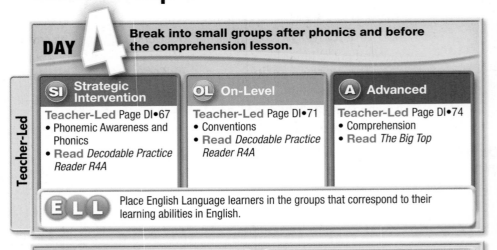

DAY 4 Break into small groups after phonics and before the comprehension lesson.

Teacher-Led

SI Strategic Intervention	**OL On-Level**	**A Advanced**
Teacher-Led Page DI•67	**Teacher-Led** Page DI•71	**Teacher-Led** Page DI•74
• Phonemic Awareness and Phonics	• Conventions	• Comprehension
• **Read** *Decodable Practice Reader R4A*	• **Read** *Decodable Practice Reader R4A*	• **Read** *The Big Top*

ELL Place English Language learners in the groups that correspond to their learning abilities in English.

Practice Stations	**Independent Activities**
• Read for Meaning	• Read independently/Reading log on *Reader's and Writer's Notebook* p. RR1. • Audio Text of Main Selection

Phonics—Build Fluency
Consonant *h* /h/, Short Vowel *o* /o/

Model

Envision It!

Have children turn to page 94 in their Student Edition. Look at the pictures on this page. I see a picture of a *helicopter* and a picture of an *octopus*. When I say *helicopter*, I begin with the sound /h/. The /h/ sound is spelled with an *h*. When I say *octopus*, I begin with the sound /o/. The /o/ sound is spelled with an *o*.

Guide practice

For each word in "Words I Can Blend," ask for the sound of each letter. Make sure that children identify the correct sound for *h* or *o*. Then have children blend the whole word.

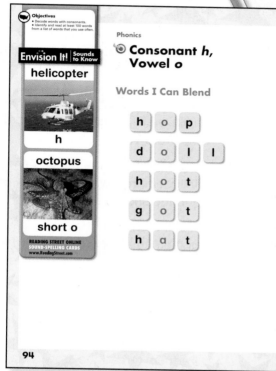

Student Edition p. 94

Corrective feedback

If... children have difficulty blending a word,
then... model blending the word, and then ask children to blend it with you.

Differentiated Instruction

A Advanced

Extend Blending Provide children who can segment and blend all the words correctly with more challenging words such as: *held, hopped, hand, hilltop, hockey, stop, blot, holly, pond,* and *pocket.*

Spelling Patterns

/h/ Spelled *h* The sound /h/ is usually spelled *h*.

/o/ Spelled *o* The sound /o/ is usually spelled *o* at the beginning or in the middle of a word.

Objectives
- Apply knowledge of sound-spellings to decode unknown words when reading.
- Decode words in context and in isolation.
- Practice fluency with oral rereading.
- Read high frequency words.

Decodable Practice Reader R4A
🎯 Consonants d /d/, h /h/ and Short o: o

Decode words in isolation	Have children turn to page 49. Have children decode each word.
Review high-frequency words	Review the previously taught words was, look, and I. Have children read each word as you point to it on the Word Wall.
Preview Decodable Reader	Have children read the title and preview the story. Tell them they will read words with sounds /d/, /h/, and the short o sound.
Print awarenress	Remind children that reading is done from the top of the page to the bottom and from left to right with a return sweep. Have them read aloud the first few pages of the Decodable Practice Reader using their fingers to track the print. Monitor children as they read aloud, making sure they are tracking the print correctly.
Decode words in context	Pair children for reading and listen carefully as they decode. One child begins. Children read the entire story, switching readers after each page. Partners reread the story. This time the other child begins.

On Top
Written by Crystal Tsang

Decodable Practice Reader R4A

Tom sat.
Tom was on top.

Look, Mom.
I am on top.

50

51

Decodable Reader R4A

Dot sat.
Dot was on top.

Look, Mom.
I am on top.

52

53

Tom was hot.

Dot was hot.

54

55

Tom was not on top.
Dot was not on top.

56

Corrective feedback

If... children have difficulty decoding a word,
then... refer them to the Sound-Spelling Cards to
identify the sounds in the word. Prompt them to blend
the word.

- What is the new word?
- Is the new word a word you know?
- Does it make sense in the story?

Check decoding and comprehension

Have children retell the story to include characters, setting, and
events. Then have children locate words with /o/ spelled *o* in the
story. List words that children name. Children should supply *Tom,
on, top, Mom, Dot, hot,* and *not.* Ask children how they know these
words have the /o/ sound. *(They all have o.)*

Reread for Fluency

Have children reread Decodable Reader R4A to develop automaticity decoding words with the short *o* sound.

   ROUTINE   **Oral Rereading**

(1) **Read** Have children read the entire book orally.

(2) **Reread** To achieve optimal fluency, children should reread the text
three or four times.

(3) **Corrective Feedback** Listen as children read. Provide corrective
feedback regarding their fluency and decoding.

Routines Flip Chart

English Language Learners
Short o: o

Beginning After reading, lead
children through a picture walk
through *On Top*. Have children
tell what Tom or Dot is doing in
each picture.

Intermediate After reading,
have children make up a sentence about one of the characters, Tom, Dot, or Mom. Monitor
children's pronunciation.

Advanced/Advanced High
After reading, draw a T-chart
with the headings: *Names with
o* and *Words with o.* Have children write the short o names
and words from the story in
the appropriate column. Then
have them select four to use in
sentences.

Objectives
- Identify the features of realistic fiction.
- Review high-frequency words.

Genre
Realistic Fiction

Identify features of realistic fiction

Use the story *The Big Top* to have children identify the features of realistic fiction.

- The reading selection, *The Big Top*, tells about two girls and a cat. In the story, the girls play with a doll and a top. The cat hits the doll and then jumps on the top.
- Are these things that could happen in real life? How do you know? (Possible response: Yes, I have played with these things and I know a cat can get into trouble.)
- What about if the doll came to life and danced with the cat? Could that happen in real life? How do you know? (No, a doll can't come to life and real cats do not dance.)
- We use what we read and what we know to tell that *The Big Top* is a made-up story that could happen in real-life. It is realistic fiction.

Guide practice

Explain that the class will now use the story *Snap!* to compare realistic fiction to something that is actually true. Use Graphic Organizer 4 or draw a T-Chart. Label the left column *Snap!* and

T-Chart	
Snap!	**True Story**
made-up characters, made-up setting, made-up events that could really happen	In a true story, the people and setting are real, and the events really did happen.

Graphic Organizer Flip Chart 4

the right column "True Story." Have children help you list the characteristics of the story and the characteristics of a true story, or nonfiction. What are some things that a realistic story like *Snap!* includes? (made-up characters, made-up setting, made-up events that could really happen). How are these things different with a true story? (In a true story, the people and setting are real, and the events really did happen).

On their own

Have groups of children work together to create their own realistic short stories. Have them draw pictures to tell their story and then tell and show the story to the class. Ask them to explain why their stories are realistic fiction and not true stories.

High-Frequency Words
Build Fluency

Read words in isolation

Remind children that there are some words we learn by remembering the letters, rather than by saying the sounds. Then have them read each of the highlighted high-frequency words aloud.

Read words in context

Chorally read the I Can Read! passage along with the children. Then have them read the passage aloud to themselves. When they are finished, ask children to reread the high-frequency words.

Team Talk Have children choose two high-frequency words and give them time to create a sentence in which both words are used properly. Then have them share the sentence with a partner.

 I Can Read!

I have a big doll. Doll can hop. Hop, Doll, hop! Doll can hop on a hill.

Two can look at Doll hop.

It got hot on that hill. The two got a hat. They are not hot.

You've learned

- Consonants d, l, h
- Vowel o

High-Frequency Words
are have they that two

95

Student Edition p. 95

Differentiated Instruction

A Advanced

Extend High-Frequency Words
Have pairs of students tell their own sentences about the doll. Have them use this week's high-frequency words in their sentences.

Objectives
- Build background about neighborhoods.
- Preview and predict.
- Use structure and elements of realistic fiction to improve understanding of text.
- Set a purpose for reading text.

Build Background
The Big Top

Background Building Audio

Have children listen to the CD. Tell them to listen especially for all the people and things the dog sees on the block.

 Background Building Audio

Discuss neighborhoods

Team Talk Have children turn to a partner and use these questions for discussion:

- What is a neighborhood?
- What are some things you can find in a neighborhood?
- Who are your neighbors?

Draw a map

Draw a block map. Title it *My Neighborhood.* Have children help you fill in the map with buildings and places you would find in a neighborhood.

Connect to selection

We heard about a pet and its view of the block. What are some of the things the dog sees? (The dog sees people who live on the block, a fire hydrant, stop signs, a park, an apartment building, a library, and a store.) We're going to read *The Big Top.* It is a story about two friends and a troublesome cat. We'll read to find out what happens when the friends play together.

Student Edition pp. 96–97

Main Selection—Let's Read
The Big Top

Practice the skill

 Realism and Fantasy Remind children that realistic fiction is a made-up story that could happen and a fantasy is a story that could never happen. Have children name a story that is realistic fiction and a story that is a fantasy. Have them tell how they know.

Introduce the strategy

Questioning Explain that readers ask themselves questions to make sense of what they read. Have children turn to page EI•13 in their Student Edition.

Envision It!

Think Aloud Look at what is happening in the picture. What is the child asking? (why the bell is cracked) Why is the child probably asking this? (Possible response: The child is confused about the crack in the bell and wants to understand why it is there.) Good readers ask themselves questions before and during reading. This helps them understand what happens in the selection.

Student Edition EI•13

Introduce genre

Let's Read Together **Realistic fiction** is a made-up story that could happen in real life. As they read *The Big Top,* have children look for realistic parts of the story.

Preview and predict

Have children identify the title of the story, the author, and the illustrator. Read aloud the names of the author and illustrator and have children describe the role of each. Help children activate prior knowledge by asking them to look through the selection and use the illustrations to predict what might happen in the story.

Set a purpose

Good readers read for a purpose. Setting a purpose helps us to think and understand more as we read.

Have children read the story to find out what happens on the block.

Tell children that today they will read *The Big Top.* Use the Guide Comprehension notes to help children develop their comprehension of the reading selection.

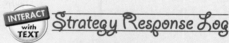

Objectives
○ Ask questions about narrative text to clarify understanding.
• Describe the plot (problem and solution) in a narrative text.

The Big Top

by Molly O'Keefe
illustrated by Hector Borlasca

Genre Stories that are **realistic fiction** tell about events could happen in the lives of real people and animals. This story is about two friends who play together.

Question of the Week
What can we do with our neighborhood friends?

96

97

Student Edition pp. 96–97

Comprehension Strategy
Questioning

Teach   Read the question on p. 97 aloud: *What can we do with our neighborhood friends?* Explain that questioning helps us make sense of what we read. Good readers always ask questions about what they read. Thinking of questions to ask makes it easier to pay attention and be interested in the story.

Model   **Think Aloud** When I read a story, I ask myself questions to help me understand, to remember, and to learn more about what I am reading. When I preview *The Big Top,* I ask questions such as "Who are the kids in the illustration? Are they friends? Where does this story take place? What is the big top?" I will read to find the answer. I will continue asking myself questions as I read the story.

Guide practice   Have children ask their own questions as they preview the story. Record the questions on the board and tell children to read to find the answers.

Pam and Dot can hop and hop.

One, two. They can hop fast.

98

Dot and Pam sat.

Dot and Pam are on the mat.

99

Student Edition pp. 98–99

Comprehension Skill
Review Plot

Teach

Remind children that the plot of a story is made up of the events that happen in the beginning, middle, and end of the story. What happens at the beginning of *The Big Top*?

If... children have difficulty answering the question,

then... model how to use the text and illustrations to recognize the plot of the story.

Model

 Think Aloud As I read, I ask myself what is happening in this story. I know that in the beginning, Pam and Dot are hopping on their block. Then they are tired. They sit on a mat. I will keep reading to find out what happens next.

Guide practice

Ask children why it is helpful to look for what happens at the beginning and in the middle of the story.

Differentiated Instruction

 A Advanced

Discuss Neighborhoods Use the pictures and text to talk about the type of neighborhood in the story. Discuss different places to live, such as houses, apartments, and townhouses. Compare the block in the story with the neighborhoods they live in. How are they different? How are they the same?

Strategic Reading

Remind children that good readers use comprehension strategies, such as questioning, as they read.

English Language Learners
Picture Walks Use picture walks to preview the text and the concept of neighborhoods. Use the pictures to introduce characters and the setting, and to give a simple summary of the story.

The Big Top **98–99**

Objectives

○ Distinguish realism from fantasy.
• Read words in context.
• Read words with *d* /d/, *h* /h/, *l*, *ll* /l/, and short *o* /o/.
• Read nondecodable words.

A <u>doll</u> sat <u>on</u> the mat.

Tip hit the <u>doll</u>. <u>Stop</u>, Tip, <u>stop</u>!

100

A big <u>top</u> sat <u>on</u> the mat.

Tip can see it.

101

Student Edition pp. 100–101

Comprehension Skill
Realism and Fantasy

Teach

Remind children that realism is about made-up events that could happen in real life, while fantasy is about things that could never really happen. Could this story happen in real life? How can you tell?

| If... children have difficulty answering the questions,
| then... model how to distinguish fantasy from realistic fiction.

Model

Think Aloud

I know that kids can sometimes play outside on the block by their houses. Real children have friends on their block that they play with. People play with dolls and tops, too. The pictures on these pages show children and a cat that look real. These things tell me that this story could really happen.

Guide practice

Have children study the pictures on pages 100 and 101 and describe what clues tell them this story is realistic fiction. (Possible response: The toys look real, and the block looks like a real street. The cat acts like a real cat.)

Dot got the big top.

Tip did not like that top!

Tip hid.

Dot and Pam sat.

Student Edition pp. 102–103

Phonics/High-Frequency Words
Word Reading

Teach

Remind children that they have learned some new sounds and letters this week.

Model

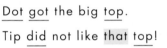 Some words on page 102 have the short *o* sound spelled *o*. *Dot* is one of these words. Knowing short *o* will help me read this word: /d/ /o/ /t/, *Dot*. What are some other short *o* words on this page? **(got, top, not)** You also learned some other words this week that you don't have to blend the sounds to read. You already know these words. *That* on page 102 is one of these words. What are some other words like this in the story? **(two, they, are, have)**

Guide practice

If... children come to a decodable word or high-frequency word they don't know,

then... reteach the problematic word and blend it with them.

Objectives
○ Ask questions about narrative text to clarify understanding.

Tip hit the big top.

Tip bit it. Stop, Tip, stop!

104

Pam and Dot stop Tip.

Pam and Dot have the big top.

105

Student Edition pp. 104–105

Comprehension Strategy
Questioning

Teach

Remind children that questioning while we read helps us learn more about the text and make sense of it. Good readers always ask questions about what they read. Think about the questions you had at the beginning of the story. Have those questions been answered? Did you have any more as you read?

Model

 I wanted to know who the kids were and if they were friends. Those questions were answered right away. I also wanted to know where the story took place. Even though it didn't say exactly where, I was able to figure it out as I kept reading. I also learned what the big top was. I had a lot more questions as I read. I wanted to know what Tip would do with the top and if Pam and Dot would be able to get him to stop biting it.

Guide practice

Have children review with a partner their own questions at the beginning of the story. Have them discuss whether the questions were answered.

Comprehension Check

Have children discuss each question with a partner. Ask several pairs to share their responses.

☑ **Realistic fiction** What clues show *The Big Top* is a realistic story or a fantasy? (Possible response: The children look real. They do things that real kids would do, such as playing with things outside. The cat looks and acts real, too. These clues show it is a realistic story.)

☑ **Questioning** How did asking questions help you as you read? (Possible response: Asking questions helped me understand the story better because I looked for answers as I read.)

☑ **Confirm predictions** How did you use the pictures and words to confirm what happened in the story? (Possible response: I read the part that tells about what Tip did with the top. I used the picture of Tip jumping on the top.)

☑ **Connect text to self** Dot and Pam like to play outside. Think about a time you played outside. What did you play? Did you play with a friend? Explain what happened. (Possible response: I played tag in my backyard with my friend Billy. We had a lot of fun running, but I tripped and fell. Mom said to be more careful.)

Strategy Self-Check

Have children talk about any problems they encountered as they read and what they did to solve them.

Questioning

• What did they want to know about as they read the story?

Remind children that good readers use many strategies as they read.

English Language Learners

Support Discussion Have children identify the characters and setting in the story. Then help them describe the events of the story on each page.

Objectives
- Retell a narrative.
- Identify if a story is realism or fantasy.
- Write clear, coherent sentences.

Check Retelling
SUCCESS PREDICTOR

Objectives
- Describe the problem and the solution of a story. Retell a story's beginning, middle, and end in the order in which the events happened. • Read on your own for a period of time.

Envision It! Retell

READING STREET ONLINE
STORY SORT
www.ReadingStreet.com

106

Think Critically

1. Tip did not like the big top. Tell what you would do to help. Text to Self

3. Could this story really happen? Explain.

 Realism and Fantasy

4. **Look Back and Write**
Look back at pages 98 and 99. What do Pam and Dot like to do? Write about it.

TEST PRACTICE Extended Response

Meet the Illustrator

Hector Borlasca

Hector Borlasca loves to illustrate books because it brings a new surprise every day. He hopes that children see something new every time they look at his illustrations.

AGUSTINA se duerme

Here is another book illustrated by Hector Borlasca.

Use the Reading Log in the *Reader's and Writer's Notebook* to record your independent reading.

107

Student Edition pp. 106–107

Retelling

Envision It! Have children work in pairs retelling the story. Remind children that their partners should include the characters, setting, and events from the beginning, middle, and end of the story. Children should use the retelling strip in the Student Edition as they retell. Monitor children's retelling.

Scoring rubric

Top-Score Response A top-score response makes connections beyond the text, elaborates on the author's purpose, and describes in detail the characters, setting, and plot.

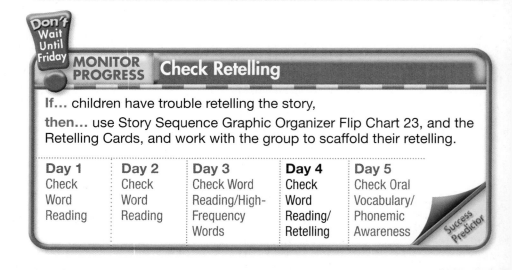

Don't Wait Until Friday

MONITOR PROGRESS Check Retelling

If... children have trouble retelling the story,

then... use Story Sequence Graphic Organizer Flip Chart 23, and the Retelling Cards, and work with the group to scaffold their retelling.

Day 1	Day 2	Day 3	Day 4	Day 5
Check Word Reading	Check Word Reading	Check Word Reading/High-Frequency Words	Check Word Reading/ Retelling	Check Oral Vocabulary/ Phonemic Awareness

Success Predictor

Think Critically

Text to Self

1. Possible response: I would show Tip the top. I would let him see it up close. Then he would not be scared.

 Realism and Fantasy

2. Possible response: Yes, this story could really happen. The characters do things that real people do. The setting is like a real setting.

Writing on Demand

3. **Look Back and Write** For writing fluency, assign a 5 minute time limit. As children finish, encourage them to reread their responses and proofread for errors.

Scoring rubric

> **Top-Score Response** A top-score response uses details from the text and the pictures to tell what Pam and Dot like to do. For example:
>
> Pam and Dot like to hop. They hop fast. Pam and Dot sit on a mat.

Meet the illustrator

Read aloud page 107 as children follow along. Ask children:

• What does an illustrator do? (draws the pictures that go with the story)

Have them look back at the pictures in *The Big Top*. Tell them that if they liked this story, they may want to read other books illustrated by Hector Borlasca.

Differentiated Instruction

A Advanced

Look Back and Write Ask children who show proficiency with the writing prompt to discuss other things that Pam and Dot might like to do outside.

 INTERACT with TEXT

Strategy Response Log

Genre Have children use p. RR10 in their *Reader's and Writer's Notebook* to add additional information about realistic fiction.

Plan to Assess Retelling

☐ Week 1: Strategic Intervention

☐ Week 2: Advanced

☐ Week 3: Strategic Intervention

☑ This week: Assess On-Level children

☐ Week 5: Strategic Intervention

☐ Week 6: Assess any children you have not yet checked during this unit.

Retelling

Success Predictor

Objectives

- Identify a simple sentence.
- Produce a simple sentence.
- Write a simple sentence that states a complete idea.

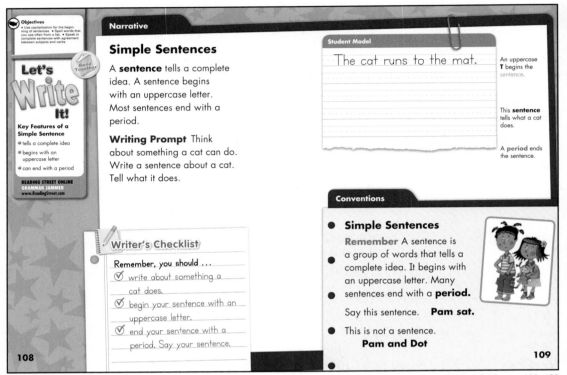

Student Edition pp. 108–109

Writing—Sentences

Teach

Look at p. 108 in the Student Edition. Read aloud the Key Features of a Simple Sentence. Help children better understand the Writing Prompt by reading it aloud and discussing the Writer's Checklist with children.

Review the student model

Then read the Student Model on p. 109 to children. Point out that the sentence expresses a complete idea. Ask children what the sentence starts with. (an uppercase letter) Ask them what the sentence ends with. (a period) What is the sentence about? (the cat) What does the cat do? (runs)

Guide practice

Now it is time to write your sentence. Think about what a cat can do. Then tell about it. Remember, your sentence should be complete and include a verb and a noun. Guide children as they write a sentence about what a cat does. Encourage them to remember things they have seen real cats do. If children cannot write a complete sentence, provide them with a sentence frame, such as, *The cat _____*. Have them fill in the blank and complete the sentence. If children are unable to write decodable words, have them orally suggest the words and model writing them in the blank. (For example: The cat *can nap*.)

Conventions
Simple Sentences

Read aloud the Conventions note on p. 109 as children follow along. Have them explain what a sentence is and then read with you the example of a complete sentence and an incomplete sentence. Have them identify the uppercase letter at the beginning of the complete sentence and the period at the end.

On their own

Use *Reader's and Writer's Notebook* p. 76.

Reader's and Writer's
Notebook p. 76

Objectives
- Understand the purpose of a map.
- Interpret map symbols.
- Use correct letter size when writing.
- Write Oo.

Research
Maps

Teach

Explain that a **map** is a special kind of drawing that shows places such as roads, cities, or states. There are many different kinds of maps. People use maps to get from one place to another. Drawings called **symbols** stand for things on a map, such as houses, schools, or parks. The **map key** is a section on the map that shows what each symbol stands for.

Display Research Transparency R4. This is a map showing streets in a neighborhood. It has a map key with symbols. Read the street names. Point out the map key and read the name of each symbol. We will use the map to find answers to the questions below it. Read the first question and model how to find the answer.

Research Transparency R4

Model

 Think Aloud When I look at the map key, I see the symbol that stands for a road. Then I look for a road that is labeled Bliss Street. I see there is a picture of a building with a flag on top. The map key tells me that this symbol stands for a school. For the answer to the first question, I will write *a school.*

Guide practice

Continue reading the questions. Help children read the map and interpret the key to find the answer. Review the information once you've recorded all the responses.

On their own

Use *Reader's and Writer's Notebook* p. 77.

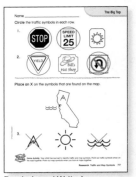

Reader's and Writer's Notebook p. 77

Handwriting
Letter Size

Model letter formation

Display upper- and lower-case letters: *Oo*. Use the stroke instructions pictured below to model proper letter formation.

D'Nealian™   Ball and Stick

Model letter size

Remind children that some letters are tall, some are small, some fall below the line, and some go above the mid-line. I will pay attention to letter size when I write a word. Model the four different letter sizes by writing *Pop, fan,* and *cot.* Have children identify the size of each letter.

Guide practice

Write the following sentence: *Tom sat on top.*

Team Talk Tell children you will point to a letter. Have pairs work together to decide if the letter is tall, small, falls below the line, or goes above the mid-line. Point to different letters in the sentence and monitor children's responses.

On their own

Use the *Reader's and Writer's Notebook* p. 78.

Reader's and Writer's Notebook p. 78

Wrap Up Your Day

✔ **Vowel *Oo* /o/** Write *mop* and *Odd.* Point to the *o* in *mop* and the *O* in *Odd* as you say the words aloud. Have children repeat them after you. Remind children that this is the short *o* sound of *o.*

✔ **Realism and Fantasy** Is the story "My Puppy Sings the Blues" realistic or an animal fantasy? How do you know? (Possible response: It is realistic because it is a story that could happen in real life.)

✔ **Questioning** Remind children that good readers ask questions about text and look for the answers as they read.

Differentiated Instruction

 Advanced

Draw a Map Have children with good map skills pair up and draw a simple map of the school. Ask them to include symbols in the map and a map key. Then have the pair present the map to the class.

Academic Vocabulary

map a special kind of drawing that shows places

map key a section on a map that tells what each map symbol stands for

symbols drawings that stand for things

Preview DAY 5

Tell children that today they heard about a new girl in Autumn's neighborhood. Tomorrow they will hear about Autumn again.

Objectives

- Review concepts: friends and neighborhoods
- Build oral vocabulary.
- Identify details in text.

Today at a Glance

Oral Vocabulary
Review

Print Awareness
Sequence Letters

Phonemic Awareness
Blend onsets and rimes

Phonics
Review Consonants *Dd* /d/, *Ll* /l/, *Hh* /h/, and Short *o*

High-Frequency Words
Review

Comprehension
◉ Realism and Fantasy

Listening and Speaking
Give Instructions

Vocabulary
Sort Decriptive Words

Handwriting
Proper Letter Size

Writing and Conventions
Simple Sentences

Check Oral Vocabulary
SUCCESS PREDICTOR

Concept Wrap Up

Question of the Week

What can we do with our neighborhood friends?

Review Concept

This week we have read and listened to stories about friends and neighborhoods Today you will listen to find out how the new neighbors introduce themselves to each other. **Read the story.**

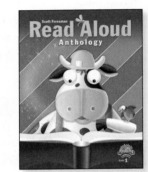

"My Puppy Sings the Blues"

- How do Laura and Autumn introduce themselves to each other? (Laura says "Hi!" and tells Autumn her name and her dog's name. Then Autumn tells Laura her name and her dog's name.)

Review Amazing Words

Orally review the meaning of this week's Amazing Words. Then display this week's concept map. Have children use Amazing Words such as *introduce, neighbor*, and *porch,* as well as the concept map, to answer the question: "What can we do with our neighborhood friends?"

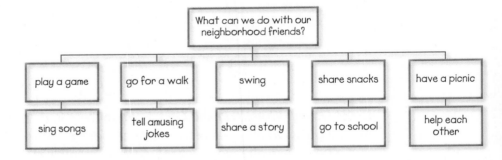

What can we do with our neighborhood friends?

| play a game | go for a walk | swing | share snacks | have a picnic |
| sing songs | tell amusing jokes | share a story | go to school | help each other |

E L L **Check Concepts and Language** Use the Day 5 instruction on ELL Poster R4 to monitor children's understanding of the lesson concept.

E L L Poster R4

Oral Vocabulary
Amazing Ideas

Connect to the Big Question

Team Talk Pair children and have them discuss how the Question of the Week connects to this unit's Big Question, "What is all around me?" Tell children to use the concept map and what they've learned from this week's Anchored Talks and reading selections to form an Amazing Idea — a realization or "big idea" about **my world**. Then ask each pair to share their Amazing Idea with the class.

Amazing Ideas might include these key concepts:

• We can swing and play games with neighborhood friends.

• Neighbors can help each other when there is trouble.

It's Friday

MONITOR PROGRESS | **Check Oral Vocabulary**

Call on individuals to use this week's Amazing Words to talk about what neighborhood friends can do with each other. Prompt discussion with the questions below. Monitor children's ability to use the Amazing Words and note which words children are unable to use.

• **What *amusing* things can we do with our *neighbors*?**

• **How would you *introduce* your friend to a new neighbor?**

• **What neighborhood friends would you meet if you walked to the *corner* of your street?**

• **How would you help a neighborhood friend who was having some *trouble*?**

If... children have difficulty using the Amazing Words,

then... reteach the unknown words using the Oral Vocabulary Routines, pp. 89b, 92b, 94b, 94n.

Day 1 Check Word Reading	**Day 2** Check Word Reading	**Day 3** Check Word Reading/ Retelling	**Day 4** Check High-Frequency Words/Retelling	**Day 5** Check Oral Vocabulary

Success Predictor

Amazing Words

amusing	trouble
introduce	deliver
neighbor	porch
corner	squirrel

Differentiated Instruction

A **Advanced**
Alternative Ending Have children work with a partner. Have pairs create an alternative ending for the Read-Aloud story "My Puppy Sings the Blues." Ask them to share their alternative ending with another pair or with the rest of the class.

English Language Learners
Amazing Words Pair English language learners with native English speakers. Have English learners answer as much as they can. Have English speakers share the pair's responses with the class.

Oral Vocabulary
Success Predictor

Objectives

- Understand that the letters of the alphabet are arranged in a sequence.
- Sequence the letters of the alphabet from *q* through *z*.
- Blend onsets and rimes.

Print Awareness
Sequence Letters

Introduce

Earlier this week, we studied the order of some letters in the alphabet. First, we ordered the letters from *a* to *g*. Then, we put the letters from *h* to *p* in order. Today, we'll order the last ten letters.

Model

Write lower-case letters from *q* through *z* on the board. Touch each letter in turn and name it. Be aware that children have formally studied only *r, s,* and *t* of these letters so far this year, though children may remember other letters from kindergarten or from ordinary classroom experiences.

 Think Aloud I need to find a way to remember the order of these letters. Let me see...I'll say them in groups. I'll say *q, r, s,* and I'll put a box around these three letters. Say it with me: *q, r, s.* Next comes *t, u, v.* I'll draw another box around those three letters. What do we have so far? *q, r, s.* Then *t, u, v.* At the end I'll say *w, x, y, z,* and draw a box around those four letters too. Say them with me! **Say the letter names carefully and slowly, pausing between each group, and have children say the names with you.**

Guide practice

Point to the letter groups in order: first *q, r, s,* then *t, u, v,* and finally *w, x, y, z.* Have children say them first with you, then without you. Then break the class into three parts. Point to one group at random and have them say *q, r, s.* Point to another group and have them say *t, u, v.* Then have the last group say *w, x, y, z.* Repeat several times.

On their own

Use *Reader's and Writer's Notebook* p. 79.

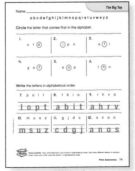

Reader's and Writer's
Notebook p. 79

Phonological Awareness
Blend Onsets and Rimes

Model

I'm thinking of a word. The first part of my word is /d/. Say it with me: /d/. The last part of my word sounds like this: /ol/. Say it with me: /ol/. The first part is /d/. The second part is /ol/. You can find out what my word is by blending the sounds in order. Listen: /d/, /ol/, /dol/. My word is *doll.*

Guide practice

I will say two parts of a word. Then you blend the sounds to tell me my word. /h/ /ot/. Blend the sounds with me: /h/ /ot/, /hot/, hot. Now blend the sounds without me.

Have children blend the sounds of the following words: /st/ /op/, *stop;* /bl/ /ack/, *black;* /h/ /op/, *hop;* /h/, /eld/, *held;* /l/ /ots/, *lots.*

Corrective feedback

If children make an error, model the correct response. Return to the word later in the practice.

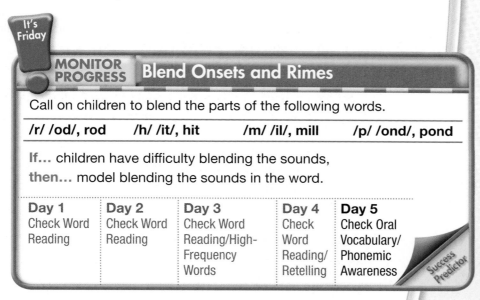

It's Friday

MONITOR PROGRESS | **Blend Onsets and Rimes**

Call on children to blend the parts of the following words.

| /r/ /od/, rod | /h/ /it/, hit | /m/ /il/, mill | /p/ /ond/, pond |

If... children have difficulty blending the sounds,
then... model blending the sounds in the word.

Day 1	Day 2	Day 3	Day 4	Day 5
Check Word Reading	Check Word Reading	Check Word Reading/High-Frequency Words	Check Word Reading/Retelling	Check Oral Vocabulary/Phonemic Awareness

Success Predictor

Objectives
- Review consonants *d* /d/, *h* /h/, *l* /l/, and short *o* /o/.
- Identify upper- and lower-case letters.
- Review high-frequency words *a, do, like, look, see, the, was, we, you.*

Fluent Word Reading
Spiral Review

Read words in isolation

Display these words. Tell children that they can blend some words on this list but others are Word Wall words.

Have children read the list three or four times until they can read at the rate of two to three seconds per word.

big	Bill	a	on	you
the	was	hill	look	Gil
dog	hid	do	in	log
we	Bob	see	doll	like

Word Reading

If... children have difficulty reading whole words,
then... have them use sound-by-sound blending for decodable words or have them say and spell high-frequency words.

If... children cannot read fluently at a rate of two to three seconds per word,
then... have pairs practice the list until they can read it fluently.

Read words in context

Display these sentences. Then randomly point to review words and have children read them. To help you monitor word reading, high-frequency words are underlined and decodable words are italicized.

<u>Look</u>! <u>Do</u> <u>you</u> <u>see</u> *Bill*?

Bob <u>was</u> *on* <u>the</u> *hill*.

<u>We</u> <u>like</u> <u>the</u> *big dog*.

Gil hid <u>the</u> *doll in* <u>a</u> *log*.

Sentence Reading

Corrective feedback

If... children are unable to read an underlined high-frequency word,
then... read the word for them and spell it, having them echo you.

If... children have difficulty reading an italicized decodable word,
then... guide them in using sound-by-sound blending.

Spell Words

Guide practice

Now we are going to spell words with the sounds and letters we learned this week. The first word we will spell is *lid*. What sounds do you hear in *lid*? (/l/ /i/ /d/) What is the letter for the sound /l/? Let's all write *l*. What is the letter for the sound /i/? Write *i*. What is the letter for the sound /d/? Write *d*. Have children confirm their spellings by comparing them with what you've written. Continue practice with *doll, nod, hot, lit, hog,* and *got* as time allows.

High-Frequency Words

Review

Point to the words *are, have, that, they,* and *two* one at a time on the Word Wall. Have children read and spell each word chorally. Have children work with a partner to use each word in a sentence. Ask several pairs to share their sentences.

Cumulative review

Point to the remaining Word Wall words one at a time. Have children read the words chorally.

On their own

Use *Reader's and Writer's Notebook* p. 80.

Reader's and Writer's
Notebook p. 80

Spiral Review

These activities review

- previously taught high-frequency words *a, do, like, look, see, the, was, we,* and *you*
- Consonants *b* /b/, *d* /d/, *g* /g/, *h* /h/, and *l* /l/
- upper- and lower-case letters

Differentiated Instruction

SI Strategic Intervention

Organize Information Have children work with a partner. Give each pair a 2-circle Venn diagram. Label one circle *Words with* d and the other circle *Words with* o. Show children how to place the word *dip* in the left-hand circle, the word *cot* in the right circle, and the word *rod* in the overlapping area. Then have children add more words to the diagram. Repeat with *Words with* i and *Words with* l.

Small Group Time

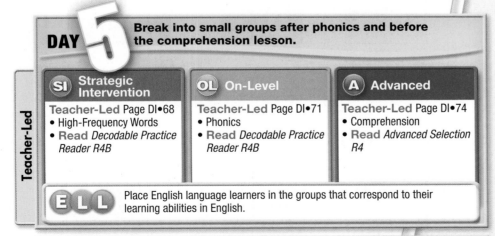

DAY 5

Break into small groups after phonics and before the comprehension lesson.

Teacher-Led

SI Strategic Intervention
Teacher-Led Page DI•68
- High-Frequency Words
- **Read** *Decodable Practice Reader R4B*

OL On-Level
Teacher-Led Page DI•71
- Phonics
- **Read** *Decodable Practice Reader R4B*

A Advanced
Teacher-Led Page DI•74
- Comprehension
- **Read** *Advanced Selection R4*

 Place English language learners in the groups that correspond to their learning abilities in English.

Practice Stations
- Get Fluent
- Let 'Write'

Independent Activities
- *Reader's and Writer's Notebook* p. RR1.
- Concept Talk Video
- AudioText of Paired Selection

English Language Learners
Fluent Word Reading Have children take turns echo-reading the words with a partner. Have partners read the sentences together several times.

High-Frequency Words
Practice

Review

Review this week's Words to Read: *are, they, have, that, two.*

- Point to a word. Say and spell it.
- Use each word in a sentence.

Guide practice

Have children say and spell each word twice. Then have them use each high-frequency word in a sentence.

On their own

Have pairs of children take turns using each high-frequency word in a sentence. Remind children to listen politely and to speak clearly at an appropriate pace. Have pairs of children share some of their sentences with the class.

Don't Wait Until Friday

MONITOR PROGRESS   ⟳ High-Frequency Words

Point to these words on the Word Wall and have the class read them. Listen for children who miss words during the reading. Call on those children to read some of the words individually.

are	they	have	that	two	Spiral Review
do	you	look	was	we	← **Row 2** reviews previously taught high-frequency words

If... children cannot read these words,

then... use the Small Group Time Strategic Intervention lesson, p. 66, to reteach the words. Monitor children's fluency with these words during reading, and provide additional practice.

Day 1	Day 2	Day 3	Day 4	Day 5
Check Word Reading	Check Word Reading	Check Word Reading/ High-Frequency Words	Check Word Reading/ Retelling	Check Oral Vocabulary/ Phonemic Awareness

Success Predictor

Differentiated Instruction

 Advanced

Extend Language If pairs of children easily produce sentences using the high-frequency words, have them practice using two or more high-frequency words in each sentence. Challenge them to use previously taught high-frequency words from the Word Wall.

Decodable Practice Reader R4B
Review Consonant Sounds /d/, /l/, /h/, /b/, /f/, /g/ and Short /i/, /o/

Decode words in isolation
Review high-frequency words

Have children turn to the first page. Have children decode each word.

Review the previously taught words *we* and *you*. Have children read each word as you point to it on the Word Wall.

Preview Decodable Reader

Have children read the title and preview the story. Tell them they will read words with consonant sounds /d/, /l/, /h/, /b/, /f/, /g/ and short *i* and *o* in this story.

Print awarenress

Remind children that reading is done from the top of the page to the bottom and from left to right with a return sweep. Have them read aloud the first few pages of the Decodable Practice Reader using their fingers to track the print. Monitor children as they read aloud, making sure they are tracking the print correctly.

Decode words in context

Pair children for reading and listen carefully as they decode. One child begins. Children read the entire story, switching readers after each page. Partners reread the story. This time the other child begins.

Decodable Practice Reader R4B

Decodable Reader R4B

Corrective feedback

If... children have difficulty decoding a word, **then...** refer them to the Sound-Spelling Cards to identify the sounds in the word. Prompt them to blend the word.

- What is the new word?
- Is the new word a word you know?
- Does it make sense in the story?

Check decoding and comprehension

Have children retell the story to include characters, setting, and events. Then have children locate words with /d/ spelled *d* in the story. List words that children name. Children should supply *did, dig, dab, Dot, and dip.* Ask children how they know these words have the /d/ sound. (They all have *d.*) Continue in the same way with /l/ spelled *l* and *ll (Sal, fill, Lil, Bill, Hal),* spelled *h (hop, hit, Hal),* and /o/ spelled *o (hop, Tom, dot, pop).*

Reread for Fluency

Have children reread Decodable Reader R4B to develop automaticity decoding words with the sounds /d/, /l/, /h/ and /o/.

 Oral Rereading

1. **Read** Have children read the entire book orally.
2. **Reread** To achieve optimal fluency, children should reread the text three or four times.
3. **Corrective Feedback** Listen as children read. Provide corrective feedback regarding their fluency and decoding.

Routines Flip Chart

ELL

English Language Learners
Review /o/, /d/, /l/, /h/

Beginning Pronounce and then act out the verbs in the story: *hop, fill, hit, dig, dab, dip,* and *pop.* Then have children say the words as you pantomime the actions again.

Intermediate
After reading, have children ELPS 1.B, 2.Eng the words *hop, fill, dig,* and *dab.* Monitor children's pronunciation.

Advanced/Advanced High
After reading, have children use the illustrations to make up their own sentences that tell what each story character is doing.

Objectives
- Read signs and symbols.
- Recognize structure and elements of procedural text.
- Relate prior knowledge to new text.
- Set purpose for reading.

Read Together

Social Studies in Reading

Preview and predict

Read the title and the first sentence of the selection. Have children look through the selection and predict what they might learn. (Possible response: They might learn about different signs and symbols.) Ask them what clues helped them make that prediction. (They might say the pictures of the different signs in the selection and the first sentence.)

Genre

Procedural Text Tell children that they will read a **procedural text**. Review the key features of a procedural text: some selections include words as well as signs and symbols. A **sign** tells you what to do. A **symbol** stands for something else. Explain that this selection is a procedural text because it has words as well as signs and symbols.

Activate prior knowledge

Ask children to recall what their neighborhoods look like and the signs they might see there. (There are stop signs on the street for cars. There are street signs that tell the names of the streets people live on. There are railroad signs for trains.)

Set a purpose for reading

Let's Read Together As children read, have them pay attention to clues that would indicate other types of signs you would find in a neighborhood.

Objectives
• Explain what different signs and symbols mean.

Social Studies in Reading

Genre
Procedural Text

• Some selections use words along with signs and symbols.
• A sign tells you what to do.
• A symbol stands for something else.
• Read "Around the Block." As you read, remember what you learned about signs and symbols.

Around the Block

 Read Together

There are many signs and symbols in our neighborhood.

110

Signs and symbols help us drive.

Let's Think About...
What signs and symbols do you see on these pages?
Procedural Text

Signs and symbols help us ride.

Let's Think About...
What do the signs and symbols tell you?
Procedural Text

Signs and symbols help keep us safe.

Let's Think About...
Reading Across Texts What kinds of street signs might Pam see in her neighborhood?
Writing Across Texts Draw a picture of some signs and symbols Pam might see in her neighborhood. Write a label for each.

111

Student Edition pp. 110–111

Academic Vocabulary

sign an object that tells you what to do

symbol a picture that stands for something

Differentiated Instruction

(A) **Advanced**

Discuss "Around the Block" Have children recall what they learned about neighborhood signs from the selection. Ask children to talk about what signs and symbols would **most likely** be found on a neighborhood block, and why these signs and symbols are important.

Guide Comprehension

Guide practice

Think Aloud I know that signs tell us what to do, and symbols stand for something else. As I look at the signs on page 110, I see a big read sign that says "Stop." I know I need to stop when I am driving on the road and see that sign. I also see a yellow sign with two capital *Rs* on it and a big *X*. I know that this symbol tells me that I am about to cross a railroad track. Continue modeling what each sign and symbol on page 110 means.

Let's Think About...

Procedural Text

Possible response: The signs and symbols tell you how to get around your neighborhood safely.

Reading Across Texts Have children think about Pam's neighborhood in *The Big Top* and discuss the signs and symbols they learned about in "Around the Block."

Writing Across Texts Children should draw pictures of the signs they discussed above and label each sign.

English Language Learners
Idioms Talk about the term "around the block." Help children understand that you can go "around the block" by walking to the end of the street and then turning the corner. They can walk all the way "around the block," never having to cross the street, and come back to where they started. Ask children to walk around their block in their minds and describe what buildings, people, and houses they see.

Objectives
- Give instructions
- Speak clearly.
- Listen attentively.
- Sort descriptive words.
- Write using proper letter size.

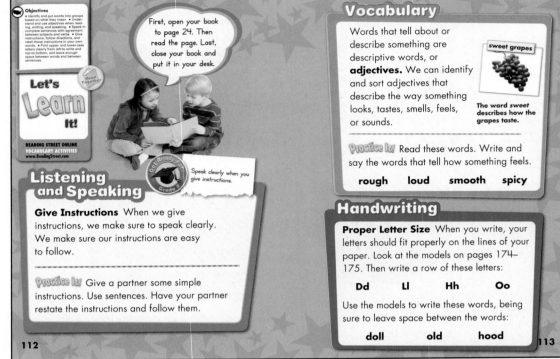

Student Edition pp. 112–113

Listening and Speaking
Give Instructions

Teach

Have children turn to pages 112–113 of the Student Edition. Read and discuss what the children are doing. Remind children that good speakers speak clearly. They make sure the other person can understand them.

Analyze model

One child in the picture is giving instructions. What is the first thing the child wants the other child to do? (open the book to page 24) What is the second part of the instructions? (read the page). What is the last part of the instructions? (close the book and put it in your desk). Very good. These instructions are clear and easy to follow.

Introduce prompt

Read the Practice It! prompt with the class. Remind children that their instructions should be clear and easy to follow.

Team Talk Have pairs take turns giving and following instructions. Tell children that good speakers speak clearly and make sure their instructions are easy to follow. Good listeners repeat the instructions to be sure they understand what to do.

Vocabulary
Sort Descriptive Words

Teach Read and discuss the Vocabulary lesson on page 113 of the Student Edition. Use the model to explain sorting adjectives.

Model Point to the photographs. What do you see in the first picture? (a blanket) How does the blanket feel? (soft) The word *soft* describes how something feels. What do you see in the second picture? (grapes) What do grapes taste like? (sweet) The word *sweet* describes how something tastes.

Guide practice Read the instructions for the Vocabulary Practice It! Activity. Have children study the words.

The first word is *rough.* Does this word describe how something feels? (Yes) What is something that feels rough? (Possible responses: sandpaper, a cat's tongue) That's right, *rough* is a words that describes how something feels.

On their own Have children continue with the other adjectives on the page.

Corrective feedback Circulate around the room and listen as children choose adjectives that describe how things feel. Provide assistance as needed.

Handwriting
Proper Letter Size

Teach Read and discuss the Handwriting instructions. Review proper letter size.

Write letters Give children a moment to look at the letter models. Then have them write a row for each of these letters: *Dd, Ll, Hh, Oo.* After children have finished writing their letters, have them write the following words: *doll, old, hood.*

Assess

◉ Blend words with consonants *d*
/d/, *l* /l/, *h* /h/ and short *o*.
• Read high-frequency words.

Assessment
Monitor Progress

Phonemic Awareness
For a written assessment of consonants *d* /d/, *l* /l/, *h* /h/, short *o*, and high-frequency words, use Weekly Test 4, pp. 19–24.

Assess words in isolation
Word reading Use the following reproducible page to assess children's ability to read words in isolation. Call on children to read the words aloud. Start over if necessary.

Assess words in context
Sentence reading Use the following reproducible page to assess children's ability to read words in context. Call on children to read two sentences aloud. Start over with sentence one if necessary.

MONITOR PROGRESS | **Word Reading and Sentence Reading**

If... children have trouble reading words with consonants *d* /d/, *l* /l/, *h* /h/ and short *o*,

then... use the Reteach Lesson on pp. 187 and 191 of *First Stop*.

If... children cannot read all the high-frequency words,

then... mark the missed words on a high-frequency word list and have the child practice reading the words with a fluent reader.

Success Predictor

Monitor accuracy
Record scores Use the Word/Sentence Reading Chart for this unit on p. 64 of *First Stop*.

Name _____

Read the Words

hop	hog
lot	are
that	cod
dog	have
two	log
Don	hot
they	doll

Read the Sentences

1. That dog can dig.

2. Two can have a hot dog.

3. They see the doll.

4. We are in the dog lot.

MONITOR PROGRESS
- Consonants *d* /d/, *l* /l/, *h* /h/
- Short *o*
- High-frequency words

The Big Top   **113c**

Objectives
- Identify a simple sentence.
- Produce a simple sentence.
- Write a simple sentence that states a complete idea.
- Develop the concept: neighborhoods.

Conventions
Simple Sentences

Review simple sentences

Hop up and down. What am I doing? *I hop.* Pantomime running. *I can run.* The sentences *I hop* and *I can run* tell complete ideas. They tell what I am doing. Write the sentences on the board and read them with children.

Guide practice

Have children think of farm animals that move in different ways. Write the name of each animal on the board, and then have children tell how each animal moves. Then write simple sentences and read them aloud.

Connect to oral language

Have the class complete these sentence frames orally.

> **Ducks can _____.**
>
> **_____ run fast.**

On their own

Put children in groups of three or four. Have them take turns naming animals and what they do. Have other children in the group suggest simple sentences, using these nouns and verbs. Have them share with the class.

Writing—Sentences

Wrap up the weekly concept

Remind children that they have been talking about neighborhoods all week.

I want to tell about my friends Amy and Max. They live next door and like to play soccer. I will write a sentence that tells about this. I will use the verb *play* and the nouns *kids* and *soccer*. Write and read the following sentence.

Model

> **The kids play soccer.**

Guide practice

Have children name nouns and verbs that tell what they do with their own friends. Then encourage them to tell a complete sentence, using these nouns and verbs. Work with children to write sentences on the board. You may suggest a sentence frame, such as *We _____* or *_____ have fun*.

On their own

Write the following sentence frame on the board and read it aloud.

> **I _____.**

Tell children they will write a sentence about something they do at home. Instruct children to complete the sentence with decodable words. If children are unable to write decodable words, have them suggest the words and model writing them in the blank.

Wrap Up Your Week!

Question of the Week

What can we do with our neighborhood friends?

Think Aloud This week we explored the topic of neighborhoods and what we can do with our neighborhood friends. In the story *The Big Top,* we read about two girls who play on a neighborhood block. In the song *New Neighbor,* we sang about a new neighbor who likes to play. The children in both selections do fun things with their neighborhood friends. **Have children recall their Amazing Ideas about neighborhoods. Then have children use these ideas to help them demonstrate their understanding of the Question of the Week.**

ELL

English Language Learners

Poster Preview Prepare children for next week by using Week 5, ELL Poster R5. Read the Poster Talk-Through to introduce the concept and vocabulary. Ask children to identify and describe objects and actions in the art.

Selection Summary Send home the summary of *School Day* in English and the child's home language if available. Children can read the summary with family members.

Preview NEXT WEEK

Tell children that next week they will read about a boy and his friends in a neighborhood school.

Weekly Assessment

Use pp. 19–24 of *Weekly Tests* to check:

✔ **Phonemic Awareness** Rhyming Words

✔ **Phonics** /d/d/, /l/l/, /h/h/, /o/o/

✔ **Comprehension Skill** Realism and Fantasy

✔ **High-Frequency Words**

are	they
have	two
that	

Weekly Tests

A
Advanced

OL
On-Level

SI
Strategic Intervention

Differentiated Asssessment

Use pp. 19–24 of *Fresh Reads for Fluency and Comprehension* to check:

✔ **Comprehension Skill** Realism and Fantasy

✔ Review **Comprehension Skill** Plot

Fresh Reads for Fluency and Comprehension

Managing Assessment

Use *Assessment Handbook* for:

✔ **Weekly Assessment Blackline Masters for Monitoring Progress**

✔ **Observation Checklists**

✔ **Record-Keeping Forms**

✔ **Portfolio Assessment**

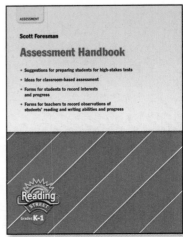

Assessment Handbook

Hat Day on Lot Hill

What kind of party was fun? The Hat Day Party was fun! It was on top of Lot Hill. Pals played games. They ate good food. They looked at hats. They stayed all day long.

Rob asked Mom for her hat. It was a hard hat for work. Hal wore Dad's floppy hat. It had spots. Miss Dodd had a big red hat with large white dots.

"I like your red hat, Miss Dodd," said Hal.

"I am glad you like it, Hal. That hat looks good on you," Miss Dodd said.

Some hats were tall. Some hats were long. One hat had duck ears!

Then a strong wind came. Hats flew off. It looked like the end of Hat Day.

"Look! A dog with a hat!" said Hal and Rob. The hat was tied on with string. That hat did not fly off! Hal and Rob ran. They got string. They gave it to all their pals. It was not the end of Hat Day. The pals stayed all day long!

Advanced Selection R4   **Vocabulary:** pal, floppy

Small Group Time

Pacing Small Group Instruction

20–30 min.

5 Day Plan

DAY 1	• Phonemic Awareness/ Phonics
DAY 2	• Phonemic Awareness/ Phonics
DAY 3	• Phonemic Awareness/ Phonics • Leveled Reader
DAY 4	• Phonemic Awareness/ Phonics • Decodable Reader
DAY 5	• High-Frequency Words • Decodable Reader

3 or 4 Day Plan

DAY 1	• Phonemic Awareness/ Phonics
DAY 2	• Phonemic Awareness/ Phonics
DAY 3	• Phonemic Awareness/ Phonics • Leveled Reader
DAY 4	• Phonemic Awareness/ Phonics • Decodable Reader

3 Day Plan: Eliminate the shaded box.

SI *Strategic Intervention*

DAY 1

Phonemic Awareness•Phonics

■ **Isolate Initial, Medial, and Final Phonemes** Reteach pp. 90–91 of the Teacher's Edition. Model isolating and matching initial, medial, and final /d/ in these words. Then have children practice isolating and matching /d/ on their own.

dark initial /d/   **desk** initial /d/   **road** final /d/

buddy medial /d/   **side** final /d/   **ready** medial /d/

Next, tell children that you are thinking of a word that starts with /d/. I'm thinking of an animal that usually lives in a lake or a pond. My animal is a bird. It can swim and fly, and it makes a sound like this: Quack! I am thinking of a —. Have children fill in the missing word *duck*. Repeat with *door* and *dime*.

■ ◉ **Consonant d /d/** Reteach p. 91a of the Teacher's Edition. Then have children hold up a letter tile for *d* when you say a word that begins with *d*. Have them keep their tiles down if the word does not begin with *d*.

• This word is *pin*. Does it begin with the letter *d*? (No)

• This word is *dinner*. Does it begin with the letter *d*? (Yes)

• This word is *dive*. Does it begin with the letter *d*? (Yes)

• This word is *deep*. Does it begin with the letter *d*? (Yes)

• This word is *rake*. Does it begin with the letter *d*? (No)

Repeat with words that end with the letter *d*. Use the following words: *slid, red, like, pad, tray, cloud.*

Objectives
• Isolate initial sounds in one-syllable spoken words.
• Isolate final sounds in one-syllable spoken words.

DAY 2

More Reading
Use text at the children's instructional level.

Phonemic Awareness•Phonics

■ **Isolate Initial, Medial, and Final Phonemes** Reteach p. 92d of the Teacher's Edition. Model isolating and matching initial, medial, and final /l/ in these words. Then have children practice isolating and matching /l/ on their own.

jelly medial /l/ **lab** initial /l/ **falling** medial /l/

late initial /l/ **will** final /l/ **bowl** final /l/

Tell children that you are thinking of a word that begins with /l/. I'm thinking of a large animal that lives in Africa. It's like a cat, but it is much, much larger, and it makes a very loud noise. I am thinking of a—. Have children fill in the missing word *lion*. Repeat with *lemon* and *lake*.

■ ◉ **Consonant *l, ll* /l/** Reteach p. 92e of the Teacher's Edition. Then have children hold up the letter tile for *l* when you read a word that begins with *l*. Have them keep the tiles down for other words.

• This word is *lucky*. Does it begin with *l*? (Yes)

• This word is *ride*. Does it begin with *l*? (No)

• This word is *chase*. Does it begin with *l*? (No)

• This word is *laugh*. Does it begin with *l*? (Yes)

• This word is *loop*. Does it begin with *l*? (Yes)

Repeat with words that end with *ll*. Use these words: *tell, more, soon, still, pull, shell.*

Objectives
• Isolate initial sounds in one-syllable spoken words.
• Isolate final sounds in one-syllable spoken words.

SI Strategic Intervention

Phonemic Awareness•Phonics

■ **Rhyme Words** Reteach p. 94d of the Teacher's Edition. Point out which pairs of words rhyme and which pairs do not rhyme. Emphasize that the vowel sounds (and final consonants, if any) must be the same for words to rhyme.

Continue the activity with the following examples. Say each pair of words aloud and ask children whether they rhyme.

lid, kid (yes)	**sip, hip** (yes)	**tap, tip** (no)	**big, cat** (no)
win, fin (yes)	**stiff, stick** (no)	**dish, fish** (yes)	**swim, clam** (no)

■ ◉ **Consonant h /h/** Reteach p. 94e of the Teacher's Edition. Then read the following words aloud: *hot, find, hair, hope, wait, hills, high.* Have children hold up a letter tile for *h* if the word begins with consonant *h*. Have them keep their tiles down for words that begin with some other letter.

Concept Literacy Leveled Reader

■ **Preview and Predict** Read the title and author's name. Have children look at the cover and ask them to describe what they see. How many children are there? What are they doing? Are they having fun? How do you know? Help children activate their prior knowledge by asking them to look through the book and to use the pictures to predict what the story might be about.

■ **Set a Purpose** Remind children that setting a purpose for reading can help them better understand what they read. Have children read to see what things children can do with their friends. Ask them to think about the things they can do with their own friends.

■ **Read** Provide corrective feedback as children read the story orally. When they are finished reading, ask them if they could confirm any of the predictions they made prior to reading the story.

If... children have difficulty reading the story individually,
then... read a sentence aloud as children point to each word. Then have the group reread the sentences as they continue pointing. Continue reading in this way until children read individually.

■ **Retell** Have children take turns retelling the story and identifying the things that the text says the narrator can do with friends. Provide support by asking, What are the friends doing on page __?

Concept Literacy

Objectives
• Isolate initial sounds in one-syllable spoken words.
• Establish purpose for reading selected texts.

SI Strategic Intervention

DAY **4**

Phonemic Awareness•Phonics

■ **Segment and Blend Phonemes** Reteach p. 94p of the Teacher's Edition. Model blending and segmenting the phonemes in these words.

Continue the activity with the following examples.

Blend /h/ /o/ /t/	**Blend /d/ /o/ /l/**	**Segment** *lot*	**Segment** *hop*
Blend /r/ /o/ /d/	**Blend /d/ /o/ /t/**	**Segment** *Don*	**Segment** *Todd*

■ 🔊 **Short Vowel o** Reteach p. 94q of the Teacher's Edition. Then read the following words aloud: *box, top, Ron, rap, tick, lot, rock.* Have children use their hands to form the letter *o* when the word includes short vowel *o.* Have them keep their hands down for words that include some other vowel sound.

Decodable Practice Reader R4A

Decodable Practice Reader R4A

■ **Review** Use the word lists to review short vowel o and the consonants *d* /d/ and *h* /h/, as well as the high-frequency words at the bottom of the page. Model how to blend the words *Dot* and *hot* and have children repeat. Then have children read the story, pointing to the words as they say them.

> **If…** children have difficulty reading the story individually,
> **then…** read a sentence aloud as children point to each word. Then have the group reread the sentences as they continue pointing. Continue reading in this way until children read individually.

Check comprehension by having children retell the story in sequence. Have children locate three-letter words in the story that include short vowel *o.* List the words children identify. Ask children whether the words end with *om, op,* or *ot.* Then have children sort the words into a chart and read them aloud.

-om	-op	-ot
Tom	top	hot
Mom		Dot
		not

Objectives
• Isolate medial sounds in one-syllable spoken words.
• Decode words in isolation by applying common letter-sound correspondences, including: single letters (vowels) including short.

More Reading

Use text at the children's instructional level.

High-Frequency Words

■ **Review** Write *they, have, two, that, are* on the board. Model saying each word. Then have children read each word, spell each word as you point to each letter, and have them say each word again. Allow time for children to practice reading these high-frequency words using the word cards.

Decodable Practice Reader R4B

Decodable Reader R4B

■ **Review** Use the word lists to review the sounds /i/, /o/, /l/, /d/, and /h/, the letters *i, o, l, d,* and *h,* and the high-frequency words *you* and *we.* Then review how to blend individual phonemes into words, using the sounds /h/ /o/ /p/ to create the word *hop.* Then have children read the story, pointing to the words as they speak them.

> **If...** children have difficulty reading the story individually, **then...** read a sentence aloud as children point to each word. Then have the group reread the sentences as they continue pointing. Continue reading in this way until children read individually.

Check comprehension by having children name the things the children do in the story. Then have children locate words in the story that have short *o,* consonant *l, ll,* consonant *d,* and consonant *h.* List the words children identify. Then help children classify the words according to the letters they contain. Note that some words will be in more than one category.

o	l, ll	d	h
hop	Sal	bid	hop
Tom	fill	dig	hit
Dot	Bill	dab	Hal
pop	Lil	Dot	
	Hal	dip	

Objectives
• Decode words in isolation by applying common letter-sound correspondences, including: single letters (vowels) including short o.

 On-Level   **DAY 1**

Phonemic Awareness•Phonics

■ **Isolate Initial, Medial, and Final Phonemes** Say the words below. Have children say them with you. Then have children generate other words that have an initial, medial, or final /d/ sound.

     bed   **dark**   **deer**   **down**

Repeat with words that end with /d/. Use *wide* and *red* as examples. Then repeat with words that include medial /d/, such as *middle* and *reading*.

■ **Consonant d /d/** Remind children that the letter d usually stands for the sound /d/. Have children hold up a letter tile for *d* to identify which of these words begins with *d: day, dog, pine, dish, bang, doors.* Repeat with words that end with *d,* using these words: *sad, like, bed, food, slid, storm.*

Objectives
• Isolate initial sounds in one-syllable spoken words.
• Isolate final sounds in one-syllable spoken words.

 On-Level   **DAY 2**

Phonics•High-Frequency Words

■ **Consonant l, ll /l/** Read the following words aloud. Have children identify whether the word has *l* at the beginning or *ll* at the end.

   will   **late**   **line**   **fell**   **look**   **spell**   **last**   **call**

Write some of the words on the board. Have children come to the board and circle the initial *l* or the final *ll.*

■ **High-Frequency Words** Hold up this week's High-Frequency Word Cards and review proper pronunciation. Have children chorally read each word. To help children demonstrate their understanding of the words, provide them with oral sentence frames such as: The number that comes after one is _____. (two)

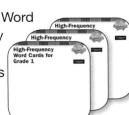

Objectives
• Isolate initial sounds in one-syllable spoken words.

Pacing Small Group Instruction
 20–30 min.

5 Day Plan

DAY 1	• Phonemic Awareness • Phonics
DAY 2	• Phonics • High-Frequency Words
DAY 3	• Leveled Reader
DAY 4	• Conventions • Decodable Reader
DAY 5	• Phonics • Decodable Reader

3 or 4 Day Plan

DAY 1	• Phonemic Awareness • Phonics
DAY 2	• Phonics • High-Frequency Words
DAY 3	• Leveled Reader • Decodable Reader
DAY 4	• Conventions • Decodable Reader

3 Day Plan: Eliminate the shaded box.

 On-Level

DAY 3

Concept Literacy Leveled Reader

On-Level

■ **Preview and Predict** Read the title and the author's name. Have children look at the cover and ask them to describe in detail what they see. Help children preview the story by asking them to look through the book. Have them use the photos to predict what the story will be about.

■ **Realism and Fantasy** Before reading, review the differences between realism and fantasy. Ask children whether a story about a dragon would be realism or fantasy (fantasy); then ask the same question regarding a story about a girl who goes to a school like theirs (probably realism). Then challenge children to determine whether "My Friends" is realism or fantasy as they read.

■ **Read** During reading, monitor children's comprehension by providing higher-order thinking questions. Ask:

• Which of these activities do you like to do with your friends? Why?

• Think of some activities you do with your friends that are not mentioned in the book. What are some of these activities?

To help children gain a better understanding of the text, build upon their responses with a group discussion.

■ **Questioning** Explain that asking and answering questions about a text can help children better understand what they read. Use questions such as the following to model the process of questioning. Then have children generate and answer each other's questions about the text.

• Would you like to live in the neighborhood pictured in the book? Explain.

• Does it ever rain in this neighborhood? How do you know?

■ **Text to Self** Help children make personal connections to the story. Ask:

• What do you like best about running/hopping/riding with your friends?

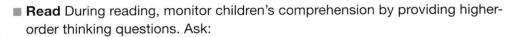

Objectives
• Ask relevant questions about stories.

 OL On-Level

DAY 4

More Reading
Use text at the children's instructional level.

Conventions•Decodable Practice Reader

■  **Simple Sentences** Remind children that a sentence is a complete idea that begins with a capital letter and ends with a period or other punctuation mark. Write the following on the board and have children find the sentences:

on top　　*We see a hat.*　　*the pan*　　*The man can hop.*

■ **Decodable Practice Reader R4A** Review words with *d* /d/, *h* /h/, and short *o* and all high-frequency words in the text. Have children blend and read these words from the story: *Dot, hot.* Point out that *Dot* is a name. Have children reread the text orally. To achieve optimal fluency, children should reread the text three or four times.

Decodable Reader R4A

Objectives
• Recognize distinguishing features of a sentence.

 OL On-Level

DAY 5

Phonics Review•Decodable Practice Reader

■  **Consonants *d* /d/, *l, ll* /l/, *h* /h/ and Short Vowel *o*** Have children practice blending and reading words that contain this week's target phonics skills.

hop　　hot　　doll　　did　　hill　　mop　　hid　　lot　　had

Then have children identify the words that have the /d/, /l/, /h/, or /o/ sounds.

■ **Decodable Practice Reader R4B** Review words with *d, h, l,* and *o* and the high-frequency words *you* and *we*. Then have children blend and read these words from the story: *hop, dig, Lil.* Have children reread the text orally. To achieve optimal fluency, children should reread the text three or four times.

Decodable Reader R4B

Objectives
• Decode words in isolation by applying common letter-sound correspondences, including: single letters (vowels), including short *o*.

Small Group Time

5 Day Plan

DAY 1	• Phonics
DAY 2	• Phonics • Comprehension
DAY 3	• Leveled Reader
DAY 4	• Comprehension
DAY 5	• Comprehension

3 or 4 Day Plan

DAY 1	• Phonics • Advanced Selection
DAY 2	• Phonics • Comprehension
DAY 3	• Leveled Reader
DAY 4	• Comprehension

3 Day Plan: Eliminate the shaded box.

A Advanced — **DAY 1**

Phonics

■ **Consonant d /d/** Have children practice with longer words containing *d* /d/. Say these words. Then have children say *Beginning, Middle,* or *End* to tell where in the word the letter *d* belongs.

salad	modern	wedding	ready
doorbell	dishes	ahead	daughter

Then tell children that you are thinking of a word that ends with *d* and is the name of a color (*red*)…ends with *d* and is something you eat (*bread* or *food*)…ends with *d* and means the opposite of quiet (*loud*).

Objectives
• Isolate initial sounds in one-syllable spoken words.
• Isolate final sounds in one-syllable spoken words.

A Advanced — **DAY 2**

Phonics•Comprehension

■ **Consonant l, ll /l/** Have children practice reading and writing words with consonant *l* and *ll*. Have children use letter tiles to create the word *fill*. Then have them make changes.

• Change the *f* in *fill* to *b*. What word did you make? (bill)

• Change the *ll* in *bill* to *t*. What word did you make? (bit)

• What should we do to turn *bit* into *lit*? (replace *b* with *l*)

■ **Comprehension** Reread this week's Read Aloud, "A Neighborhood Picnic," with children. Review the concepts of fantasy and realism. Ask children to identify whether the story is fantasy or realism and explain how they know.

A Neighborhood Picnic

Objectives
• Decode words in context by applying common sound-letter correspondences, including single letters (consonants), including l.

 A *Advanced*

DAY 3

Concept Literacy Leveled Reader

- **Activate Prior Knowledge** Read the title and the author's name. Have children look at the cover and ask them to describe in detail what they see. Then activate children's prior knowledge by asking them to tell a partner about a time they did something fun with a friend.

- **Realism and Fantasy** Before reading, remind children that some stories are realistic and some are fantasy. Have children describe the difference between realism and fantasy; then ask them to give examples of books they know that fit into these genres. Have them predict whether "My Friends" will be realistic or fantasy, and have them check their prediction as they read.

- **Read** During reading, monitor children's comprehension by providing higher-order thinking questions. Ask:

  - What do you like best about the neighborhood where these children live? Why?

  - Suppose you were writing a book about the things you do with your friends. What activities would you write about?

  Build on children's answers to help them gain a better understanding of the text.

- **Questioning** Ask the following questions and have children discuss their responses with a partner. Then have children ask and answer questions of their own. Remind them that asking and answering questions can help them understand what they read.

  - What kinds of weather do they have in this neighborhood? How do you know?

  - Look at the picture on page 6. Where do you think the photographer was standing?

- **Text to World** Help children connect the story to the world around them. Ask:

  - What activities could people do during the summer/the winter/the fall/the spring?

Concept Literacy

More Reading

Use text at the children's instructional level.

Small Group Time

More Reading

Use text at the children's instructional level.

A Advanced

DAY 4

Comprehension

■ 🔊 **Comprehension** Have children silently read this week's main selection, "The Big Top." Have them identify the characters and describe the story's plot. Then have them retell the events of the story in sequence.

Remind children that realistic fiction is about things that did not happen, but seem as if they could. Ask if "The Big Top" is an example of realistic fiction. Have children explain how they know.

■ **Text to Self** Ask children if they would rather spend time with their friends playing hopscotch, playing with a doll, or playing with a spinning top. Have them explain why.

The Big Top

Objectives
• Describe the plot (problem and solution).
• Retell a story's beginning, middle, and end, with attention to sequence of events.

A Advanced

DAY 5

Comprehension

■ **Comprehension** After they have finished reading the selection, have children describe the part of the story they liked best. Then, on the back of the selection page, have them write three sentences that describe a hat they would wear if they went to a Hat Day party.

Advanced Selection R4

Objectives
• Read aloud grade-level appropriate text with fluency and comprehension.

Concept Development

What can we do with our neighborhood friends?

■ **Activate Prior Knowledge** Write the question of the week and read it aloud. Underline the word *neighborhood* and have children say it with you. Your neighborhood is where you live. Ask children to name some things they might find in their neighborhood. Then have them describe some activities they do with friends.

■ **Connect to New Concept** Have children turn to pages 88–89 in the Student Edition. Read the title aloud and have children track the print as you read it. Point to the pictures one at a time and use them to guide a discussion about what we can do with our neighborhood friends. For example, point to the girls swinging. What are these girls doing? (swinging) These girls are friends. They like to swing together. What do you like to do with your friends?

■ **Develop Concepts** Display ELL Poster R4 and have children identify where the party is happening. (in the street, on the sidewalks) What kinds of neighbors do you see? Have children point to the people on the poster. (girls, boys, parents, older people) Use the leveled prompts below to assess understanding and build oral language. Point to pictures on the poster as you guide discussion. Encourage children to seek clarification as needed.

Beginning Ask yes/no questions, such as Are people talking? Are people riding bikes?

Intermediate Ask children questions that can be answered with simple sentences. What are the girls with the box doing? What kinds of animals are their puppets? What are the children drawing on the sidewalk?

Advanced/Advanced High Have children answer the Question of the Week by giving examples from the poster and naming things they do in their neighborhood.

■ **Review Concepts and Connect to Writing** Review children's understanding of the concept at the end of the week. Ask them to write in response to these questions: What are some things we can do with our neighborhood friends? What English words did you learn this week? Have students use new academic vocabulary in sentences. Write and display key ideas from the discussion.

Objectives
- Isolate final sounds in one-syllable spoken words.
- Internalize new basic and academic language by using and reusing it in meaningful ways in speaking and writing activities that build concept and language attainment.

Content Objectives
- Describe what we can do with neighborhood friends.

Language Objectives
- Share information orally and seek clarification.
- Use new academic vocabulary to describe what we can do with neighborhood friends.

Daily Planner
The ELL lessons are organized by strands. Use them to scaffold the weekly lesson curriculum or during small-group time.

Daily Planner	
DAY 1	• Concepts and Oral Vocabulary • Listening (Read Aloud) • Match final phonemes. • Consonant d /d/
DAY 2	• Concepts • High-Frequency Words • Consonants d /d/ and l /l/
DAY 3	• Concepts • Realism and Fantasy • Read *The Big Top*
DAY 4	• Concepts • ELL/ELD Readers
DAY 5	• Concepts • Sentences • Revising

See the ELL Handbook for ELL Workshops with targeted instruction.

Language Objectives

• Match final phonemes.

Transfer Skills

Consonants In Spanish, words often end in vowels. However, the consonant *d* can end words in Spanish. Have Spanish-speaking children name words in their home language that end with the /d/ sound.

ELL Teaching Routine

For more practice with blending words, use the Sound-by-Sound Blending Routine (*ELL Handbook*, page 493).

Phonemic Awareness: Match Final Phonemes

■ **Preteach Final Phonemes**

• Have children open to pages 122–123. Point to the field. Where is the boy on the horse? (in a field) Say the word *field* slowly. I am going to say the sounds in *field*. Listen for the ending sound: /f/ /ie/ /l/ /d/. The ending sound I hear is /d/. Say /d/ with me. Say the words *red* and *kid* as you point to the picture. Emphasize the final /d/ in each word.

• Have children repeat the words *red* and *kid*. Ask them to say the ending /d/ sound aloud.

• Then say pairs of words as you point to the corresponding images on the picture. For each pair, ask if the two words end with the same sound.

    man/kid   cat/dog   lid/glad   dad/bud

■ **Practice** Say the words *ball* and *grill*. Help children hear the final /l/. As you say these pairs of words, have children tell which pairs end with the same sound: *call, cup; pal, doll; fall, pig; fill, full.*

Phonics: Consonant d /d/

■ **Preteach** Display Sound-Spelling Card 5. This is a dime. What sound do you hear at the beginning of *dime*? (/d/) Say it with me: /d/. Point to *d*. The /d/ sound in *dime* is spelled with a *d*.

■ **Listen and Write** Distribute Write and Wipe Boards.

• Have children write the letter *d* on their board. Tell children that you will write and say a word. If the word begins or ends with /d/, they are to say /d/ and show the *d* on their board. Say the following words: *sad, tree, add, dot*.

For more practice pronouncing these sounds, use the Modeled Pronunciation Audio CD Routine (*ELL Handbook*, page 501).

Objectives
• Recognize elements of the English sound system in newly acquired vocabulary such as long and short vowels, silent letters, and consonant clusters.

 ELL English Language Learners

■ **Reteach and Practice**

• Write the word *doll* on the board. Say the letters with me: *d, o, l, l*. Now say the sounds for the letters: /d/ /o/ l/, *doll*.

• Write the letter *d* on the board. I will say a word. If the word ends with /d/, say /d/. Say these words one at a time: *hill, sad, tall, bed*. Write the words with the /d/ sound on the board.

 Leveled LS Support

Beginning Have children read the words aloud. Monitor for accurate pronunciation. Ask them to repeat the /d/ sound orally.

Intermediate Have children read the words aloud. Monitor for accurate pronunciation. Ask them to the name the consonant sound spelled by *d*.

Advanced/Advanced High Have children read the words aloud and name other words that begin or end with the /d/ sound.

Phonics: Consonant *l, ll* /ll/

■ **Preteach** Have children turn to Envision It! on page 92 of the Student Edition.

• The word for the picture is *ladder*. Point to the ladder to indicate the meaning. What sound do you hear at beginning of *ladder*? (/l/) Say it with me: /l/. Explain that the /l/ sound can also be spelled *ll* as in *ball*. Write *ball* on the board and have children repeat, emphasizing the /l/ sound spelled *ll*.

■ **Practice** Distribute Letter Tiles *f, i, l, d, r, s,* and *t* to pairs. Give each pair two *l* Letter Tiles.

• Blend the sounds in *fill* and have pairs spell *fill* with their tiles: /f/ /i/ /ll/, *fill*.

• Replace the *f*. Spell *drill*.

• Replace the *d* and *r*. Spell *still*.

Language Objectives

• Associate the consonant sound /d/ with the letter *d*.

• Read words that begin or end with the consonant *l, ll* /ll/.

 Transfer Skills

Final Consonants Double final consonants such as *ll* do not exist in Spanish. Speakers of these languages may need extra spelling practice with these words.

Objectives
• Recognize elements of the English sound system in newly acquired vocabulary such as long and short vowels, silent letters, and consonant clusters.
• Learn relationships between sounds and letters of the English language to represent sounds when writing in English.

Support for English Language Learners

Content Objectives
- Monitor and adjust oral comprehension.

Language Objectives
- Discuss oral passages.
- Use a graphic organizer to take notes.

ELL Teacher Tip
To help children identify what happens at the beginning, middle, and end of a story, divide the Read Aloud into sections and have children discuss what happens in each section.

ELL English Language Learners

Listening Comprehension

Indoor Fun

Patty Pig and Jenny Hen were neighbors. They saw a sign on a tree. "Come to a picnic at Duck Lake. Bring food to share. There will be games and races."

Jenny Hen wanted to bring a fruit salad. Patty Pig wanted to bring sandwiches.

On Saturday, it was raining. It was raining too hard to have a picnic at Duck Lake. So, Jenny Hen and Patty Pig decided to have the picnic inside. They pushed the furniture up against the walls. They used umbrellas to cover the walkway between their houses.

Soon, their friends arrived. Everyone had fun at the picnic. They sang songs, told jokes, and shared stories. They had such a good time that everyone decided to have more indoor picnics during rainy or cold weather.

Prepare for the Read Aloud The modified Read Aloud above prepares children for listening to the oral reading "A Neighborhood Picnic" on page 91e.

■ **First Listening: Listen to Understand**

1. Write the title of the Read Aloud on the board. This story is about friends who want to have a picnic. What happens to their plan? What do they do instead?

2. After reading, ask children to discuss picnics they might have had.

■ **Second Listening: Listen to Check Understanding** Using a Story Map graphic organizer (*ELL Handbook,* page 506), work with children to identify what happened at the beginning, middle, and end of the story as you complete the organizer. Review the completed maps together as a class.

Objectives
- Understand the general meaning, main points, and important details of spoken language ranging from situations in which topics, language, and contexts are familiar to unfamiliar.
- Demonstrate listening comprehension of increasingly complex spoken English by following directions, and taking notes commensurate with content and grade-level needs.

ELL English Language Learners

High-Frequency Words

■ **Preteach** Use the Poster Talk-Through on ELL Poster R4 to preteach this week's high-frequency words: *they, have, two, that, are.* Display the words and read each one slowly and clearly aloud as you track the print. Have children repeat each word with you. Monitor children's pronunciation. Provide daily practice using the activities on the poster.

■ **Practice** Give each pair of children two copies of the Word Cards (*ELL Handbook,* page 47). Then have children use these cards in a matching game. Partners should take turns turning over the cards to find pairs of matching words. Model the correct pronunciation of each word. Have children say the word aloud as they turn each card over. Guide children as they read the word.

■ **Speaking/Writing with High-Frequency Words**

• **Teach/Model** Review high-frequency words. Give each child a set of Word Cards. Model drawing a picture to illustrate one high-frequency word.

• **Practice** Have children illustrate each high-frequency word. Then have children describe their drawings, using language as appropriate. Correct any misconceptions. After reteaching, have children label their drawings.

Leveled LS Support

Beginning/ Intermediate Have children illustrate each high-frequency word. Then have students describe each picture to a partner.

Advanced/Advanced High Have children illustrate each high-frequency word. Have children label their drawings and describe each picture to a partner.

Language Objectives

• Understand and use basic vocabulary.

• Understand and read high-frequency words.

• Understand important details in spoken language.

Beginners Support

Display the high-frequency word *they* to children. Explain to children that *they* is a pronoun. Provide a list of pronouns to children such as *I, you, he, she,* and *it.*

Mini-Lesson: Listening for Details

Prepare children for reading the paired reading on p. 95 of the Student Edition. Read aloud and ask them to listen for important details. Prompt their thinking with questions: What can doll do? Where does she do this? What does doll do so that she is not hot? Children can then read the page with partners.

Objectives
• Use strategic learning techniques such as concept mapping, drawing, memorizing, comparing, contrasting, and reviewing to acquire basic and grade-level vocabulary.
• Speak using learning strategies such as requesting assistance, employing non-verbal cues, and using synonyms and circumlocution (conveying ideas by defining or describing when exact English words are not known).

Content Objectives
• Identify a story as realism or fantasy.

Language Objectives
• Use the words *realism* and *fantasy* to describe reading materials.

Cognates
Share the cognate pairs realism/realismo and fantasy/fantasia with Spanish-speaking children.

Guide Comprehension
Realism and Fantasy

■ **Preteach** Show children a picture of an animal as a character in a story. Then show children a picture of a person as a character in a story. A story may include people (point to people). A story may include animals (point to an animal). The people or animals in stories are called characters. Sometimes, things happen in stories that aren't real.

Practice Have children turn to Envision It! on pages EI•2 and EI•3 in the Student Edition. Point to the pictures of the bears. Have children respond to questions about the story. Which bears are real? Which bears are make believe?

■ **Reteach/Practice** Distribute copies of the Picture It! (*ELL Handbook*, p. 48). Have children look at the images. Remind children that some stories have fantasy, things that cannot happen in real life, in them. Read the story to children. Ask them to find something that is fantasy. Reread the story chorally with children, asking them to find things that are reality. (**Answers**: fantasy: a tiger talking; reality: a tiger sleeping, a boy running, and a boy talking.)

Beginning Read the passage to children. Ask them to think about what could happen in real life and what could not. Then choral read each paragraph with children. Make a T-chart on the board, labeled *reality* and *fantasy*. After each paragraph, ask children to discuss if each event could really happen. Record the events on the T-chart.

Intermediate/Advanced/Advanced High Read the passage to children. Ask them to think about what is reality and fantasy. Write: *A boy can _____ . A tiger can _____. A tiger cannot _____."* on the board. Then, guide children in filling in each sentence frame and identifying if the sentence shows reality or fantasy.

Objectives
• Express opinions, ideas, and feelings ranging from communicating single words and short phrases to participating in extended discussions on a variety of social and grade-appropriate academic topics.

 ELL English Language Learners

Reading Comprehension
The Big Top

■ **Frontloading**

- **Background Knowledge** Read aloud the title and discuss it. Point to the houses and the neighborhood. Discuss the concept of a neighborhood. This is a story about two friends that play together.

- **Preview** Guide children on a picture walk through the story, asking them to identify people, places, and actions. Reteach these words using visuals in the Student Edition: *neighborhood* (page 97), *hop* (page 98), *mat* (page 99), and *top* (page 101).

- **Predict** Why do you think Tip is scared of the top?

Sheltered Reading Ask questions such as the following to guide children's comprehension:

- p. 98: Point to Pam and Dot. What can Pam and Dot do?

- p. 100: Point to the doll. What did Tip do to the doll?

- p. 103: Point to Tip. What did Tip do when he saw the top?

- p. 104: Point to Tip. What did Tip do to the top?

After Reading Help children summarize the text with the Retelling Cards. Ask questions that prompt children to summarize the important parts of the text.

Content Objectives
- Monitor and adjust comprehension.
- Use contextual support.
- Make and adjust predictions.

Language Objectives
- Summarize text using visual support.

Audio Support
Children can prepare for reading *The Big Top* by using the main selection eText online or the Audio Text CD. See the Audio Text CD Routine (*ELL Handbook*, page 500) for suggestions on using these learning tools.

Objectives
- Understand the general meaning, main points, and important details of spoken language ranging from situations in which topics, language, and contexts are familiar to unfamiliar.
- Demonstrate comprehension of increasingly complex English by participating in shared reading, retelling or summarizing material, and taking notes commensurate with content area and grade level needs.

ELL/ELD Reader

Comprehension:
On Our Street

■ **Before Reading** Distribute copies of the ELL and ELD Readers, *On Our Street*, to children at their reading level.

• **Preview** Read the title aloud with children: This is a story about what we can find on a street in a neighborhood. **Activate prior knowledge.** The story in our book was about what we can find in a neighborhood. The street you live on is part of your neighborhood.

• **Set a Purpose for Reading** Let's read to find out what you can do on a street with your friends.

■ **During Reading** Follow this Reading Routine for both reading groups.

1. Read the entire Reader aloud slowly as children follow along and finger point.

2. Reread the Reader one sentence at a time, having children echo read after you.

■ **After Reading** Use the exercises on the inside back cover of *On Our Street* and invite children to share drawings and writing. In a whole-group discussion, ask children to discuss the different things that can be done with friends in their neighborhood. Encourage children to compare what the children in the story do to what they do with their friends.

ELD Reader

■ **pp. 2** Point to the children. Are the children jumping rope? (yes)

■ **p. 7** Point to the girl raking leaves. Is the girl playing or helping? (She is helping.)

Writing Draw a picture of one thing the children do on their street. Label your picture. Ask children to work in pairs and share their picture with the whole class.

ELL Reader

■ **pp. 4–5** Point to the children. What do friends do on the street? (They play ball and draw.)

■ **p. 8** Point to the children washing a dog. How are the children helping? (They are washing a dog.)

Study Guide Distribute copies of the ELL Reader Study Guide (*ELL Handbook*, page 52). Scaffold comprehension by asking children what they like to do on their street. List responses. Review their responses together. (**Answers** See *ELL Handbook*, pp. 245–248.)

Objectives
• Understand the general meaning, main points, and important details of spoken language ranging from situations in which topics, language, and contexts are familiar to unfamiliar.

 English Language Learners

Conventions
Simple Sentences

■ **Preteach** Write *The children play.* Read the sentence aloud and have children repeat. Explain that this is called a sentence. Point to the capital letter and period. A sentence begins with an uppercase letter and ends with a period.

■ **Practice** Model how to write a simple sentence with a noun and a verb by writing a sentence frame on the board: *The* _____ _____. Hold up an item such as a pen. Drop the pen on the floor. Complete the sentence by writing the noun and verb in the blanks. The pen fell. The word *pen* is a noun. The word *fell* is a verb. Have children draw a simple picture of a noun showing an action. Suggest choices, such as *frog hops, dog runs, children play.* Then have each child write or dictate the noun and verb to complete the sentence: *The* _____ _____.

Beginning/Intermediate Write the following sentence frame on the board: The _____ _____. Have one child provide the noun and another child provide the verb. Write their responses in the blanks. Then have children read the sentences aloud.

Advanced/Advanced High Using the sentence frame, have children write a noun and a verb to complete the sentence and draw a picture of it. Then have them read the sentence to the group.

■ **Reteach**

• Write this sentence on the board and read it aloud: *I read.* Point out that this is a sentence. It starts with an uppercase letter and ends with a period.

■ **Practice**

Beginning/Intermediate Use sticky notes to label pictures of people, places, and things in the classroom, such as *girl, boy, book, pencil.* Write the following sentence frame on the board: The _____ _____. Have children write or dictate words that could complete the sentence frame.

Advanced/Advanced High Have children copy and complete the sentence frame and draw a picture that illustrates their sentence. Display one picture at a time. Have the other children guess the noun and the verb the picture is showing.

Objectives

• Speak using a variety of grammatical structures, sentence lengths, sentence types, and connecting words with increasing accuracy and ease as more English is acquired.

Content Objectives

• Identify the parts of sentences.

Language Objectives

• Use nouns and verbs in simple sentences.

• Write simple sentences.

 Transfer Skills

Capital Letters Children with literacy skills in Cantonese may need practice in starting sentences with a capital letter since these conventions exist only in alphabetic systems. Provide practice with starting sentences with capital letters.

Grammar Jammers

For more practice with sentences, use the Grammar Jammers for this target skill. See the Grammar Jammers Routine (*ELL Handbook*, page 501) for suggestions on using this learning tool.

Practice Page

ELL Handbook page 380 provides practice with recognizing and writing sentences.

Support for English Language Learners

Content Objectives
- Identify nouns and verbs.
- Identify simple sentences.

Language Objectives
- Write simple sentences.
- Share feedback for editing and revising.

Write Simple Sentences

- **Introduce Terms** Point to the children on pages 88–89 in the Student Edition. Write on the board *The children play.* Read the sentence aloud and have children repeat. Explain that this is called a sentence. Circle *children* and underline *play.* Tell children that *play* is a verb and *children* is a noun. Point to the capital letter and period. A sentence begins with an uppercase letter and ends with a period.

- **Introduce Simple Sentences** Write the following on the board as you point to the images on the pages *The children walk. The girls swing.* Read the sentences aloud and have children repeat. Tell children that these are sentences. Point out the uppercase letter at the beginning and the period at the end.

- **Model** Draw a two-column chart on the board. Label them *Nouns* and *Verbs.* Engage children in naming nouns that describe what they might see in their neighborhood. Record their responses in the first column of the chart. Then ask children to name action words that might describe things they like to do in their neighborhood. Record responses in the second column of the chart.

Nouns	Verbs
friends	play
dog	runs
cat	hides

- **Write** Have children use the words in the chart to orally create sentences as you write them on the board. Then have children underline the nouns and circle the verbs in each sentence. Make sure to include an uppercase letter and a period in each sentence. Have children draw a simple picture of the sentence.

Beginning Guide children in writing or dictating the noun and verb for you to write. Children can copy your writing.

Intermediate Have children write or dictate the noun and verb to complete the sentence about their drawing.

Advanced/Advanced High Have children write the noun and verb for their pictures. Read each completed sentence, and have the child repeat it.

Objectives
- Internalize new basic and academic language by using and reusing it in meaningful ways in speaking and writing activities that build concept and language attainment.
- Write using newly acquired basic vocabulary and content-based grade-level vocabulary.

This Week's ELL Overview

ELL Handbook

- Maximize Literacy and Cognitive Engagement
- Research Into Practice
- Full Weekly Support for Every Selection

  ### School Day
  - Multi-Lingual Summaries in Five Languages
  - Selection-Specific Vocabulary Word Cards
  - Frontloading/Reteaching for Comprehension Skill Lessons
  - ELD and ELL Reader Study Guides

- Transfer Activities
- Professional Development

Daily Leveled ELL Notes

ELL notes appear throughout this week's instruction and ELL Support is on the DI pages of your Teacher's Edition. The following is a sample of an ELL note from this week.

English Language Learners

Beginning Before reading, explain that the word *fit* has more than one meaning. In this story, *fit* means healthy and strong. Act out some of the action words (*hop, jog, jig*) as you say them. Have children repeat them after you.

Intermediate Walk through the story and identify the characters. Have children point out the proper names and say them aloud. Monitor children's pronunciation.

Advanced After reading, have children tell how the characters in the story get fit and healthy. Ask children what other things they can do to get fit and healthy.

Advanced High After reading, have children compare and contrast how the characters in the story get fit and healthy. Ask children to tell which character they are most like and what they like best about getting fit.

ELL by Strand

The ELL lessons on this week's Support for English Language Learners pages are organized by strand. They offer additional scaffolding for the core curriculum. Leveled support notes on these pages address the different proficiency levels in your class. See pages DI•96–DI•105.

ELL Guy
Dr. Jim Cummins

——— The Three Pillars of ELL Instruction ———

ELL Strands	Activate Prior Knowledge	Access Content	Extend Language
Vocabulary p. DI•100	Preteach	Teach/Model	Practice
Reading Comprehension p. DI•101	Preteach	Reteach	Leveled Practice Activities
Phonics, Spelling, and Word Analysis pp. DI•97–DI•98	Preteach	Listen and Write	Leveled Practice Activities
Listening Comprehension p. DI•99	Prepare for the Read Aloud	First Listening	Second Listening
Conventions and Writing pp. DI•104–DI•105	Preteach	Leveled Practice Activities	Leveled Practice Activities; Leveled Writing Activities
Concept Development p. DI•96	Activate Prior Knowledge	Develop Concepts	Review Concepts and Connect to Writing

This Week's Practice Stations Overview

Six Weekly Practice Stations with Leveled Activities can be found at the beginning of each week of instruction. For this week's Practice Stations, see pp. 114h–114i.

Small Group Teacher-led

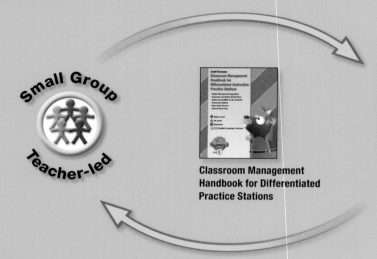

Classroom Management Handbook for Differentiated Practice Stations

Practice Stations

Daily Leveled Center Activities

⬤ Below   ◼ Advanced

△ On-Level   **E L L**

Practice Stations Flip Charts

	Listen Up!	**Word Work**	**Words to Know**	**Let's Write!**	**Read for Meaning**	**Get Fluent**
Objectives	• Identify words with the /d/, /l/, /h/, /o/ sounds. • Distinguish between initial and final /d/, /l/, /h/, /o/.	• Identify words with the consonants d, l, h. • Pronounce and spell words with d, l, h, and short o.	• Identify high-frequency words *they, have, two, that, are*. • Pronounce and spell high-frequency words *they, have, two, that, are*.	• Write complete sentences that begin with an uppercase letter. • Write complete sentences that end with a period.	• Identify the plot of a story. • Identify what aspects of the story are real. • Identify what aspects of the story are fantasy.	• Develop fluency by listening and following along with familiar texts.
Materials	• *Listen Up!* Flip Chart Activity R5 • Picture Cards • paper and crayons	• *Word Work* Flip Chart Activity R5 • ELL Poster • Letter Tiles • Picture Cards	• *Words to Know* Flip Chart Activity R5 • Word Cards • paper • pencils	• *Let's Write!* Flip Chart Activity R5 • Picture Cards • paper • pencils	• *Read for Meaning* Flip Chart Activity R5 • Student Edition Unit R • paper • pencils • crayons	• AudioText CD for *School Day* and "How Do You Get to School?" • Student Edition • CD player

Week 5

This Week on Reading Street!

My World

Question of the Week
What is around us at school?

Daily Plan

Don't Wait Until Friday

Whole Group

- ◉ Consonants *r, w, k*
- ◉ Short e: *e*
- ◉ Plot
- • Vocabulary

MONITOR PROGRESS	Success Predictor			
Day 1 Check Word Reading	Day 2 Check Word Reading	Day 3 Check Word Reading Check High-Frequency Words	Day 4 Check Word Reading: Check Retelling	Day 5 Check Oral Vocabulary: Check Phonemic Awareness

Small Group

Teacher-Led

- • Reading Support
- • Skill Support

Practice Stations

Independent Activities

Customize Literacy More support for a Balanced Literacy approach, see CL•1–CL•47.

Customize Writing More support for a customized writing approach, see CW•11–CW•20.

Whole Group

- • Writing: Sentences with Adjectives
- • Conventions: Adjectives

Assessment

- • Weekly Tests
- • Day 5 Assessment
- • Fresh Reads

You Are Here! Unit R Week 5

This Week's Reading Selections

Main Selection
Genre: **Realistic Fiction**

Paired Selection

Decodable Practice Readers

Concept Literacy Reader

ELL and ELD Readers

Resources on Reading Street!

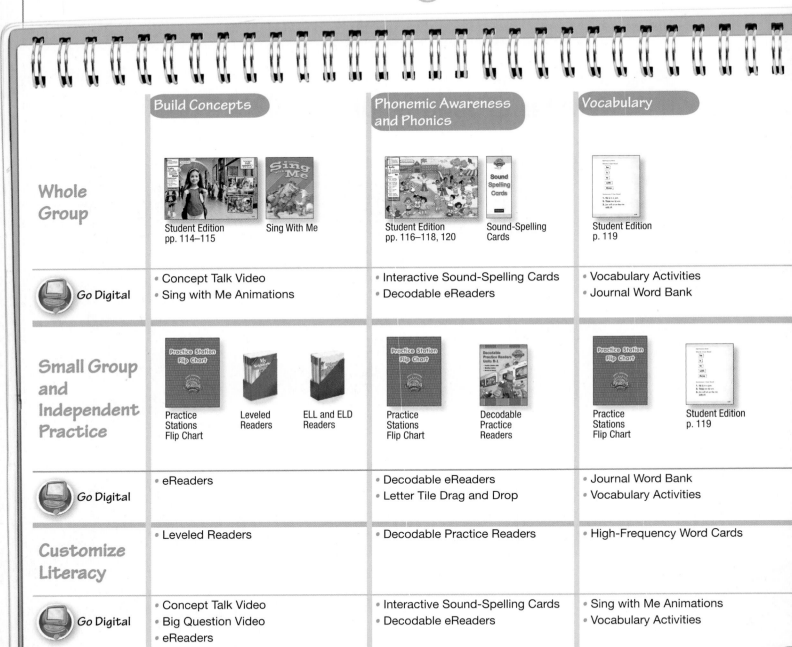

	Build Concepts	Phonemic Awareness and Phonics	Vocabulary
Whole Group	Student Edition pp. 114–115 / Sing With Me	Student Edition pp. 116–118, 120 / Sound-Spelling Cards	Student Edition p. 119
Go Digital	• Concept Talk Video • Sing with Me Animations	• Interactive Sound-Spelling Cards • Decodable eReaders	• Vocabulary Activities • Journal Word Bank
Small Group and Independent Practice	Practice Stations Flip Chart / Leveled Readers / ELL and ELD Readers	Practice Stations Flip Chart / Decodable Practice Readers	Practice Stations Flip Chart / Student Edition p. 119
Go Digital	• eReaders	• Decodable eReaders • Letter Tile Drag and Drop	• Journal Word Bank • Vocabulary Activities
Customize Literacy	• Leveled Readers	• Decodable Practice Readers	• High-Frequency Word Cards
Go Digital	• Concept Talk Video • Big Question Video • eReaders	• Interactive Sound-Spelling Cards • Decodable eReaders	• Sing with Me Animations • Vocabulary Activities

Question of the Week
What is around us at school?

Week 5

Comprehension

Student Edition
pp. 122–133

- Envision It! Animations
- eSelections

Practice Stations Flip Chart

Leveled Readers

ELL and ELD Readers

- eReaders

- Envision It! Skills and Strategies Handbooks
- Leveled Readers

- Envision It! Animations
- eReaders

Conventions and Writing

Student Edition
pp. 134–135

- Grammar Jammer
- Online Journal

Practice Stations Flip Chart

Reader's and Writer's Notebook

- Grammar Jammer
- Online Journal

- Reader's and Writer's Notebook

- Grammar Jammer
- Online Journal

You Are Here!
Unit R
Week 5

My 5-Day Planner for Reading Street!

SUCCESS PREDICTOR
Don't Wait Until Friday

	Check Word Reading **Day 1** pages 114j–117i	Check Word Reading **Day 2** pages 118a–119e

Get Ready to Read	**Concept Talk,** 114j–115
	Oral Vocabulary, 115a–115b
	  classmate, education, polite
	Phonemic Awareness, 116–117
	  Isolate Initial, Medial, Final Phonemes
	Phonics, 117a–117c
	  ◉ Consonant *r* /r/
		Concept Talk, 118a–118b
		Oral Vocabulary, 118b
		  principal, recess
		Print Awareness, 118c
		  Identify Information
		Phonemic Awareness, 118d
		  Isolate Initial Phonemes
		Phonics, 118e–118
		  ◉ Consonants, *j* /j/, *w* /w/

Read and Comprehend	**Listening Comprehension,** 117d–117e
	  ◉ Plot
		Comprehension, 119a
		  ◉ Plot
		Vocabulary, 119a
		  Use Descriptive Words
		High-Frequency Words, 119
		  Introduce *he, is, three, to, with*

Language Arts	**Conventions,** 117f
	  Adjectives
	Handwriting, 117g
	  Letter *R* and *r*; Proper Letter Size
	Writing, 117h
	  Sentences with Adjectives
	Listening and Speaking, 117i
	  Ask Questions
		Conventions, 119b
		  Adjectives
		Handwriting, 119c
		  Letters *Ww* and *Jj*; Proper Body/Paper Position
		Writing, 119d
		  Sentences with Adjectives
		Listening and Speaking, 119e
		  Follow Directions

You Are Here!
Unit R
Week 5

What is around us at school?

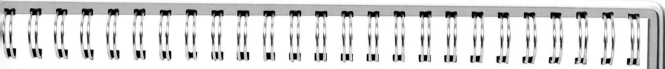

Check Word Reading: **Check High-Frequency Words** **Day 3** pages 120a–120l	**Check Word Reading:** **Check Retelling** **Day 4** pages 120m–135c	**Check Oral Vocabulary:** **Check Phonemic Awareness** **Day 5** pages 136a–139e
Concept Talk, 120a–120b **Oral Vocabulary,** 120b *science* **Print Awareness,** 120c Identify Information **Phonological Awareness,** 120d Rhyme Words **Phonics,** 120e–120g ⊙ Consonant *k* /k/	**Concept Talk,** 120m–120n **Oral Vocabulary,** 120n *applaud, complicated, success* **Print Awareness,** 120o Sequence Letters **Phonemic Awareness,** 120p Segment and Blend Phonemes **Phonics,** 120q–120 ⊙ Short *e: e* **READ Decodable Practice Reader** R5A, 121a–121b	**Concept Wrap Up,** 136a Review **Oral Vocabulary,** 136b **Print Awareness,** 136c Sentence Features **Phonological Awareness,** 136d Identify Syllables Review **Fluent Word Reading,** 136e Review **Phonics,** 136f ⊙ Consonants *r* /r/, *w* /w/, *j* /j/, *k* /k/ ⊙ Short *e: e* Review **High-Frequency Words,** 136f **READ Decodable Practice Reader** R5B, 136g–136h
High-Frequency Words, 120h Practice *he, is, three, to, with*	**Literary Text,** 121c Fiction and Nonfiction **High-Frequency Words,** 121 Build Fluency *he, is, three, to, with* **Build Background,** 122a **READ Main Selection,** 122b–133a *School Day*	**Social Studies in Reading,** 136i **READ Paired Selection,** 136–137 "How Do You Get to School?" **Listening and Speaking,** 138–139 Ask Questions **Vocabulary,** 139a Use Descriptive Words **Handwriting,** 139a Body Position **Assessment,** 139b–139c Monitor Progress
Conventions, 120i Adjectives **Handwriting,** 120j Letter *K* and *k*; Self-Evaluation **Writing,** 120k Sentences with Adjectives **Listening and Speaking,** 120l Restate Directions	**Conventions,** 134–135 Adjectives **Writing,** 135a Sentences with Adjectives **Research,** 135b Calendar **Handwriting,** 135c Letter *E* and *e*; Letter Size	Review **Conventions,** 139d Adjectives **Writing,** 139d Sentences with Adjectives **Wrap Up Your Week,** 139e Question of the Week ⊙ What is around us at school?

Week 5

Grouping Options for Differentiated Instruction
Turn the page for the small group time lesson plan.

Planning Small Group Time on Reading Street!

SMALL GROUP TIME RESOURCES

Look for this Small Group Time box each day to help meet the individual needs of all your children. Differentiated Instruction lessons appear on the DI pages at the end of each week.

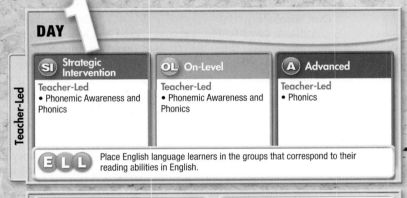

DAY 1

Teacher-Led

SI Strategic Intervention	OL On-Level	A Advanced
Teacher-Led	**Teacher-Led**	**Teacher-Led**
• Phonemic Awareness and Phonics	• Phonemic Awareness and Phonics	• Phonics

ELL Place English language learners in the groups that correspond to their reading abilities in English.

Practice Stations
• Listen Up
• Word Work

Independent Activities
• Reader's and Writer's Notebook
• Concept Talk Video

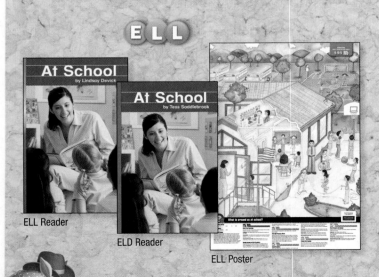

ELL

ELL Reader

ELD Reader

ELL Poster

Day 1

SI Strategic Intervention	**Phonemic Awareness and Phonics, DI•85**
OL On-Level	**Phonemic Awareness and Phonics, DI•90**
A Advanced	**Phonics, DI•93**
ELL English Language Learners	DI•96–DI•105 **Concepts and Oral Vocabulary Listening (Read Aloud)**

You Are Here! Unit R Week 5

Reading Street
Intervention Kit

Reading Street
Practice Stations Kit

Question of the Week
What is around us at school?

SI Strategic Intervention

OL On-Level

A Advanced

Concept Literacy Reader

Decodable Practice Readers

Concept Literacy Reader

Concept Literacy
Reader

Advanced Selection

Small Group Weekly Plan

Day 2	Day 3	Day 4	Day 5
Phonemic Awareness and Phonics, DI•86	**Phonemic Awareness and Phonics,** DI•87 **Read Concept Literacy Leveled Reader,** DI•87	**Phonemic Awareness and Phonics,** DI•88 **Read Decodable Practice Reader** R5A, DI•88	**High-Frequency Words,** DI•89 **Read Decodable Practice Reader** R5B, DI•89
Phonics and High-Frequency Words, DI•90	**Read Concept Literacy Leveled Reader,** DI•91	**Conventions,** DI•92	**Phonics Review,** DI•92
Phonics and Comprehension, DI•93	**Read Concept Literacy Leveled Reader,** DI•94	**Comprehension,** DI•95	**Comprehension,** DI•95
DI•96–DI•105 **Concepts** **Vocabulary** **Phonics and Spelling** **Conventions**	DI•96–DI•105 **Concepts** **Vocabulary** **Comprehension Skill** **Main Selection**	DI•96–DI•105 **Concepts** **Vocabulary** **ELL/ELD Readers** **ELL Workshop**	DI•96–DI•105 **Concepts** **Vocabulary** **Sentences with Adjectives**

Week 5

Practice Stations for Everyone on Reading Street!

Listen Up!
Match sounds and pictures.

Objectives
- Identify words with the /d/, /l/, /h/, /o/.
- Distinguish between initial and final /d/, /l/, /h/, /o/.

Materials
- *Listen Up!* Flip Chart Activity R5
- Picture Cards
- Paper and crayons

Differentiated Activities

⬤ Find Picture Cards with things that start or end like the first sound in *dad.* Then find things that start or end with the first sounds in *lip, hip,* and *on.*

▲ Find Picture Cards with things that start or end like the first sound in *dad.* Then find things that start or end with the first sounds in *lip, hip,* and *on.* Draw pictures of other thing that begin or end with these sounds.

◼ Find Picture Cards with things that start or end like the first sound in *dad.* Then find things that start or end with the first sounds in *lip, hip,* and *on.* Sort them into piles for beginning sounds and ending sounds.

Technology
- Interactive Sound-Spelling Cards

Word Work
Identify the sounds of *d, l, h,* and short *o.*

Objectives
- Identify words with the consonants *d, l, h.*
- Pronounce and spell words with *d, l, h,* and short *o.*

Materials
- *Word Work* Flip Chart Activity R5
- ELL Poster
- Letter Tiles
- Picture Cards

Have children look at the Picture Cards and the ELL Poster for ideas.

Differentiated Activities

⬤ Find Picture Cards that show things with *d, l, h,* or short *o.* Quietly say each word. Match one or more of the Letter Tiles to each Picture Card that pictures a word with the sound of the letter.

▲ Find Picture Cards that show things with *d, l, h,* or short *o.* Quietly say each word. Then use Letter Tiles *d, l, h, o, p, s, t, n,* and *a* to spell three words.

◼ Think of words with the *d, l,* or *h* sound at the beginning or end and short vowels *a, l,* or *o* in the middle. Use Letter Tiles to spell five words. Quietly say each word.

Technology
- Interactive Sound-Spelling Cards

Words To Know
Practice high-frequency words.

Objectives
- Identify high-frequency words *they, have, two, that,* and *are.*
- Pronounce and spell high-frequency words *they, have, two, that,* and *are.*

Materials
- *Words to Know* Flip Chart Activity R5
- Word Cards
- paper
- pencils

Differentiated Activities

⬤ Look at the Word Cards for *they, have, two, that,* and *are.* Match the letters in each word with Letter Tiles.

▲ Look at the Word Cards for they, have, two, that, and are. Copy the words on your paper.

◼ Look at the Word Cards for look, *do, you, was, yellow, they, have, two, that,* and *are.* Write sentences using as many of the words as you can.

Technology
- Online Tested Vocabulary Activities

You Are Here!
Unit R
Week 5

Use this week's materials from the Reading Street Practice Stations Kit to organize this week's stations.

Key
- Below
- On-Level
- Advanced

Let's Write!
Write in complete sentences.

Objectives
- Write complete sentences that begin with an uppercase letter.
- Write complete sentences that end with a period.

Materials
- *Let's Write!* Flip Chart Activity R5
- Picture Cards
- paper
- pencils

Differentiated Activities
- A **complete sentence** has a subject and verb. It tells a complete thought.
- **End punctuation** is a mark at the end of a sentence. It can be a period (**.**), an exclamation mark (**!**), or a question mark (**?**).

Choose a Picture Card. Write a complete sentence about it including a noun and a verb. Begin with a capital letter. End with a period.

Choose two Picture Cards of people. Write a complete sentence about each picture. Each sentence should include a noun and a verb. Remember to use capital letters and end punctuation.

Choose a Picture Card of an animal. Write sentences telling how the animal moves, where it lives, and how it eats. Use complete sentences. Use capital letters and end punctuation.

Technology
- Online Journals

Read For Meaning
Identify realism and fantasy.

Objectives
- Identify the plot of a story.
- Identify what aspects of the story are real.
- Identify what aspects of the story are fantasy.

Materials
- *Read for Meaning* Flip Chart Activity
- Student Edition Unit R
- paper
- pencils
- crayons

Differentiated Activities
- **Realism** refers to a story that could happen in real life.
- **Fantasy** refers to a story that could not happen in real life.

Reread *A Big Mess.* Identify the main character. Identify a key plot event. Draw a picture that shows if the story is realism or fantasy.

Reread *A Big Mess.* Think about the character and the plot. Is the story realistic or fantasy? Answer in a sentence, and tell why. Draw a picture to go with your sentence.

Reread *A Big Mess.* Think about its characters and plot. Is the story realistic or fantasy? Write a list identifying the story's realistic or fantastic parts.

Technology
- Online Student Edition

Get Fluent
Listen to fluent reading.

Objective
- Develop fluency by listening and following along with familiar texts.

Materials
- AudioText CD for *School Day* and "How Do You Get to School?"
- Student Edition
- CD player

Activity
Open your book to the selection *School Day.* Track the print as you listen to the AudioText CD. Notice how the reader says the words on each page. Then listen to "How Do You Get to School?"

Technology
- Online Main Selection and Paired Selection eText

Week 5

Objectives
- Introduce concepts: schools.
- Share information and ideas about the concept.

Today at a Glance

Oral Vocabulary
classmate, education, polite

Phonemic Awareness
Isolate Initial, Medial, and Final Phonemes

Phonics
⊙ Consonant *r* /r/

Comprehension
⊙ Plot

Conventions
Adjectives

Handwriting
R and r/Proper Letter Size

Writing
Sentences with Adjectives

Listening and Speaking
Ask Questions

Concept Talk

Question of the Week

What is around us at school?

Introduce the concept

To build concepts and to focus children's attention, tell them that this week they will talk, sing, read, and write about schools. Write the Question of the Week, and track the print as you read it.

ROUTINE **Activate Prior Knowledge** **Team Talk**

1. **Think** Have children think for a minute about schools.
2. **Pair** Have pairs of children discuss the question.
3. **Share** Have children share information and their ideas with the group. Remind children to ask questions to clarify information. Guide discussion and encourage elaboration with prompts such as:
   - What else can you see at a school?

Routines Flip Chart

Anchored Talk

Develop oral language

Have children turn to pages 114–115 in their Student Editions. Read the title and look at the photos. Use these questions to guide discussion and create the "What is around us at school?" concept map.

- What does the first picture show? **(children)** I'll draw a box and label it *People*. I'll write *schoolchildren* in that box. I also see a hallway, so I'll make a box labeled *Places*. I'll write *hallways* in this box. I see doors to classrooms too, so *classrooms* goes in the *Places* box.

- What do you see in the top picture? **(children at tables)** What things are in the picture? **(tables, chairs, books, a computer, a globe)** I'll make a box and label it *Things*. Write *tables, chairs, books, computers,* and *globes* in the *Things* box.

- What is in the third picture? **(a person teaching art)** I'll put *teachers* in the *People* box and *art supplies* in the box labeled *Things*.

Oral Vocabulary

Objectives
• Listen closely to speakers and ask questions to help you better understand the topic. • Share information and ideas about the topic. Speak at the correct pace.

Let's Talk About

Read Together

Neighborhoods
● Share information about what is around us at school.
● Share ideas about what we do at school each day.

READING STREET ONLINE
CONCEPT TALK VIDEO
www.ReadingStreet.com

You've learned
0 3 0
Amazing Words ☆
so far this year!

114   115

Student Edition pp. 114–115

classmate	science
education	complicated
polite	success
principal	applaud
recess	

Writing on Demand

Develop Writing Fluency Ask children to write about what they know about schools. Have them write for two to three minutes. Children should write as much as they can. Tell them to try to do their best writing. You may want to discuss what children wrote during writing conferences.

Connect to reading

Explain to children that this week, they will read another story about Sam. Tell children that this story is about Sam meeting his friends at school. Have children talk about what they like to do with their friends at school. Let's add *friends* to our map. Should I write *friends* in the *People* box, the *Places* box, or the *Things* box? That's right, the *People* box, because friends are people.

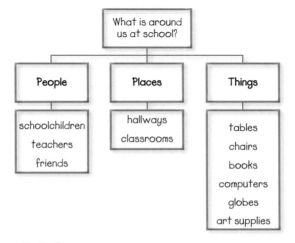

```
          What is around
          us at school?

   People        Places        Things

schoolchildren  hallways       tables
               classrooms
  teachers                     chairs

  friends                      books

                             computers

                              globes

                             art supplies
```

ELL Preteach Concepts Use the Day 1 instruction on ELL Poster R5 to assess and build background knowledge, develop concepts, and build oral vocabulary.

ELL

English Language Learners
Listening Comprehension
English learners will benefit from additional visual support to understand the key terms in the concept map. Use the pictures on pp. 114–115 to scaffold understanding. For example, when talking about teachers and children, point to the picture of the woman helping the children with their art projects.

ELL Support Additional ELL support and modified instruction is provided in the *ELL Handbook* and in the ELL Support Lessons on pp. DI•96–DI•105.

ELL Poster R5

School Day   **114–115**

Objectives
- Build oral vocabulary.
- Discuss the concept to build oral language.
- Share information and ideas about the concept.

Oral Vocabulary
Amazing Words

Introduce Amazing Words

Display p. R5 of the *Sing with Me* Big Book. Tell children they are going to sing a song about being at school. Ask children to listen for the Amazing Words *classmate*, *education*, and *polite* as you sing. Sing the song again and have children join you.

 Sing with Me Big Book Audio

Sing with Me Big Book, p. R5

Teach Amazing Words

Amazing Words Oral Vocabulary Routine

1 **Introduce the Word** Relate the word *polite* to the song: In the song, everybody is *polite* at school. Supply a child-friendly definition: When you are *polite*, you have good manners and you show respect for other people. Have children say the word.

2 **Demonstrate** Provide examples to show meaning: It is *polite* to say "please" and "thank you." Listening when others speak is *polite*. It is not *polite* to push somebody out of your way.

3 **Apply** Have children demonstrate their understanding: Give me an example of when you are being *polite*.

See p. OV•2 to teach *classmate* and *education*.

Routines Flip Chart

Sing with Me Animations

Whole Group

Check understanding of Amazing Words

As you continue the discussion, have children use today's Amazing Words, *classmate*, *education*, and *polite*. If children have difficulty using the words, remind them of the definitions. Guide them to respond in complete sentences.

Look at the pictures on page 114–115 of your books. How are the children in the pictures like your *classmates*? Use *classmates* in your answer. (Possible response: My classmates wear backpacks, do art projects, and raise their hands when they want to talk.)

How are these children getting an *education*? Use the word *education*. (Possible response: They are getting an education from their books and their teacher.)

How can these children be *polite* to each other? Use the word *polite*. (Possible response: They can be polite by listening to each other, sharing, and saying "please" and "thank you.")

Apply Amazing Words

Have children demonstrate their understanding of the Amazing Words by completing these sentences orally.

Some things I like to do with my **classmates** are _____.

You will get a good **education** if you _____.

It makes sense to be **polite** to other people because _____.

Corrective feedback

If... children have difficulty using the Amazing Words,
then... remind them of the definitions and provide opportunities for children to use the words in sentences

Preteach Academic Vocabulary

Write the following on the board:

- plot
- realistic fiction
- adjectives

Have children share what they know about this week's Academic Vocabulary. Use children's responses to assess their prior knowledge. Preteach the Academic Vocabulary by providing a child-friendly description, explanation, or example that clarifies the meaning of each term. Then ask children to restate the meaning of the Academic Vocabulary in their own words.

Amazing Words

classmate	science
education	complicated
polite	success
principal	applaud
recess	

Differentiated Instruction

A **Advanced**

Telling Stories Have children work with a partner. Have them make up a short story that uses all three of the day's Amazing Words. Encourage them to tell other children or to write down parts of it. Have them make and label illustrations as well.

ELL

English Language Learners
Cognates The word *education* has a cognate in Spanish: *educacion*. Relating the Spanish word to the English may help children learn this new Amazing Word.

School Day **115b**

Objectives

- Isolate initial, medial, and final phonemes.
- Match initial, medial, and final phonemes.
- Associate consonant *r* with the sound /r/.
- Recognize and name the letters *Rr*.
- Write the letters *Rr*.

Skills Trace

◉ **Consonant *r*/r/**
Introduce URW5D1
Practice URW5D4; URW5D5
Reteach/Review URW5D2;
URW5D3; URW5D4; URW5D5
Assess/Test Weekly Test URW5
Benchmark Test UR

Student Edition pp. 116–117

Phonemic Awareness
Match Initial, Medial, Final Phonemes

Introduce   Read together the first two bulleted points on pages 116–117 of the Student Edition. Find the children who are having a race. *Race* starts with the /r/ sound. I see a small animal wiggling in the dirt. What animal is it? (a worm) The sound /r/ is in the middle of *worm*. I see a boy kicking a soccer ball. *Soccer* ends with the /r/ sound.

Model   Listen to the first sound of *race*: /r/. Say the sound with me: /r/. *Race* begins with /r/. Listen to the middle of *worm*: /r/. The sound /r/ is in the middle of *worm*. Listen to the end of *soccer*: /r/. *Soccer* ends with /r/. Repeat with *red, girl,* and *ear*.

Guide practice   Have children say: *ribbon, running, recycle, warm, shirt, picture, sneaker.*

Corrective feedback   **If...** children make an error,
then... model by saying the sound again, along with a word that begins or ends with the sound, and have them repeat the sound and the word.

Phonics
Consonant r /r/

Hear

Today you will learn how to spell the sound /r/. Listen: /r/, /r/, /r/. When you say /r/, your voice box is turned on and the tip of your tongue goes up and toward the roof of your mouth. Say /r/ and feel the tip of your tongue go up and toward the roof of your mouth. **Watch and listen as children produce the sound.** Say /r/ with me: /r/, /r/, /r/.

Say

Display Sound-Spelling Card 20. This is a picture of a *rocket*. Say it with me: *rocket*. The first sound in *rocket* is /r/. Listen: /r/, *rocket*. Say it with me: /r/, *rocket*. What is the first sound in *rocket*?

See

Point to *r*. This is *r*. The sound /r/ is usually spelled *r*. *Rocket* begins with /r/. *Rocket* begins with the letter *r*. Have children say /r/ several times as you point to *r*.

Read ABC Rhyme Time

Display ABC Rhyme Time, p. 23. Point to the letters *Rr* at the top of the page. The name for both these letters is *r*. Point to *R*. This is an upper-case *R*. Point to *r*. This is a lower-case *r*. Point to each letter again and ask: What is the name of this letter?

This rhyme is about a robot that cleans a room. Read the rhyme aloud, tracking the print with your finger. Then read it again. Point to examples of upper- and lower-case *r*'s as you read each word aloud.

Write

Now I will show you how to write upper-case *R* and lower-case *r*. Write *R*. Watch as I trace upper-case *R* with my finger. Follow the stroke instructions pictured. Now you write upper-case *R*. Repeat for lower-case *r*.

Sound-Spelling Card 20

ABC Rhyme Time p. 23

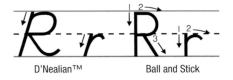
D'Nealian™   Ball and Stick

Professional Development

Oral Responses When children respond orally as a class, it can be difficult to know whether individual children are responding correctly. For the sound /r/, however, looking at the position of children's lips can help you determine if they are saying the sound properly.

Spelling Pattern

/r/r The sound /r/ is almost always spelled *r*.

Academic Vocabulary

phoneme smallest meaningful unit of sound in spoken language

ELL

English Language Learners
Pronounce Words with the Sound /r/ Speakers of Chinese, Japanese, Korean, and Vietnamese may confuse the sound /r/ with the sound /l/. Help children practice distinguishing these sounds and letters in word pairs such as *rap/lap, rid/lid,* and *row/low.*

Objectives
○ Blend, read, and spell words with consonant *r* /r/.
○ Associate the consonant *r* with the sound /r/.
• Write the letters *Rr*.
• Recognize and name the letters *Rr*.

Phonics—Teach/Model
↺ Consonant *r* /r/

Sound-Spelling Card 20

ROUTINE Blending Strategy

1. **Connect** Connect consonant *r* to the sound /r/. Write *r*. This is *r*. The sound for *r* is /r/. Say the sound with me: /r/, /r/, /r/. When you see the letter *r*, what sound will you say?

2. **Model** Model how to blend *ran*. Write *r*. What is the sound for this letter? Say the sound with me: /r/. Write *a*. Say this sound with me: /a/. Write *n*. Say this sound with me: /n/. Listen as I blend all the sounds together: /r/ /a/ /n/, *ran*. Blend the sounds with me: /r/ /a/ /n/, *ran*. Now blend the sounds without me.

3. **Guide Practice** Continue the process in Step 2 with the following words: *rag, rob, rip, rat, lot, hot, hat, lap,* and *pal*. First we say the sounds, then we blend the sounds to read the word. **For corrective feedback, model blending the sounds to read the word. Then have children blend the sounds and read it with you.**

4. **Review** What do you know about reading words that begin with the letter *r*? The sound for *r* is /r/.

Routines Flip Chart

Spell Words Now we are going to spell words with the sound /r/ spelled *r*. The first word we will spell is *rod*. What sounds do you hear in *rod*? (/r/ /o/ /d/) What is the letter for /r/? Let's all write *r*. What is the letter for /o/? Write *o*. What is the letter for /d/? Write *d*. **Have children confirm their spellings by comparing them with what you have written.** Continue the practice with *ram, rib,* and *rot*.

On their own Use the *Reader's and Writer's Notebook* p. 81 for additional practice with consonant *r* /r/.

Reader's and Writer's Notebook p. 81

Phonics
Identify Lower-Case and Upper-Case Letters

Guide Practice

Write a lower-case *r* and point to it. What letter is this? (lower-case *r*) Write an upper-case *R* and point to it. What letter is this? (upper-case *R*) Write a series of upper- and lower-case *r*'s. Have children identify each as upper-case *R* or lower-case *r*.

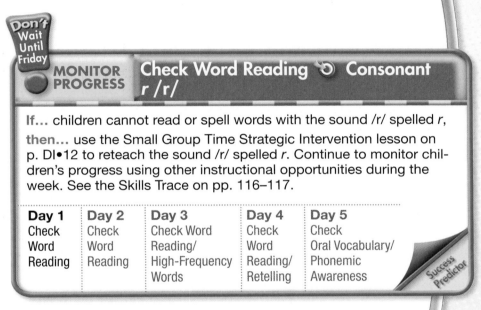

Don't Wait Until Friday

MONITOR PROGRESS **Check Word Reading** 🔊 **Consonant r /r/**

If... children cannot read or spell words with the sound /r/ spelled *r*,

then... use the Small Group Time Strategic Intervention lesson on p. DI•12 to reteach the sound /r/ spelled *r*. Continue to monitor children's progress using other instructional opportunities during the week. See the Skills Trace on pp. 116–117.

Day 1	**Day 2**	**Day 3**	**Day 4**	**Day 5**
Check Word Reading	Check Word Reading	Check Word Reading/ High-Frequency Words	Check Word Reading/ Retelling	Check Oral Vocabulary/ Phonemic Awareness

Success Predictor

Small Group Time

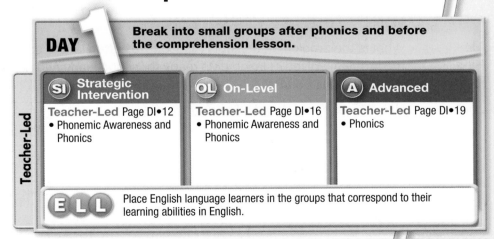

DAY 1

Break into small groups after phonics and before the comprehension lesson.

Teacher-Led

SI Strategic Intervention
Teacher-Led Page DI•12
• Phonemic Awareness and Phonics

OL On-Level
Teacher-Led Page DI•16
• Phonemic Awareness and Phonics

A Advanced
Teacher-Led Page DI•19
• Phonics

ELL Place English language learners in the groups that correspond to their learning abilities in English.

Practice Stations
• Listen Up
• Word Work

Independent Activities
• Read independently/Reading log on *Reader's and Writer's Notebook* p. RR1.
• Concept Talk Viideo

Differentiated Instruction

SI Strategic Intervention

Writing *r* Help children connect the lower-case letter *r* with the sound /r/ by having them make the sound /r/ as they write the letter. Have their voices go down in pitch as they make the down-stroke on the letter, then raise the pitch as they do the upstroke and the final curve.

ELL

English Language Learners
Vocabulary The words that children blend in this lesson are all ordinary English words, but ELL children often will not know what the words mean. When possible, give a child-friendly definition for each word and use it in a sentence. Add gestures if necessary. For *rag*, for example, you might say *A rag is an old piece of cloth,* and then add, using a polishing motion, *I used a* rag *to help wash my car.* If time permits, help children create sentences of their own with these words.

Objectives
○ Recognize plot in realistic fiction.

Skills Trace
◉ **Plot**
Introduce URW3D1; URW5D1; U1W2D1; U5W1D1
Practice URW3D2; URW3D3; URW3D4; URW5D2; URW5D3; URW5D4; U1W2D2; U1W2D3; U1W2D4; U5W1D2; U5W1D3; U5W1D4
Reteach/Review URW3D5; URW4D2; URW5D2; U1W1D2; U1W2D5; U1W4D2; U2W2D2; U3W4D2; U4W6D2; U5W1D5; U5W6D2
Assess/Test Weekly Tests URW3; URW5; U1W2; U5W1 Benchmark Tests UR

Listening Comprehension
Plot

Introduce

Envision It!

The **plot** of a story is what happens at the beginning, middle, and end of the story. The plot explains the problem in the story and the solution to the problem, which means how the problem is solved. Good readers pay attention to the plot because it helps them understand what is happening in the story. Readers understand a story best when they know the problem in the story and understand the solution to the problem.

Student Edition EI•5

Have children turn to p. EI•5 in their Student Edition. These pictures show an example of a plot. **Ask:**

- What happens at the beginning of the story? (the rabbits wake up)
- The middle of this story explains the problem. What is the problem in the story? (one of the rabbits will not wake up)
- What do the other rabbits do to solve the problem? You can find out by looking at the end of the story. (The other rabbits make a lot of noise so that the sleeping rabbit will wake up.)

Model

Today we will read a story about two boys who meet at school. Read "Early for School" and model how to recognize and understand its plot.

 Think Aloud When I read, I pay attention to the plot of the story. I read to find out what the problem in the story will be. Then I read to find out how the characters solve the problem. I want to know what happens in the beginning, the middle, and the end. At the beginning of "Early for School," I read that Jason is late to school. That sounds like a problem to me!

Guide practice

What is the problem in the story? (Jason was often late to school.) How is the problem solved? (Jason gets ready for school early and is ready when Peter rings his doorbell.)

On their own

Use *Reader's and Writer's Notebook* p. 82.

Reader's and Writer's Notebook p. 82

Read Aloud

Early for School

Jason liked school a lot, but he was often late. Today he had spent too much time day-dreaming over breakfast until Mom told him what time it was. Luckily, Jason lived only a block from school. He ran down the block, walked quickly through the large school doors, and hurried down the long hall to his classroom. He tiptoed quietly in and took his seat.

"Good morning, Jason," said his teacher, Miss Parsons. "I was just introducing our new student, Peter Rogers, to the class. Peter and his family moved here from another state, and as it turns out, he lives on your block. So perhaps after school, you and Peter can walk home together."

"Sure, Miss Parsons," said Jason. "It's nice to meet you, Peter." Jason was a very polite boy.

Peter smiled and said thanks, and then the class took out their reading books and started working. During the day, Jason showed Peter where to find things. He showed his new classmate the library area. He showed him where the pencils and crayons were kept, and the chart that listed the class jobs. After lunch, they played ball on the playground.

At the end of the day, Jason and Peter walked home together. They had a lot to talk about. Jason liked his new friend and Peter felt the same way. The boys reached Jason's house first, but before they said good-bye, they made a plan to meet the next morning to walk to school together.

"I'll ring your doorbell early tomorrow, so we can take our time," said Peter.

"That sounds great!" said Jason. "I'll be ready." And he was!

Academic Vocabulary

plot a series of related events at the beginning, middle, and end of a story; includes a problem and its solution

Objectives
- Understand and use adjectives.
- Use proper letter size when writing.
- Write *Rr*.

Conventions
Adjectives

Model

Explain that an **adjective** is a describing word that tells about a noun. Adjectives can tell what size, what color, or how many. *Red, big,* and *three* are all adjectives.

Display Grammar Transparency R5. Read the definition aloud. Model reading the example and comparing it to the picture shown. Then read the directions and model number 1.

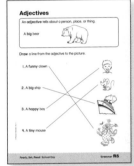

Grammar Transparency R5

- The adjective here is *funny*. It is in bold letters to show it is an adjective. I see a lot of pictures on the page. The first three pictures don't show anything funny. The last picture shows a clown that looks funny as he juggles. This picture matches the adjective *funny*.

- I will draw a line from the words *A funny clown* to the picture of the funny clown at the bottom of the page.

Guide practice

Continue with items 2–4, having children draw a line from each adjective to the matching picture.

Connect to oral language

Have the class complete these sentence frames orally using adjectives.

1. I wear _____ shoes.

2. My friend wears _____ socks.

On their own

Team Talk Pair children and have them talk about the things they see in the classroom. Then have them take turns using adjectives in sentences to describe these things.

Handwriting
Letter *R* and *r;*
Proper Letter Size

Model letter formation

Display upper- and lower-case letters: *Rr*. Use the stroke instructions pictured below to model proper letter formation.

D'Nealian™   Ball and Stick

Model proper letter size

Remind children that it is important to use correct letter size in our writing. The lines on our writing paper help us to keep our letters the correct size. The letters cannot be too small or too large. Say: When I write upper-case *R*, I start at the top line. When I write lower-case *r*, I start at the middle line. Repeat this action several times. Then write the letters *Rr* on the board to model correct letter size.

Guide practice

Write the following words on the board: *rip, Rob, Ron, rid*

Team Talk Have children work together in pairs to identify the letters *Rr*. Then have them copy the words on lined paper. Remind them to use proper letter size.

On their own

Use the *Reader's and Writer's Notebook* p. 83.

Reader's and Writer's Notebook p. 83

Differentiated Instruction

SI Strategic Intervention

Adjectives Restate the definition of an adjective. Write the sentence *Tasha has yellow boots.* Underline *yellow.* Explain that it is an adjective that describes the noun *boots.* Continue modeling with other sentences. Then ask the group to supply other adjectives they could use in the sentences.

Academic Vocabulary

adjective a word that tells which one, what kind, how many, or how much

noun a word that names a person, place, animal, or thing

Daily Fix-It

1. i will look at Kim.
   I will look at Kim.
2. I kan se Kim
   I can see Kim.

Discuss the Daily Fix-It with children. Review sentence capitalization and punctuation, capitalization of I, and spelling.

English Language Learners
Options for Conventions Support To provide children with practice with adjectives, use the modified conventions lessons on pp. 402–403 in the *ELL Handbook.*

Objectives
- Produce adjectives.
- Write complete sentences with vivid adjectives.
- Listen attentively and ask questions.

Writing—Sentences

Connect to conventions

Review adjectives: an **adjective** is a describing word that tells about a person, place, animal, or thing. Remind children that a sentence tells a complete idea. It begins with a capital letter and often ends with a period. Some sentences have adjectives to tell more about a person, place, animal, or thing.

Model

Write *I see small children. They wear green shoes.* Read these sentences aloud. *Small* and *green* are words that tell about the children and their shoes. *Small* and *green* are adjectives. Circle *small* and *green*. Explain how these words help describe the children and shoes and make them easier for us to picture. Discuss the importance of word choice when choosing an adjective.

Guide practice

Let's think of words that tell more about what we wear. As children give examples of what they are wearing, list the adjectives on the board. Then write these sentence frames and read them aloud.

> I wear _____ pants.
> I wear a _____ shirt.

Model completing the first sentence frame with an adjective from the chart you created together. This first sentence will tell about the pants I am wearing. I know that it must be an adjective. What are some adjectives that describe my pants? *Blue* is an adjective. My pants are blue. I will write *blue* in the blank to complete the sentence. Have children suggest adjectives from the list that could complete the second sentence, guiding them to choose a vivid adjective that is descriptive.

Shared writing

Have children use other adjectives from the list to create new sentences about their clothes. As they suggest adjectives and sentences, write their suggestions on the board. Invite other children to identify the adjective in each sentence.

On their own

Some children may be ready to write on their own. Write several more sentence frames on the board, each with a blank for an adjective. Reread the list of adjectives and have children use them to complete the sentences on their own. Children may also write new sentences, if they can. Have children circle the adjective in each sentence.

Listening and Speaking
Ask Questions

Teach asking questions

Tell children that we ask questions when we are confused. Explain that getting answers helps us understand more. When you do not understand something, you should ask questions.

- Do not interrupt the speaker.
- Ask politely. Tell the speaker what you do not understand.
- Face the speaker and make eye contact.

Model

My friend goes to a different school. She told me what her school looks like, but I did not understand if it was as big as my school. I waited for my friend to reach a good stopping place while she was speaking. Then I politely asked: Is your school as big as my school? She told me that it was.

Guide practice

Briefly discuss things you like about your school. Have children ask questions when they do not understand something. Remind them to follow the rules for listening that were established in Week 1.

On their own

Team Talk Have pairs of children take turns sharing information about a school subject and asking questions.

Wrap Up Your Day

✔ **Consonants *Rr* /r/** Write *Ron* and *ran*. Point to the *R* in *Ron* and the *r* in *ran* as you say the words aloud. Have children repeat them after you.

✔ **Plot** Have children identify plot in "Early for School" by telling the problem and solution.

✔ **Build Concepts** To develop the concept of Neighborhoods, ask children to name places near the school.

✔ **Homework** Send home this week's Family Times Newsletter from Let's Practice It! pp. 17–18 on the *Teacher Resource DVD-ROM*.

Let's Practice It!
TR DVD • 17–18

Preview DAY 2

Tell children that tomorrow they will hear about Henry's first day in first grade.

Objectives
- Discuss the concept of schools to develop oral language.
- Build oral vocabulary.

Today at a Glance

Oral Vocabulary
principal, recess

Print Awareness
Identify Information

Phonemic Awareness
Isolate Initial Phonemes

Phonics and Spelling
◉ Consonants *w* /w/, *j* /j/

High-Frequency Words
is, he, three, with, to

Comprehension
◉ Plot

Vocabulary
Give Descriptions

Conventions
Adjectives

Handwriting
Proper Body/Paper Position

Writing
Sentences with Adjectives

Listening and Speaking
Follow Directions

Concept Talk

Question of the Week
What is around us at school?

Build concepts

To reinforce concepts and to focus children's attention, have children sing "At School" from the *Sing with Me* Big Book. What do the children in the song do at school? (read, work with classmates) Do they enjoy school? How do you know? (yes; they say it's cool and fun)

 Sing with Me Big Book Audio

Introduce Amazing Words

Display the Big Book, *First Grade, Here I Come!* Read the title and identify the author. Explain that in the story, the author uses the word *principal* to describe an important person in Henry's school. Have children listen to the story to find out what the principal does.

Big Book

ELL **Reinforce Vocabulary** Use the Day 2 instruction on ELL Poster R5 to teach Selection Vocabulary and discuss the lesson concept.

ELL Poster R5

Oral Vocabulary
Amazing Words

Amazing Words

Teach Amazing Words

 **Amazing Words** **Oral Vocabulary Routine**

1. **Introduce the Word** Relate the word *principal* to the book. Henry brought a note to the *principal*. Supply a child-friendly definition: The *principal* is the leader of the school. Have children say the word.

2. **Demonstrate** Provide examples to show meaning. The *principal* of our school is named _____. The *principal* helps teachers. The *principal* makes the rules for our school.

3. **Apply** Have children demonstrate their understanding. Ask: What does our *principal* do?

   See p. OV•2 to teach *recess*.

Routines Flip Chart

Anchored Talk

Add to the concept map

Display the concept map you began on Day 1. Explain that the class will now add to it. Review the information on the map. What else have you learned that is around us at school?

- Recall the song "At School." Who does the singer work with in school? **(classmates)** I'll add *classmates* to the *People* box.

- Let's remember the Read Aloud story "Early for School." Jason shows Peter where the pencils are kept. Where should I write *pencils*? **(in the *Things* box)** Where do Jason and Peter play ball? **(on the playground)** Add *playground* to the *Places* box.

- Recall the Big Book First *Grade, Here I Come!* Remind children that they just learned about an important person in Henry's school. Who is that person? **(the principal)** In which box should I write *principal*? **(*People*)**

Amazing Words

classmate	science
education	complicated
polite	success
principal	applaud
recess	

Differentiated Instruction

SI **Strategic Intervention**

Pronunciation If children pronounce the sound /l/ with a vowel-like quality at the end of words, they may say the *al* in *principal* as if it were *u*. Help children learn the formal pronunciation by saying the word clearly, emphasizing the final sound /l/, and having children repeat it several times.

English Language Learners
Extend Language To reinforce the meaning of the words on the concept map, have children work with a partner to find and name places and things they see in the classroom, including items already on the concept map as well as items that are not yet on the map. Encourage them to create sentences of their own that use these words.

Objectives
- Identify information provided by books, such as title and author.
- Identify the tables of contents in a book and explain its purpose.
- Match initial phonemes.

Print Awareness
Identify Information

Teach

Using the Big Book *First Grade, Here I Come!*, review with children that books have a title, an author, and an illustrator. This information can be found on the cover of the book. Sometimes we can find more information in books. Some books have a *table of contents*. A table of contents is found in the front of a book. It tells you what is in the book and what page that information is on.

Model

Have children open their Student Editions to page 4. Some long books give you another important piece of information as well. That information is called a *table of contents*. A table of contents comes at the front of a book. It tells you what is in the book and where in the book you can find it. Here is the table of contents for our reading book. How many pages long is this table of contents? (4) Point out the text on the left and the page numbers on the right.

Guide practice

Hold up a book that has a table of contents, such as a student math textbook, a nonfiction trade book written for children, or a teacher resource book. I'm going to look at this book to find the title, the author, and other important information. Indicate the title and author on the cover and again on the title page. Read this information aloud. If an illustrator's name is given, read that aloud as well and remind children that illustrators are people who make pictures for books. Then open the book to the table of contents. I see the words *Table of Contents* on the page. I can also tell that this is the table of contents because it has words over *here* and page numbers over *here*. Indicate words and page numbers as you speak.

On their own

Use *Reader's and Writer's Notebook* p. 84.

Reader's and Writer's
Notebook, p. 84

Phonemic Awareness
Isolate Initial Phonemes

Model isolating sounds

Read together the second two bullet points on pages 116–117. I see some things in this picture that start with the sound /w/. Find a *worm* and a *watch*. The first sound in *worm* and *watch* is /w/. I also see some things that begin with the sound /j/: a *jug*, a *jump rope*, and a *jet*. The first sound in *jug*, *jump rope*, and *jet* is /j/.

Student Edition pp. 116–117

Model matching phonemes

Listen to the first sound of *worm*: /w/. Say the sound with me: /w/. Listen to the first sound of *jug*: /j/. Say the sound with me: /j/. Continue modeling with *woman* and *juice*.

Guide practice

Now we're going to listen to the first sound of some words. Say *w-w-w-wow*! if the first sound you hear is /w/. Don't say anything if the first sound is <u>not</u> /w/. **Say the words:** *with, way, can, wet, ice, will*.

Here are some more words. This time we'll decide if the first sound of each word is /j/. Give me a thumbs up if the sound you hear is /j/. Put your thumbs down if it is not /j/. **Say the words:** *jump, cat, go, jam, Jen, tape.*

Corrective feedback

If... children make an error,

then... model again the sound in isolation, along with a word that begins with the sound, and have them repeat the sound and the word.

On their own

Have children look at the picture and name more items that begin with the sounds /w/ and /j/.

Differentiated Instruction

A **Advanced**

The Sound /j/ If children are easily able to distinguish the sound /j/ from the initial sounds of words such as *cat, go,* and *tape,* challenge children to distinguish words beginning with /j/ from words such as *chest, drop,* and *train.* The phoneme /ch/ and the blends /dr/ and /tr/ are quite close to the sound /j/.

ELL

English Language Learners
Vocabulary The phrase *table of contents* may be confusing to some English language learners, since the primary meaning of *table* refers to a piece of furniture. Explain that the word *table* can also mean a kind of chart. Use classroom charts, such as a job chart, to make your meaning clear.

Objectives

- Associate the consonant *w* with the sound /w/.
- Associate the consonant *j* with the sound /j/.
- Write the letters *Ww* and *Jj*.
- Blend, read, and spell words with *w* and *j*.
- Recognize and name the letters *Ww* and *Jj*.

Phonics
Consonant w /w/, j /j/

Hear Today you will learn how to spell the sound /w/. Listen: /w/, /w/, /w/. When you say /w/, your lips make a circle. Say /w/ and feel your lips make a circle. Watch and listen as children produce the sound. Now let's learn how to spell the sound /j/. Listen: /j/, /j/, /j/. When you say /j/, your tongue is up and your lips are open. Say it with me: /j/, /j/, /j/.

Say Display Sound-Spelling Card 26. This is a picture of a *waterfall*. The first sound in waterfall is /w/. Say it with me: /w/, *waterfall*.

Display Sound-Spelling Card 12. This is a picture of a *jacket*. The first sound in *jacket* is /j/. Say it with me: /j/, *jacket*.

See Point to *w*. This is *w*. The sound /w/ is usually spelled *w*. *Waterfall* begins with /w/. *Waterfall* begins with the letter *w*. Have children say /w/ several times as you point to *w*.

Point to *j*. The sound /j/ is usually spelled *j*. *Jacket* begins with *j*.

Read ABC Rhyme Time Display ABC Rhyme Time, p. 28. Point to the letters *Ww* at the top of the page. This is an upper-case *W*. This is a lower-case *w*. This rhyme is about a *wombat*. Read the rhyme aloud, tracking the print with your finger. Then read it again. Point to examples of upper- and lower-case *w*'s as you read each word aloud.

Display ABC Rhyme Time, p. 15. Point to the letters *Jj* at the top of the page. This is an upper-case *J*. This is a lower-case *j*. This rhyme is called "Joyful Jackrabbit." Read the rhyme aloud, tracking the print with your finger. Read it again. Point to examples of upper- and lower-case *j*'s as you read each word.

Write Now I will show you how to write upper-case *W* and lower-case *w*. Write *Ww*. Follow the stroke instructions pictured. Now I will show you how to write upper-case *J* and lower-case *j*. Write *Jj*. Follow the stroke instructions pictured.

Sound-Spelling Card 26

Sound-Spelling Card 12

Wandering Wombat

Would a wombat wander
Across the Wild West?
Would he walk through windy weather
In a warm and woolly vest?

ABC Rhyme Time p. 28

Joyful Jackrabbit

Joyful little jackrabbit,
Jogging through the town.
You're such a jolly joker,
Jumping up and down.

Are you wearing jammies
Or just a furry jacket?
Goodness, little jackrabbit,
You're making such a racket!

ABC Rhyme Time p. 15

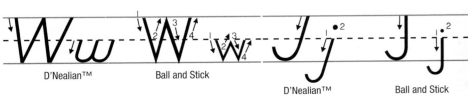

D'Nealian™   Ball and Stick   D'Nealian™   Ball and Stick

Interactive Sound-Spelling Cards

Phonics—Teach/Model
 Consonants *w* /w/, *j* /j/

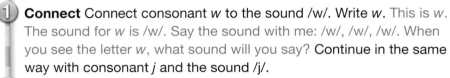

ROUTINE Blending Strategy

1 **Connect** Connect consonant *w* to the sound /w/. Write *w*. This is *w*. The sound for *w* is /w/. Say the sound with me: /w/, /w/, /w/. When you see the letter *w*, what sound will you say? Continue in the same way with consonant *j* and the sound /j/.

2 **Model** Model how to blend *win*. Write *w*. What is the sound for this letter? Say the sound with me: /w/. Write *i*. Say this sound with me: /i/. Write *n*. Say this sound with me: /n/. Listen as I blend all the sounds together: /w/ /i/ /n/, *win*. Blend the sounds with me: /w/ /i/ /n/, *win*. Now blend the sounds without me. Follow the same procedure to model blending the word *job*.

3 **Guide Practice** Continue the routine in Step 2 with the words that follow. Remember, first we say the sounds. Then we blend the sounds to read the word.

wig	will	wag	jam	jog	jab
rim	ram	ham	him	hog	fog

For corrective feedback, model blending the sounds to read the word. Then have children blend the sounds and read the word with you.

4 **Review** What do you know about reading words that begin with the letter *w* or *j*? (The sound for *w* is /w/; the sound for *j* is /j/.)

Routines Flip Chart

Sound-Spelling Card 26

Sound-Spelling Card 12

Spell words Now we are going to spell words with the sound /w/ spelled *w* and the sound /j/ spelled *j*. The first word we will spell is *wag*. What sounds do you hear in *wag*? (/w/ /a/ /g/) What is the letter for /w/? Let's all write *w*. What is the letter for /a/? Write *a*. What is the letter for /g/? Write *g*. Have children confirm their spellings by comparing them with what you have written. Continue practice with *win, wig, job, jam,* and *jig*.

On their own Use the *Reader's and Writer's Notebook* p. 85 for additional practice with consonants *w* /w/ and *j* /j/.

Reader's and Writer's Notebook p. 85

Differentiated Instruction

SI **Strategic Intervention**
Sounds /j/ and /ch/ The only difference between the sounds /j/ and /ch/ is that /j/ is voiced, while /ch/ is not voiced. If children say /ch/ when they should be saying /j/, have them touch their throats while saying the two sounds to feel the vibrations created by saying /j/.

Spelling Pattern

/w/w The sound /w/ is usually spelled *w*.

/j/j The sound /j/ is usually spelled *j* at the beginning of a word. /j/ can also be spelled *g* when followed by *e, i,* or *y,* and is usually spelled *ge* or *dge* at the end of a word or syllable.

English Language Learners
Words with Sounds /w/ and /j/ Spanish does not have exact equivalents for these two English sounds. The letter *w* is used only in words of foreign origin, and the letter *j* is associated with a different sound with no exact match in English. Give Spanish speakers plenty of practice in saying and writing words with these letters.

Objectives

- Associate consonant *w* with the sound /w/.
- Associate consonant *j* with the sound /j/.
- Blend and read words with *w*.
- Blend and read words with *j*.
- Recognize and name the letters *Ww* and *Jj*.

Phonics
Identify Lower-Case and Upper-Case Letters

Guide Practice

Write a lower-case *w* and point to it. What letter is this? (lower-case *w*) Write an upper-case *W* and point to it. What letter is this? (upper-case *W*) Write more upper- and lower-case *w*'s. Have children identify each as upper-case *W* or lower-case *w*. Repeat with upper-case *J* and lower-case *j*.

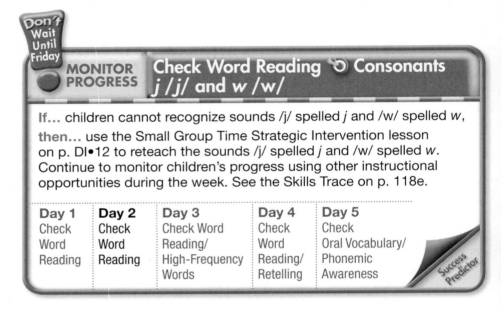

Don't Wait Until Friday

MONITOR PROGRESS **Check Word Reading** **Consonants** *j* /j/ and *w* /w/

If... children cannot recognize sounds /j/ spelled *j* and /w/ spelled *w*,

then... use the Small Group Time Strategic Intervention lesson on p. DI•12 to reteach the sounds /j/ spelled *j* and /w/ spelled *w*. Continue to monitor children's progress using other instructional opportunities during the week. See the Skills Trace on p. 118e.

Day 1	**Day 2**	**Day 3**	**Day 4**	**Day 5**
Check Word Reading	Check Word Reading	Check Word Reading/ High-Frequency Words	Check Word Reading/ Retelling	Check Oral Vocabulary/ Phonemic Awareness

Success Predictor

Small Group Time

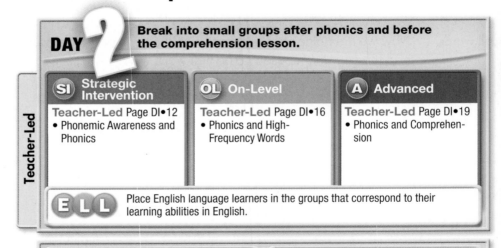

DAY 2 Break into small groups after phonics and before the comprehension lesson.

Teacher-Led

(SI) Strategic Intervention
Teacher-Led Page DI•12
- Phonemic Awareness and Phonics

(OL) On-Level
Teacher-Led Page DI•16
- Phonics and High-Frequency Words

(A) Advanced
Teacher-Led Page DI•19
- Phonics and Comprehension

E L L Place English language learners in the groups that correspond to their learning abilities in English.

Practice Stations
- Listen Up
- Word Work

Independent Activities
- Read independently/Reading log on *Reader's and Writer's Notebook* p. RR1.

Phonics—Build Fluency
 Consonants *r* /r/, *w* /w/, and *j* /j/

Model

Envision It!

Have children turn to page 118 in their Student Edition. Look at the pictures on this page. I see a picture of a *rocket*, a picture of a *waterfall*, and a picture of a *jacket*. When I say *rocket*, I begin with the sound /r/. The /r/ sound is spelled with an *r*. When I say *waterfall*, I begin with the sound /w/. The /w/ sound is spelled with a *w*. When I say *jacket*, I begin with the sound /j/. The /j/ sound is spelled with a *j*.

Guide practice

For each word in "Words I Can Blend," ask for the sound of each letter. Make sure that children identify the correct sound for *r, w,* or *j*. Then have children blend the whole word.

Corrective feedback

If... children have difficulty blending a word,
then... model blending the word, and then ask children to blend it with you.

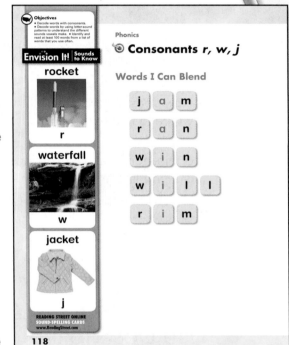

Student Edition p. 118

Differentiated Instruction

A Advanced

Extend Blending Provide children who can segment and blend all the words correctly with more challenging words such as: *rags, roast, rabbit, wind, want, willow, jacket, James, jobs,* and *joking.*

Spelling Patterns

/r/r The sound /r/ is usually spelled *r*.

/w/w The sound /w/ is usually spelled *w*.

/j/j The sound /j/ is usually spelled *j* at the beginning of a word. /j/ can also be spelled *g* when followed by *e, i,* or *y,* and is usually spelled *ge* or *dge* at the end of a word or syllable.

Objectives

- Identify the plot (problem and solution) in a narrative text.
- Understand and use descriptive adjectives.
- Read high-frequency words

Skills Trace

⊙ Setting

Introduce URW3D1; URW5D1; U1W2D1; U5W1D1

Practice URW3D2; URW3D3; URW3D4; URW5D2; URW5D3; URW5D4; U1W2D2; U1W2D3; U1W2D4; U5W1D2; U5W1D3; U5W1D4

Reteach/Review URW3D5; URW4D2; URW5D2; U1W1D2; U1W2D5; U1W4D2; U2W2D2; U3W4D2; U4W6D2; U5W1D5; U5W6D2

Assess/Test Weekly Tests URW3; URW5; U1W2; U5W1

Benchmark Tests UR

Comprehension
Plot

Review plot

Remember, **plot** is made up of the events that happen in the beginning, middle, and end of a story. It usually includes a problem and a solution. Readers better understand a story when they pay attention to the plot.

Guide practice

Reread the story **"Early for School"** aloud. Have children listen for clues to tell them about the plot of the story. Write children's answers to the questions below.

- How does Jason help Peter in the middle of the story? (He shows Peter where to find things. He plays with Peter. He walks home with Peter.)
- What clues help you figure out Jason's problem? (It says in the beginning of the story that Jason liked school, but was often late. This hints that it is a problem for Jason.)

On their own

Have children think about the story *The Big Top*. Discuss the plot, including problem and solution. Then have children draw a picture of something that happens in the story.

Vocabulary
Use Descriptive Words

Discuss descriptive words

Explain to children that when we talk or write about something that happened, we can use descriptive words to help our readers picture what we mean.

Model

Write the following descriptions on the board. Read the sentences aloud and identify the descriptive words.

> **You rode to school in the <u>yellow</u> bus.**
>
> **We saw <u>six</u> <u>big</u> dogs at the park.**

Guide practice

Ask children to add their own statements with descriptive words that tell about things they saw on the first day of school. Write these descriptive words on the board.

On their own

Have children work in pairs. Ask them to use descriptive words to complete the following sentence: **This is a _____ school.** Have children share their descriptive words with the class.

High-Frequency Words

Introduce

ROUTINE Nondecodable Words

① **Say and Spell** Look at p. 119. Some words we have to learn by remembering the letters rather than saying the sounds. We will say and spell the words to help learn them. **Point to the first word.** This word is *he*. The letters in *he* are h-e, *he*.

② **Identify Familiar Letter-Sounds** Point to the first letter in *he*. This letter says its name. What is the letter and what is its sound? (*e /ē/*)

③ **Demonstrate Meaning** Tell me a sentence using the word *he*. Repeat this routine with the other Words I Can Read.

Routines Flip Chart

Read words in isolation — Have children read the words on p. 119 aloud. Add the words to the Word Wall.

Read words in context — Have children read the sentences aloud. Have them identify this week's High-Frequency Words in the sentences.

On their own — Use *Reader's and Writer's Notebook* p. 90.

Differentiated Instruction

SI **Strategic Intervention**

Plot Recall some of the stories you have read together as a class, such as *Snap!,* Give children clues about the story—characters, setting, or what happens in the beginning, middle, or end. After each clue, ask children what story plot you are describing. Continue with other children giving the plot clues.

High-Frequency Words

Words I Can Read

he
is
to
with
three

Sentences I Can Read

1. He is in a jam.
2. Three ran to win.
3. Jim will sit on the rim with Jill.

119

English Language Learners
Identify High-Frequency Words Write the following sentences: *He is with three cats; He is at a store.* Have children identify the high-frequency words. Have children practice repeating the sentences.

Reader's and Writer's Notebook p. 90

Student Edition p. 119

School Day **119**

Objectives
- Understand and use adjectives.
- Use proper body and paper position when writing.
- Write *Ww* and *Jj*

Conventions
Adjectives

Model nouns
Write *The flag has white stars* on the board. Point to each word as you read it. Ask children to identify the adjective. (white) An adjective is a word that can tell what color, what size, or how many. The word *white* is a noun because it tells what color. What are some other adjectives you know? (Possible responses: small, four, blue, wide, one) All of these words are adjectives.

Guide practice
Write the following sentences on the board. Read the sentences aloud and have the children repeat after you. Have children identify the adjective in each sentence.

1. **Rob and Ron are two boys.**   **(two)**
2. **Rob will run on a high hill.**   **(high)**
3. **Ron will sit on a big rock.**   **(big)**

Connect to oral language
Have the class complete these sentence frames orally using adjectives.

1. **Wanda will rock the _____ baby.**
2. **Rick will cut the _____ watermelon.**

On their own
Use *Reader's and Writer's Notebook* p. 86.

Reader's and Writer's Notebook p. 86

Handwriting
Letter *Ww* and *Jj*;
Proper Body and Paper Position

Model letter formation

Display upper- and lower-case letters: *Ww* and *Jj*. Use the stroke instructions pictured below to model proper letter formation.

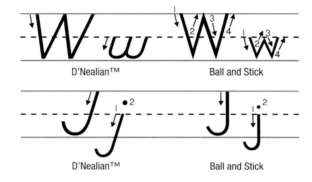

D'Nealian™   Ball and Stick

D'Nealian™   Ball and Stick

Model proper body and paper position

Remind children that when we write, it is important to have correct body and paper position. Model correct positions as you explain. When I get ready to write, I make sure I sit up straight. I have both feet on the floor in front of me and I keep my arms on the table or desk. I am also careful to position my paper correctly. If I am right-handed, I place the paper so that it slants from the left at the top to the right at the bottom. If I am left-handed, I place it so that the paper slants from the right at the top to the left at the bottom.

Guide practice

Write the following words on the board: *wag, Will, Jan, job.*

Team Talk Have children work together in pairs to identify the letters *Ww* and *Jj*. Then have them copy the words on lined paper. Remind them to use proper body and paper positions while writing.

On their own

Use the *Reader's and Writer's Notebook* p. 87.

Reader's and Writer's Notebook p. 87

Daily Fix-It

3. Kim wil see jill.
   Kim wi**ll** see **J**ill.
4. Thay Met Sam.
   Th**ey** **m**et Sam.

Discuss the Daily Fix-It corrections with children. Review sentence capitalization, capitalization of names, and spelling.

English Language Learners

Adjectives In languages such as Spanish, Hmong, and Vietnamese, adjectives often follow the noun. Point out that in English, the adjective usually comes before the noun. Then provide several simple sentences containing adjectives, and read them with children. Have them identify the adjective in each sentence.

Objectives
- Produce adjectives.
- Write complete sentences with vivid adjectives.
- Follow directions.

Writing — Sentences

Model

Have children recall the Read Aloud, "Early for School." In the beginning of the story, Jason is late for school. Let's write a sentence that tells what happens later in the story. Write the sentence below. Read the sentence, and identify the adjective *new.* Explain that it describes the noun *friend.*

> **Jason meets a new friend.**

Guide practice

Write more sentences about what Jason does in the story. Then read the sentences and have children identify the adjectives.

> **Jason runs down the short block.**
>
> **Jason walks through the large doors.**

Connect to phonics

Reread the sentences with children and have them point to the words with /r/ spelled *r,* /w/ spelled *w,* and /j/ spelled *j.*

Shared writing

Rewrite the second sentence with a blank replacing the word *large.* Have children suggest different adjectives to complete the sentence. Remind them to think of vivid, descriptive words for the noun *doors.* Point out the importance of word choice: different words will tell different things about a noun. Write children's suggestions on the board.

On their own

Some children may be ready to write on their own. Write another sentence on the board about what happens in the story. Leave a blank for an adjective. Have children think of an adjective to complete the sentence on their own. Children may also write new sentences, if they can. Have children circle the adjectives in their sentence. Then have them read their sentence aloud, name the adjective, and tell what the adjective describes.

Listening and Speaking
Follow Directions

Teach following directions

Tell children that **directions** tell how to do or make something. It is important to follow directions in the **order** in which they are given. Order is the way one thing follows another.

- Good listeners listen carefully to each step of the directions.
- They restate the directions in their own words to make sure they understand what to do.
- Good listeners also follow the directions in the order they are given.

Model

Think Aloud Last week, I went to a craft class where I learned how to make a vest from a paper bag. I listened carefully to each step of the directions. Then I restated the directions to make sure I understood what to do. Once I knew what to do, I followed the directions and made a really nice vest.

Guide practice

Give two-step directions for writing the letter *T*. Have children restate the directions and come to the board to write the letter. Make sure they follow the directions in the order they were given.

On their own

Assign each child a partner. Give two-step directions for drawing a house. Have children take turns restating the directions to each other and following the directions in the order they were given. Remind children to follow the rules for listening that they established in Week 1.

Wrap Up Your Day

✔ **Consonants *Ww* /w/ and *Jj* /j/** Write the letters *Ww* and *Jj*. Have children identify the letters. Write *Winn* and *wig*. Write *Jim* and *jig*. Point to *W, w, J,* and *j* as you say the words aloud. Have children repeat them after you.

✔ **Build Concepts** Monitor children's use of oral vocabulary as they respond. Recall the Big Book, *First Grade, Here I Come!* Have children tell if they think Henry's neighborhood school is a good place to get an education.

Academic Vocabulary

directions how to do something or make something

order the way one thing follows another; sequence

E L L

English Language Learners
Activate Prior Knowledge
Have children talk about some things that require directions. Help children activate prior knowledge about why directions are necessary. Ask them to give short directions for the ideas they discuss.

Preview DAY 3

Tell children that tomorrow they will listen again to a story about Henry's first day in first grade.

Objectives

- Build oral vocabulary.
- Identify details in text.
- Share information and ideas about the concept.

Today at a Glance

Oral Vocabulary
science

Print Awareness
Identify Information

Phonological Awareness
Rhyme words

Phonics
⊙ Consonant *k* /k/

High-Frequency Words
is, he, three, with, to

Convention
Adjectives

Handwriting
Self-Evaluation

Writing
Sentences with Adjectives

Listening and Speaking
Restate Directions

Concept Talk

 Question of the Week
What is around us at school?

Build concepts

To reinforce concepts and to focus children's attention, have children sing "At School" from the *Sing with Me* Big Book. What do you enjoy the most about school? (possible responses: being with friends, learning to read)

 Sing with Me Big Book Audio

Monitor listening comprehension

Display the Big Book, *First Grade, Here I Come!* Read the book aloud. Tell children to think about what Henry's teacher does on the first day of school.

- What are some things we learned about Henry's teacher, Mr. McCarthy? (He likes Henry's pet worm, has a cool science center, teaches the children math and a science fact, takes them to the library, plays kickball with them, and asks Henry to deliver a note to the principal.)

Big Book

ELL **Expand Vocabulary** Use the Day 3 instruction on ELL Poster R5 to help children expand vocabulary.

ELL Poster R5

Oral Vocabulary
Amazing Words

Teach Amazing Words

 Amazing Words — **Oral Vocabulary Routine**

1 **Introduce the Word** Relate the word *science* to the book. Henry says that Mr. McCarthy has a cool *science* corner. Supply a child-friendly definition: *Science* is learning about things in nature, like stars, rocks, plants, and animals. Have children say the word.

2 **Demonstrate** Provide examples to show meaning. In our *science* books we learn that animals need food and water. A *science* museum might have dinosaur bones. We will do a *science* experiment by planting seeds.

3 **Apply** Have children demonstrate their understanding. What do you like to learn about in *science*?

Routines Flip Chart

Anchored Talk

Add to the concept map

Use these questions to discuss what people can see in schools as you add to the concept map.

- Recall the Big Book, *First Grade, Here I Come!* What are some places in his school that Henry talks about? (science corner, library, bathroom, lunchroom, principal's office) I'll add all these words to our *Places* box.

- Who are some people at Henry's school that we haven't listed yet? (lunchroom workers) I'll write *lunchroom workers* in the *People* box.

- Let's look through the book and see what things are in Henry's school. I see plants, animals, and rocks in the science corner. What else do you see? (desks with names, paper, chalkboard, chalk) List items in the *Things* box as children name them.

Amazing Words

classmate	science
education	complicated
polite	success
principal	applaud
recess	

Differentiated Instruction

A **Advanced**

Writing Have children work in pairs. Ask them to work together to write a short poem about science. Remind them that poems do not necessarily have to rhyme. Have children share their poems with other pairs or with the class as a whole.

 ELL

English Language Learners
Double-Meaning Words Tell children that the word *cool* has two meanings. It can mean *not warm*. It can also be a slang word meaning *great*. Ask children which meaning they think Henry is using when he calls the science corner *cool*.

Objectives
- Identify information provided by books, such as title and author.
- Identify the tables of contents in a book and explain its purpose.
- Write the table of contents for a simple book.
- Rhyme words.
- Determine whether two given words rhyme.

Print Awareness
Identify Information

Review   Let's review the information that books give us. The name of a book is called its— Pause and let children fill in *title*, or provide it yourself. Repeat with the author and illustrator. Then remind children that the table of contents tells where to find certain topics or information in the book. Point out these features on actual books as you name them.

Model   I'm going to write a book. Here is the first page. I'll label it page 1. Sketch a simple picture of a bird on a large sheet of paper. Then write *Lots of birds can fly*. Read the words aloud with children.

Guide practice   Repeat with a fish, a dog, and a cat, asking children to tell you a fact about each of these animals.

Now I need to make a cover with some information about my book. First, I need the title. I think we should call this book *All About Animals*. Write those words on a large sheet of paper. There. That's the title, or the name of this book. Point to the title and read it aloud.

Now I need the name of the author. That's all of us! I'll write *By _____'s Class* below the title. Remember, the author is the person or the people who wrote the words for the book. Repeat with illustrator, writing your own name and using *Illustrated by* or *Pictures by*.

A table of contents will help our readers find their favorite animals easily. Write *Table of Contents* on a new sheet of paper and read it aloud. The first page is about birds. So, I'll write *birds* here on the left, and *page 1* across from it on the right. Continue in this manner for pages 2, 3, and 4. Point out that the table of contents tells exactly which page tells about each animal.

On their own   Use *Reader's and Writer's Notebook* p. 88

Reader's and Writer's Notebook p. 88

Phonological Awareness
Rhyme Words

Model producing rhyming words

Have children look at the picture on pages 116–117 in their Student Editions. Today we are going to use this picture to help us produce rhyming words. Remember that **rhyming words** are words that end with the same sounds. It looks like a *hot* day in this picture, doesn't it? Let's all say *hot*. The word *hot* ends with the sounds /o/, /t/, /ot/. What other words in the picture end that way? Oh, I know—I see a *lot* of children! *Hot* and *lot* rhyme. They both end with the same sound, /ot/. Say those words and listen for the sounds at the end: *hot, lot*. I also see a *nest*. *Nest* does not rhyme with *hot* and *lot*. *Nest* does not end with the same sounds.

Student Edition pp. 116–117

Guide practice

Guide children to use the picture to produce words that rhyme with *wet* (*net* or *jet*) and *rock* (*sock*). Then help children determine if the following word pairs rhyme: *race/ring* (no), *key/tree* (yes), *juice/mess* (no).

On their own

Have children produce words that rhyme with the following words.

hop	rob	log
jaw	mad	pin

Team Talk Have children tell a partner two words. Have the partner determine whether they rhyme.

Differentiated Instruction

 Strategic Intervention

Rhymes Some children may believe that CVC words rhyme if their final consonant is the same or if their vowel sounds are identical. Use the following to explain that these words are not rhymes: *Top* and *nap* both end with the sound /p/, but the vowels are different. Listen: /top/, /op/, /o/; /nap/, /ap/, /a/. *Top* and *nap* don't rhyme. *Shop* and *rock* do not rhyme because they do not end with the same consonant. Listen: /shop/, /op/, /p/; /rok/, /ok/, /k/. But *top* and *shop* are rhyming words: /top/, /op/; /shop/, /op/.

Academic Vocabulary

rhyming words words that end with the same sound

ELL

English Language Learners

Distinguish Sounds /a/ and /o/ Speakers of languages such as Chinese, Korean, Spanish, and Urdu may not easily distinguish sounds /o/ from /a/. Thus, they may think that words such as *rack* and *lock* rhyme. To help children distinguish these sounds, it can be useful to have them say /a/, /o/, /a/, /o/, while paying close attention to the positions of their lips.

Objectives
- Associate the consonant *k* with the sound /k/.
- Write the letters *Kk*.
- Blend, read, and spell words with initial *k*.
- Recognize and name the letters *Kk*.

Phonics
Consonant *k* /k/

Hear

You already know that you can spell the sound /k/ with the letter *c*. Today you will learn another way to spell the sound /k/. Listen: /k/, /k/, /k/. When you say /k/, the back of your tongue is humped and in the back of your mouth. Say /k/ and feel that the back of your tongue is humped and in the back of your mouth. **Watch and listen as children produce the sound.** Say /k/ with me: /k/, /k/, /k/.

Say

Display Sound-Spelling Card 13. This is a picture of a *kite*. Say it with me: *kite*. The first sound in *kite* is /k/. Listen: /k/, *kite*. Say it with me: /k/, *kite*. What is the first sound in *kite*?

Sound-Spelling Card 13

See

Point to *k*. This is *k*. The sound /k/ can be spelled *k*. What other letter can spell the sound /k/? That's right—the letter *c* can spell /k/. *Kite* begins with /k/. *Kite* begins with the letter *k*. The word *card* begins with /k/, but in *card* the /k/ sound is spelled *c*. What sound goes with the letter *k*? **Have children say /k/ several times as you point to *k*.**

Read ABC Rhyme Time

Display ABC Rhyme Time, p. 16. Point to the letters *Kk* at the top of the page. The name for both of these letters is *k*. Point to *K*. This is an upper-case *K*. Point to *k*. This is a lower-case *k*. Point to each letter again and ask: What is the name of this letter?

This rhyme is called "Karate Kangaroo." What do you think it might be about? **Read the rhyme aloud, tracking the print with your finger. Then read it again. Point to examples of upper- and lower-case *k*'s as you read each word aloud.**

ABC Rhyme Time p. 16

Write

Now I will show you how to write upper-case *K* and lower-case *k*. Write *K*. **Watch as I trace capital *K* with my finger. Follow the stroke instructions pictured. Now you write upper-case *K*. Repeat for lower-case *k*.**

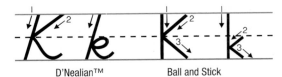

D'Nealian™   Ball and Stick

Phonics—Teach/Model
⟳ Consonant k /k/

ROUTINE **Blending Strategy**

1 **Connect** Connect consonant *k* to the sound /k/. Write *k*. This is *k*. What is the sound for *k*? The sound for *k* is /k/. Say the sound with me: /k/, /k/, /k/. When you see *k*, what sound will you say?

2 **Model** Model how to blend *kid*. Write *k*. What is the sound for this letter? Say the sound with me: /k/. Write *i*. Say this sound with me: /i/. Write *d*. Say this sound with me: /d/. Listen as I blend all the sounds together: /k/ /i/ /d/, *kid*. Blend the sounds with me: /k/ /i/ /d/, *kid*. Now blend the sounds without me.

3 **Guide Practice** Continue the routine in Step 2 with the words that follow. Remember, first we say the sounds. Then we blend the sounds to read the word.

kit	kin	kiss	Kim	Kip
rot	jot	wig	wag	rat	jog

For corrective feedback, model blending the sounds to read the word. Then have children blend the sounds and read the word with you.

4 **Review** What do you know about reading words that begin with the letter *k*? The sound for *k* is /k/.

Routines Flip Chart

Spell Now we are going to spell words with the sound /k/ spelled *k*. The first word we will spell is *kit*. What sounds do you hear in *kit*? (/k/ /i/ /t/) What is the letter for /k/? Let's all write *k*. What is the letter for /i/? Write *i*. What is the letter for /t/? Write *t*. Have children confirm their spellings by comparing them with what you have written. Continue practice with *Kim, kiss, Kip,* and *kin*.

On their own Use the *Reader's and Writer's Notebook* p. 89 for additional practice with /k/ spelled *k*.

Reader's and Writer's Notebook p. 89

Differentiated Instruction

SI **Strategic Intervention**
Stop Sounds The sound /k/ is a stop sound; that is, it is said only briefly, unlike vowel sounds or consonant sounds such as /s/, /f/, and /l/, which can be held for several seconds. Words beginning with stop sounds can be harder for children to sound out. Have children look at the letter combination *ki* for the words used in the lesson, and help them get used to saying /kiiii/ if they are having difficulty with this sound. Saying /kiiii/ can help them glide more smoothly into the next sound.

Spelling Pattern

/k/k The sound /k/ is usually spelled *k* when it is followed by *e* or *i*, and may be spelled *k* when followed by other letters as well. The sound /k/ may also be spelled *c* or *ck*.

ELL

English Language Learners
Spell Words with k The sound /k/ is represented in Spanish by the letters *c* or *qu*. Give native Spanish speakers extra practice spelling and reading words with the letter *k*.

Objectives
- Identify upper- and lower-case *Kk*.
- Practice high-frequency words.

Phonics
Identify Lower-Case and Upper-Case Letters

Guide practice

Write a lower-case *k* and point to it. What letter is this? (lower-case *k*) Write an upper-case *K* and point to it. What letter is this? (upper-case *K*) Write a series of upper- and lower-case *k*'s. Point to each and have children identify each as upper-case *K* or lower-case *k*.

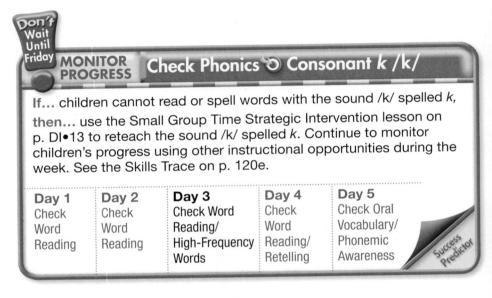

Don't Wait Until Friday

MONITOR PROGRESS | **Check Phonics ↻ Consonant *k* /k/**

If... children cannot read or spell words with the sound /k/ spelled *k*,

then... use the Small Group Time Strategic Intervention lesson on p. DI•13 to reteach the sound /k/ spelled *k*. Continue to monitor children's progress using other instructional opportunities during the week. See the Skills Trace on p. 120e.

Day 1	**Day 2**	**Day 3**	**Day 4**	**Day 5**
Check Word Reading	Check Word Reading	Check Word Reading/ High-Frequency Words	Check Word Reading/ Retelling	Check Oral Vocabulary/ Phonemic Awareness

Success Predictor

Small Group Time

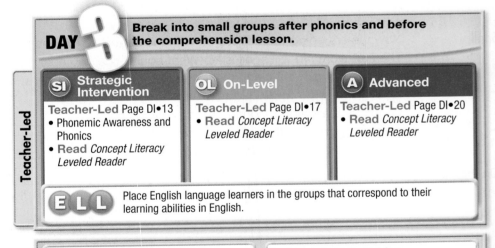

DAY 3 Break into small groups after phonics and before the comprehension lesson.

Teacher-Led

SI Strategic Intervention
Teacher-Led Page DI•13
- Phonemic Awareness and Phonics
- Read *Concept Literacy Leveled Reader*

OL On-Level
Teacher-Led Page DI•17
- Read *Concept Literacy Leveled Reader*

A Advanced
Teacher-Led Page DI•20
- Read *Concept Literacy Leveled Reader*

E L L Place English language learners in the groups that correspond to their learning abilities in English.

Practice Stations
- Words to Know

Independent Activities
- Read independently/Reading log on *Reader's and Writer's Notebook* p. RR1.

High-Frequency Words
Practice

Review

Review this week's Words to Read: *he, is, to, with, three.*

• Point to a word. Say and spell it.

• Use each word in a sentence.

Guide practice

Have children say and spell each word twice. Then have them use each high-frequency word in a sentence.

On their own

Have pairs of children take turns using each high-frequency word in a sentence. Remind children to listen politely and to speak clearly at an appropriate pace. Have pairs of children share some of their sentences with the class.

Don't Wait Until Friday

MONITOR PROGRESS | ↻ **High-Frequency Words**

Point to these words on the Word Wall and have the class read them. Listen for children who miss words during the reading. Call on those children to read some of the words individually.

he	is	to	with	three	**Spiral Review**
are	have	they	that	two ←	**Row 2** reviews previously taught high-frequency words.

If... children cannot read these words,

then... use the Small Group Time Strategic Intervention lesson, p. DI•87, to reteach the words. Monitor children's fluency with these words during reading, and provide additional practice.

Day 1	**Day 2**	**Day 3**	**Day 4**	**Day 5**
Check Word Reading	Check Word Reading	Check Word Reading/ High-Frequency Words	Check Word Reading/ Retelling	Check Oral Vocabulary/ Phonemic Awareness

Success Predictor

English Language Learners
Spell Words with *k* In Spanish, the sound /k/ spelled *k* only occurs in borrowed words. The sound /k/ in Spanish words is spelled *c (a), c (o),* or *c (u).* Give children practice spelling words with sound /k/ spelled *k.*

Conventions
Adjectives

Review Adjectives

Remind children that an adjective is a word that tells about a noun. It can tell what color, what size, or how many. Hold up five fingers and say *I hold up five fingers. Five* is an adjective because it tells how many.

Guide practice

Write this sentence on the board and read it aloud.

Jill had a big job.

What other adjectives could we use instead of *big* in this sentence? (Possible responses: fun, small, hard, easy, good) How would the meaning of the sentence be different with the new adjective?

Team Talk Have children say the sentence using their adjectives.

Connect to oral language

Have children complete these sentence frames orally using adjectives.

1. **Jim bit into a _____ fig.**
2. **Jill smiled and gave a _____ shout.**

On their own

Use *Reader's and Writer's Notebook* p. 91.

Reader's and Writer's Notebook 91

Handwriting
Letter *K* and *k*; Self-Evaluation

Model letter formation

Display upper- and lower-case letters: *Kk*. Use the stroke instructions pictured below to model proper letter formation.

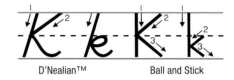

D'Nealian™   Ball and Stick

Model self-evaluation

Remind children that when we write a word, we need to go back and check our writing. Do the upper-case and lower-case letters look the way they should? Did I use the lines on the paper to write the letters the correct size? Did I write them from left to right on the page and use correct spacing between them? Remind children to completely erase any mistakes they find before rewriting.

Guide practice

Write the following sentence with obvious errors in letter size and left-to-right progression.

Kim can hop on the yak.

Read the sentence aloud as you track the words. Have children find the errors in the sentence.

Team Talk Have children work in pairs to rewrite the sentence correctly and evaluate their work.

On their own

Use the *Reader's and Writer's Notebook* p. 92.

Reader's and Writer's Notebook p. 92

Differentiated Instruction

A Advanced

Self-Evaluation Pair up children who have strong evaluation skills with those who need help. Have them work together to evaluate their handwriting and fix any errors.

Daily Fix-It

5. Jil is with kim.
   Jill is with Kim.
6. Kin can see the bage.
   Kim can see the bag.

Discuss the Daily Fix-It corrections with children. Review capitalization of names and spelling.

English Language Learners

Adjectives for Sizes In Spanish, adjectives often have endings that reflect the number and gender of the noun they modify. If children add endings to adjectives (*the bigs bags*), provide additional practice.

Writing—Sentences

Model

Have children recall the Big Book, *First Grade, Here I Come!* Yesterday and today we heard a story about what first grade is like for Henry. Let's write a sentence about something special Henry does. Write the sentence below.

> **Henry sees a furry pet.**

Read the sentence and identify the adjective *furry*. Point out that *furry* describes the noun *pet*.

Guide practice

Write more sentences about Henry's first day in first grade. Then read the sentences and have children identify the adjectives.

> **Henry meets a nice kid.**
>
> **He plays a fun game of kickball.**

Connect to phonics

Reread the sentences with children and have them point to the words with /k/ spelled *k*.

Shared writing

Write the following sentence frame on the board: *This is a _____ story.* Have children suggest different adjectives to complete the sentence. Tell children to think about the story and choose an adjective to help describe it. Remind them to choose their words carefully when thinking of adjectives. Use children's suggestions to complete the sentence.

On their own

Some children may be ready to write on their own. Write the following sentence frame on the board: *The boy has a _____ cat.* Leave a blank for an adjective. Have children think of an adjective to complete the sentence on their own. Children may also write new sentences, if they can. Have children circle the adjective in the sentence. Then have them read their sentence aloud, name the adjective, and tell what the adjective describes.

Listening and Speaking
Restate Directions

Review
Restating directions

Have children recall what they know about following directions. Directions tell how to do or make something. It is important to restate directions that are given to you.

- Good listeners restate directions to make sure they understand what to do.

- They also restate directions to make sure they know the correct order of the directions.

Model

 Think Aloud My sister gave me directions for planting a flower. First you dig a hole in the ground. Then you place the flower in the hole and fill the hole with dirt. I wanted to make sure I understood what to do and the correct order to do it, so I restated the directions. First I dig a hole. Then I put the flower and dirt in it.

Guide practice

Give directions for weeding a garden. Have children restate the directions in their own words.

On their own

Have pairs of children take turns giving and restating directions for washing their hair. Remind children to follow the rules for listening that they established in Week 1.

Wrap Up Your Day

✔ **Consonants Kk /k/** Write the letters K and k. Have children identify the letters. Write *kit and Kim.* Point to the k in *kit* and the K in *Kim* as you say the words aloud. Have children repeat them after you.

✔ **High-Frequency Words** Point to the words *is, he, three, with,* and *to* on the Word Wall. Have children read each word and use it in a sentence.

✔ **Build Concepts** Monitor children's use of oral vocabulary as they respond. Recall the Big Book, *First Grade, Here I Come!* Have children explain some of Henry's favorite things about his neighborhood school.

Differentiated Instruction

 Strategic Intervention
Visualize If children have difficulty restating directions in order, tell them to visualize the steps as the directions are given to them. Then have them picture the steps in their head before restating.

A Advanced
Restate Order Give more complicated, multi-step directions to children who exhibit good restating skills. Give directions for making breakfast, washing a car, or playing a game. Ask children to restate the directions in the same order they were given.

Preview DAY 4

Tell children that tomorrow they will read about Sam and his friends at school.

Objectives

- Discuss the concept to develop oral language.
- Build oral vocabulary.
- Identify details in text.

Today at a Glance

Oral Vocabulary
applaud, complicated, success

Print Awareness
Sequence Letters

Phonemic Awareness
Blend and segment phonemes

Phonics
◉ Short *e*

Genre
Fiction and Nonfiction

High-Frequency Words
is, he, three, with, to

Comprehension
◉ Plot
◉ Monitor and Clarify

Writing and Conventions
Adjectives: Revise

Research
Calendar

Handwriting
Letter Size

Concept Talk

Question of the Week

 What is around us at school?

Build concepts

To reinforce concepts and to focus children's attention, have children sing "At School" from the *Sing with Me* Big Book. When do we work with classmates in our classroom? (possible response: paired reading time)

🔘 Sing with Me Big Book Audio

Monitor listening comprehension

Help children recall that in the Big Book, *First Grade, Here I Come!,* Henry brings his pet worm to school and shows it to Mr. McCarthy. Tell children that today you will read a story about a show-and-tell where children bring their pets and other interesting things to school. Read the selection.

"Show and Tell"

ELL Produce Oral Language Use the Day 4 instruction on ELL Poster R5 to extend and enrich language.

ELL Poster R5

Oral Vocabulary
Amazing Words

Teach Amazing Words

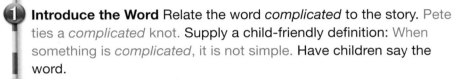

Amazing Words · **Oral Vocabulary Routine**

1 Introduce the Word Relate the word *complicated* to the story. Pete ties a *complicated* knot. Supply a child-friendly definition: When something is *complicated*, it is not simple. Have children say the word.

2 Demonstrate Provide examples to show meaning. A *complicated* problem is not easy to solve. You have to work hard to understand a *complicated* story. It is hard to do a *complicated* job.

3 Apply Have children demonstrate their understanding. What are some things that seem *complicated* to you?

See p. OV•2 to teach *applaud* and *success*.

Routines Flip Chart

Anchored Talk

Add to the concept map

Use these questions to discuss what is around us at school as you add to the concept map.

- In the poem "Show and Tell," what are some things children brought to school? (a lizard, a plant, lightning bugs, hamster, bird's nest, teddy bears, rope) Most of these things would belong in a science corner. I'll write *show-and-tell things* to include them all, and I'll write that in the *Things* box on the map.

Amazing Words

classmate	science
education	complicated
polite	success
principal	applaud
recess	

Differentiated Instruction

SI **Strategic Intervention**
Amazing Words Have children clap to demonstrate the meaning of *applaud*. To further connect the concept to the word, have children chant *When I clap, I applaud* to the rhythm of the clapping.

 **E L L**

English Language Learners
Sentences Use the Read Aloud "Show and Tell" as a springboard for having English language learners do their own show and tell. They can use objects from the classroom such as pencils and scissors. Help them name the objects and form a sentence or two about each.

Print Awareness
Sequence Letters

Review

Have children name some letters of the alphabet. Write them in lower-case form on the board. Then tell children that the letters of the alphabet go in a certain order. The first letter of the alphabet is *a.* Draw a long horizontal line on the board and write *a* on the left. Then indicate the right end of the line. Does anybody know what letter goes here at the end? That's right, *z.* The last letter of the alphabet is called *z,* and it looks like this. Write *z* at the end of the line. The order of the letters goes from *a* to *z.*

Model

Write lower-case letters on the board as you say the following:

 Think Aloud I know there are 26 letters in the alphabet. The first letter is *a.* The next letter is *b; b* comes right after a. Then the next letter is *c,* which comes right after *b.* The first three letters are *a, b, c.* I start here at the left and I go to the right. *a, b, c.*

Touch the letters *a, b, c* on the board and name them. Say it with me: *a, b, c.* Continue, adding *d, e, f,* and *g.*

Guide practice

So far, the order is *a, b, c, d, e, f, g.* Touch the letters as you say them. But I still have to get all the way to *z.* Does anyone know what letter comes next? What letter comes right after *g?* If children are unsure, provide the letter or give them a choice of letters: Which sounds right: *a, b, c, d, e, f, g, x,* or *a, b, c, d, e, f, g, h*? Go through the rest of the alphabet in this fashion, emphasizing the phrases right after and the next by saying *Yes,* p *comes right after* o or *The next letter after* s *is* t. Continue until you have reached *z.* Then have children name the letters with you as you run your hand from left to right across the line.

On their own

Use *Reader's and Writer's Notebook* p. 93.

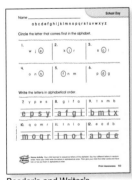

Reader's and Writer's Notebook p. 93

Phonemic Awareness
Segment and Blend Phonemes

Model

We just read about some children who brought some of their favorite things in to school for show-and-tell. One of those things was a *rope*. Listen to the sounds in *rope*: /r/ /ō/ /p/. Listen as I blend the sounds to say the word *rope*: /r/ /ō/ /p/, *rope*. Say it with me: /r/ /ō/ /p/, *rope*. **Repeat with the word** *tell*.

Guide practice

Now we're going to blend sounds to say other words. Listen to the sounds in *wet*: /w/ /e/ /t/. Say the sounds with me: /w/ /e/ /t/. Now let's blend the sounds: /w/ /e/ /t/, *wet*. **Continue with the following words. Say the sounds in each word with the children and then blend the sounds to say the word.**

/j/ /a/ /m/, jam	**/r/ /o/ /k/,** rock	**/j/ /a/ /k/,** Jack
/w/ /e/ /l/, well	**/j/ /ō/ /k/,** joke	**/r/ /e/ /d/,** red

Corrective feedback

If children make an error, model the correct response. Return to the word later in the practice.

On their own

Continue with the following words. Have children say the sounds in each word and then blend the sounds to say the word.

/j/ /e/ /f/, Jeff	**/r/ /a/ /k/,** rack	**/k/ /i/ /t/,** Kit
/j/ /u/ /j/, judge	**/w/ /ā/ /t/,** wait	**/e/ /j/,** edge

Phonics
Short e /e/

Hear

Today you will learn how to spell the sound /e/. Listen: /e/, /e/, /e/. When you say /e/, your mouth is open and your tongue is behind your bottom teeth. Say /e/. Did your mouth open? Good! Is your tongue behind your bottom teeth? Check to be sure. Say it again and pay attention to your tongue: /e/. Watch and listen as children produce the sound. Say /e/ with me: /e/, /e/, /e/.

Say

Display Sound-Spelling Card 6. This is a picture of an *elephant*. Say it with me: *elephant*. The first sound in *elephant* is /e/. Listen: /e/, *elephant*. Say it with me: /e/, *elephant*. What is the first sound in *elephant*?

Ee

e

Sound-Spelling
Card 6

See

Point to *e*. This is *e*. The sound /e/ is usually spelled *e*. *Elephant* begins with /e/. *Elephant* begins with the letter *e*. Have children say /e/ several times as you point to *e*.

Read ABC Rhyme Time

Display ABC Rhyme Time, p. 10. Point to the letters *Ee* at the top of the page. The name for both of these letters is *e*. Point to *E*. This is an upper-case *E*. Point to *e*. This is a lower-case *e*. Point to each letter again and ask: What is the name of this letter?

Enter and Exit

Elephants enter an empty elevator
To enjoy rides to higher floors.
They don't ever forget to exit
When the elevator opens its doors!

10

ABC Rhyme Time p. 10

This rhyme is called "Enter and Exit." To *enter* is to go into a place. To *exit* is to come out of a place. Both *enter* and *exit* begin with the sound *e*. They both begin with the letter *e*. Read the rhyme aloud, tracking the print with your finger. Then read it again. Point to examples of upper- and lower-case *e*'s as you read each word aloud.

Write

Now I will show you how to write upper-case *E* and lower-case *e*. Write *E*. Watch as I trace upper-case *E* with my finger. Follow the stroke instructions pictured. Now you write upper-case *E*. Repeat for lower-case *e*.

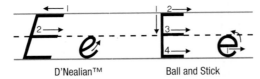

D'Nealian™   Ball and Stick

Phonics — Teach/Model
↻ Short e /e/

Blending Strategy

1 Connect Connect *e* to the sound /e/. Write *e*. This is *e*. The sound for *e* is /e/. Say the sound with me: /e/, /e/, /e/. When you see the letter *e*, what sound will you say?

2 Model Model how to blend *red*. Write *r*. What is the sound for this letter? Say the sound with me: /r/. **Write *e*.** Say this sound with me: /e/. **Write *d*.** Say this sound with me: /d/. Listen as I blend all the sounds together: /r/ /e/ /d/, *red*. Blend the sounds with me: /r/ /e/ /d/, *red*. Now blend the sounds without me.

3 Guide Practice Continue the routine in Step 2 with the words that follow. Remember, first we say the sounds. Then we blend the sounds to read the word.

met	jet	Ed	Ken	rim	rag
kiss	jam	wig	hen	bell	wet

For corrective feedback, model blending the sounds to read the word. Then have children blend the sounds and read the word with you.

4 Review What do you know about reading words that begin with the letter *e* or have *e* in the middle? **(The sound for *e* is /e/.)**

Routines Flip Chart

Spell Words   Now we are going to spell words with the sound /e/ spelled *e*. The first word we will spell is *bed*. What sounds do you hear in *bed*? (/b/ /e/ /d/) What is the letter for /b/? Let's all write *b*. What is the letter for /e/? Write *e*. What is the letter for /d/? Write *d*. Have children confirm their spellings by comparing them with what you have written. Continue practice with *men, get, led, sell,* and *fed*. Ask what letters change and what letters stay the same when you change *led* to *fed*; then ask if *led* and *fed* rhyme (yes).

On their own   Use the *Reader's and Writer's Notebook* p. 94 for additional practice with short vowel *e* /e/.

Reader's and Writer's
Notebook, p. 94

Differentiated Instruction

 Strategic Intervention

Sound /e/ Many letter names begin with the sound /e/; examples include *F, L, N, S,* and *X*. Because of this, some children may believe that a word such as *elephant* actually begins with the letter *l*, and that *enter* and *exit* begin with *n* and *x*, respectively. Remind children that letters such as *l* and *n* go with sounds of their own (/l/ and /n/) and that sounds /el/ and /en/ are different because they are a combination of sounds. You also may find it helpful to use words beginning with *e* such as *egg, edge,* and *Edward,* which are less likely to cause this kind of confusion.

Spelling Pattern

/e/e The sound /e/ is usually spelled *e* at the beginning or in the middle of a word.

ELL

English Language Learners
Visual Support Use the picture on pages 122–123 of the student book. Have children look for items with /e/ such as *bell, tent, entrance, wet,* and *mess*. Provide definitions as needed, and have children use these words in simple sentences. Close by helping children spell *wet, mess,* and *bell*.

Objectives

○ Associate consonant *k* with the sound /k/.

○ Associate vowel *e* with the sound /e/.

• Blend and read words with *k* and *e*.

• Recognize and name the letters *Kk* and *Ee*.

Phonics
Identify Lower-Case and Upper-Case Letters

Guide practice

Write a lower-case *e* and point to it. What letter is this? (lower-case *e*) Write an upper-case *E* and point to it. What letter is this? (upper-case *E*) Write a series of upper- and lower-case *e*'s. Point to each and have children identify each as upper-case *E* or lower-case *e*.

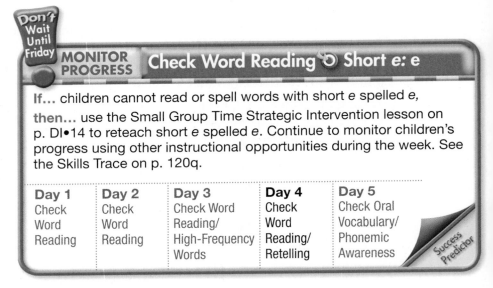

Don't Wait Until Friday

MONITOR PROGRESS | Check Word Reading ○ Short *e*: *e*

If... children cannot read or spell words with short *e* spelled *e*,

then... use the Small Group Time Strategic Intervention lesson on p. DI•14 to reteach short *e* spelled *e*. Continue to monitor children's progress using other instructional opportunities during the week. See the Skills Trace on p. 120q.

Day 1	Day 2	Day 3	Day 4	Day 5
Check Word Reading	Check Word Reading	Check Word Reading/ High-Frequency Words	Check Word Reading/ Retelling	Check Oral Vocabulary/ Phonemic Awareness

Success Predictor

Small Group Time

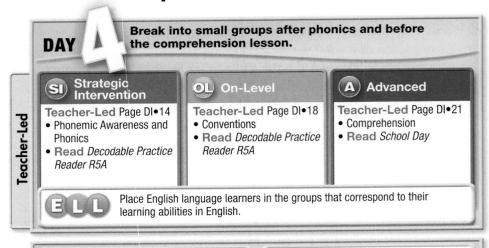

DAY 4 Break into small groups after phonics and before the comprehension lesson.

Teacher-Led

(SI) Strategic Intervention

Teacher-Led Page DI•14
• Phonemic Awareness and Phonics
• **Read** *Decodable Practice Reader R5A*

(OL) On-Level

Teacher-Led Page DI•18
• Conventions
• **Read** *Decodable Practice Reader R5A*

(A) Advanced

Teacher-Led Page DI•21
• Comprehension
• **Read** *School Day*

E L L Place English language learners in the groups that correspond to their learning abilities in English.

Practice Stations
• Read for Meaning

Independent Activities
• Read independently/Reading log on *Reader's and Writer's Notebook* p. RR1.
• AudioText of Main Selection

Phonics—Build Fluency
⟲ Consonant k /k/, Vowel e /e/

Model

Envision It!

Have children turn to page 120 in their Student Editions. Look at the pictures on this page. I see a picture of a *kite* and a picture of an *elephant*. When I say *kite*, I begin with the sound /k/. The /k/ sound in *kite* is spelled with a *k*. When I say *elephant*, I begin with the sound /e/. The /e/ sound is spelled with an *e*.

Guide practice

For each word in *Words I Can Blend*, ask for the sound of each letter. Make sure that children identify the correct sounds for *k* and *e*. Then have children blend the whole word.

Corrective Feedback

If... children have difficulty blending a word,
then... model blending the word, and then ask children to blend it with you.

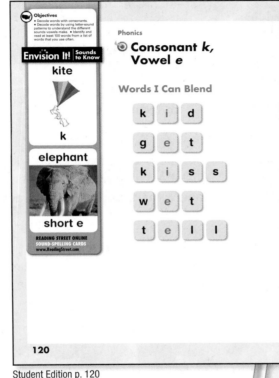

Student Edition p. 120

Differentiated Instruction

A **Advanced**

Extend Blending Provide children who can segment and blend all the words correctly with more challenging words such as: *kitty, kings, kitchen, kept, test, step, engine, Emily,* and *blend*.

Spelling Patterns

/k/ Spelled k The sound /k/ can be spelled *c, k,* or *ck*. The spelling *k* is most often used when the /k/ sound is followed by *e* or *i*.

/e/ Spelled e The sound /e/ is usually spelled *e* at the beginning or in the middle of a word.

Objectives

- Apply knowledge of sound-spellings to decode unknown words when reading.
- Decode words in context and in isolation.
- Practice fluency with oral rereading.
- Read high frequency words.

Decodable Practice Reader R5A
Consonants r /r/, w /w/, j /j/, and Short e: e

Decode words in isolation

Have children turn to page 65. Have children decode each word.

Review high-frequency words

Review the previously taught words *the, do, you,* and *see.* Have children read each word as you point to it on the Word Wall.

Preview Decodable Reader

Have children read the title and preview the story. Tell them they will read words with the short *e* sound and with the sounds /r/, /w/, and /j/.

Decodable Practice Reader R5A

Decode words in context

Pair children for reading and listen carefully as they decode. One child begins. Children read the entire story, switching readers after each page. Partners reread the story. This time the other child begins.

Deb let Meg in.

66

Meg led Pep the pig.

67

Meg did not see Big Red. Meg fell in the pen.

68

Meg fed Nell the red hen.

69

Decodable Practice Reader R5A

Do you see Nell? Get the net, Meg!

70

Meg met Jet. Jet got Meg wet.

71

Meg did well.

72

Corrective feedback

If… children have difficulty decoding a word, **then…** refer them to the Sound-Spelling Cards to identify the sounds in the word. Prompt them to blend the word.

- What is the new word?
- Is the new word a word you know?
- Does it make sense in the story?

Check decoding and comprehension

Have children retell the story to include characters, setting, and events. Then have children locate words with sound /e/ spelled *e* in the story. List words that children name. Children should supply *Deb, let, Meg, led, Pep, Red, fell, pen, fed, Nell, hen, get, net, met, Jet, wet* and *well.* Ask children how they know these words have the /e/ sound. (They all have the letter *e,* which spells the sound /e/.)

Reread for Fluency

Have children reread Decodable Practice Reader R5A to develop automaticity decoding words with the short *e* sound.

ROUTINE **Oral Rereading**

1. **Read** Have children read the entire book orally.
2. **Reread** To achieve optimal fluency, children should reread the text three or four times.
3. **Corrective Feedback** Listen as children read. Provide corrective feedback regarding their fluency and decoding.

Routines Flip Chart

ELL

English Language Learners
Short e: e
Beginning Before reading, lead children through *We Met Meg* and have them identify some of the characters. Ask them to make up a sentence about one of the characters.

Intermediate After reading, have children identify the *-ed, -ell, -en,* and *–et* words in the story that rhyme: *led, Red, fed; fell, Nell, well; pen, hen; let, get, net, met, Jet, wet.*

Advanced/Advanced High After reading, have children retell the story and ask them what happens to the character of Meg.

Objectives
- Identify the features of fiction and nonfiction.
- Review high-frequency words.

Genre
Fiction and Nonfiction

Identify features of fiction and nonfiction

Use the story *School Day* to have children determine whether a story is fiction or nonfiction.

- Nonfiction writing provides information and facts about real people, places, or events. How is nonfiction different from fiction? (Possible response: Fiction is a made-up story. It is not about real people, places, or events.)

- Today we will read a fiction story about made-up kids that go to school in the story *School Day*. How do you think the story would be different if it were non-fiction? (It would be about real kids in a real school.)

Guide practice

Use Graphic Organizer 4. Label the first column "Fiction," the second column "Nonfiction." Let's begin by listing the features of fiction in the first column. What do we know about fiction? (made-up story, characters, setting, events) Now let's list the features of nonfiction in the second column. (provides information and facts, real people, real places, real events). Refer back to this chart as your read *School Day*.

Fiction	Nonfiction
made-up story characters setting events	provides information and facts real people real places real events

Graphic Organizer Flip Chart 4

On their own

Use *Reader's and Writer's Notebook* p. 95.

Reader's and Writer's Notebook p. 95

High-Frequency Words
Build Fluency

Read words in isolation

Remind children that there are some words we learn by remembering the letters, rather than by saying the sounds. Then have them read each of the highlighted high-frequency words aloud.

Read words in context

Chorally read the I Can Read! passage along with the children. Then have them read the passage aloud to themselves. When they are finished, ask children to reread the high-frequency words.

Team Talk Have children choose two high-frequency words and give them time to create a sentence in which both words are used properly. Then have them share the sentence with a partner.

I Can Read!

Ken is three. He is a kid I met on a jet. Ken had a red bell with him.

Is a bell on a jet bad? Men on the jet tell Ken to sell that red bell. Will Ken get in a jam?

You've learned

- Consonants *r, w, j, k*
- Vowel *e*

High-Frequency Words
he   is   to   with   three

121

Student Edition p. 121

Differentiated Instruction

 Advanced

Extend High-Frequency Words Have pairs of students tell their own stories about Ken. Have them use this week's high-frequency words in their stories.

Build Background
School Day

Background Building Audio

Have children listen to the CD. Tell them to listen especially for what the first graders like to do at school.

 Background Building Audio

Discuss what children like to do at school

Team Talk Have children turn to a partner and use these questions for discussion:

- What is your favorite thing to do at school?
- What new thing would you like to try?
- What are some of the things you do in first grade that you didn't do in kindergarten?

Organize information in a web

Draw a web or display Graphic Organizer 17. Write "School" in the center circle. Have children think about things they do in school and what the children on the Audio said they like to do at school. Record their responses.

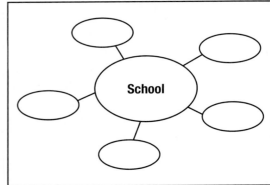

Graphic Organizer Flip Chart 17

Connect to selection

We heard about what some first graders do at their school. What are some of the things they talked about? (riding the bus to school, reading, learning math, using a computer, playing in the gym, learning new games, making new friends) We're going to read *School Day.* It is a story about Sam and some of the things he does at school. We'll read to find out what his school day is like.

Sam is sad. Kim will help him. Jill and Pat will help him.
130

They will help Fred. Sam is not sad.
131

Student Edition pp. 130–131

Main Selection—Let's Read
School Day

Practice the skill

 Plot Remind children that the plot of a story is made up of the events that happen in the beginning, middle, and end. It often includes a problem and a solution. Have children discuss why a story's plot is important.

Introduce the strategy

Monitor and Clarify Explain that good readers try to make sense of difficult words, ideas, or passages. Have children turn to page EI•11 in their Student Edition.

Student Edition EI•11

Envision It!

Think Aloud Look at what is happening in the pictures. Why does the girl seem to be confused in the first picture? (She doesn't understand what she has read.) How do you know? (Her face shows that she is confused.) What happens in the last picture? (The girl is not confused anymore.) Why? (The other girl helped her in the middle picture.) Good readers monitor their reading by asking themselves if they understand a story. They clarify what they do not understand by rereading or studying pictures.

Introduce genre

Let's Read Together Realistic fiction is a made-up story that could happen in real life. As they read *School Day,* have children look for events that indicate this could happen in real life.

Preview and predict

Have children identify the title of the story, the author, and the illustrator. Read aloud the names of the author and illustrator and have children describe the role of each. Help children activate prior knowledge by asking them to look through the selection and use the illustrations to predict what might happen in the story.

Set a purpose

Have children read to find out all the things Sam does at school.

Tell children that today they will read *School Day.* Use the Guide Comprehension notes to help children develop their comprehension of the reading selection.

INTERACT with TEXT

Strategy Response Log

Monitor and Clarify
Before reading, have children use p. RR11 of their *Reader's and Writer's Notebook* to review and use the strategy of monitor and clarify.

Academic Vocabulary

monitor and clarify make sense of what is read

realistic fiction a made-up story that could happen in real life.

 ELL

English Language Learners
Build Background Before children listen to the CD, build background and elicit prior knowledge. On the CD, you will hear about what some first graders do at their school. What are some things you do at school?

Frontload Main Selection Ask children what they already know about school using the picture on pp. 130–131. Then do a picture walk of the selection so children can talk about and see things that children do at school.

Objectives
- Reread and review to monitor and clarify.
- Distinguish realism from fantasy.

Student Edition pp. 122–123

Comprehension Strategy
Monitor and Clarify

Teach

Explain that we monitor our reading by asking ourselves if we understand a story. If something seems confusing or does not make sense, we find ways to clarify information so that we understand. Sometimes readers study the pictures or reread a part of a story if something doesn't make sense. Good readers also use their own background knowledge to help them understand things in stories.

Model

Think Aloud As I begin to read this story, I will look at the pictures and use my background knowledge to help me understand the story. I see a yellow bus on page 122, and I know that is a school bus! I already know that! On page 123, I see children with backpacks outside a building. The building looks like a school. I am using my background knowledge before I even start to read the story!

Guide practice

Have children study the picture on page 123. Tell children to use the picture to clarify what else is happening at the beginning of the story. (Possible response: I reread the title *School Day* and the first sentence: *What is around us at school?* The kids must be going to school at the beginning of the story.)

Sam is still in **bed**!

Mom **will** **get** him.

124

Grab the **red** bag, Sam!

125

Student Edition pp. 124–125

Comprehension Skill
Review Realism and Fantasy

Teach

Remind children that fantasy is about things that could never happen, while realism is about made-up events that could really happen. Look at pages 124 and 125. Could this story really happen or is it a fantasy?

If... children have difficulty answering the question, **then...** model how to distinguish realistic stories from fantasies.

Model

Think Aloud I see that Sam is sleeping in a bed. Mom is waking him up. Then Mom is handing Sam his lunch as he picks up a bag in the kitchen. Mom and Sam are characters, but they are doing things that could really happen. I think this is realistic fiction.

Guide practice

Ask children to find other clues on pages 124 and 125 that help them identify the story as realistic fiction.

Objectives
- Reread and review to monitor and clarify.
- Distinguish realism from fantasy.

Sam ran fast. **He** got on.

Sam sat **with** Fred.

126

Sam met Pat, Kim, and Jill.

The **three** tell the plan **to** Sam.

127

Student Edition pp. 126–127

Comprehension Skill
Plot

Teach

Remind children that the plot of a story is made up of the events that occur in the beginning, middle, and end of the story. What happens in the beginning of the story? What happens in the middle?

If... children have difficulty answering the question,
then... model how to use the text and the illustrations to identify the plot.

Model

Think Aloud As I read, I look carefully at the illustrations to help me identify the plot of the story. In the beginning, Sam is sleeping in bed and the text says Mom will get him. In the middle of the story, Sam runs to the bus stop and then meets his friends at school.

Guide practice

Have children study the picture on page 126 and describe how it illustrates Sam's problem in the beginning of the story. (Possible response: The picture shows Sam running for the bus because he is late. This shows that Sam might miss the bus.)

Pat did a jet kit. Jill will jig.

Kim will sit on a mat.

128

The red bag had a rip!

Fred will drop! Stop him!

129

Student Edition pp. 128–129

Comprehension Strategy
Monitor and Clarify

Teach

Remind children that we monitor our reading by asking ourselves if we understand a story. If we do not understand, we find ways to clarify information. Look at pages 128–129. Explain who Fred is. What could you do if you don't know the answer?

Model

Think Aloud To understand who Fred is, I can reread the words and look at the pictures. I read that Sam sits on the bus with Fred earlier in the story. I only see Sam with a bag. But I also see that a frog drops out of Sam's bag on page 129. Fred must be the frog! I can figure that out by using my own background knowledge.

Guide practice

Have children use the pictures on pages 128–129 to explain why rereading part of the story and looking at pictures might help them understand something that confused them. (Possible response: It may give me information I missed the first time I read it.)

Sam is sad. Kim will help him.

Jill and Pat will help him.

130

They will help Fred.

Sam is not sad.

131

Student Edition pp. 130–131

Phonics/High-Frequency Words
Word Reading

Teach   Remind children that they have learned some new sounds and letters this week.

Model   *Think Aloud* One of the words on page 130 begins with the letter *j, Jill*. We learned this week that the letter *j* has the sound /j/. That will help me read this word: /j/ /i/ /l/, *Jill*. There is a word with the sound /k/ on this page, too. Can you find it? **(Kim)** You also learned some other words this week that you don't have to blend the sounds to read. You already know these words. *Is* on page 131 is one of these words. What are some other words like this in the story? **(he, with, three, to)**

Corrective feedback

Decoding
If... children come to a decodable word they don't know,
then... review the sound-letter relationships in isolation and then blend.

High-Frequency Words
If... children have a problem reading a new high-frequency word,
then... reteach the problematic word and read it in context.

Comprehension Check

Have children discuss each question with a partner. Ask several pairs to share their responses.

☑ **Realistic fiction** How do you know that this story is realistic fiction? (Possible response: This story is realistic fiction because it could happen in real life. The kids in the story do things that real kids do.)

☑ **Plot** What is Sam's problem at the end of the story? How does he solve his problem? (Possible response: Sam drops his frog Fred at the end of the story. He solves his problem by gluing it back together with his friends.)

☑ **Confirm predictions** How did you use the pictures and words to confirm what happened in the story? (Possible response: I read the part that tells about what Sam does at school. I used the pictures of Sam and his friends at school to confirm that he has show-and-tell with his friends.)

☑ **Connect text to self** Have you ever had something go wrong for you at school? What happened? (Possible response: Yes, I once brought in a paper doll I made to show the class, but it got caught in my book and ripped.)

Strategy Self-Check

Have children talk about any problems they encountered as they read and what they did to solve them.

Monitor and Clarify

• What did they do when they didn't understand words or ideas?

Remind children that good readers use many strategies as they read.

English Language Learners

Support Discussion Pair English learners with English speakers. Ask children to help each other answer the questions by rewording the questions, if necessary. Children can write or draw their ideas and share them with the rest of the class.

Objectives
- Retell a narrative.
- ○ Identify the plot of a story
- Write clear, coherent sentences.

Check Retelling
SUCCESS PREDICTOR

1.9.A.2 Retell a story's beginning middle, and end, with attention to sequence of events.

1.19.C.1 Write brief comments on literary texts.

RC-1.D.2 Use textual evidence to support understanding.

Objectives
- Retell a narrative.
- ◉ Identify the plot of a story
- Write clear, coherent sentences.

Check Retelling
SUCCESS PREDICTOR

Objectives
Describe the problem and the solution of a story. Retell a story's beginning, middle, and end, in the order in which the events happened.

Envision It! Retell

READING STREET ONLINE
STORY SORT
www.ReadingStreet.com

132

Think Critically

1. How is Sam's school like your school? Text to Self

2. What happens in the beginning of the story? What happens at the end?
   ◉ Plot

3. **Look Back and Write** Look back at page 128. What will Kim, Jill, and Pat do?

   TEST PRACTICE Extended Response

School Bus

Friendly fellow
Dressed in yellow
Greets his kids
With a beep-beep hello!

by Dee Lillegard
illustrated by Dean MacAdam

133

Student Edition pp. 132–133

Retelling

Envision It! Have children work in pairs to retell the story. Remind children to include the characters, setting, and events from the story. Children should use the retelling strip in the Student Edition. Monitor children's retelling.

Scoring rubric

Top-Score Response A top-score response makes connections beyond the text, elaborates on the author's purpose, and describes in detail the characters, setting, and plot.

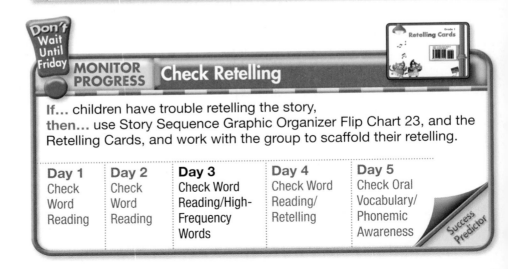

Don't Wait Until Friday

MONITOR PROGRESS Check Retelling

Grade 1
Retelling Cards

If... children have trouble retelling the story,
then... use Story Sequence Graphic Organizer Flip Chart 23, and the Retelling Cards, and work with the group to scaffold their retelling.

Day 1	Day 2	Day 3	Day 4	Day 5
Check Word Reading	Check Word Reading	Check Word Reading/High-Frequency Words	Check Word Reading/ Retelling	Check Oral Vocabulary/ Phonemic Awareness

Success Predictor

Think Critically

Text to Self

1. Possible response: Some children take the bus to my school. We have show-and-tell sometimes in my school, too.

 Plot

2. Possible response: At the beginning of the story, Sam wakes up late and might miss the bus. At the end of the story, Sam and his friends work together to fix Fred, his frog.

Writing on Demand

3. **Look Back and Write** For writing fluency, assign a five-minute time limit. As children finish, encourage them to reread their responses and proofread for errors.

Scoring rubric

> **Top-Score Response** A top-score response uses details from the text and the pictures to tell what Kim, Jill, and Pat will do. For example:
>
> Kim, Jill, and Pat will help Sam. They will fix Fred. They are Sam's friends.

Read poetry

Read aloud page 133 as children follow along. Point out the rhythm of the poem as you read. Children can tap the rhythm with a pencil. Ask children to identify the words that rhyme as you read. Ask children:

- How is this poem like the story *School Day*? (They both have a school bus in them.)
- What are some other ways we might get to school? (train, walk, bike, car)
- How do you get to school?

Differentiated Instruction

 Advanced

Look Back and Write Ask children who show proficiency with the writing prompt to explain why they think Sam's friends want to help Sam.

Strategy Response Log

Genre Have children use p. RR11 in their *Reader's and Writer's Notebook* to identify the characteristics of realistic fiction.

Plan to Assess Retelling

- ☐ Week 1: Strategic Intervention
- ☐ This week: Advanced
- ☐ Week 3: Strategic Intervention
- ☐ Week 4: On-Level
- ☑ This Week: Assess Strategic Intervention children
- ☐ Week 6: Assess any children you have not yet checked during this unit.

Retelling

Success Predictor

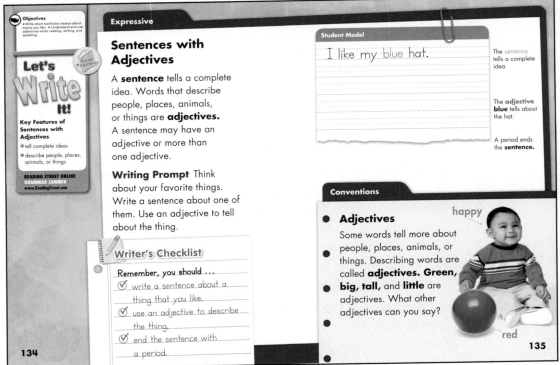

Objectives
• Write short nonfiction essays about topics you like. • Understand and use adjectives when reading, writing, and speaking.

Let's Write It!

Key Features of Sentences with Adjectives
• tell complete ideas
• describe people, places, animals, or things

READING STREET ONLINE
GRAMMAR JAMMER
www.ReadingStreet.com

Expressive

Sentences with Adjectives

A **sentence** tells a complete idea. Words that describe people, places, animals, or things are **adjectives**. A sentence may have an adjective or more than one adjective.

Writing Prompt Think about your favorite things. Write a sentence about one of them. Use an adjective to tell about the thing.

Writer's Checklist

Remember, you should . . .
☑ write a sentence about a thing that you like.
☑ use an adjective to describe the thing.
☑ end the sentence with a period.

134

Student Model

I like my blue hat.

The *sentence* tells a complete idea.

The **adjective blue** tells about the hat.

A period ends the **sentence**.

Conventions

• **Adjectives**
Some words tell more about people, places, animals, or things. Describing words are called **adjectives. Green, big, tall,** and **little** are adjectives. What other adjectives can you say?

happy

red

135

Student Edition pp. 134–135

Writing—Sentences

Teach

Look at p. 134 in the Student Edition. Read aloud the Key Features of Sentences with Adjectives. Help children better understand the Writing Prompt by reading it aloud and discussing the Writer's Checklist with children.

Review the student model

Then read the Student Model on p. 135 to children. Point out that the sentence expresses a complete idea. Ask children what the sentence ends with. (a period) Have children identify what the adjective *blue* describes. (the noun *hat*)

Guide practice

Now it is time to write your sentence. Think about your favorite things. Then tell about one of those things. Remember, your sentence should include an adjective that describes a noun. Choose an adjective that will help the reader understand exactly what you mean. Guide children as they write a sentence about a favorite thing. If children cannot write a complete sentence, provide them with a sentence frame, such as, *I like my _____ _____.* Have them fill in the blanks with an adjective and a noun that tell about a favorite thing. If children are unable to write decodable words, have them orally suggest the words and then model writing them in the blank. (For example: I like my *big top.*)

Conventions
Adjectives

Read aloud the Conventions note on p. 135 as children follow along. Have them explain what an adjective is and then read with you the examples of adjectives that are on the page (*green, big, tall,* and *little*). Then have them think of other descriptive adjectives and share them with the class. As they share, list adjectives on the board.

On their own

Use the *Reader's and Writer's Notebook* p. 96.

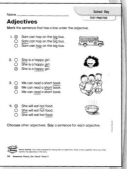

Reader's and Writer's Notebook p. 96

Read aloud the Conventions note on p. 135

Differentiated Instruction

 Advanced

Adjectives Have one group of children create a list of color adjectives and another group of children create a list of size adjectives. Then have the groups exchange lists and use crayons to draw pictures of the adjectives on the list. Have them present their pictures to the class and use each adjective in a sentence.

English Language Learners

Adjectives for Colors Speakers of Polish and other languages may express choices among objects using adjectives without nouns: *I want the blue.* Help children add the noun.

Objectives
- Understand and use adjectives.
- Use proper letter size when writing.
- Write *Ee.*

Research
Calendar

Teach

Display the classroom calendar. Explain that a calendar shows the days, weeks, and months of a year. There are twelve months in a year. List the names of the months. The name of this month is (give current month). Each month is made up of weeks. Each week is made up of days. List the days of the week. Today is (give current day). Each number on the calendar stands for a date. Today's date is (give current date).

Display Research Transparency R5. This is a blank calendar. Fill in the month and dates on the calendar with the children. Review the names of the days of the week. We will use the calendar to find answers to the questions below it. Read the first two questions and model how to find the answers.

Research Transparency R5

Model

Think Aloud

The first question asks me the name of the month. When I look at the calendar, I see the month is (give current month). I will write the word (give current month) on the line. The second question asks me the date of the first Wednesday of the month. First I will find the word *Wednesday* on the calendar. Then I will look at the calendar to find the first Wednesday of the month. The first Wednesday is (give date). I will write that date on the line.

Guide practice

Continue reading the questions. Help children interpret the calendar to find the answers. Review the information once you've recorded all the responses.

On their own

Use *Reader's and Writer's Notebook* p. 97.

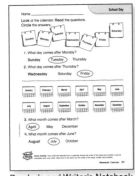
Reader's and Writer's Notebook p. 97

Handwriting
Letter *E* and *e;*
Letter Size

Model letter formation

Display upper- and lower-case letters: *Ee*. Use the stroke instructions pictured below to model proper letter formation.

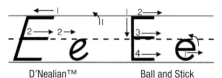

D'Nealian™   Ball and Stick

Model letter size

Remind children that some letters are tall, some are small, some fall below the line, and some go above the mid-line. I will use the lines on the paper to help me use correct letter size when writing. Model the four different letter sizes by writing *Lip, jet,* and *met.* Have children identify the size of each letter.

Guide practice

Write the following sentence: *Dad fed the dog Ed.*

Team Talk Tell children you will point to a letter. Have pairs work together to decide if the letter is tall, small, falls below the line, or goes above the mid-line. Point to different letters in the sentence and monitor children's responses.

On their own

Use the *Reader's and Writer's Notebook* p. 98.

Reader's and Writer's Notebook, p. 98

Wrap Up Your Day

✔ **Vowel *Ee* /e/** Write the letters *E* and *e.* Have children identify the letters. Write *Ed* and *pet.* Say the words aloud. Have children repeat after you. Remind children that this is the short *e* sound of *e.*

✔ **Plot** Have children explain a problem and its solution in the story *School Day.*

✔ **Monitor and Clarify** Remind children that good readers use pictures and reread to help them understand what they read.

Differentiated Instruction

 Strategic Intervention

Forming the Letters *Ee* Explain that while many capital and lower-case letters share the same basic shape, the letters *Ee* do not. Point out that upper-case *E* is made up of straight lines, while lower-case *e* is formed by a curved line. Have children write several upper- and lower-case *Ee*'s. Then have them underline the letters they formed using all straight lines and circle the letters they formed using a curved line.

 Advanced

Extend Research Skill Talk about the things you might find on a calendar. Discuss holidays. Have them find Thanksgiving on a calendar. Write the holiday on the board and the month it falls. Continue with other holidays, recording each one as it is found on the calendar. Then have children place the holidays in order from January to December.

Academic Vocabulary

calendar shows the days, weeks, and months of a year

Preview DAY 5

Tell children that tomorrow they will read about Sam and his friends at school.

Objectives

- Review concepts: neighbor-hoods and schools.
- Build oral vocabulary.
- Identify details in text.

Today at a Glance

Oral Vocabulary
Review *classmate, education, polite, principal, recess, science, applaud, complicated, success*

Print Awareness
Sentence Features

Phonological Awareness
Identify syllables

Phonics
Review Consonants *Rr* /r/, *Ww* /w/, *Jj* /j/, *Kk* /k/, and Short *e* /e/

High-Frequency Words
Review

Comprehension
⊙ Plot

Vocabulary
Give Descriptions

Listening and Speaking
Ask Questions

Handwriting
Proper Body Position

Writing and Conventions
Sentences with Adjectives

Check Oral Vocabulary
SUCCESS PREDICTOR

Concept Wrap Up

Question of the Week

What is around us at school?

Review
Concept

This week we have read and listened to stories about school Today you will listen to find out why the speaker becomes a success. **Read the story.**

- What does the speaker do that makes his class-mates applaud him as a success? (He finds Benny's missing lizard.)

Review
Amazing
Words

Orally review the meaning of this week's Amazing Words. Then display this week's concept map. Have children use Amazing Words such as *science, class-mate,* and *principal,* as well as the concept map, to answer the question: "What is around us at school?"

Read Aloud Anthology
"Show-and-Tell"

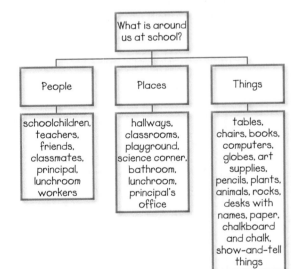

ELL **Check Concepts and Language** Use the Day 5 instruction on ELL Poster R5 to monitor chil-dren's understanding of the lesson concept.

ELL Poster R5

Oral Vocabulary
Amazing Ideas

Connect to the Big Question

Team Talk Pair children and have them discuss how the Question of the Week connects to this unit's Big Question, "What is all around me?" Tell children to use the concept map and what they've learned from this week's Anchored Talks and reading selections to form an Amazing Idea — a realization or "big idea" about **My World**. Then ask each pair to share their Amazing Idea with the class.

Amazing Ideas might include these key concepts:

- Schools are full of people, places, and things.
- You learn about science and other things at school, and you can also play games at recess.

It's Friday

MONITOR PROGRESS — **Check Oral Vocabulary**

Call on individuals to use this week's Amazing Words to talk about neighborhood schools. Prompt discussion with the questions below. Monitor children's ability to use the Amazing Words and note which words children are unable to use.

- **Why is it important for *classmates* to be *polite* to one another?**
- **How do schools help us get an *education*?**
- **What does a *principal* do?**
- **Why is it harder to be a *success* when you're doing something *complicated*?**

If... children have difficulty using the Amazing Words,

then... reteach the unknown words using the Oral Vocabulary Routines, pp. 115a, 118b, 120b, 120n.

Day 1	Day 2	Day 3	Day 4	Day 5
Check Word Reading	Check Word Reading	Check Word Reading/High-Frequency Words	Check Word Reading/Retelling	Check Oral Vocabulary/Phonemic Awareness

Success Predictor

Amazing Words

classmate	science
education	applaud
polite	complicated
principal	success
recess	

Differentiated Instruction

A Advanced

Amazing Words If children can easily answer the questions about the Amazing Words, ask these questions as well: *What do we learn about in science?*, *What do you like best about recess?*, and *When would you applaud a classmate?*

ELL

English Language Learners

Amazing Words If children have difficulty using the Amazing Words to answer the questions, model how to rephrase the questions by using sentence frames such as *Classmates should be polite because* _____ or *A principal can* _____.

Oral Vocabulary

Success Predictor

Objectives

- Recognize that sentences have initial upper-case letters and final periods.
- Write sentences with initial upper-case letters and final periods.
- Identify syllables.

Print Awareness
Sentence Features

Introduce

Say the following sentence: *Three men met a wet hen*. This is a sentence. It tells a complete idea. Get a picture in your mind of what is happening. How many men are there? **(three)** What did they do? **(they met a hen)** What was strange about that hen? **(it was wet)** The sentence tells us *who* and it tells us *what*. It is a complete idea, so it is a sentence. I'm going to write the sentence down, with your help. There are a couple of important rules I'll need to follow, though!

Model

Think Aloud The first word is *three*. I bet some of you know how to spell that word by now, and I'm sure you all know the first two letters—*th*. Write *three*; then frown. Whoops! The word *three* is the first word in my sentence. There's a rule about how to start sentences. The first letter of every sentence has to be an upper-case letter. Carefully erase the *t* in *three* and replace it with *T*. Now have children help you spell the remaining words of the sentence, paying close attention to the /e/ sound in several of the words. After writing *hen*, frown again and say: Oh, and there's one more important rule. I have to end my sentence with a special mark. One of those marks is called a period. Here's what a period looks like. My sentences need to end with a period or another mark.

Guide practice

Repeat with the sentences *The cat will nap* and *He ran to the net*. Have children tell you what needs to go at the beginning of each sentence (an upper-case letter) and at the end (a period); then have them help you spell the words to write the sentence.

On their own

Use *Reader's and Writer's Notebook* p. 99

Reader's and Writer's Notebook p. 99

Phonological Awareness
Identify Syllables

Model

In "Show-and-Tell," Benny brings in a lizard. *Benny* is an interesting name. I'm going to clap to the word *Benny*. Clap twice, once as you say *Ben*, and once as you say *ny*. *Ben-ny, Ben-ny.* Each clap stands for what we call a *syllable*. We say that *Benny* has two syllables: *Ben-ny, one, two.* Clap the syllables one more time and have children clap with you. Repeat with *rope* (one clap) and *animal* (three claps).

Guide practice

I will say a word, then you tell me how many syllables it has. *Recess: re-cess.* How many syllables are there in *recess*?

Continue this exercise using the words: *polite, classmate, education, school, teacher,* and *principal*.

Corrective feedback

If children make an error, model the correct response. Return to the word later in the practice.

It's Friday

MONITOR PROGRESS | **Identify Syllables**

Call on children to tell you how many syllables they hear in the following words.

| puppy | far | success | tapping |
| waterfall | over | cats | radio |

If... children have difficulty counting the syllables,

then... model counting syllables in the word again.

| **Day 1** | **Day 2** | **Day 3** | **Day 4** | **Day 5** |
| Check Word Reading | Check Word Reading | Check Word Reading/ High-Frequency Words | Check Word Reading/ Retelling | Check Oral Vocabulary/ Phonemic Awareness |

Success Predictor

Academic Vocabulary

syllable a word part that contains a single vowel sound

Differentiated Instruction

SI Strategic Intervention

Final *en* Some children may pronounce the short *e* in *hen* and *men* as if it were /i/. Say the words slowly and distinctly to help children master the formal pronunciation of these words, /hen/ and /men/.

ELL

English Language Learners

Syllables English allows any syllable of a word to be stressed, but some languages are much more restrictive about where an accent can be placed. Be sure children understand that *success* and *tapping*, for example, are both two-syllable words even though the accents are placed on different syllables.

Oral Vocabulary

Success Predictor

Objectives

- Review consonants *r* /r/, *w* /w/, *j* /j/, *k* /k/, *d* /d/, *l*, *ll* /l/, and *h* /h/, and vowels *e* /e/ and *o* /o/.
- Review high-frequency words *are, do, have, like, look, see, that, they, two, you, is, he, three, with, to.*
- Identify upper- and lower-case letters.
- Spell CVC words.

Fluent Word Reading
Spiral Review

Read words in isolation

Display these words. Tell children that they can blend some words on this list but others are Word Wall words.

Have children read the list three or four times until they can read at the rate of two to three seconds per word.

hop	two	Don	do	jog
that	hog	like	hill	they
men	see	look	you	red
will	den	are	wig	have

Word Reading

Corrective feedback

If... children have difficulty reading whole words,
then... have them use sound-by-sound blending for decodable words or have them say and spell high-frequency words.

If... children cannot read fluently at a rate of two to three seconds per word,
then... have pairs practice the list until they can read it fluently.

Read words in context

Display these sentences. Then randomly point to review words and have children read them. To help you monitor word reading, high-frequency words are underlined and decodable words are italicized.

I <u>see</u> *Don jog* on the *hill*.

<u>Two</u> *men* <u>are</u> in the *den*.

<u>Do</u> <u>you</u> <u>like</u> the *red wig*?

Sentence Reading

Corrective feedback

If... children are unable to read an underlined high-frequency word,
then... read the word for them and spell it, having them echo you.

If... children have difficulty reading an italicized decodable word,
then... guide them in using sound-by-sound blending.

Spell Words

Guide practice

Now we are going to spell words with the sounds and letters we learned this week. The first word we will spell is *wet*. What sounds do you hear in *wet*? (/w/ /e/ /t/) What is the letter for the sound /w/? Let's all write *w*. What is the letter for the sound /e/? Write *e*. What is the letter for the sound /t/? Write *t*. Have children confirm their spellings by comparing them with what you've written. Continue practice with *Ken, red, jet, hop, well,* and *jog* as time allows.

High-Frequency Words

Review

Point to the words *is, he, three, with,* and *to* one at a time on the Word Wall. Have children read and spell each word chorally. Have children work with a partner to use each word in a sentence. Ask several pairs to share their sentences.

Cumulative review

Point to the remaining Word Wall words one at a time. Have children read the words chorally.

On their own

Use *Reader's and Writer's Notebook* p. 100

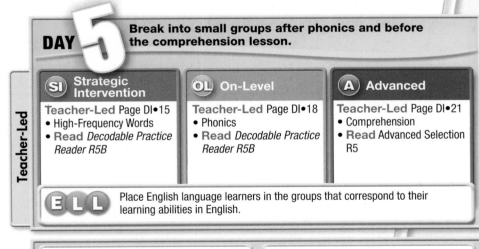

Reader's and Writer's Notebook, p. 100

Small Group Time

DAY 5 Break into small groups after phonics and before the comprehension lesson.

Teacher-Led

SI Strategic Intervention	**OL On-Level**	**A Advanced**
Teacher-Led Page DI•15	Teacher-Led Page DI•18	Teacher-Led Page DI•21
• High-Frequency Words	• Phonics	• Comprehension
• **Read** *Decodable Practice Reader R5B*	• **Read** *Decodable Practice Reader R5B*	• **Read** Advanced Selection R5

ELL Place English language learners in the groups that correspond to their learning abilities in English.

Practice Stations
• Get Fluent
• Let 'Write'

Independent Activities
• *Reader's and Writer's Notebook* p. RR1.
• Concept Talk Video
• AudioText of Paired Selection

Spiral Review

These activities review

• previously taught high-frequency words *are, do, have, like, look, see, that, they, two, you, is, he, three, with, to.*

• Consonants *r* /r/, *w* /w/, *j* /j/, *k* /k/, *d* /d/, *l, ll* /l/, and *h* /h/, and vowels *e* /e/ and *o* /o/.

Differentiated Instruction

SI Strategic Intervention

Chanting If children have trouble telling high-frequency words apart, have them do simple chants with motions for the spellings of some of the words,. To distinguish *look* from *like*, for example, have children chant the letters of *look* while placing their fingers in the shape of O's around their eyes.

English Language Learners

Sentences Help children form oral sentences with some or all of the words used for reading in the lesson. Examples might include *The dog is* wet or He is *my friend*.

Objectives

- Apply knowledge of sound-spellings to decode unknown words when reading.
- Use context to confirm the word that was read.
- Practice fluency with oral rereading.
- Read high-frequency words.

Decodable Practice Reader R5B

Review /r/, /w/, /j/, /k/, /e/

Decode words in isolation

Have children turn to the first page. Have children decode each word.

Decodable Practice Reader R5B

Review high-frequency words

Review the previously taught words *I, see,* and *a.* Have children read each word as you point to it on the Word Wall.

Preview Decodable Reader

Have children read the title and preview the story. Tell them they will read words with /r/ spelled *r,* /w/ spelled *w,* /j/ spelled *j,* /k/ spelled *k,* and /e/ spelled *e* in this story.

Decode words in context

Pair children for reading and listen carefully as they decode. One child begins. Children read the entire story, switching readers after each page. Partners reread the story. This time the other child begins.

Rob will jog with Red.
Get fit!

74

Jen will hop a lot.
Get fit!

75

Wes will do a jig.
Get fit!

76

Kit will hit the rim.
Get fit!

77

Decodable Practice Reader R5B

Ken is on a mat.
Get fit!

78

It can get hot.
We will get wet.

79

We will get fit.

80

Corrective Feedback

If... children have difficulty decoding a word, **then...** refer them to the Sound-Spelling Cards to identify the sounds in the word. Prompt them to blend the word.

- What is the new word?
- Is the new word a word you know?
- Does it make sense in the story?

Check decoding and comprehension

Have children retell the story to include characters, setting, and events. Then have children locate words with /r/ spelled r in the story. List words the children name. Children should supply *Rob, Red,* and *rim.* Ask them how they know these words have the /r/ sound. (They all have *r.*) Continue in the same way with /w/ spelled *w (will, Wes, wet),* /j/ spelled *j (jog, Jen, jig),* /k/ spelled *k (Kit, Ken),* and /e/ spelled *e (Red, get, Jen, Wes, Ken, wet).*

Reread for Fluency

Have children reread Decodable Reader R5B to develop automaticity decoding words with the sounds /w/ spelled *w,* /k/ spelled *k,* /j/ spelled *j,* /r/ spelled *r* and /e/ spelled *e.*

 Oral Rereading

1. **Read** Have children read the entire book orally.
2. **Reread** To achieve optimal fluency, children should reread the text three or four times.
3. **Corrective Feedback** Listen as children read. Provide corrective feedback regarding their fluency and decoding.

Routines Flip Chart

English Language Learners
Review /w/, /k/, /j/, /r/, and /e/
Beginning
Before reading, explain that the word *fit* has more than one meaning. In this story, *fit* means healthy and strong. Act out some of the action words *(hop, jog, jig)* as you say them. Have children repeat them after you.

Intermediate
Walk through the story and identify the characters. Have children point out the proper names and say them aloud. Monitor children's pronunciation.

Advanced/Advanced High
After reading, have children tell how the characters in the story get fit and healthy. Ask children what other things they can do to get fit and healthy.

Objectives

- ○ Reread and review to monitor and clarify.
- • Recognize structure and elements of a photo essay.
- • Relate prior knowledge to new text.
- • Set purpose for reading.

Read Together

Social Studies in Reading

Preview and predict

Read the title and the first sentence of the selection. Have children look through the selection and predict what they might learn. (Possible response: They might learn how children get to school.) Ask them what clues helped them make that prediction. (They might say the title of the selection or the photographs.)

Genre

Photo Essay Tell children that they will read a **photo essay**. Review the key features of a photo essay: it uses photographs and words to give information or to entertain. The photographs help readers understand the words. Explain that this selection is a photo essay because it shows photographs of children going to school and has words about them.

Activate prior knowledge

Ask children to recall different ways that they can go to school. (They can go to school by train or car. They can also ride a bike or walk to school.) Ask them to recall other selections they have read or heard that tell something about ways in which children get to school. (Jason and Peter walk to school in "Early for School." Sam takes the bus in *School Day*. Henry takes the bus in *First Grade, Here I Come!*

Set a purpose for reading

Let's Read Together As children read, have them pay attention to clues that would indicate the different ways that children get to school.

Objectives
• Understand the reasons for different types of media with help from a teacher or a parent.

Social Studies in Reading

Genre
Photo Essay

• The words and photographs in a photo essay are about the same topic. The words tell and the photographs show.

• The photographs in a photo essay are usually very beautiful and memorable. The photographer wants you to feel as if you were there.

• Photographs help readers connect with real people, places, and events, even from different parts of the world.

• Read "How Do You Get to School?" Think about what you learned about photo essays.

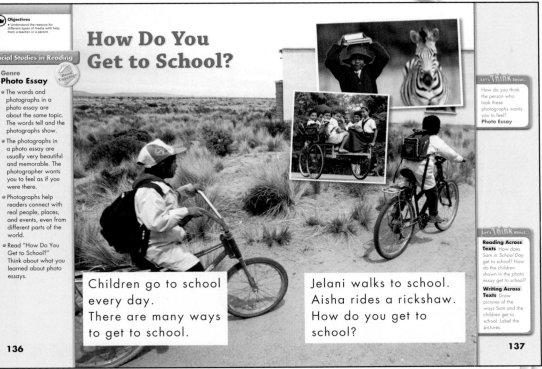

How Do You Get to School?

Let's THINK About...

How do you think the person who took these photographs wants you to feel?
Photo Essay

Let's THINK About...

Reading Across Texts How does Sam in *School Day* get to school? How do the children shown in the photo essay get to school?

Writing Across Texts Draw pictures of the ways Sam and the children get to school. Label the pictures.

Children go to school every day.
There are many ways to get to school.

Jelani walks to school.
Aisha rides a rickshaw.
How do you get to school?

136

137

Student Edition pp. 136–137

Guide Comprehension
Monitor and Clarify

Guide practice

Think Aloud

When I read "Aisha rides a rickshaw," I wasn't sure what a rickshaw was. I stopped and looked at the photographs to see if they helped. One picture shows a bike, so the other picture must show a rickshaw. It looks similar to a cart, but with someone in front riding a bike to pull it.

Let's Think About...

Photo Essays

Possible response: I think the photographer wants me to be interested in how other people go to school.

Reading Across Texts Have children compare Sam in *School Day* to the people in the photographs and explain how they each get to school.

Writing Across Texts Children should draw pictures of what they discussed above and label the transportation in each.

Academic Vocabulary

photo essay a kind of writing made up of photographs and words where the photographs help explain the words

Differentiated Instruction

A Advanced

Discuss "How Do You Get to School?" Have children recall the ways children get to school in the selection. Ask: Do you think it might be easier to walk or ride a bike to school in a large city? Explain. How do the details in the photographs help you decide this?

English Language Learners
Activate Prior Knowledge Talk about the ways in which each child gets to school. Encourage them to use the English words *walk, bus, car,* and *bike.* Make a chart of all the ways children get to school and note how many come by bus, by car, on their bikes, or on foot.

Objectives

- Ask questions
- Listen attentively.
- Use descriptive words
- Write using proper body position.

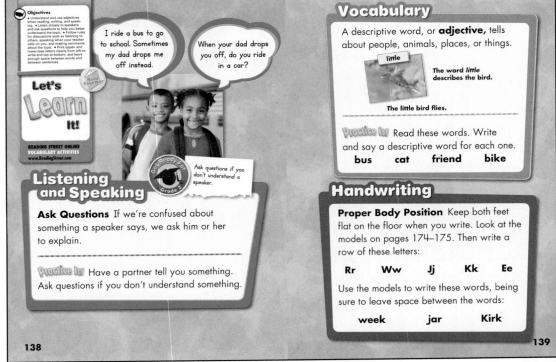

Student Edition pp. 138–139

Listening and Speaking
Ask Questions

Teach Have children turn to pages 138–139 of the Student Edition. Read and discuss what the children are doing. Remind children that good listeners ask questions to clarify things they do not understand.

Analyze model The children in the picture are having a discussion. The second child asks a question about something he doesn't understand. How will asking the question help him to understand? (The other child will answer his question.)

Introduce prompt Read the Practice It! prompt with the class. Have partners take turns talking about things they do for fun and asking one another questions.

Team Talk Have pairs take turns speaking about things they do for fun. The listener should ask questions to clarify information. Tell children that good listeners ask questions when they are confused about something the speaker said. Good speakers answer the questions to help the listeners understand what they mean.

Vocabulary
Use Descriptive Words

Teach

Read and discuss the Vocabulary lesson on page 139 of the Student Edition. Use the model to explain adjectives.

Model

Point to the photographs. What do you see in the picture? (a bird) What size is the bird? (little) The word *little* describes the bird.

Guide practice

Read the instructions for the Vocabulary Practice It! Activity. Have children study the words.

The first word is *bus.* What are some words that describe a bus? (Possible responses: big, yellow) *Big* and *yellow* are adjectives that describe a bus.

On their own

Have children continue assigning adjectives to the other nouns on the page.

Corrective feedback

Circulate around the room and listen as children choose adjectives. Provide assistance as needed.

Handwriting
Proper Body Position

Teach

Read and discuss the Handwriting instructions. Review proper body position.

Write letters

Give children a moment to look at the letter models. Then have them write a row for each of these letters: *Rr, Ww, Jj, Kk, Ee.* When children have finished, have them write the following words: *week, jar, Kirk.*

Differentiated Instruction

 Strategic Intervention
Visualize Skills Some children might find it helpful to see additional visual representations of the vocabulary skill, adjectives.

Ask Questions
Children at Grade 2 should be able to ask questions of others using a variety of question words. They should ask relevant questions that are easy to understand using words such as *when, how,* and *why.* Their questions should be specific enough that the speaker can easily answer them.

ELL

English Language Learners
Produce Language Have children practice using adjectives to describe animals they know of. Remind children that adjectives might describe the color, size, or shape of things.

Objectives
- Blend words with consonants *r* /r/, *w* /w/, *j* /j/, *k* /k/, and *short e*.
- Read high-frequency words.2

Assessment
Monitor Progress

For a written assessment of consonants *r* /r/, *w* /w/, *j* /j/, *k* /k/, short *e*, and high-frequency words, use Weekly Test R5, pp. 25–30.

Assess words in isolation

Word reading Use the following reproducible page to assess childrenís ability to read words in isolation. Call on children to read the words aloud. Start over if necessary.

Assess words in context

Sentence reading Use the following reproducible page to assess childrenís ability to read words in context. Call on children to read two sentences aloud. Start over with sentence one if necessary.

MONITOR PROGRESS **Word and Sentence Reading**

If ... children have trouble reading words with consonants *r* /r/, *w* /w/, *j* /j/, *k* /k/, and short *e*,

then ... use the Reteach Lesson on p. XX of *First Stop*.

If ... children cannot read all the high-frequency words,

then ... mark the missed words on a high-frequency word list and have the child practice reading the words with a fluent reader.

Success Predictor

Monitor accuracy

Record scores Use the Word/Sentence Reading Chart for this unit on p. 64 of *First Stop*.

Name _____

Read the Words

red	he
wet	Ken
is	three
Jeff	jet
to	with
pen	kit
jot	well

Read the Sentences

1. Jeff is with Ken.

2. Is he in the red jet?

3. Wet Jed is with him.

4. Three can hop to the red well.

MONITOR PROGRESS
• Consonants r /r/, w /w/, j /j/, k /k/
• Short e
• High-frequency words

School Day **139c**

Objectives
- Identify adjectives.
- Produce adjectives.
- Write complete sentences with vivid adjectives.
- Develop the concept: neighborhoods.

Conventions
Adjectives

Review adjectives

Suppose I want to draw a straight line. *Straight* is an adjective because it tells what kind of line. Draw a wavy line. What kind of line is this? (wavy) *Wavy* is an adjective because it tells about the line.

Guide practice

Have children find other classroom objects that they can describe with an adjective. Write the name of each object on the board. Write an adjective next to the object and have children use the pair in oral sentences.

Connect to oral language

Have the class complete these sentence frames orally using adjectives.

> I use the _____ eraser.
>
> You have the _____ pencil.

On their own

Put children in groups of three or four. Have them take turns saying sentences that name classroom objects and adjectives that describe them.

Writing—Sentences

Wrap up the weekly concept

Remind children that they have been talking about neighborhoods all week. Ask children to name adjectives that describe what is around them at school. Have them tell sentences that use the adjectives they named.

Model

I want to tell about my desk. It is smooth on top. *Smooth* is an adjective. I will write a sentence about my desk using the adjective *smooth*. Write the following sentence and read it aloud.

> I use my smooth desk.

Guide practice

Have children name adjectives that describe things around them at school. Then encourage them to tell a complete sentence, using the adjectives they provided. Work with children to write sentences on the board. You may suggest a sentence frame, such as *I am in a _____ classroom.*

On their own

Write the following sentence frame on the board and read it aloud.

> Sam hops on the _____ bus.

Instruct children to complete the sentence with a decodable word. If children are unable to write a decodable word, have them suggest the word and model writing it in the blank.

Wrap Up Your Week!

Question of the Week

What is around us at school?

Think Aloud This week we explored the topic of what is around us at school. In the story *School Day*, we read about something that goes wrong for a boy at school. In the story *First Grade, Here I Come!*, we read all about Henry's first day of first grade. And in "Early for School," we listened to a story about a boy who makes a new friend. All of these children had interesting experiences at school. **Have children recall their Amazing Ideas about school. Then have children use these ideas to help them demonstrate their understanding of the Question of the Week.**

Amazing Words

You've learned **0 0 9** words this week!

You've learned **0 3 9** words this year!

English Language Learners

Poster Preview Prepare children for next week by using Week 6, ELL Poster R6. Read the Poster Talk-Through to introduce the concept and vocabulary. Ask children to identify and describe objects and actions in the art.

Selection Summary Send home the summary of *The Farmers Market* in English and the child's home language if available. Children can read the summary with family members.

Preview NEXT WEEK

Tell children that next week they will read about the people and the things they see in their neighborhood.

Weekly Assessment

Use pp. 25–30 of *Weekly Tests* to check:

✔ ◎ **Phonics** *r/r/, w/w/, k/k/, e/e/*

✔ ◎ **Comprehension Skill** Plot

✔ **High-Frequency Words**

he	to
is	with
three	

Weekly Tests

Advanced

On-Level

Strategic Intervention

Differentiated Asssessment

Use pp. 25–30 of *Fresh Reads for Fluency and Comprehension* to check:

✔ ◎ **Comprehension Skill** Plot

✔ Review **Comprehension Skill** Realism and Fantasy

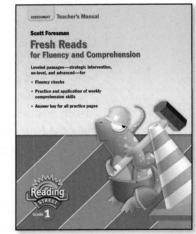

Fresh Reads for Fluency and Comprehension

Managing Assessment

Use *Assessment Handbook* for:

✔ **Weekly Assessment Blackline Masters for Monitoring Progress**

✔ **Observation Checklists**

✔ **Record-Keeping Forms**

✔ **Portfolio Assessment**

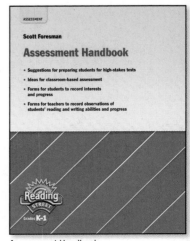

Assessment Handbook

The Best Pet

Pets are fun. Some kids have pets at home. Some kids have pets at school.

A fish can be a class pet. Fish must live in water. They do not need a bed. They just swim in a tank. They eat just a little. But you must feed fish. You must clean the fish tank. Can you get a fish from a tank? You must use a net. You must put a fish back fast. Fish must stay wet. Does your class have a fish tank?

Can a bug be a pet? Bugs can live in small jars. Your class may have ten bugs in a jar. But you cannot pet a bug. Can a pig be a pet? You can pet a pig. Pigs are big. A pig will not stay on a rug. It will run around the room. Most pigs live in a pen.

A skunk can make a bad smell. A duck likes a pond. A robin likes a nest. They will not be good class pets.

What pet is in your school? Is it a good class pet?

Advanced Selection R5   **Vocabulary:** tank, pen

Small **Group Time**

Pacing Small Group Instruction

20-30 min.

5 Day Plan

DAY 1	• Phonemic Awareness/ Phonics
DAY 2	• Phonemic Awareness/ Phonics
DAY 3	• Phonemic Awareness/ Phonics • Leveled Reader
DAY 4	• Phonemic Awareness/ Phonics • Decodable Reader
DAY 5	• High-Frequency Words • Decodable Reader

3 or 4 Day Plan

DAY 1	• Phonemic Awareness/ Phonics
DAY 2	• Phonemic Awareness/ Phonics
DAY 3	• Phonemic Awareness/ Phonics • Leveled Reader
DAY 4	• Phonemic Awareness/ Phonics • Decodable Reader

3 Day Plan: Eliminate the shaded box.

SI *Strategic Intervention*   **DAY 1**

Phonemic Awareness•Phonics

■ **Isolate Initial, Medial, and Final Phonemes** Reteach pp. 116–117 of the Teacher's Edition. Model isolating and matching initial, medial, and final /r/ in these words. Then have children practice isolating and matching /r/ on their own.

rag initial /r/	**far** final /r/	**scare** final /r/
sorry medial /r/	**rhyme** initial /r/	**worm** medial /r/

Then tell children that you are thinking of a word that begins with /r/. I'm thinking of something you can find on the ground. It's hard, and it can be big or small. You can also call it a *stone* It is a—. Have children fill in the word *rock*. Repeat with *rabbit* and *run*.

■ **Consonant *r* /r/** Reteach p. 117a of the Teacher's Edition. Then have children hold up a letter tile for *r* when you say a word that begins with *r*. Have them keep the letter tile down if the word does not begin with *r*.

• This word is *raft*. Does it begin with the letter *r*? (Yes)

• This word is *lamp*. Does it begin with the letter *r*? (No)

• This word is *wish*. Does it begin with the letter *r*? (No)

• This word is *ring*. Does it begin with the letter *r*? (Yes)

• This word is *rug*. Does it begin with the letter *r*? (Yes)

Repeat with words that end with the letter *r*. Use the following words: *for, star, shoe, hill, care, wire*. Then repeat with words that include medial *r*, using the words *carry, boring, ocean, parade, stuff*.

Objectives
• Isolate initial sounds in one-syllable spoken words.
• Isolate final sounds in one-syllable spoken words.

Phonemic Awareness•Phonics

■ **Isolate Initial Phonemes** Reteach p. 118d of the Teacher's Edition. Model isolating and matching initial /w/ and /j/ in these words. Then have children practice isolating and matching /w/ and /j/ on their own.

well initial /w/	**jet** initial /j/	**wave** initial /w/
Josh initial /j/	**job** initial /j/	**warm** initial /w/

Then tell children that you are thinking of a word that begins with /w/. I'm thinking of an important part of a bird. Birds flap them so they can fly. I am thinking of—. Have children fill in the word *wings*. Repeat with *wall*. Then repeat with initial /j/ and the words *jump* and *jelly*.

■ **Consonants *w* /w/ and *j* /j/** Reteach p. 118e of the Teacher's Edition. Then have children hold up a letter tile for *w* when you read a word that begins with *w*. Have them hold up a letter tile for *j* when you read a word that begins with *j*.

• This word is *just*. Does it begin with *w* or *j*? (j)

• This word is *joy*. Does it begin with *w* or *j*? (j)

• This word is *wind*. Does it begin with *w* or *j*? (w)

• This word is *jacket*. Does it begin with *w* or *j*? (j)

• This word is *walk*. Does it begin with *w* or *j*? (w)

• This word is *wake*. Does it begin with *w* or *j*? (w)

More Reading
Use text at the children's instructional level.

Objectives
• Isolate initial sounds in one-syllable spoken words.

 Strategic Intervention

Phonemic Awareness•Phonics

■ **Rhyme Words** Reteach p. 120d of the Teacher's Edition. Point out which pairs of words rhyme and which pairs do not. Remind children that rhyming words must have the same vowel sounds and final consonants, if any.

Continue the activity with the following examples. Say each pair of words aloud and ask children if they rhyme.

top, mop (yes)	**lot, box** (no)	**sock, lock** (yes)	**cot, cat** (no)
rock, sack (no)	**shop, stop** (yes)	**hot, held** (no)	**Mom, Tom** (yes)

■ ◉ **Consonant _k_ /k/** Reteach p. 120e of the Teacher's Edition. Then read the following words aloud: _king, kite, share, kept, some, tap, Kim._ Have children hold up a letter tile for _k_ if the word begins with consonant _k_. Have them keep their tiles down for words that begin with some other letter.

Concept Literacy Leveled Reader

■ **Preview and Predict** Read the title and author's name. Ask children to look at the cover and describe what they see. Help children activate prior knowledge by having them look through the story and use the pictures to predict things that might take place.

■ **Set a Purpose** Remind children that setting a purpose for reading can help them better understand what they read. Guide children to pay attention to what the story tells about the narrator's school.

■ **Read** Provide corrective feedback as children read the story orally. Point out that they can use the pictures to help them with unfamiliar words. During reading, ask them if they were able to confirm any of the predictions they made prior to the story.

If... children have difficulty reading the story individually,
then... read a sentence aloud as children point to each word. Then have the group reread the sentences as they continue pointing. Continue reading in this way until children read individually.

■ **Retell** Have children take turns retelling the story. Help them identify things that are in the school by asking, What does page _____ tell us about?

Concept Literacy

SI *Strategic Intervention*   DAY 4

More Reading
Use text at the children's instructional level.

Phonemic Awareness•Phonics

■ **Blend and Segment Phonemes** Reteach p. 120p of the Teacher's Edition. Model blending and segmenting the phonemes in these words.

Continue the activity with the following examples.

Blend /w/ /e/ /l/   **Blend /j/ /e/ /t/**   **Segment** *Jess* **Segment** kept

■ 🔊 **Short Vowel** *e* Reteach p. 120q of the Teacher's Edition. Then read the following words aloud: *net, cup, west, bed, send, then, pat, Nick, step*. Have children hold up a letter card *e* for words that include short vowel *e*. Have them keep their cards down for words that include some other vowel sound.

Decodable Practice Reader R5A

■ **Review** Use the word lists to review short vowel *e* and the high-frequency words *the, do, you*, and *see*. Review the process of blending, using the words *wet* and *Red*. Have children read the story together, pointing to the words as they speak them.

> **If…** children have difficulty reading the story individually,
> **then…** read a sentence aloud as children point to each word. Then have the group reread the sentences as they continue pointing. Continue reading in this way until children read individually.

Check comprehension by having children retell the events of the story in order. Then have children locate words in the story that end with the following letter combinations: *-et, -ell, -en, -ed*. List the words children identify and write them in a chart on the board. Then have children read the words in isolation.

We Met Meg
Written by Desirée Moody

Decodable Reader R5A

-et	-ell	-en	-ed
Jet	fell	pen	led
wet	Nell	hen	red
net	well		fed
met			
let			
get			

Objectives
• Isolate medial sounds in one-syllable spoken words.

Small Group Time

More Reading

Use text at the children's instructional level.

SI *Strategic Intervention*

High-Frequency Words

■ **Review** Write *is, he, three, with, to* on the board. Model saying each word. Then have children read each word, spell each word as you point to each letter, and have them say each word again. Allow time for children to practice reading these high-frequency words using the word cards.

Decodable Practice Reader R5B

■ **Review** Use the word lists to review the sounds /r/, /w/, /j/, /k/, and /e/, the letters *r, w, j, k,* and *e,* and the high-frequency words *with, do, is, a, the,* and *we.* Then have children read the story chorally, pointing to the words as the speak them.

> **If...** children have difficulty reading the story individually,
> **then...** read a sentence aloud as children point to each word. Then have the group reread the sentences as they continue pointing. Continue reading in this way until children read individually.

Check comprehension by having children describe some of the ways that the children in the story get fit. Then have children locate words in the story that begin with consonants *r, w, j,* or *k.* List the words children identify. Then help children classify the words according to the letters they contain.

Decodable Reader R5B

r	*w*	*j*	*k*
Rob	will	jog	kit
Red	Wes	Jen	Ken
rim	wet	jig	
sat			

Objectives
- Decode words in context by applying common letter-sound correspondences, including: single letters (vowels) including short e.
- Read at least 100 high-frequency words from a commonly used list.

OL On-Level **DAY 1**

Phonemic Awareness•Phonics

■ **Isolate Initial, Medial, and Final Phonemes** Say the words below and have children repeat them with you. Then have children generate other words that begin with the sound /r/.

rug	room	rocks	rope

Repeat with words that end with /r/. Use *far*, *sure*, and *stair* as examples. Then continue with words with /r/ in the middle, such as *sharing*, *hurry*, and *very*.

■ ⊙ **Consonant r /r/** Remind children that the sound /r/ goes with the letter *r*. Have children identify whether the *r* is at the beginning, middle, or end of these words: *store, bear, rip, forest, right, berry*.

Objectives
• Isolate initial sounds in one-syllable spoken words.
• Isolate final sounds in one-syllable spoken words.

Pacing Small Group Instruction 20-30 min.

5 Day Plan

DAY 1	• Phonemic Awareness • Phonics
DAY 2	• Phonics • High-Frequency Words
DAY 3	• Leveled Reader
DAY 4	• Conventions • Decodable Reader
DAY 5	• Phonics • Decodable Reader

OL On-Level **DAY 2**

Phonics•High-Frequency Words

■ ⊙ **Consonants w /w/ and j /j/** Read the following words aloud. Have children identify whether the words begin with *w* or *j*.

well	Jane	joke	want
juggle	waving	jumped	we

Then write some of the words on the board. Have children come to the board and circle the *w* or the *j*.

■ **High-Frequency Words** Hold up this week's High-Frequency Word Cards and review proper pronunciation. Continue holding the cards and have children chorally read each word. To help children demonstrate their understanding of the words, provide them with oral sentence frames such as: Goldilocks met _____ bears. (Three)

Objectives
• Isolate initial sounds in one-syllable spoken words.
• Read at least 100 high-frequency words from a commonly used list.

---

3 or 4 Day Plan

DAY 1	• Phonemic Awareness • Phonics
DAY 2	• Phonics • High-Frequency Words
DAY 3	• Leveled Reader
DAY 4	• Conventions • Decodable Reader

3 Day Plan: Eliminate the shaded box.

OL On-Level

DAY **3**

Concept Literacy Leveled Reader

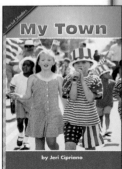

Concept Literacy

■ **Preview and Predict** Read the title and the author's name. Have children look at the cover and ask them to describe in detail what they see. Help children preview the story by asking them to look through the story and to use the photos to predict things that might take place.

■ ⊚ **Realism and Fantasy** Before reading the story, review with children the difference between realism and fantasy. Then have children predict by looking at the pictures whether the story will be realistic or a fantasy. Have them check their predictions as they read the story.

• **Read** During reading, monitor children's comprehension by providing higher-order thinking questions. Ask:

• How is the school in the story like our school?

• How is the school in the story different from our school?

To help children gain a better understanding of the text, build upon their responses with a group discussion.

■ ⊚ **Monitor and Clarify** Remind children that good readers always monitor their reading by making sure they understand the information in the story and by asking if what they are reading makes sense. Remind children that they can reread parts of the story or use picture clues to help them. Ask:

• Does it make sense to have a picture of a school bus in a book about a school?

• Where do you think the children pictured on page 4 are going? How do you know?

■ **Text to Self** Help children connect the story to their own experiences. Ask:

• Would you like to go to the school in the picture? Why or why not?

Objectives
• Ask relevant questions about stories.
• Monitor comprehension, making corrections when that understanding breaks down.

 OL On-Level · DAY **4**

Conventions•Decodable Practice Reader

■ **Adjectives** Have children use the sentence frame *I saw a _____* to name an animal, such as a dog, bird, or frog. Then have them repeat the sentence, this time inserting an adjective, such as *I saw a big dog/ red bird/wet frog.*

■ **Decodable Practice Reader R5A** Review words with short vowel *e* and the high-frequency words *the, do, you,* and *see.* Then have children blend and read these words from the story: *Jet, well, red.* Be sure that children understand that many capitalized words in the story, such as *Jet,* are the names of farm animals or people. Have children reread the text orally. To achieve optimal fluency, children should reread the text three or four times.

Decodable Practice Reader R5A

More Reading

Use text at the children's instructional level.

Objectives
• Understand and use descriptive adjectives in the context of reading, writing, and speaking.

OL On-Level · DAY **5**

Phonics Review•Decodable Practice Reader

■  **Consonants *r* /r/, *w* /w/, *j* /j/, *k* /k/ and Short Vowel *e*** Have children practice blending and reading words that contain this week's target phonics skills:

red	jet	well	Ken	Jim	kit
wet	ram	will	ten		

Have children identify the words that have the /r/, /w/, /j/, /k/, or /e/ sounds.

■ **Decodable Practice Reader R5B** Review words with *r, w, j, k,* and *e* and the high-frequency words listed in the front. Have children blend and read these words from the story: *Ken, wet, Red, Jen.* Have children reread the text orally. To achieve optimal fluency, children should reread the text three or four times.

Decodable Practice Reader R5B

Objectives
• Decode words in context by applying common letter-sound correspondences, including: single letters (vowels), including short e.

Small Group Time

Pacing Small Group Instruction

20-30 min.

3 Day Plan: Eliminate the shaded box.

A — Advanced — DAY 1

Phonics

■ ◉ **Consonant r /r/** Have children practice with longer words containing consonant r. Read aloud the following words. Have children say *beginning*, *middle*, or *end* to indicate where in the word the letter r would go.

center	rhythm	Carol	forest	boring
summer	relatives	conductor	rosebushes	rockets

Write some of the words on the board. Have children come to the board one by one to circle the letter r.

Objectives
• Isolate initial sounds in one-syllable spoken words.
• Isolate final sounds in one-syllable spoken words.

A — Advanced — DAY 2

Phonics • Comprehension

■ ◉ **Consonants w /w/ and j /j/** Have children spell the word *bill* with letter tiles. Then have children make changes.

• Change the *b* in bill to w. What word did you spell? (will)

• Change the *ll* in will to g. What word did you spell? (wig)

• What letter would you change to turn *wig* into *jig*? (w to j)

• What letter would you change to turn *jig* into *jog*? (i to o)

• **Comprehension** Reread this week's Read Aloud, "Early for School," with children. Remind children that the plot of a story is the problem and the solution the characters find to the problem. Have children identify the problem in the story and describe how Jason and Peter solve the problem.

Early for School

Objectives
• Isolate initial sounds in one-syllable spoken words.
• Describe the plot (problem and solution).

 A Advanced | DAY **3**

Concept Literacy Leveled Reader

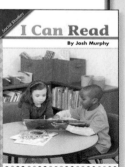

Concept Literacy

More Reading
Use text at the children's instructional level.

■ **Activate Prior Knowledge** Read the title and the author's name. Have children look at the cover and describe in detail what they see. Ask them to picture your school and classroom in their minds as they read the story. Instruct them to focus on how the school in the photographs is like their own school and how the two schools are different.

■ 🔊 **Realism and Fantasy** Before reading, have children tell a partner about the meanings of the terms realism and fantasy. Have children give examples of stories they know that are realistic and stories that are fantasies. Have children predict whether the story *My School* will be realism or fantasy, and have them explain how they will know if their predictions are correct.

• **Read** During reading, monitor children's comprehension by providing higher-order thinking questions. Ask:

• Would you like to attend the school in the picture? Why or why not?

• If you made a picture book about your own school, what would you show in the pictures? Why?

Build on children's answers to help them gain a better understanding of the text.

■ 🔊 **Monitor and Clarify** Remind children that they will be better readers if they are constantly checking to make sure the story makes sense. Explain that they can use words and pictures to help them check. Ask the following questions to guide their thinking.

• Name some of the objects in the pictures. Are they things you would expect to find in a school? Are there any objects you would not expect to find?

• What do you the class is doing on page 8? Explain your answer.

■ **Text to World** Help children connect the story to the experiences of people around them. Ask:

• How might schools in other places be different from the school in the book? How might schools in other places be different from our school?

Objectives
• Ask relevant questions about stories.

Small Group Time

More Reading

Use text at children's instructional level.

A Advanced **DAY 4**

Comprehension

- **Comprehension** Have children silently read this week's main selection, *School Day*. Have them retell the story to a partner. Ask them to describe the characters and the setting. Then have them summarize what they think is the most important idea in the story.

  Talk about whether *School Day* is fiction or nonfiction. Ensure that children understand that the story is fiction, because it is a made-up story that comes out of the author's imagination.

- **Text to Text** Have children compare the school in *School Day* to the school pictured in the concept literacy reader *My School*.

School Day

Objectives
- Describe characters in a story.
- Identify important details in text, heard or read.

A Advanced **DAY 5**

Comprehension

- **Comprehension** After they have finished reading the selection, have children review the story by repeating some of the information the text gives about pets. Then, on the back of the selection page, have them write three sentences indicating what kind of pet they would choose for the classroom and explaining why.

Advanced Selection R5

Objectives
- Read aloud grade-level appropriate text with fluency and comprehension.
- Write brief compositions about topics of interest to the student.

Concept Development

What is around us at school?

- **Activate Prior Knowledge** Write the question of the week and read it aloud. Underline the word *school* and have children say it with you. You are at school right now. What are some of the things you do at school? Have children name activities they do at school and in their classroom.

- **Connect to New Concept** Have children turn to pages 114–115 in the Student Edition. Read the title aloud and have children track the print as you read it. Point to the pictures one at a time and use them to guide a discussion about what is around us at school. For example, point to children making an art project. What are these children doing? (making an art project) These children are making an art project. Their teacher is helping them. Emphasize the English vocabulary routinely used in the classroom. Have children use the word school in a sentence about something that happens in your school day.

- **Develop Concepts** Display ELL Poster R5 and have children identify the setting of the poster. (school) What things do you see at this school? Have children point to things at the school on the poster. (flag, playground, buses, classroom) Use the leveled prompts below to assess understanding and build oral language. Point to pictures on the poster as you guide discussion.

Beginning Ask yes/no questions, such as Do teachers watch the children outside? Does a boy hold open a door?

Intermediate Ask children questions that can be answered with simple sentences. What games are the children playing? What do the children learn in the classroom? How many buses are parked outside?

Advanced/High Advanced Have children answer the Question of the Week by giving specific examples from the poster and their own experiences at school.

Review Concepts and Connect to Writing Review children's understanding of the concept at the end of the week. Ask them to write in response to these questions: What types of things do you see at school each day? What English words did you learn this week? Write and display key ideas from the discussion.

Objectives
- Use prior knowledge and experiences to understand meanings in English.
- Internalize new basic and academic language by using and reusing it in meaningful ways in speaking and writing activities that build concept and language attainment.

Content Objective
- Describe what is around us at school.
- Use English vocabulary routinely used in the classroom.

Language Objective
- Share information orally.
- Use basic vocabulary for describing what is around us at school.

Daily Planner
The ELL lessons are organized by strands. Use them to scaffold the weekly lesson curriculum or during small-group time.

Daily Lesson Planner

DAY 1	• Concepts and Oral Vocabulary • Listening (Read Aloud) • Match Initial And Final Phonemes • Consonant *r* /r/
DAY 2	• Concepts • High-Frequency Words • Consonant *w* /w/; Consonant *j* /j/
DAY 3	• Concepts • Story Words • Plot • Read *School Day*
DAY 4	• Concepts • Story Words • ELL/ELD Readers
DAY 5	• Concepts • Story Words • Use Vivid Word for Understanding • Revising

Language Objectives

- Match initial and final phonemes.
- Recognize consonant *r* /r/.
- Sound out words.

Transfer Skills

Consonants The English /r/ causes difficulty to speakers of many languages, and they tend to substitute a sound that is similar to one in their home language. For example, Arabic-speaking children substitute a stressed or a rolled /r/.

ELL Teaching Routine

For more practice with consonants use the Sound-by-Sound Blending Routine (*ELL Handbook*, p. 496).

ELL *English Language Learners*

Phonemic Awareness: Match Initial and Final Phonemes

■ **Preteach Initial and Final Phonemes**

- Have children open to pp. 116–117. Say the word *run* as you point to the children running. Emphasize the beginning /r/ sound. Pronounce /r/.
- Write the letters *Rr* on the board. Tell children /r/ is spelled with a *r* or a *R*. Write the word *race* on the board and ask children what sound they hear at the beginning (/r/) and what letter spells that sound (r). Repeat with *rake*.
- Model producing /w/, and have children repeat the sound. Write the letters *W* and *w* on the board. Point to each, and have children name the letter with you. Then say the word *worm* as you point the worm on the p. 117, Have children repeat the word. Remind them that *worm* begins with the letter *w*. Repeat the process for *jump*. Emphasize the skills that you are using to decode, or sound out, the words.

■ **Practice** Tell children that you will write and say a word. If the word has the /r/ sound at the beginning, they are to growl like a lion, grrr. Use these words: *red*, *pat*, *rim*, *mop*. Have children say *win* as a child writes *w* on the board and others write the letter in the air. Continue with *wet, sun, top, well, box, went*. For each word that begins with /w/, have children write the letter *w*. Then continue for the /j/ sound with the words *jam, cake, jar, June, mat, sit*.

Phonics: Consonant *r* /r/

■ **Preteach** Display Sound-Spelling Card 20. This is a rocket. What sound do you hear at the beginning of *rocket*? (/r/) Say it with me: /r/. Point to *r*. The /r/ sound is spelled using *r* or sometimes *R*. Write the word *red* and read it aloud. Ask children what sound they hear at the beginning of *red* (/r/) and what letter spells that sound (r). Repeat with *rag*. Review the letters *Oo, Ll, Hh* and their corresponding sounds using the words *ocean, land*, and *hat*.

■ **Listen and Write** Distribute Write and Wipe Boards.

- Write the word *rabbit* on the board. Copy this word. As you write *r*, say the sound to yourself. /r/. Now say the sound aloud. (/r/) Underline *r* in *rabbit*. The letter *r* spells /r/ in *rabbit*.

Objectives

- Recognize elements of the English sound system in newly acquired vocabulary such as long and short vowels, silent letters, and consonant clusters.

 English Language Learners

■ **Reteach and Practice**

- Write the following words on the board and have children read them aloud with you: *rug, rag, run, ran, rest, robin*. Segment and blend each word with children. Point out the beginning /r/ sound in each word.

- Leave the words on the board, but erase the letter *r* and replace it with a blank. Have children fill in the missing *r*.

 Leveled Support

Beginning Have children read the word aloud. Monitor for accurate pronunciation. Ask them to repeat the /r/ sound.

Intermediate Have children read the word aloud. Monitor for accurate pronunciation. Ask them to the say the consonant sound spelled by *r*.

Advanced/High Advanced Have children read the word aloud and name another word with the same beginning /r/ sound.

Phonics: Consonant *w* /w/, *j* /j/

■ **Preteach** Have children turn to Envision It! on page 118 of the Student Edition.

- The word for the second picture is *waterfall*. Use your fingers to mimic water falling. What sound do you hear at the beginning of *waterfall*? (/w/) Say it with me: /w/. The word for the third picture is *jacket*. Act out putting on a jacket. What sound do you hear at the beginning of *jacket*? (/j/) Say it with me: /j/. Review the letters *Rr*, *Oo*, *Hh* and their corresponding sounds using the words *rabbit, open,* and *hot*.

■ **Preteach** Distribute Letter Tiles *j, w, a, m, i, n,* and *l* to pairs. Give each pairs two *l* Letter Tiles.

- Blend the sounds in *jam* and have pairs spell *jam* with their tiles: /j/ /a/ /m/, jam.

- Blend the sounds in *win* and have pairs spell *win* with their tiles: /w/ /i/ /n/, win.

- Replace the *n* with *w*. Spell *will*.

Language Objectives

- Associate the sound /r/ with the consonant letter *r*.

- Read and spell words with the consonant sounds /w/ and /j/.

Catch Up The consonant letter *w* is pronounced by pursing the lips together.

 Transfer Skills

Consonant Sounds Spanish speakers may have difficulty pronouncing and perceiving the sounds /j/, /r/, /v/, /w/, and /z/. Vietnamese and Cantonese speakers may have difficulty pronouncing and perceiving the /j/ sound. Haitian-Creole speakers may have difficulty pronouncing and perceiving the English sound /r/. Provide modeling with attention to children's production and remediation of these sounds.

Practice Page

*ELL Handbook pages 255–256 provides additional practice for this week's skill.

Objectives
- Recognize elements of the English sound system in newly acquired vocabulary such as long and short vowels, silent letters, and consonant clusters.

Content Objectives

- Monitor and adjust oral comprehension.

Language Objectives

- Discuss oral passages.
- Use a graphic organizer to take notes.

ELL Teacher Tip

To help children identify what happens at the beginning, middle, and end of a story, divide the Read Aloud into sections and have children discuss what happens in each section.

ELL English Language Learners

Listening Comprehension

A New Friend

Jason was late to school a lot. Today, he was almost late because he took his time at breakfast. He ran to school very fast. He walked into his classroom quietly. He sat down.

His teacher told Jason about Peter. Peter was a new student. Peter lived near Jason. His teacher told Peter and Jason to walk home together.

Jason helped Peter for the rest of the day. He showed him where to find things. They played together on the playground.

After school, they walked home together. They talked a lot. They liked each other. They agreed to leave early the next day so they could talk some more. Jason was early to school the next day!

Prepare for the Read Aloud The modified Read Aloud above prepares children for listening to the oral reading "Early for School" on page 117E.

■ **First Listening: Listen to Understand**

1. Write the title of the Read Aloud on the board. This story is about a boy who is often late for school. He meets a new friend. What happens in the story?

2. After reading, ask children to discuss what happens at the end of the story.

■ **Second Listening: Listen to Check Understanding** Using a Story Map graphic organizer (*ELL Handbook*, page 506), work with children to identify what happened at the beginning, middle, and end of the story. Review the completed maps together as a class.

Objectives

- Understand the general meaning, main points, and important details of spoken language ranging from situations in which topics, language, and contexts are familiar to unfamiliar.
- Demonstrate listening comprehension of increasingly complex spoken English by following directions, retelling or summarizing spoken messages, and taking notes commensurate with content and grade-level needs.

 English Language Learners

High-Frequency Words

■ **Preteach** Use the Poster Talk-Through on ELL Poster R5 to preteach this week's high-frequency words: *is, he, three, with, to*. Display the words and read each one slowly and clearly aloud as you track the print. Have children repeat each word with you. Monitor children's pronunciation. Provide daily practice using the activities on the poster.

■ **Practice** Teach children the following song, to the tune of "Row, Row, Row Your Boat," to practice this week's high-frequency words. Distribute a Word Card to each child. As you sing the song with children, point to one child at a time to supply that child's word. Have the child show the card and read the word aloud. *Say, Say, Say new words, Say them every day. My word is _____, and it is new, I learned a new word today.*

■ **Speaking/Writing with High-Frequency Words**

• **Teach/Model** Review high-frequency words. Give each child a set of Word Cards. Model drawing a picture to illustrate one high-frequency word and then speaking about the drawing.

• **Practice** Have children illustrate each high-frequency word. Then have children describe their drawings, speaking using the content-area vocabulary. Correct any misconceptions. After reteaching, have children label their drawings.

 Leveled LS Support

Beginning/Intermediate Have children illustrate each high-frequency word. Then have children describe each picture to a partner.

Advanced/High Advanced Have children illustrate each high-frequency word. Have children label their drawings and describe each picture to a partner.

Language Objectives

• Understand and use basic vocabulary.

• Understand and read high-frequency words.

• Understand the general meaning of spoken language.

• Speak using content-area vocabulary.

Beginners Support

Have children listen to the following sentence: There are three children playing. Repeat the sentence several times as children clap their hands when they hear the word *three*. Repeat the activity using the remaining high-frequency and concept words.

Mini-Lesson: Listening

Ask children to listen as you read the paired reading selection on p. 121 of the Student Edition. To be sure they understand both the general meaning and the context of the passage, ask What can you tell me about Ken? "Getting in a jam" means getting in trouble. Why might Ken get in a jam?

Objectives
• Use strategic learning techniques such as concept mapping, drawing, memorizing, comparing, contrasting, and reviewing to acquire basic and grade-level vocabulary.
• Understand the general meaning, main points, and important details of spoken language ranging from situations in which topics, language, and contexts are familiar to unfamiliar.

Content Objectives
- Identify the plot of a story.

Language Objectives
- Describe the plot of a story by including what happens at the beginning, middle, and end.

ELL — English Language Learners

Guide Comprehension
Plot

■ **Preteach** The plot of a story is what happens in the beginning, middle, and end. The events that happen in a story are part of the plot. Most stories have a problem. The problem is usually solved by the end of the story.

Practice Have children turn to Envision It! on pages El•4 and El•5 in the Student Edition. Point to the pictures on both pages. Let's name what happens to the bunnies on the page. Have children respond to questions about the story. Who wakes up in the beginning? Who stays asleep? How does the bunny family wake up Brother?

• **Reteach** Distribute copies of the Picture It! (*ELL Handbook*, p. 54). Have children look at the images. Remind them that they should pay attention to the events that happen in the story. Read the story to the children. Ask the children to use the pictures to tell the key events. (**Answers:** Sister gets in the pool. Dad gets in the pool. Mom gets in the pool, and it breaks.)

Beginning Read the passage to the children. Ask them to listen for the events as you read. Then reread each paragraph with the children, as they follow along. After each paragraph, have the children retell what happened in their own words. Write their retellings on the board. Then, have the children choral read the sentence with you.

Intermediate/Advanced/High Advanced Read the passage to the children. Ask them to think about the main events. Have children retell the story to a partner, using the pictures if needed. Then, draw three boxes on the board. Have the children tell the three main events in the story. Record their responses in the boxes.

MINI-LESSON

Survival Vocabulary

Talk about the word *house* and have children point out house-related items on the Envision It! pages. Have children seek clarification of words as needed.

Objectives
- Use accessible language and learn new and essential language in the process.
- Express opinions, ideas, and feelings ranging from communicating single words and short phrases to participating in extended discussions on a variety of social and grade-appropriate academic topics.

Reading Comprehension
School Day

■ **Frontloading**

- **Background Knowledge** Read aloud the title and discuss it. Point to the school bus. This is a school bus. Some children ride to school on a school bus. How do you get to school each day?

- **Preview** Guide children on a picture walk through the story, asking them to identify people, places, and actions. Reteach these words using visuals in the Student Edition: *grab* (page 125), *ran* (page 126), *jet* (page 128), and *drop* (page 129). Turn to p. 124 in the Student Edition to emphasize directionality. When I read, I start at the top and the left. I read across the line. Then I start on the next line and read across. Have children track the print as you model tracking and read aloud. Then have them track the print on another page on their own.

- **Predict** Why is Sam sad?

Sheltered Reading Ask questions such as the following to guide children's comprehension:

- p. 124: Point to Sam. Who is still in bed?

- p. 126: Point to the bus. Why is Sam running fast?

- p. 128: Point to Pat. What did Pat do?

- p. 129: Point to Fred. What did Fred do?

After Reading Help children summarize the text with the Retelling Cards. Ask questions that prompt children to summarize the important parts of the text. Record their retelling points in a graphic organizer with Beginning, Middle, and End. You might also lead a discussion about directionality in print. Turn to page 124, for example. Have children describe how to track the print on the page (from top to bottom and left to right). They can demonstrate by using their fingers to track.

Content Objectives
- Monitor and adjust comprehension.
- Make and adjust predictions.
- Recognize directionality in the selection.

Language Objectives
- Summarize text using visual support.

Graphic Organizer
Beginning _____
Middle _____
End _____

Audio Support
Children can prepare for reading *School Day* by using the main selection eText online or the Audio Text CD. See the Audio Text CD Routine (*ELL Handbook*, page 500) for suggestions on using these learning tools.

Objectives
- Understand the general meaning, main points, and important details of spoken language ranging from situations in which topics, language, and contexts are familiar to unfamiliar. 4.B Recognize directionality of English reading such as left to right and top to bottom.

Support for English Language Learners

ELL English Language Learners

Comprehension:
At School

ELL/ELD Reader 1.U.5

- **Before Reading** Distribute copies of the ELL and ELD Readers, *At School*, to children at their reading level.

  - **Preview** Read the title aloud with children and allow for them to look through the pages. This is a story about what we do at school. Activate prior knowledge. The story in our book was also about what we do at school. What can we do at school? What do you like to do at school?

  - **Set a Purpose for Reading** Let's read to find out what these children do at school.

- **During Reading** Follow this Reading Routine for both reading groups.

1. Read the entire Reader aloud slowly as children follow along and finger point.

2. Reread the Reader one sentence at a time, having children echo read after you.

- **After Reading** Use the exercises on the inside back cover of *At School* and invite children to share drawings and writing. In a whole-group discussion, ask children to list the things the children do at school. Encourage them to compare the list with the activities they do at school.

ELD Reader

- **p. 3** Point to the lockers. Do coats go here? (yes)

- **p. 7** Point to the child. Is this class listening to the teacher read? (no)

Writing Draw a picture of something the children do at school. Label your picture. Ask children to work in pairs and share their picture with the whole class. Have them compare the differences in their pictures and tell the different activities children do at school.

ELL Reader

- **p. 3** What do children do with their coats? (Put them away.)

- **p. 8** Point to the bus. How do the children get home? (They take the bus.)

Study Guide Distribute copies of the ELL Reader Study Guide (*ELL Handbook*, page 58). Scaffold comprehension by talking about things that happen at your school. Review their responses together. (**Answers** See *ELL Handbook*, pp. 245–248.)

Objectives
- Understand the general meaning, main points, and important details of spoken language ranging from situations in which topics, language, and contexts are familiar to unfamiliar.

Conventions
Adjectives

■ **Preteach** Show a blue crayon. This is a blue crayon. Point to other items in the classroom and have children describe each item after you. Make a list on the board of items as they are named. Add adjectives to describe each noun. A word that describes something is an adjective. Ask children to name words that describe your school.

■ **Practice**

Beginning /Intermediate Write the following sentence frame on the board: *I see the _____ book.* Have one child point to a book in the room, describe the book, and write or dictate the adjective. Have other children repeat the sentence.

Advanced/Advanced High Using the sentence frame, have children write an adjective to complete the sentence and draw a picture of it. Then have them read the sentence to the group.

■ **Reteach**

• Remind children that an adjective is a word that describes something. Write *I see a yellow bus.* Point to the word *yellow*. The adjective in this sentence is *yellow*. The word *yellow* describes the bus.

Beginning /Intermediate Write the following sentence frame on the board: *I have a _____ _____.* Have children draw something they play with at home. Read the sentence frame, and have children write or dictate a noun and an adjective to complete the sentence.

Advanced/Advanced High Have children copy the sentence frame. Have them think of something they play with and then write the word and the adjective that describes it to complete the sentence. Have them read their sentences aloud.

Content Objectives
• Identify and use adjectives.

Language Objectives
• Use adjectives to describe objects.

• Write sentences with adjectives.

• Monitor written language production.

Transfer Skills

Adjectives In Spanish, Vietnamese, Hmong, and Haitian Creole, adjectives usually follow the noun. Point out that in English, the adjective usually comes before the noun. Provide practice with phrases and sentences containing adjectives that follow the noun.

Grammar Jammers

For more practice with adjectives, use the Grammar Jammers for this target skill. See the Grammar Jammers Routine (*ELL Handbook*, page 501) for suggestions on using this learning tool.

Objectives
• Speak using a variety of grammatical structures, sentence lengths, sentence types, and connecting words with increasing accuracy and ease as more English is acquired.

Support for English Language Learners

ELL — English Language Learners

Write Sentences with Adjectives

■ **Introduce Terms** Write *adjective* on the board. Remind children that an adjective is a word gives more information about a noun. Write and read the following phrases: *blue sky, brown shoes, green tree, red heart, yellow sun*. Have children repeat the phrases after you. Then ask the children questions about the phrases such as What color is the sky? (blue) How would you describe the tree? (green) Then have children brainstorm a list of other colors and describe items in the classroom.

■ **Introduce Sentences with Adjectives** Put four or five objects in front of the classroom, such as a book, globe, piece of chalk, and box. Ask questions that require children to identify objects by shape and color. Which one is blue? Which one is round? Write children's responses in the form of sentences. *The round ball is blue.*

■ **Model** Draw a two-column chart on the board. Label the columns *Adjective* and *Object*. Engage children in naming adjectives that describe the color and shape of objects in the classroom

Adjective	Object
yellow	*pencil*

■ **Write** Have children copy this sentence frame: *The _____ _____ is _____.* Have them use words from both columns to fill in the blanks. Use the Student Edition to provide a visual cue. Turn to p. 126 and elicit children's ideas about the bus. Ask questions to encourage children to describe with increasing specificity: What size is the bus? What color is the bus? At what speed does the bus go?

LS — Leveled Support

Beginning/Intermediate Ask children to choose two or more objects in the classroom to describe by writing or dictating the shape and color. Provide the frames: *The paper is _____. The shape is a _____.*

Advanced/Advanced High Have children write sentences about two or three objects in the classroom, describing them by shape and color.

Content Objectives
- Identify adjectives that describe.

Language Objectives
- Write sentences with adjectives.
- Employ self-corrective techniques for editing and revising.
- Describe with increasing specificity and detail.

Objectives
- Monitor oral and written language production and employ self-corrective techniques or other resources.
- Narrate, describe, and explain with increasing specificity and detail as more English is acquired. **5.B** Write using newly acquired basic vocabulary and content-based grade-level vocabulary.

This Week's ELL Overview

ELL Handbook

- Maximize Literacy and Cognitive Engagement
- Research Into Practice
- Full Weekly Support for Every Selection

Farmers Market
- Multi-Lingual Summaries in Five Languages
- Selection-Specific Vocabulary Word Cards
- Frontloading/Reteaching for Comprehension Skill Lessons
- ELD and ELL Reader Study Guides

- Transfer Activities
- Professional Development

Daily Leveled ELL Notes

ELL notes appear throughout this week's instruction and ELL Support is on the DI pages of your Teacher's Edition. The following is a sample of an ELL note from this week.

English Language Learners

Beginning Before reading, identify Quin and Bev for children. After reading, lead children on a picture walk through *The Quiz.* Have children tell what Quin is doing in each picture, using the sentence frame: *Quin is _____.*

Intermediate After reading, have children answer the following questions with complete sentences: *What are Quin and Bev going to do? When do Quin and Bev quit? How do you know that Quin and Bev did well on the quiz?*

Advanced After reading, have children point to all the words with the sound /kw/ (*Quin, quit, quiz*). Ask them to make up a few sentences using those words. Monitor children's pronunciation.

Advanced High After reading, make a T-chart on the board and label it *Words with qu-.* Invite children to help make a class list of words that have the sound /kw/. Then have children make up a sentence using as many *qu-* words as possible.

ELL by Strand

The ELL lessons on this week's Support for English Language Learners pages are organized by strand. They offer additional scaffolding for the core curriculum. Leveled support notes on these pages address the different proficiency levels in your class. See pages DI•117–DI•126.

ELL Guy
Dr. Jim Cummins

The Three Pillars of ELL Instruction

ELL Strands	Activate Prior Knowledge	Access Content	Extend Language
Vocabulary p. DI•121	Preteach	Teach/Model	Practice
Reading Comprehension p. DI•122	Preteach	Reteach	Leveled Practice Activities
Phonics, Spelling, and Word Analysis pp. DI•118–DI•119	Preteach	Listen and Write	Leveled Practice Activities
Listening Comprehension p. DI•120	Prepare for the Read Aloud	First Listening	Second Listening
Conventions and Writing pp. DI•125–DI•126	Preteach	Leveled Practice Activities	Leveled Practice Activities; Leveled Writing Activities
Concept Development p. DI•117	Activate Prior Knowledge	Develop Concepts	Review Concepts and Connect to Writing

This Week's Practice Stations Overview

Six Weekly Practice Stations with Leveled Activities can be found at the beginning of each week of instruction. For this week's Practice Stations, see pp. 140h–140i.

Practice Stations

Small Group Teacher-led

Classroom Management Handbook for Differentiated Practice Stations

Daily Leveled Center Activities

● Below   ■ Advanced
▲ On-Level   **ELL**

Practice Stations Flip Charts

	Listen Up!	Word Work	Words to Know	Let's Write!	Read for Meaning	Get Fluent
Objectives	• Identify things with sounds /r/, /w/, /j/, /k/, and /e/. • Distinguish between initial and final sounds.	• Identify words with the sounds of consonants *r, w, j,* and *k*. • Identify the short vowel sound of *e*.	• Identify high-frequency words *is, he, three, with, to*. • Spell high-frequency words *is, he, three, with, to*.	• Use adjectives in a complete sentence. • Use adjectives to describe nouns in sentences.	• Identify the plot of a story. • Identify the problem in a plot. • Identify the solution to the problem.	• Develop fluency by listening and following along with familiar texts.
Materials	• *Listen Up!* Flip Chart Activity R6 • Picture Cards	• *Word Work* Flip Chart Activity R6 • Picture Cards • Letter Tiles • ELL Posters	• *Words to Know* Flip Chart Activity R6 • Word Cards • Letter Tiles • paper • pencils	• *Let's Write!* Flip Chart Activity R6 • Picture Cards • paper • pencils	• *Read for Meaning* Flip Chart Activity R6 • Decodable Practice Readers R6B • paper • pencils • crayons	• AudioText CD for *Farmers Market* and "The Maid and the Milk Pail" • Student Edition • CD player

This Week on Reading Street!

Question of the Week

What can we see around our neighborhood?

My World

Daily Plan

Don't Wait Until Friday

Whole Group

- ◉ Consonants *v, y, q*
- ◉ Short *u: u*
- ◉ Realism and Fantasy
- • Vocabulary

MONITOR PROGRESS	Success Predictor			
Day 1 Check Word Reading	Day 2 Check Word Reading	Day 3 Check Word Reading Check High-Frequency Words	Day 4 Check Word Reading: Check Retelling	Day 5 Check Oral Vocabulary: Check Phonemic Awareness

Small Group

Teacher-Led

- • Reading Support
- • Skill Support

Practice Stations

Independent Activities

Customize Literacy More support for a Balanced Literacy approach, see CL•1–CL•47.

Customize Writing More support for a customized writing approach, see CW•11–CW•20.

Whole Group

- • Writing for Thesis: Brief Composition
- • Conventions: Exclamatory Sentences

Assessment

- • Weekly Tests
- • Day 5 Assessment
- • Fresh Reads

You Are Here!
Unit R Week 6

This Week's Reading Selections

Main Selection
Genre: **Realistic Fiction**

Paired Selection

Decodable Practice Readers

Concept Literacy Reader

ELL and ELD Readers

Resources on Reading Street!

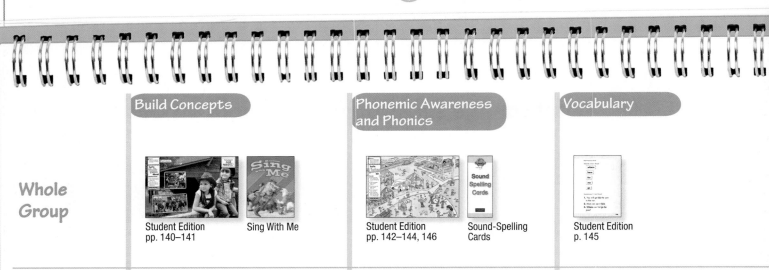

	Build Concepts	Phonemic Awareness and Phonics	Vocabulary
Whole Group	Student Edition pp. 140–141 / Sing With Me	Student Edition pp. 142–144, 146 / Sound-Spelling Cards	Student Edition p. 145
Go Digital	• Concept Talk Video • Sing with Me Animations	• Interactive Sound-Spelling Cards • Decodable eReaders	• Vocabulary Activities • Journal Word Bank
Small Group and Independent Practice	 Practice Stations Flip Chart / Leveled Readers / ELL and ELD Readers	Practice Stations Flip Chart / Decodable Practice Readers	Practice Stations Flip Chart / Student Edition p. 145
Go Digital	• eReaders	• Decodable eReaders • Letter Tile Drag and Drop	• Journal Word Bank • Vocabulary Activities
Customize Literacy	• Leveled Readers	• Decodable Practice Readers	• High-Frequency Word Cards
Go Digital	• Concept Talk Video • Big Question Video • eReaders	• Interactive Sound-Spelling Cards • Decodable eReaders	• Sing with Me Animations • Vocabulary Activities

What can we see around our neighborhood?

Comprehension	**Conventions and Writing**
 Student Edition pp. 148–159	Student Edition pp. 160–161
• Envision It! Animations • eSelections	• Grammar Jammer • Online Journal
Practice Stations Flip Chart Leveled Readers ELL and ELD Readers	Practice Stations Flip Chart Reader's and Writer's Notebook
• eReaders	• Grammar Jammer • Online Journal
• Envision It! Skills and Strategies Handbooks • Leveled Readers	• Reader's and Writer's Notebook
• Envision It! Animations • eReaders	• Grammar Jammer • Online Journal

Week 6

You Are Here!
Unit R
Week 6

My 5-Day Planner for Reading Street!

Don't Wait Until Friday
SUCCESS PREDICTOR

Check Word Reading	Check Word Reading
Day 1 pages 140j–143i	**Day 2** pages 144a–145e

Get Ready to Read

Concept Talk, 140j–141 **Oral Vocabulary,** 141a–141b *bargain, browse, bustling* **Phonemic Awareness,** 142–143 Isolate Initial and Medial Phonemes **Phonics,** 143a–143c ◎ Consonant *v* /v/	**Concept Talk,** 144a–144b **Oral Vocabulary,** 144b *library* **Print Awareness,** 144c Sentence Features **Phonemic Awareness,** 144d Match Initial and Final Phonemes **Phonics,** 144e–144 ◎ Consonants *y* /y/, *z, zz* /z/

Read and Comprehend

Listening Comprehension, 143d–143e ◎ Realism and Fantasy	**Comprehension,** 145a ◎ Realism and Fantasy **Vocabulary,** 145a Sort Nouns for People, Animals, Places, and Thing **High-Frequency Words,** 145 Introduce *for, go, here, me, where*

Language Arts

Conventions, 143f Sentences **Handwriting,** 143g Letter *V* and *v*; Proper Letter Size **Writing,** 143h Sentences with Nouns, Verbs, and Adjectives **Listening and Speaking,** 143i Ask Questions	**Conventions,** 145b Sentences **Handwriting,** 145c Letters *Yy* and *Zz*; Proper Body/Paper Position **Writing,** 145d Sentences with Nouns, Verbs, and Adjectives **Listening and Speaking,** 145e Retell Stories

You Are Here!
Unit R Week 6

What can we see around our neighborhood?

Check High-Frequency Words: Check Retelling	Check Fluency	Check Oral Vocabulary
Day 3 pages 146a–146l	**Day 4** pages 146m–161c	**Day 5** pages 162a–165e
Concept Talk, 146a–146b **Oral Vocabulary,** 146b *fact* **Print Awareness,** 146c Sentence Features **Phonological Awareness,** 146d Identify Syllables **Phonics,** 146e–146g ◉ Short *u: u*	**Concept Talk,** 146m–146n **Oral Vocabulary,** 146n *cost, customer, scale* **Print Awareness,** 146o Sentence Features **Phonemic Awareness,** 146p Segment and Blend Phonemes **Phonics,** 146q–146 ◉ Consonant *q, qu* /kw/ **READ Decodable Practice Reader** R6A, 147a–147b	**Concept Wrap Up,** 162a Review **Oral Vocabulary,** 162b **Print Awareness,** 162c **Phonological Awareness,** 162d Review **Fluent Word Reading,** 162e Review **Phonics,** 162f ◉ Consonants *v* /v/, *y* /y/, *z, zz* /z/, *q, qu* /kw/ ◉ Short *u: u* Review **High-Frequency Words,** 162f **READ Decodable Practice Reader** R6B, 162g–162h
High-Frequency Words, 146h Practice *for, go, here, me, where*	**Literary Text,** 147c Realistic Fiction **High-Frequency Words,** 147 Build Fluency *for, go, here, me, where* **Build Background,** 148a **READ Main Selection,** 148b–159a *The Farmers Market*	**Social Studies in Reading,** 162i **READ Paired Selection,** 162–163 "The Maid and the Milk Pail" **Listening and Speaking,** 164–165 Relate an Experience in Sequence **Vocabulary,** 165a Sort Nouns **Handwriting,** 165a Self-Evaluation **Assessment,** 165b–165c Monitor Progress
Conventions, 146i Sentences **Handwriting,** 146j Letter *U* and *u*; Self-Evaluation **Writing,** 146k Sentences with Nouns, Verbs, and Adjectives **Listening and Speaking,** 146l Relate an Experience in Sequence	**Conventions,** 160–161 Sentences **Writing,** 161a Sentences with Nouns, Verbs, and Adjectives **Research,** 161b Library/Media Center **Handwriting,** 161c Letters *Qq, Qu,* and *qu*; Letter Size	Review **Conventions,** 165d Sentences **Writing,** 165d Sentences with Nouns, Verbs, and Adjectives **Wrap Up Your Week,** 165e Question of the Week What can we see around our neighborhood?

Week 6

Grouping Options for Differentiated Instruction
Turn the page for the small group time lesson plan.

Planning Small Group Time on Reading Street!

SMALL GROUP TIME RESOURCES

Look for this Small Group Time box each day to help meet the individual needs of all your children. Differentiated Instruction lessons appear on the DI pages at the end of each week.

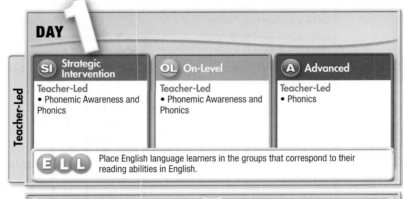

DAY 1

Teacher-Led

SI Strategic Intervention	**OL** On-Level	**A** Advanced
Teacher-Led	Teacher-Led	Teacher-Led
• Phonemic Awareness and Phonics	• Phonemic Awareness and Phonics	• Phonics

ELL Place English language learners in the groups that correspond to their reading abilities in English.

Practice Stations
• Listen Up
• Word Work

Independent Activities
• Reader's and Writer's Notebook
• Concept Talk Video

ELL

ELL Reader

ELD Reader

ELL Poster

Day 1

SI Strategic Intervention		Phonemic Awareness and Phonics, DI•106
OL On-Level		Phonemic Awareness and Phonics, DI•111
A Advanced		Phonics, DI•114
ELL English Language Learners		DI•117–DI•126 **Concepts and Oral Vocabulary** **Listening (Read Aloud)**

Reading Street
Intervention Kit

Reading Street
Practice Stations Kit

Question of the Week
What can we see around our neighborhood?

SI Strategic Intervention

OL On-Level

A Advanced

Concept Literacy Reader

Decodable Practice Readers

Concept Literacy Reader

Concept Literacy
Reader

A Yard for Bugs and Ducks

Advanced Selection

Small Group Weekly Plan

Day 2	Day 3	Day 4	Day 5
Phonemic Awareness and Phonics, DI•107	**Phonemic Awareness and Phonics,** DI•108 **Read Concept Literacy Leveled Reader,** DI•108	**Phonemic Awareness and Phonics,** DI•109 **Read Decodable Practice Reader R6A,** DI•109	**High-Frequency Words,** DI•110 **Read Decodable Practice Reader R6B,** DI•110
Phonics and High-Frequency Words, DI•111	**Read Concept Literacy Leveled Reader,** DI•112	**Conventions,** DI•113	**Phonics Review,** DI•113
Phonics and Comprehension, DI•114	**Read Concept Literacy Leveled Reader,** DI•115	**Comprehension,** DI•116	**Comprehension,** DI•116
DI•117–DI•126 **Concepts** **Vocabulary** **Phonics and Spelling** **Conventions**	DI•117–DI•126 **Concepts** **Vocabulary** **Comprehension Skill** **Main Selection**	DI•117–DI•126 **Concepts** **Vocabulary** **ELL/ELD Readers** **ELL Workshop**	DI•117–DI•126 **Concepts** **Vocabulary** **Sentences with Nouns, Verbs, and Adjectives**

Week 6

Practice Stations for Everyone on Reading Street!

Listen Up!
Match sounds and pictures.

Objectives
- Identify things with /r/, /w/, /j/, /k/ and /e/.
- Distinguish between initial and final sounds.

Materials
- *Listen Up!* Flip Chart Activity R6
- Picture Cards

Differentiated Activities

🔵 Find Picture Cards that begin or end like the first sound in *rat.* Then find things that begin or end with the first sounds in *wig, jog, kick,* and *end.*

🔺 Find Picture Cards that begin or end like the first sound in *rat.* Then find things that begin or end with the first sounds in *wig, jog, kick,* and *end.* Find other things in the room that begin or end with these sounds.

🟥 Find Picture Cards with things that begin or end with the firs sounds in *rat, wig, jog, kick,* and *end.* Sort them into piles for beginning sounds and ending sounds.

Technology
- Interactive Sound-Spelling Cards

Word Work
Identify the sounds of *r, w, j, k,* and *e.*

Objectives
- Identify words with the sounds of consonants *r, w, j,* and *k.*
- Identify the short vowel sound of *e.*

Materials
- Word Work Flip Chart Activity R6
- Picture Cards
- Letter Tiles
- ELL Posters

Differentiated Activities

Have children look at the ELL Poster and objects in the room for ideas.

🔵 Find Picture Cards that show things with *r, w, j, k,* or short *e.* Quietly say each word. Match one or more of the Letter Tiles to each Picture Card that pictures a word with the sound of the letter

🔺 Find Picture Cards that show things with *r, w, j, k,* or short *e.* Then use Letter Tiles *r, w, j, k, e, t, m, a, d, i, l,* and *n* to spell new words. Say each word quietly.

🟥 Think of words that begin or end with the sounds of *r, w, j,* or *k* and have short *e, a, o,* or *i* in the middle. Use Letter Tiles to spell as many words like this as you can. Quietly say each word.

Technology
- Interactive Sound-Spelling Cards

Words To Know
Identify high-frequency words.

Objectives
- Identify high-frequency words *is, he, three, with, to.*
- Spell high-frequency words *is, he, three, with, to.*

Materials
- Words to Know Flip Chart Activity R6
- Word Cards
- Letter Tiles
- paper
- pencils

Differentiated Activities

🔵 Look at the Word Cards for *is, he, three, with, to.* Match Letter Tiles to the letters on the cards. Say each word quietly.

🔺 Look at the Word Cards for *is, he, three, with, to.* Copy the words on your paper. Say each word quietly.

🟥 Look at the Word Cards for look, *do, you, was, yellow, is, he, three, with, to.* Write two sentences using as many of these words as you can.

Technology
- Online Tested Vocabulary Activities

You Are Here!
Unit R
Week 6

Use this week's materials from the Reading Street Practice Stations Kit to organize this week's stations.

Let's Write!
Write descriptive sentences with adjectives.

Objectives
• Use adjectives in a complete sentence.
• Use adjectives to describe nouns in sentences.

Materials
• *Let's Write!* Flip Chart Activity R6
• Picture Cards
• paper
• pencils

Differentiated Activities
• An **adjective** describes a noun or another adjective:
The <u>green</u> house stood on a <u>big</u> hill.

● Choose a Picture Card noun. Think of an adjective to describe the noun in the picture. Write a sentence using the adjective to describe the noun. Underline the adjective.

▲ Choose a Picture Card noun. Write a sentence with one or more adjectives describing the pictured noun. Underline the adjective or adjectives in your sentence.

■ Choose two Picture Card animals. Write sentences comparing the way the animals look. Underline the adjectives.

Technology
• Online Journals

Read For Meaning
Identify a story's plot.

Objectives
• Identify the plot of a story.
• Identify the problem in a plot.
• Identify the solution to the problem.

Materials
• *Read for Meaning* Flip Chart Activity
• Decodable Practice Readers R6B
• paper
• pencils
• crayons

Differentiated Activities
• A **plot** is what happens in a story. A plot often sets up a problem and builds to a solution.

● Read your book. Identify the plot in the story. Draw a picture that shows the problem.

▲ Read your book. Think about the story's plot. Write two sentences that explain the problem. Draw a picture to go with your sentence.

■ Read your book. Think about the plot of the story. Write two sentences that explain the problem. Then write a sentence that tells its solution.

Technology
• Online Student Edition

Get Fluent
Listen to fluent reading.

Objective
• Develop fluency by listening and following along with familiar texts.

Materials
• AudioText CD for *Farmers Market* and "The Maid and the Milk Pail"
• Student Edition
• CD player

Differentiated Activities

Open your book to the selection *Farmers Market*. Track the print as you listen to the Audio-Text CD. Notice how the reader says the words on each page.

Then listen to "The Maid and the Milk Pail."

Technology
• Online Main Selection and Paired Selection eText

Week 6

Objectives
- Introduce concepts: neighborhoods
- Share information and ideas about the concept.

Today at a Glance

Oral Vocabulary
bargain, browse, bustling

Phonemic Awareness
Isolate Initial and Medial Phonemes

Phonics
◉ Consonant *v* /v/

Comprehension
◉ Realism and Fantasy

Conventions
Sentences

Handwriting
V and *v*/Proper Letter Size

Writing
Sentences with Nouns, Verbs, and Adjectives: Introduce

Listening and Speaking
Ask Questions

Concept Talk

Question of the Week
What can we see around our neighborhood?

Introduce the concept

To build concepts and to focus children's attention, tell them that this week they will talk, sing, read, and write about neighborhoods. Write the Question of the Week, and track the print as you read it.

ROUTINE — **Activate Prior Knowledge** — **Team Talk**

1. **Think** Have children think for a minute about neighborhoods.
2. **Pair** Have pairs of children discuss the question.
3. **Share** Have children share information and their ideas with the group. Remind them to ask questions and clarify information. Guide discussion and encourage elaboration with prompts such as:
   - What are some things can you see around your neighborhood?

Routines Flip Chart

Anchored Talk

Develop oral language

Have children turn to pages 140–141 in their Student Editions. Read the title and look at the photos. Use these questions to guide discussion and create the "What can we see around our neighborhood?" concept map (shown on the next page).

- Find the picture of the two girls. Where are they? (at home) We'll start our map with this idea. I'll write *We can see people at home* in this box.
- What are the people in the small pictures doing? (walking or shopping) I'll write *We can see people walking* in this box. I'll write *We can see people shopping* in this box.
- Look at the picture of the people shopping. Where are they shopping? (at a farmers market) How can I add that to our map?

Oral Vocabulary

Let's Talk About
Neighborhoods

- Share information about what we see around our neighborhood.
- Share ideas about places we can go and things we can do in our neighborhood.

READING STREET ONLINE
CONCEPT TALK VIDEO
www.ReadingStreet.com

Objectives
● Listen closely to speakers and ask questions to help you better understand the topic. ● Share information and ideas about the topic. Speak at the correct pace.

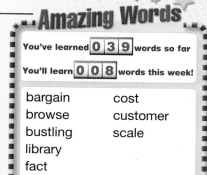

You've learned **0 3 9**
Amazing Words ⭐
so far this year!

140 141

Student Edition pp. 140–141

Amazing Words ⭐

You've learned **0 3 9** words so far

You'll learn **0 0 8** words this week!

bargain	cost
browse	customer
bustling	scale
library	
fact	

⏱ Writing on Demand

Develop Writing Fluency Ask children to write about what they know about neighborhoods. Have them write for two to three minutes. Children should write as much as they can. Tell them to try to do their best writing. You may want to discuss what children wrote during writing conferences.

Connect to reading

Explain to children that this week, they will read a story about Sam's father and sister. In the story they go to a farmers market. The market is in a park. You can often see a park in a neighborhood. Add *We can see parks* to the map.

```
          What can we
        see around our
         neighborhood?
    ┌──────┬──────┬──────┬──────┐
 We can see  We can see  We can      We can see
 people at   people walking.  see people   parks
 home.                shopping
                         │
                  Neighborhoods
                  can have
                  farmers
                  markets.
```

ELL **Preteach Concepts** Use the Day 1 instruction on ELL Poster R6 to assess and build background knowledge, develop concepts, and build oral vocabulary.

ELL Poster R6

ELL

English Language Learners

Vocabulary Have children use words they know to describe parts of the picture in as much detail as possible. Provide words as needed, and encourage children to help each other.

ELL Support Additional ELL support and modified instruction is provided in the *ELL Handbook* and in the ELL Support Lessons on pp. DI•117–DI•126.

Farmers Market **140–141**

Objectives
- Build oral vocabulary.
- Discuss the concept to develop oral language.
- Share information and ideas about the concepts.

Oral Vocabulary
Amazing Words

Introduce Amazing Words

Display p. R6 of the *Sing with Me* Big Book. Tell children they are going to sing a song about shopping in a neighborhood. Ask children to listen for the Amazing Words *bargain*, *browse*, and *bustling* as you sing. Sing the song again and have children join you.

 Sing with Me Big Book Audio

Sing with Me Big Book
p. R6

Teach Amazing Words

Amazing Words Oral Vocabulary Routine

1. **Introduce the Word** Relate the word *bustling* to the song: The outdoor market is a *bustling* place. Supply a child-friendly definition: *Bustling* means crowded, busy, and noisy. Have children say the word.

2. **Demonstrate** Provide examples to show meaning: Our school is *bustling* with children in the morning. A beehive is *bustling* with busy bees. Stores are *bustling* with shoppers at holiday times.

3. **Apply** Have children demonstrate their understanding: Which place would be *bustling* with people: a city sidewalk or a mountain trail?

See p. OV•3 to teach *bargain* and *browse*.

Routines Flip Chart

Check understanding of Amazing Words

Have children look at the picture at the bottom of page 140–141. That street is sure *bustling* with people. What places have you visited that are *bustling* with people? Use *bustling* in your answer. (Possible response: I have visited a bustling store. Other responses: a baseball stadium; an airport; a busy post office.)

Would you like to get a *bargain* when you are shopping? Why or why not? (Possible response: Yes; if I get a bargain then I am getting something good for not a lot of money.)

What do you do when you *browse* through the books in the classroom library? (Possible response: I look at each one for a short time.)

Apply Amazing Words

Have children demonstrate their understanding of the Amazing Words by completing these sentences orally.

> This coat is a **bargain** because _____.
>
> It's fun to **browse** through _____.
>
> We walked into the **bustling** _____.

Corrective feedback

If... children have difficulty understanding the Amazing Words, **then...** remind them of the definitions and provide opportunities for children to use the words in sentences.

Preteach Academic Vocabulary

Write the following on the board:

- realism and fantasy
- realistic fiction
- sentences

Have children share what they know about this week's Academic Vocabulary. Use children's responses to assess their prior knowledge. Preteach the Academic Vocabulary by providing a child-friendly description, explanation, or example that clarifies the meaning of each term. Then ask children to restate the meaning of the Academic Vocabulary in their own words.

Amazing Words

bargain	fact
browse	cost
bustling	customer
library	scale

Differentiated Instruction

SI **Strategic Intervention**

Act It Out If children are having difficulty with the meanings of the three Amazing Words, it may help to have them act the words out. For example, have children pantomime browsing through a pile of books, or finding a bargain at a store. Say *Jeff is browsing in the library/walking in a bustling crowd* and have children repeat.

English Language Learners

Pronounce -ing The phoneme /ng/ is extremely common in English, but is not as prevalent in some other languages. Help children hear the differences between *bustlin* and *bustling.* Say *bustling* and *bustling* several times as they listen for the final /ing/. Then have them produce the sounds themselves.

Objectives
○ Isolate initial and medial phonemes.
○ Match initial and medial phonemes.
• Associate consonant v with the sound /v/.
• Recognize and name the letters *Vv.*
• Write the letters *Vv.*

Skills Trace
◉ **Consonant v/v/**
Introduce URW6D1
Practice URW6D4; URW6D5
Reteach/Review URW6D2; URW6D3; URW6D4; URW6D5
Assess/Test Weekly Test URW6
Benchmark Test UR

Student Edition pp. 142–143

Phonemic Awareness
Match Initial and Medial Phonemes

Introduce

Read together the first bullet point on pages 142–143 of the Student Edition. What does the woman by the truck have? (vegetables) *Vegetable* begins with the sound /v/. Have children find four more things that begin with /v/. (van, violin, violet, vine) Sometimes words have the sound /v/ in the middle. I see a *river*: Say *river* with me. Listen for /v/. The sound /v/ comes in the middle of the word *river*.

Model

Listen to the first sound of *violin*: /v/. Say the sound with me: /v/. *Violin* begins with /v/. Listen to the middle sound of *seven*: /v/. Seven has /v/ in the middle. Continue modeling with *van* and *driver*.

Guide practice

Guide children as they practice saying the following words: *van, never, oval, valley, vine, living, vote, delivery.*

Corrective feedback

If... children make an error,
then... model by saying the sound again, along with a word that has the sound at the beginning or middle, and have them repeat the sound and the word.

Phonics
Consonant v /v/

Hear

Today you will learn how to spell the sound /v/. Listen: /v/, /v/, /v/. When you say /v/, your top teeth touch your bottom lip and your throat moves a little. Say /v/ and feel how your top teeth touch your bottom lip. Watch and listen as children produce the sound. Say /v/ with me: /v/, /v/, /v/.

Say

Display Sound-Spelling Card 25. This picture shows a *volcano*. Say it with me: *volcano*. The first sound in *volcano* is /v/. Listen: /v/, *volcano*. Say it with me: /v/, *volcano*. What is the first sound in *volcano*?

See

Point to *v*. This letter is *v*. The sound /v/ is usually spelled *v*. *Volcano* begins with /v/. *Volcano* begins with the letter *v*. Have children say /v/ several times as you point to *v*.

Read ABC Rhyme Time

Display ABC Rhyme Time, p. 27. Point to the letters *Vv* at the top of the page. The name for both of these letters is *v*. Point to *V*. This is an upper-case *V*. Point to *v*. This is a lower-case *v*. Point to each letter again and ask: What is the name of this letter?

This rhyme is about vultures on a volcano. Vultures are big birds. Read the rhyme aloud, tracking the print with your finger. Then read it again. Point to examples of upper- and lower-case *v*'s as you read each word aloud.

Sound-Spelling Card 25

ABC Rhyme Time p. 27

Write

Now I will show you how to write upper-case *V* and lower-case *v*. Write *V*. Watch as I trace upper-case *V* with my finger. Follow the stroke instructions pictured. Now you write upper-case *V*. Repeat for lower-case *v*.

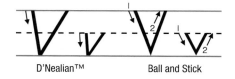

D'Nealian™   Ball and Stick

Differentiated Instruction

SI Strategic Intervention
Words with medial sound /v/ generally have two syllables, which may make the sound /v/ difficult for some children to hear. You can help by saying *driver* twice, once normally and once divided into syllables: *dri-ver*. Have children repeat the syllables, emphasizing the sound /v/. Then say the first syllable and have children supply the second syllable of the word, again emphasizing sound /v/. Repeat with *oval* and *waving*.

Spelling Pattern
/v/v The sound /v/ is almost always spelled *v*.

Academic Vocabulary
phoneme smallest meaningful unit of sound in spoken language

English Language Learners
Pronounce *v* In some languages, the English phoneme /v/ does not exist. Demonstrate how your top teeth touch your bottom lip when you make the sound /v/.

Objectives

- Blend, read, and spell words with consonant *v*/v/.
- Associate the consonant *v* with the sound /v/.
- Write the letters *Vv*.
- Recognize and name the letters *Vv*.

Phonics—Teach/Model
↻ Consonant *v* /v/

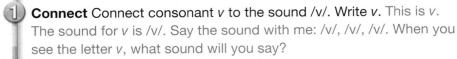

Vv

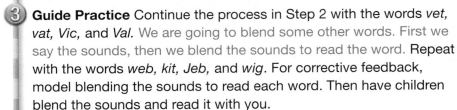

v

Sound-Spelling
Card 25

ROUTINE **Blending Strategy**

1. **Connect** Connect consonant *v* to the sound /v/. Write *v*. This is *v*. The sound for *v* is /v/. Say the sound with me: /v/, /v/, /v/. When you see the letter *v*, what sound will you say?

2. **Model** Model how to blend van. Write *v*. What is the sound for this letter? Say the sound with me: /v/. Write *a*. Say this sound with me: /a/. Write *n*. Say this sound with me: /n/. Listen as I blend all the sounds together: /v/ /a/ /n/, van. Blend the sounds with me: /v/ /a/ /n/, van. Now blend the sounds without me.

3. **Guide Practice** Continue the process in Step 2 with the words *vet, vat, Vic,* and *Val.* We are going to blend some other words. First we say the sounds, then we blend the sounds to read the word. Repeat with the words *web, kit, Jeb,* and *wig.* For corrective feedback, model blending the sounds to read each word. Then have children blend the sounds and read it with you.

4. **Review** What do you know about reading words that begin with the letter *v*? The sound for *v* is /v/.

Routines Flip Chart

Spell Words   Now we are going to spell words with the sound /v/ spelled *v*. The first word we will spell is *vet*. What sounds do you hear in *vet*? (/v/ /e/ /t/) What is the letter for /v/? Let's all write *v*. What is the letter for /e/? Write *e*. What is the letter for /t/? Write *t*. Have children confirm their spellings by comparing them with what you have written. Continue the practice with *vest* and *Vic.*

On their own   Use the *Reader's and Writer's Notebook* p. 101 for additional practice with consonant *v* /v/.

Reader's and Writer's Notebook
p. 101

Phonics
Identify Lower-Case and Upper-Case Letters

Write a lower-case *v*. What letter is this? (lower-case *v*) Write an upper-case *V*. What letter is this? (upper-case *V*) Write a series of upper- and lower-case *v*'s. Point to each and have children identify each as upper-case *V* or lower-case *v*.

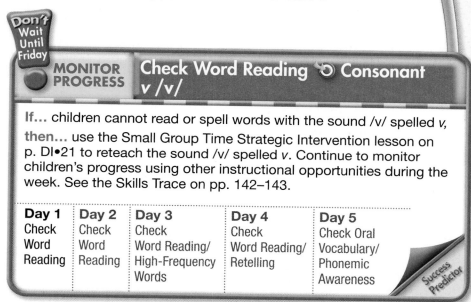

Don't Wait Until Friday

MONITOR PROGRESS

Check Word Reading ↺ Consonant v /v/

If... children cannot read or spell words with the sound /v/ spelled *v*,

then... use the Small Group Time Strategic Intervention lesson on p. DI•21 to reteach the sound /v/ spelled *v*. Continue to monitor children's progress using other instructional opportunities during the week. See the Skills Trace on pp. 142–143.

Day 1	Day 2	Day 3	Day 4	Day 5
Check Word Reading	Check Word Reading	Check Word Reading/ High-Frequency Words	Check Word Reading/ Retelling	Check Oral Vocabulary/ Phonemic Awareness

Success Predictor

Small Group Time

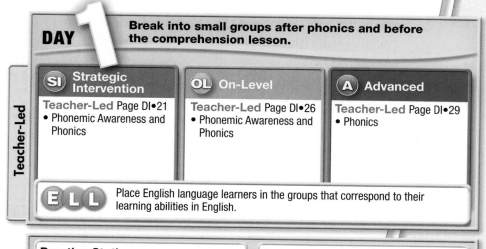

DAY 1

Break into small groups after phonics and before the comprehension lesson.

SI Strategic Intervention
Teacher-Led Page DI•21
• Phonemic Awareness and Phonics

OL On-Level
Teacher-Led Page DI•26
• Phonemic Awareness and Phonics

A Advanced
Teacher-Led Page DI•29
• Phonics

ELL Place English language learners in the groups that correspond to their learning abilities in English.

Practice Stations
• Listen Up
• Word Work

Independent Activities
• Read independently/Reading log on *Reader's and Writer's Notebook* p. RR1.
• Concept Talk Video

Differentiated Instruction

A Advanced
Rhyming Words Have children work with partners. Ask them to generate words that rhyme with the words *van, vat,* and *vet.* Encourage them to use the spelling patterns they know to write these words as well.

ELL

English Language Learners
Letters *v* and *b* In Spanish, the letter *v* is associated with the same sound as the letter *b*. You can help children distinguish these sounds in English by having children spell and pronounce word pairs such as *van/ban* and *vet/bet.*

Objectives
○ Distinguish realism from fantasy.

Skills Trace

◎ **Realism and Fantasy**
Introduce/Teach URW4D1; URW6D1
Practice URW4D2; URW4D3; URW4D4; URW6D2; URW6D3; URW6D4
Reteach/Review URW4D5; URW6D5; U1W3D2
Assess/Test
Weekly Tests URW4; URW6
Benchmark Tests UR

Listening Comprehension
🔊 Realism and Fantasy

Introduce

Realistic fiction is a story that could actually happen in real life. A **fantasy** is a made-up story that could never happen in real life. Good readers look for clues that tell them whether a story is realistic fiction or a fantasy.

Have children turn to pp. EI•2–EI•3 in their Student Edition. These pictures show examples of realism and fantasy. Ask:

Student Edition EI•2–EI•3

- Which picture is realistic? (the girl reading) How do you know? (The girl looks like a real girl; real girls read books.)

- Which picture is a fantasy? (the bears eating) Why do you think so? (Real bears don't wear clothes or live in houses.)

Model

Today we will read a story about two friends spending the day together. Read "A Busy Day" and model how to tell fantasy and realistic fiction apart.

Think Aloud I know this story is fantasy. Real bears don't talk, and real bears don't go to the library.

Guide practice

What other clues help you know that the story is a fantasy? (The bears buy fruit at the farmers market.) But bears like real fruit. Why isn't this part of the story real? (Possible response: Bears don't buy food at markets.

On their own

Use *Reader's and Writer's Notebook* p. 102.

Reader's and Writer's Notebook p. 102

 Read Aloud

A Busy Day

Bonnie Bear and Betty Bear were neighbors and good friends. Today they sat down to make a list of errands they both needed to do. They had to go to the library, the market, and their favorite hat shop.

Their first stop was the library. Bonnie liked books about the moon, stars, and planets. So she wanted to browse and look for those kinds of books. Betty liked to read stories about people. So she wanted to find books like that. When they found books they liked, they checked them out.

"Isn't it curious that we are such good friends, yet we like different kinds of books?" asked Betty as they left the library.

"Yes, I suppose it is," answered Bonnie.

Next, the bears went to an outdoor market to buy fruit. Today the market was bustling with activity. Bonnie filled up her basket with apples and pears. Betty filled her basket with oranges and grapes.

"Isn't it curious that we are such good friends, yet we like different kinds of fruit?" asked Betty as they left the market.

"Yes, I suppose it is," answered Bonnie.

Then the bears went to their favorite hat shop. Betty tried on a white hat with red polka dots. "I love the color white and I love polka dots!" she said. "This is the hat for me. Besides, it's a bargain."

Bonnie tried on a pale blue hat. It had no polka dots. "Blue is my favorite color," she said. "This is the hat I will buy."

"Isn't it curious that we are such good friends, but yet we like different kinds of hats?" asked Betty as they left the hat shop.

"Yes, I suppose it is," said Bonnie.

Since the bears were done with their errands, they sat down in the park to eat their fruit. "I've been thinking about your questions," said Bonnie. "We may not like the same books, fruit, or hats, but we really like each other, and that's why we're such good friends!" And Betty, of course, agreed.

Academic Language

realistic fiction a made-up story that could happen in real life

fantasy a made-up story that could never really happen

Objectives
- Identify a sentence.
- Recognize and use punctuation marks at the ends of sentences.
- Space letters appropriately.
- Write letters *Vv*.

Conventions
Sentences

Model

Remind children that a **sentence** is a group of words that tells a complete idea. Explain that all sentences contain a verb and many sentences contain a noun and an adjective. *Vic got a green bike* is a sentence because it tells a complete idea. Tell children that a sentence always starts with a capital letter. It often ends with a period.

Display Grammar Transparency R6. Read the title aloud. Model identifying the parts of the sentence in the example. Then read the directions and model number 1.

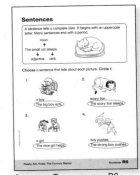

Grammar Transparency R6

- The first choice just says *a boy*. The picture shows a boy. But a boy is not a sentence. It does not tell a complete idea. A sentence would tell something about the boy. For example, it might tell what the boy is doing.

- The second choice tells what the boy is doing. It tells a complete idea. So, it is a sentence. I can also tell it is a sentence because it begins with a capital letter and ends with a period.

Guide practice

Continue with items 2–4, having children identify which of the two answer choices is the sentence.

Connect to oral language

Have the class complete these sentence frames orally so they are complete ideas. Have them identify the capital letter and period in each sentence.

> **1. The _____ sweater fits.**
>
> **2. The _____ dog sings.**

On their own

Team Talk Pair children and have them talk about presents they would like to get or presents they have gotten. Be sure they use complete sentences as they talk.

Handwriting
Letter *V* and *v*;
Proper Letter Size

Model letter formation

Display upper- and lower-case letters: *Vv*. Use the stroke instructions pictured below to model proper letter formation.

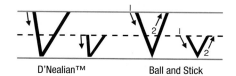

D'Nealian™   Ball and Stick

Model proper letter size

Remind children that when we write a word, we need to make the letters the proper sizes. Draw a set of handwriting lines on the board. Then write upper case *V* so the letter touches both solid lines. Say: Upper-case letters always go from the top to the bottom. So do some lower-case letters. Write the lower-case letters *k* and *b*. Then write the lower-case letters *v, c,* and *o* and explain that these lower-case letters stay in the bottom half of the lines. Finally, write lower case *g* and *p* and remind children that these letters fall below the line.

Guide practice

Write the following words on the board: *Van, hop, jet, rim.*

Team Talk Have children work together in pairs to identify the letters that go from the top line to the bottom line, those that stay in the bottom half of the lines, and the letters that fall below the line.

On their own

Use the *Reader's and Writer's Notebook* p. 107

Reader's and Writer's Notebook p. 107

Differentiated Instruction

SI Strategic Intervention

Distinguish V and W Write upper case *V* and *W* on the board. Ask children to identify how the letters are alike and different. Have children practice writing *V W V W V W,* leaving appropriate spacing between the letters, and then name the letters in order from left to right. Repeat with lower case *v* and *w.*

Academic Vocabulary

sentence a group of words that tells a complete idea

Daily Fix-It

1. Look At teh hat.
Look <u>at</u> <u>the</u> hat.

Discuss the Daily Fix-It with children. Help children understand why this is a sentence.

ELL

English Language Learners

Verbs Help children learn new verbs and use them in their sentences by having them pantomime the action while you or classmates supply the word. For instance, children can pretend to hop like a frog to form the sentence *the frog hops.* Then have children say the sentences chorally while carrying out the action.

Objectives
- Produce a sentence.
- Write a complete sentence that contains a noun, verb, and adjective.
- Listen attentively and ask questions.

Writing—Sentences

Connect to conventions

Review sentences: a **sentence** is a group of words that tells a complete idea. It begins with a capital letter and often ends with a period. We can write sentences that contain a noun, a verb, and an adjective.

Model

Write *The teacher got a beautiful book.* This sentence tells a complete idea. It has nouns, a verb, and an adjective. Identify the nouns, verb, and adjective in the sentence. The sentence begins with a capital letter and ends with a period.

Guide practice

Let's think of other nouns, verbs and adjectives. As children give examples, write their words on the board. Then help them create sentences using these words. Have them identify if each sentence tells a complete idea and contains a noun, verb, and adjective. Then write these sentence frames and read them aloud.

> My _____ cat eats.
>
> The tall _____ runs.
>
> Her little brother _____.

Model completing the first sentence frame with an adjective. This first sentence will tell about the cat that eats. I know that it must be an adjective. What are some adjectives that would describe a cat that eats? *Hungry* is an adjective. A hungry cat would eat. I will write *hungry* in the blank to complete the sentence. Have children suggest nouns from the list that could complete the second sentence. Help them choose verbs to complete the third sentence.

Shared writing

Have children use nouns, verbs, and adjectives to create new sentences. As they suggest sentences, write their suggestions on the board. Invite other children to identify the noun, verb, and adjective in each sentence.

On their own

Some children may be ready to write on their own. Write several more sentence frames on the board, each with a blank for a noun, a verb, or an adjective. Have children complete the sentences on their own. Children may also write new sentences, if they can. Have children identify the noun, verb, and adjective in each sentence.

Listening and Speaking
Ask Questions

Teach asking questions

Explain that people tell each other information to help them learn more. Tell children that they can ask questions to help them understand things. You ask a question when you want to know something.

- Do not interrupt the speaker. Wait to ask your question until the speaker has reached a good stopping place.
- Ask politely. Tell the speaker what part you do not understand.
- Face the speaker and make eye contact.

Model

 Think Aloud Have a puppet speak the following: I went on an errand in my neighborhood! Then turn to the class and say: My puppet gave me good information, but I have questions about what she did. Look directly at the puppet and say: What was the errand? Who went with you? How did you get there?

Guide practice

Give a short statement, such as When I was young, I had two pets. Have children ask questions to learn more.

On their own

Have pairs of children take turns speaking about something in their neighborhood. Have them ask each other questions.

Wrap Up Your Day

✔ **Consonant Vv /v/** Write van and vet. Point to the v as you say the words aloud. Have children repeat them after you.

✔ **Realism and Fantasy** Have children explain how they know that the story A Busy Day is realism or fantasy. (fantasy, because the animals act like people)

✔ **Build Concepts** To develop the concept of Neighborhoods, ask children where in the neighborhood the bears browse for books.

✔ **Homework** Send home this week's Family Times Newsletter from the Let's Practice It! DVD.

Let's Practice It!
TR DVD • 21–22

Differentiated Instruction

SI Strategic Intervention
Questions If children have trouble formulating questions, provide them with key words such as *what, who,* and *where* and have them complete the question with those as the initial words.

ELL

English Language Learners
Word Order English uses a different word order for questions than for statements. The question "Can you hear me?," for example, is different from "You can hear me." Model this word order with children and help them use it when they ask questions of their own.

Preview DAY 2

Tell children that tomorrow they will hear again about Henry's first day at his neighborhood school.

Objectives
- Discuss the concept to develop oral language.
- Build oral vocabulary.

Today at a Glance

Oral Vocabulary
library

Print Awareness
Sentence Features

Phonemic Awareness
Match Initial and Final Phonemes

Phonics
- Consonant *y* /y/
- Consonant *z, zz* /z/

High-Frequency Words
go, for, here, me, where

Comprehension
- Realism and Fantasy

Vocabulary
Sort Words

Conventions
Sentences

Handwriting
Y and y, Z and z/Proper Body and Paper Position

Writing
Sentences with Nouns, Verbs, and Adjectives

Listening and Speaking
Retell Stories

Concept Talk

 Question of the Week

What can we see around our neighborhood?

Build concepts

To reinforce concepts and to focus children's attention, have children sing "Shopping Day" from the *Sing with Me* Big Book. What is it like at the market? (Possible response: there are lots of people) What kinds of things can you buy at the market? (corn, bananas, and other foods)

Sing with Me Big Book Audio

Introduce Amazing Words

Display the Big Book, *First Grade, Here I Come!* Read the title and identify the author. Explain that in the story, the author uses the word *library* to describe a place that has lots of books for people to read and browse through. Have children listen to the story to find out what Henry does in the library.

Use the Oral Vocabulary routine on the next page to teach *library*.

Big Book

ELL Reinforce Vocabulary Use the Day 2 instruction on ELL Poster R6 to reinforce the meanings of high-frequency words.

ELL Poster R6

Oral Vocabulary
Amazing Words

Teach Amazing Words

 **Amazing Words** Oral Vocabulary Routine

1 **Introduce the Word** Relate the word *library* to the book. Henry's class visits the *library*. Supply a child-friendly definition: A *library* is a place where you can read or borrow books. Have children say the word.

2 **Demonstrate** Provide examples to show meaning. I borrowed a great book from the school *library*. You can see lots of people reading in a *library*. If you get a *library* card, you can borrow books from a *library* in our town.

3 **Apply** Have children demonstrate their understanding. Ask: What can you do in a *library*?

Routines Flip Chart

Anchored Talk

Add to the concept map

Discuss the things you can see in a neighborhood.

- Recall the Read Aloud story "A Busy Day" from Day 1. What places in their neighborhood do the two bears visit? (library, outdoor market, hat shop) We already have a *farmers market*, or a *outdoor market*, on our map. Let's add *We can see libraries* to our map.

- We can also add *hat shop* to our map. Neighborhoods can have hat shops. What do you do at a hat shop? (buy hats) A hat shop is a kind of a store, so I'll draw a line that connects *hat shop* to *stores*. Add *hat shop* to the map with a line that connects it to *stores*.

Amazing Words

bargain	fact
browse	cost
bustling	customer
library	scale

Differentiated Instruction

 **Strategic Intervention**

Pronunciation Many children have difficulty pronouncing the first *r* in *library*. Break the word into syllables, emphasizing the consonant blend *br,* and have children repeat the sounds. Then have children say the whole word, focusing on the *br* blend.

ELL

English Language Learners
Synonyms The words *store* and *shop* are used interchangeably in the Read Aloud story. This may be confusing to some children. Explain that these words have the same meaning, so a *hat shop* is the same thing as a *hat store*.

Print Awareness
Sentence Features

Introduce   Write the sentence *My friend rides a bike* on the board. Include a period at the end of the sentence. Read the sentence aloud as you move your hand beneath the words. This is a sentence because it is a complete idea. Who does the sentence tell about? (my friend) What does my friend do? (ride a bike) I notice two interesting things about this sentence. One is how the sentence begins. The other is how the sentence ends. All sentences have these things. Look carefully and see if you can find the interesting things I'm talking about.

Model   Underline the first letter of the sentence. This letter is *M*. Is it a capital *M* or a lower case *m*? That's right, it's a capital *M*. It's the only capital letter in this whole sentence. Sentences always begin with capital letters. Now underline the period at the end of the sentence. Look at this symbol. It isn't a letter, and it isn't a number. It looks like a dot. It's a special mark that we call a *period*. Sentences always have a period or some other mark at the end. The period means "I'm done with my idea. This sentence is over." Briefly review by indicating the capital *M* and then the period. The capital letter begins the sentence. The period ends it.

Guide practice   Write the following on the board:

> The bear is big.
>
> you have two legs.
>
> We will play a game

Read the words aloud. Explain that each group of words makes a com- plete idea, but that they are not all written as sentences. Work with chil- dren to determine whether each group of words is written correctly. Have them help you fix the last two examples.

On their own   Use *Reader's and Writer's Notebook* p. 104

Reader's and Writer's Notebook p. 104

Phonemic Awareness
Match Initial and Final Phonemes

Model isolating sounds

Read aloud the second two bullet points on pages 142–143 in the Student Edition. Let's look for two things that start with the sound /y/. I see something that is *yellow*. What else starts with /y/? (yarn) The first sound in *yellow* and *yarn* is /y/. Now let's look for three things that start with the sound /z/. Look for a *zebra* at the *zoo*. The first sound of *zebra* and *zoo* is /z/. Can you find one more thing that starts with /z/? (zipper)

Student Edition pp. 142–143

Model matching phonemes

Listen to the first sound of *yawn*: /y/. Say the sound with me: /y/. Listen to the first sound of *zoom*: /z/. Say the sound with me: /z/. Now listen to the last sound of *buzz*: /z/. **Continue modeling with** *yell, Zach,* and *whiz.*

Guide practice

Now we're going to listen to the first sound of some words. Point to y-y-yourself if the sound you hear is /y/. Say the words: *young, ran, yes, wall, jet, yam.*

Now z-z-zip your thumb in the air if the first sound you hear is /z/. Say the words: *zing, bake, zigzag, seed.*

Now it's time to listen to the last sound of some words. Make a buzzing sound, *bzzz,* if the word ends with the sound /z/. Say the words: *fizz, Liz, jazz, door, will, ooze.*

Corrective feedback

If... children make an error,
then... repeat the sound in isolation, along with a word that begins or ends with the sound and have them repeat the sound and the word.

On their own

Have children look at the picture and name more items that begin with the sounds /y/ and /z/ or end with the sound /z/.

Objectives

- ○ Associate the consonant *y* with the sound /y/.
- • Write the letters *Yy*.
- • Blend, read, and spell words with *y*.
- • Recognize and name the letters *Yy*.

Phonics
Consonants y /y/ and z, zz /z/

Hear
Today you will spell the sound /y/. Listen: /y/, /y/, /y/. Listen as children produce the sound. Say /y/ with me: /y/, /y/, /y/.

Say
Display Sound-Spelling Card 28. This is a *yo-yo*. The first sound in *yo-yo* is /y/. Listen: /y/, *yo-yo*. Say it with me: /y/, *yo-yo*.

See
Point to *y*. This is *y*. The sound /y/ is usually spelled *y*. *Yo-yo* begins with /y/. Have children say /y/ as you point to *y*.

Read ABC Rhyme Time
Display p. 30. Point to the letters Yy at the top. This is an upper-case *Y*. This is a lower-case *y*. Point to each letter again. Read the rhyme and track the print. Read it again. Have children find examples of *y* and name the words.

Write
Now I will write upper-case *Y* and lower-case *y*. Write *Y*. Watch as I trace capital *Y* with my finger. Follow the stroke instructions pictured below. Now you write capital *Y*. Repeat for lowercase *y*.

Hear
Now let's spell the sound /z/. Listen: /z/, /z/, /z/. Listen as children produce the sound. Say /z/ with me: /z/, /z/, /z/.

Say
Display Sound-Spelling Card 29. This is a *zebra*. The first sound in *zebra* is /z/. Listen: /z/, *zebra*. Say it with me: /z/, *zebra*.

See
Point to *z*. This is *z*. The sound /z/ can be spelled *z* or *zz*. *Zebra* begins with /z/. Have children say /z/ as you point to *z*.

Read ABC Rhyme Time
Display p. 31. Point to the letters Zz at the top. This is an upper-case *Z*. This is a lower-case *z*. Point to each letter again. Read the rhyme and track the print. Read it again. Have children find other examples of *z* and *zz* and name the words.

Write
Now I will show you how to write upper-case *Z* and lower-case *z*. Write *Z*. Watch as I trace capital *Z* with my finger. Follow the stroke instructions pictured. Now you write capital *Z*. Repeat for lowercase *z*.

Sound-Spelling Card 28

ABC Rhyme Time p. 30

Sound-Spelling Card 29

ABC Rhyme Time p. 31

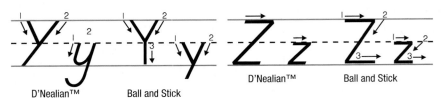

D'Nealian™   Ball and Stick   D'Nealian™   Ball and Stick

Phonics—Teach/Model
↻ Consonants y/y/, z, zz /z/

ROUTINE Blending Strategy

1 Connect Connect consonant y to the sound /y/. Write y. This is y. The sound for y is /y/. Say the sound with me: /y/, /y/, /y/. When you see the letter y, what sound will you say? Continue in the same way with /z/ and /zz/.

2 Model Model how to blend yet. Write y. What is the sound for this letter? Say the sound with me: /y/. Write e. Say this sound with me: /e/. Write t. Say this sound with me: /t/. Listen as I blend all the sounds together: /y/ /e/ /t/, yet. Blend the sounds with me: /y/ /e/ /t/, yet. Now blend the sounds without me. Repeat by blending the words zip and jazz.

3 Guide Practice Continue the routine in Step 2 with the words that follow. Remember, first we say the sounds. Then we blend the sounds to read the word.

yes   yak   yell   zip   zag   fizz   kit   vet   Kip   vat
For corrective feedback, model blending the sounds to read the word. Have children blend the sounds and read the word with you.

4 Review What do you know about reading words that begin with the letters y or z or end with the letters zz? The sound for y is /y/. The sound for z and zz is /z/.

Routines Flip Chart

Spell words Now we are going to spell words with the sound /y/ spelled y and the sound /z/ spelled z and zz. The first word we will spell is yes. What sounds do you hear in yes? (/y/ /e/ /s/) What is the letter for /y/? Let's all write y. What is the letter for /e/? Write e. What is the letter for /s/? Write s. Have children confirm their spellings by comparing them with what you have written. Continue practice with yam, yet, zap, and jazz. Ask what letters change and what letters stay the same when you change yes to yet.

On their own Use the *Reader's and Writer's Notebook* p. 105.

Reader's and Writer's Notebook p. 105

Professional Development

Articulation It may be difficult for some children to articulate the /y/ sound. If so, have them practice the sound while looking in a mirror to see the position of their tongue.

Differentiated Instruction

SI Strategic Intervention

Blending Help children blend words by having three children work together. For the word *yes,* have one child say /y/, the second /e/, and the third /s/. Have them say their sounds in order, closer and closer together, until they form the word. Then have children try blending all the sounds on their own.

Spelling Patterns

/y/y The sound /y/ is usually spelled y.

/z/z, zz The sound /z/ is most often spelled z at the beginning of a word, but can appear as zz or s at the end of a word or a syllable.

ELL

English Language Learners

Develop Vocabulary Children whose home language is not English may be unfamiliar with some of the words used in this lesson, as words with initial /y/ and /z/ are relatively rare. You can help children develop their vocabularies by using words such as yak and zoom in sentences to give children an idea of their meaning. If possible, help children produce sentences of their own with these words.

Phonics
Identify Lower-Case and Upper-Case Letters

Guide Practice

Write a lower-case *y*. What letter is this? (lower-case *y*) Write an upper-case *Y*. What letter is this? (upper-case *Y*) Write a series of upper- and lower-case *y*'s. Point to each and have children identify each as upper-case *Y* or lower-case *y*. Repeat process with upper-case *Z* and lower-case *z*.

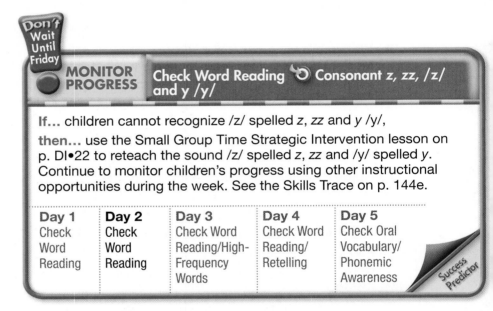

MONITOR PROGRESS — Check Word Reading ↺ Consonant *z, zz, /z/* and *y /y/*

If... children cannot recognize /z/ spelled *z, zz* and *y /y/*,

then... use the Small Group Time Strategic Intervention lesson on p. DI•22 to reteach the sound /z/ spelled *z, zz* and /y/ spelled *y*. Continue to monitor children's progress using other instructional opportunities during the week. See the Skills Trace on p. 144e.

Day 1	Day 2	Day 3	Day 4	Day 5
Check Word Reading	**Check Word Reading**	Check Word Reading/High-Frequency Words	Check Word Reading/ Retelling	Check Oral Vocabulary/ Phonemic Awareness

Success Predictor

Small Group Time

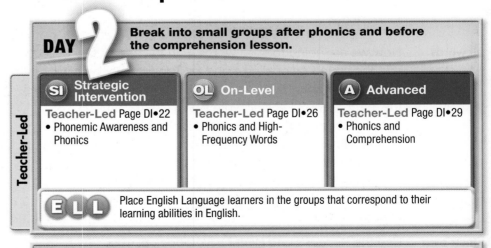

DAY 2 — Break into small groups after phonics and before the comprehension lesson.

Teacher-Led

SI Strategic Intervention
Teacher-Led Page DI•22
• Phonemic Awareness and Phonics

OL On-Level
Teacher-Led Page DI•26
• Phonics and High-Frequency Words

A Advanced
Teacher-Led Page DI•29
• Phonics and Comprehension

ELL Place English Language learners in the groups that correspond to their learning abilities in English.

Practice Stations
• Listen Up
• Word Work

Independent Activities
• Read independently/Reading log on *Reader's and Writer's Notebook* p. RR1

Phonics—Build Fluency
 Consonants v /v/, y /y/, z /z/

Model

Envision It!

Have children turn to page 144 in their Student Editions. Look at the pictures on this page. I see a picture of a *volcano*, a picture of a *yo-yo*, and a picture of a *zebra*. When I say *volcano*, I begin with the sound /v/. The /v/ sound is spelled with a *v*. When I say *yo-yo*, I begin with the sound /y/. The /y/ sound is spelled with a *y*. When I say *zebra*, I begin with the sound /z/. The /z/ sound is spelled with a *z*.

Guide practice

For each word in "Words I Can Blend," ask for the sound of each letter. Make sure that children identify the correct sound for *v, y,* or *z*. Then have children blend the whole word.

Corrective feedback

If... children have difficulty blending a word, **then...** model blending the word, and then ask children to blend it with you.

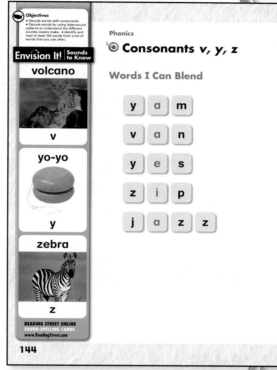

Student Edition p. 144

Objectives
- ○ Review characteristics of realistic fiction and fantasy.
- Distinguish realistic fiction from fantasy.
- Read high-frequency words

Skills Trace
◉ **Realism and Fantasy**
Introduce URW4D1; URW6D1
Practice URW4D2; URW4D3; URW4D4; URW6D2; URW6D3; URW6D4
Reteach/Review URW4D5; URW6D5; U1W3D2
Assess/Test Weekly Tests URW4; URW6
Benchmark Tests UR

Comprehension
Realism and Fantasy

Review realism and fantasy

When you read a made-up story that sounds like it could be true, that is **realistic fiction**. When you read a made-up story that cannot be true, you are reading **fantasy**.

Guide practice

Reread the story "A Busy Day" aloud. Have children listen and look for clues to tell them whether the story is realistic or fantasy. Write children's answers to the questions below.

What do the bears do in the story? (read books, buy fruit, buy hats) Would real bears do those things? (no)

The bears are doing things that people usually do. Real bears do not do these things. Is this story realistic fiction, or is it fantasy? (fantasy)

On their own

Have children work with a partner. Ask them to look through books they know. Ask them to use clues to decide if the books are fantasy or realistic.

Vocabulary
Sort Words

Discuss sorting words

Explain to children that we sort words by putting them into groups. Add that words go in the same group when they name things that are alike.

Model

Draw 3 circles on the board labeled *People, Places,* and *Things*. Explain that children can see people, places, and things in their neighborhood.

Explain that you will sort words by deciding if they tell about people, places, or things. A store is a place in a neighborhood. So, I'll write the word *store* in the circle marked *Places*. Repeat with *cars*, writing *cars* under *Things*.

Write the following words on the board. Read each word aloud and have children identify where it belongs. Write each word in the appropriate circle.

Guide practice

shoppers	sidewalk	trees	market
homes	library	neighbors	walkers

On their own

Have children work with a partner. Ask them to think of one more word to add to each circle. Have them share their words with the class.

High-Frequency Words

ROUTINE Nondecodable Words

1 **Say and Spell** Look at p. 153. Some words we have to learn by remembering the letters rather than saying the sounds. We will say and spell the words to help learn them. **Point to the word** *where*. This word is *where*. The letters in *where* are w-h-e-r-e, *where*.

2 **Demonstrate Meaning** Tell me a sentence using the word *where*. Repeat the routine with the other Words I Can Read.

Routines Flip Chart

Read words in isolation Have children reread the words on p. xx aloud. Add today's words to the Word Wall.

Read words in context Read the sentences aloud with children. Have them identify this week's High-Frequency Words in the sentences.

On their own Use *Reader's and Writer's Notebook* p. 120.

High-Frequency Words

Words I Can Read

where

here

for

me

go

Sentences I Can Read

1. Yaz will get me the yam in the van.
2. Mom can zip it here.
3. Where can Val go for jazz?

145

Student Edition p. 145

Differentiated Instruction

A **Advanced**
Make Sentences Have children work with a partner. Ask them to take turns thinking of sentences that include one of these words. Have them say their sentences aloud, omitting the high-frequency word, as in *I will ___ to the playground after school.* The partner then supplies the missing word.

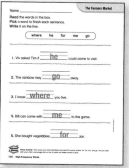

Reader's and Writer's Notebook p. 120

English Language Learners
Vocabulary Most of the words in the Guide Practice activity have been introduced, but children may not recall all of them. Use pictures to remind children of the meanings of these words. For example, point to the picture of the people walking on pages 140-141 of the Student Edition and say "These people are walking. We call them *walkers*." You may also wish to include small sketches in the sorting circles along with the words, such as sketching a tree next to the word *tree*.

Conventions
Sentences

Model sentences

Review that a sentence tells a complete idea and that most sentences end with special marks called periods. Explain that all sentences have a verb and that most sentences also have nouns and adjectives. Write *The fluffy dog barks.* on the board. Read it aloud. Ask children to identify the verb. (barks) Ask children to identify the noun and the adjective. (dog, fluffy) Finally, ask children to locate the period. Where does the period belong? (at the end of the sentence) What does the period mean? (that the sentence is over)

Guide practice

Write the followings groups of words on the board. Read each one aloud. Have children determine whether or not each group of words is written correctly. If a group of words is not written correctly, have them explain what change is needed to correct the group of words.

the big birds fly	(*the* should be capitalized)
with the new toys	(not a complete sentence; missing information)
I ran to the park	(add a period at the end of the sentence)
Pat and Kal	(not a complete sentence; missing information)

Connect to oral language

Have the class complete these sentence frames orally to form a complete sentence with a verb, a noun, and an adjective. Ask them what mark would go at the end of their sentences. (a period)

The cat _____.

I will _____.

Yesterday _____.

On their own

Use *Reader's and Writer's Notebook* p. 106.

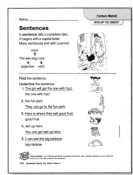

Reader's and Writer's
Notebook p. 106

Handwriting
Letters *Yy* and *Zz;*
Proper Body/Paper Position

Model letter formation

Display upper- and lower-case letters: *Yy* and *Zz.* Use the stroke instructions pictured below to model proper letter formation.

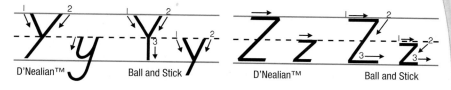

Model proper body and paper position

Explain that when people write, they must pay attention to how they are sitting and how they are holding the paper. Before I write, I make sure I am sitting up straight. Both my feet are on the floor. I am facing forward, and my arms are relaxed. Model both left-handed and right-handed paper positions; right-handed children should position the paper so the top edge slants down from the upper right corner, while left-handed children should position it so the top edge slants down from the upper left corner. Help children determine which they should use. Point out that the paper always slants in one direction or the other. Explain that slanting the paper makes it easier to form good letters and words.

Guide practice

Write the following words on the board: *yet, Zip, Yan, fizz.*

Team Talk Have one partner in each pair copy the first two words the other partner checks their work and checks that they are using correct body and paper position. Then have partners switch roles to write the last two words. Have partners discuss what they found easy and hard about using correct body and paper position.

On their own

Use *Reader's and Writer's Notebook* p. 107

Differentiated Instruction

SI Strategic Intervention

Reversals Many lower-case letters, such as *s, o,* and *a,* are formed by starting in the two-o'clock position and moving counterclockwise. The letter *z* does not fit this pattern. Partly as a result, many children write *z* backwards. You can help by having children use their fingers to trace the letter on models cut from sandpaper or another rough surface.

Academic Vocabulary

sentence a group of words that expresses a complete idea

Daily Fix-It

2. we can have fun
    We can have fun.

Discuss the Daily Fix-It corrections with children. Review the need for capital letters at the beginning of a sentence and periods or other punctuation marks at the end of a sentence.

ELL

English Language Learners
Generating Sentences Use picture cues to help children generate sentences with nouns, verbs, and adjectives. Show a picture of a dog, for instance, and ask children to name the animal. Then ask for an adjective that describes the dog (the dog is *big*), and a verb that tells what the dog is doing (the dog *runs*) to help children build *dog* into *The big dog runs.* Allow children to use gestures to convey ideas they do not yet have words for.

Reader's and Writer's Notebook p. 107

Objectives
- Produce a sentence.
- Write a complete sentence that contains a noun, verb, and adjective.
- Listen attentively.

Writing–Sentences

Model

Have children recall the Read Aloud, "A Busy Day." Bonnie and Betty do many things in this story. Let's write a sentence that tells about what they do. Write the sentence below. Read the sentence, and identify the nouns, verb, and adjective. Explain that the sentence is a complete idea.

> **The bears go to the outdoor market.**

Guide practice

Write more sentences about what you can do outside. Then read the sentences and have children identify the nouns, verbs, and adjectives.

> **The students visit the big library.**
>
> **The women zip up their yellow coats.**
>
> **Liz looks at the fresh yams.**

Connect to phonics

Reread the sentences with children and have them point to the words with /v/ spelled *v*, /y/ spelled *y*, and /z/ spelled *z*.

Shared writing

Rewrite the first sentence with a blank replacing the word *library*. Have children suggest different nouns to complete the sentence. Remind them to think of places you can go. Write children's suggestions on the board.

On their own

Some children may be ready to write on their own. Write another sentence on the board about what you can do outside. Leave a blank for a noun, a verb, or an adjective. Have children complete the sentence on their own. Children may also write new sentences, if they can. Have children identify the noun, verb, and adjective in their sentence. Then have them read their sentence aloud and explain how it tells a complete idea.

Listening and Speaking
Retell Stories

Teach retelling stories

Explain that retelling a story means to tell a story that you already know. Add that when you retell a story, you use your own words to tell what happens.

- When you retell a story, you need to tell about the characters.
- You should tell your listener what the setting of the story is.
- You also need to tell what happens in order.

Model

 Think About It I will start retelling the story "A Busy Day." *This story is about two bears named Bonnie and Betty. Bonnie and Betty were friends. They went to the library, where they got different books: Bonnie liked stories about space, and Betty got stories about people. They thought it was interesting that they liked different kinds of books, but they were friends anyway.* There! That's a good beginning. I didn't use the exact words of the story, because I'm not reading it to you — I'm retelling it.

Guide practice

Have children complete your retelling of "A Busy Day" in their own words. Encourage all children to contribute ideas.

On their own

Have pairs of children take turns retelling stories they know. Remind them to use the rules for listening established in Week 1.

Wrap Up Your Day

✔ **Consonants *Yy* /y/, *Zz* /z/** Write the letters *Yy* and *Zz*. Have children identify the letters. Have children name the sounds /y/ and /z/.

✔ **Build Concepts** Recall the Big Book *First Grade, Here I Come!.* Have children tell where Henry's teacher took the class to browse through books. Monitor children's use of oral vocabulary as they respond.

Differentiated Instruction

 Strategic Intervention

Use Pictures If children have difficulty sequencing events, have them retell a story from a picture book by leafing through the pages of the book and using the pictures as clues. Help them use time order words such as *first, next, then,* and *after that.*

Academic Vocabulary

character a person, animal, or personalized object in a story

setting where and when a story takes place

sequence the order of events

ELL

English Language Learners
Cooperative Retelling Have English language learners work in pairs with children whose home language is English. Have them work together to retell one or two stories. Have them take turns telling events in the story. This allows the native speaker to model vocabulary and sentence structure, while still including the ELL child in the activity.

Preview DAY 3

Tell children that tomorrow they will hear one last time about Henry's first day in first grade.

Objectives
- Build oral vocabulary.
- Identify details in text.
- Share information and ideas about the concept.

Today at a Glance

Oral Vocabulary
fact

Print Awareness
Sentence Features

Phonological Awareness
Identify syllables

Phonics
◉ Short u: u

High-Frequency Words
for, go, here, me, where

Conventions
Sentences

Handwriting
Letter U and u Self-Evaluation

Writing
Sentences

Listening and Speaking
Relate an Experience in Sequence

Concept Talk

 Question of the Week
What can we see around our neighborhood?

Build concepts

To reinforce concepts and to focus children's attention, have children sing "Shopping Day" from the *Sing with Me* Big Book. What are some things you know about an outdoor market? (it's big, it's full of people, you can buy things there)

🔘 Sing with Me Big Book Audio

Monitor listening comprehension

Display the Big Book, *First Grade, Here I Come!*. Read the book aloud. Tell children to think about why Henry thinks first grade is not too much for him.

- Why does Henry tell his mother that first grade is not too much for him? (Henry is a real first grader now. He's done a lot of things that real first graders do.)

FIRST GRADE, HERE I COME!

NANCY CARLSON

Big Book

ELL **Expand Vocabulary** Use the Day 3 instruction on ELL Poster R3 to help children expand vocabulary.

ELL Poster R3

Oral Vocabulary
Amazing Words

Teach Amazing Words

 **Amazing Words**   Oral Vocabulary Routine

1 **Introduce the Word** Relate the word *fact* to the book. Mr. McCarthy taught the class a *fact* about science. Supply a child-friendly definition: A *fact* is something that you can prove is true. Everybody agrees that a *fact* is true. Have children say the word.

2 **Demonstrate** Provide examples to show meaning. It is a *fact* that the name of our school is _____. It is a *fact* that the sun warms us. It is a *fact* that plants need water to grow.

3 **Apply** Have children demonstrate their understanding. Give an example of a *fact* you know.

Routines Flip Chart

Anchored Talk

Add to the concept map

Use these questions to discuss what other things people can see in their neighborhoods as you add to the concept map.

- Recall the Big Book, *First Grade, Here I Come!*. What neighborhood place do we see in this story? (Henry's school) I'll add *We can see schools* to our map of what we can see in our neighborhood.

- Point out that schools, farmers markets, parks, and libraries are all places that children can see in many neighborhoods.

bargain	fact
browse	cost
bustling	customer
library	scale

Differentiated Instruction

A **Advanced**

Fact and Opinion Explain that an opinion is something that you believe, but cannot prove is true. Have children work in pairs or small groups to generate statements that are facts and statements that are opinions.

 ELL

English Language Learners

Pronunciation Spanish, Greek, and some other languages do not have final consonant blends, such as the /kt/ that ends the word *fact*. Say /k/, /t/, and /kt/ slowly and carefully. Have children identify which sound or blend you are saying. Then have children practice saying the sounds to you and each other.

Print Awareness
Sentence Features

Review
Sentence Features

Yesterday you learned that sentences are a complete idea. You learned that sentences always begin with capital letters. You also learned that sentences usually end with periods.

Model

I'm going to write a sentence on the board. I'll have to remember to use a capital letter at the beginning and a period at the end. I'll use this song to help me. Sing the following to the tune of "Old McDonald Had a Farm," and have children sing with you:

> *Old McDonald writes a sentence, E-I-E-I-O.*
> *The sentence is a full idea, E-I-E-I-O.*
> *A capital's first*
> *A period's last*
> *Capital — period — capital — period*
> *Old McDonald writes a sentence, E-I-E-I-O.*

On the board, write the sentence *We can read lots of books*. Read it aloud with children. Then underline the initial *W*. A capital's first. Underline the period. A period's last. Touch the *W* and the period in turn as you say or sing: Capital — period — capital — period. Repeat with the sentence *The sky is blue*.

Guide practice

I want to write the sentence *It is fun to go swimming*. What word do I write first? What do I have to remember when I write this word? (to make the initial I a capital letter) Write *It's*. Now I'll write *is fun to go swimming* — What needs to come at the end? (a period) Repeat with the sentence *Dogs can run fast*.

On their own

Use *Reader's and Writer's Notebook* p. 113

Reader's and Writer's Notebook p. 113

Phonological Awareness
Identify Syllables

Model producing rhyming words

Have children look at the picture on pages 142–143 in their Student Edition. Today we are going to use this picture to help us tell how many syllables each word has. A syllable is a word part. Some words have just one syllable. Others have two syllables, or three syllables, or even more. I see a picture of a *zebra*. Find the picture of the *zebra*. The word *zebra* has two syllables. Listen carefully: *ze-bra*. I can tap my knee when I say each syllable to help me keep track. Watch. **Tap your knee twice as you say** *ze-bra*. The first syllable is *ze*. The second syllable is *bra*. *Ze-bra*. Now I see a man playing a *violin*. How many syllables are there in *violin*? Listen as I tap the syllables. Help me count. *Vi-o-lin*. **Tap your knee three times, once for each syllable.** There are three syllables in *vi-o-lin*. The first syllable is *vi*. The second syllable is *o*. The third syllable is *lin*. Say it with me and tap the syllables: *vi-o-lin*.

Student Edition pp. 142–143

Guide practice

Lead children in tapping the syllables for the following words: *zigzag, umbrella, quarter, truck*.

On their own

Have children tap the syllables and identify the number of syllables in the following words:

zipper	vine	unloading
yarn	quietly	yellow

(Team Talk) Have children work with a partner to tap and count the syllables in their names and in other words of their choice.

Phonics
Short *u*: /u/

Hear Today you will learn how to spell the sound /u/. Listen: /u/, /u/, /u/. When you say /u/, your mouth is open and your tongue is down. Say /u/. Was your mouth open? Was your tongue down? Say /u/ again. Watch and listen as children produce the sound. Say /u/ with me: /u/, /u/, /u/.

Say Display Sound-Spelling Card 24. This is a picture of an *umbrella*. Say it with me: *umbrella*. The first sound in *umbrella* is /u/. Listen: /u/, *umbrella*. Say it with me: /u/, *umbrella*. What is the first sound in *umbrella*?

Point to *u*. This is *u*. The sound /u/ is usually spelled u. *Umbrella* begins with /u/. *Umbrella* begins with the letter *u*. Have children say /u/ several times as you point to *u*.

Sound-Spelling Card 24

See Display p. 26. Point to the letters *Uu* at the top of the page. The name for both of these letters is *u*. Point to *U*. This is an upper-case *U*. Point to *u*. This is a lower-case *u*. Point to each letter again and ask: What is the name of this letter?

Read ABC Rhyme Time Point to the word *luck* in the first line of the rhyme. Here is the word *luck*. I can hear /u/ in the middle of the word. Listen: *luck, l-uck, /u/*. How is the /u/ spelled in this word? (u) We spell the /u/ in *luck* with a lower-case *u*. The sound /u/ is usually spelled with a lower-case *u*. Point to the word *Under* in the third line. This word is *Under*. It begins with the sound /u/. The sound /u/ is spelled with *u*. This time we use an upper-case *U* because the word *Under* is at the beginning of the line.

ABC Rhyme Time p. 26

Read the rhyme aloud, tracking the print with your finger. Then read it again. Point to examples of /u/ spelled *U* or *u* and name the words they begin. Point to words that have /u/ in the middle. Have children find other examples of words that begin with *u* and words that have *u* in the middle.

Write Now I will show you how to write upper-case *U* and lower-case *u*. Write *U*. Watch as I trace upper-case *U* with my finger. Follow the stroke instructions pictured. Now you write upper-case *U*. Repeat for lower-case *u*.

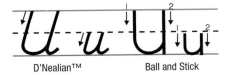

D'Nealian™   Ball and Stick

Phonics—Teach/Model
⟳ Short u: u

U u

u

Sound-Spelling
Card 24

ROUTINE   **Blending Strategy**

① **Connect** Connect *u* to the sound /u/. Write *u*. This is *u*. What is the sound for *u*? The sound for *u* is /u/. Say the sound with me: /u/, /u/, /u/. When you see *u*, what sound will you say?

② **Model** Model how to blend *run*. Write r. What is the sound for this letter? Say the sound with me: /r/. Write *u*. Say this sound with me: /u/. Write *n*. Say this sound with me: /n/. Listen as I blend all the sounds together: /r/ /u/ /n/, *run*. Blend the sounds with me: /r/ /u/ /n/, *run*. Now blend the sounds without me.

③ **Guide Practice** Continue the routine in Step 2 with the words that follow. Remember, first we say the sounds. Then we blend the sounds to read the word.

| up | bus | tug | sun | buzz | cup |

For corrective feedback, model blending the sounds to read the word. Then have children blend the sounds and read the word with you.

④ **Review** What do you know about reading words that begin with the letter *u* or have *u* in the middle of the word? The sound for *u* is /u/.

Routines Flip Chart

Spell Now we are going to spell words with the sound /u/ spelled *u*. The first word we will spell is *up*. What sounds do you hear in *up*? (/u/ /p/) What is the letter for /u/? Let's all write *u*. What is the letter for /p/? Write *p*. Have children confirm their spellings by comparing them with what you have written. Continue practice with *cut, bug, mud,* and *tub*.

On their own Use the *Reader's and Writer's Notebook* p. 109 for additional practice with /u/ spelled *u*.

Reader's and Writer's
Notebook p. 109

Professional Development

Letter Sounds While the sound /u/ is very similar to the schwa sound, the two are not identical. Avoid telling children that the *a* in *about* or *around,* for example, has the sound /u/.

Differentiated Instruction

SI Strategic Intervention

/u/ spelled *u* To help children associate the sound /u/ with the letter *u,* have them write the curved part of the letter *u* while saying /u/, their voices falling and rising as they make strokes down and then up. Then have them draw in the tail of the letter and say *U!* Have children repeat several times.

Spelling Pattern

***u*/u/** The sound /u/ is usually spelled *u* at the beginning or in the middle of a word.

ELL

English Language Learners
Vowel Discrimination The sound /u/ may be hard for some English learners to distinguish from other short vowel sounds, notably /o/. Help children by saying word pairs such as *rob/rub* and *cot/cut* and having children hold up cards with the appropriate letter.

Objectives
- Recognize and name the letters *Uu*.
- Practice high-frequency words.

Phonics
Identify Lower-Case and Upper-Case Letters

Guide Practice

Write a lower-case *u* and point to it. What letter is this? (lower-case *u*)
Write an upper-case *U* and point to it. What letter is this? (upper-case *U*)
Write a series of upper- and lower-case *u*'s. Point to each and have children identify each as upper-case *U* or lower-case *u*.

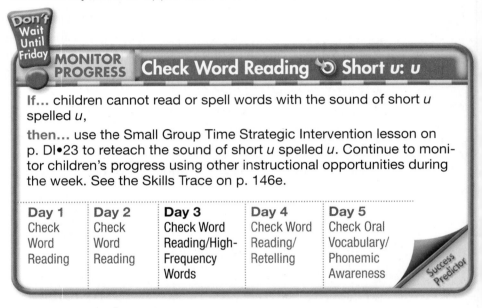

MONITOR PROGRESS Check Word Reading Short *u*: *u*

If... children cannot read or spell words with the sound of short *u* spelled *u*,

then... use the Small Group Time Strategic Intervention lesson on p. DI•23 to reteach the sound of short *u* spelled *u*. Continue to monitor children's progress using other instructional opportunities during the week. See the Skills Trace on p. 146e.

Day 1	**Day 2**	**Day 3**	**Day 4**	**Day 5**
Check Word Reading	Check Word Reading	Check Word Reading/High-Frequency Words	Check Word Reading/Retelling	Check Oral Vocabulary/Phonemic Awareness

Small Group Time

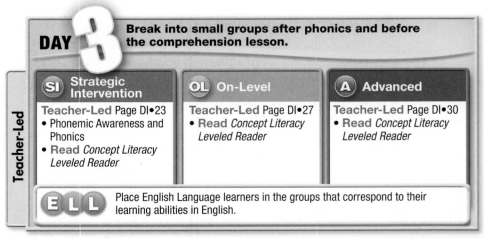

DAY 3 Break into small groups after phonics and before the comprehension lesson.

Teacher-Led

SI Strategic Intervention	**OL On-Level**	**A Advanced**
Teacher-Led Page DI•23	Teacher-Led Page DI•27	Teacher-Led Page DI•30
• Phonemic Awareness and Phonics	• **Read** *Concept Literacy Leveled Reader*	• **Read** *Concept Literacy Leveled Reader*
• **Read** *Concept Literacy Leveled Reader*		

ELL Place English Language learners in the groups that correspond to their learning abilities in English.

Practice Stations	**Independent Activities**
• Words to Know	• Read independently/Reading log on *Reader's and Writer's Notebook* p. RR1

High-Frequency Words
Practice

Review

Review this week's Words to Read: *there, go, here, for, me.*

• Point to a word. Say and spell it.

• Use each word in a sentence.

Guide practice

Point to the words in random order. Have children say and spell the words as you point to them. Then ask children to use each word in a sentence.

Have children work in pairs. Have one child say a sentence that includes one of the high-frequency words for the week. Have the other child listen for the word. Then have children switch roles.

On their own

Use *Reader's and Writer's Notebook* p. 120.

Don't Wait Until Friday

MONITOR PROGRESS ↻ High-Frequency Words

Point to these words on the Word Wall and have the class read them. Listen for children who miss words during the reading. Call on those children to read some of the words individually.

there	go	here	for	me	Spiral Review
look	is	they	to	are ←	**Row 2** reviews previously taught high-frequency words.

If... children cannot read these words,

then... use the Small Group Time Strategic Intervention lesson, p. DI•108, to reteach the words. Monitor children's fluency with these words during reading, and provide additional practice.

Day 1	Day 2	Day 3	Day 4	Day 5
Check Word Reading	Check Word Reading	Check High-Frequency Words/ Retelling	Check Fluency	Check Vocabulary

Success Predictor

Objectives
- Generate and identify sentences.
- Write *Uu*.
- Evaluate letter formation.

Conventions
Sentences

Review sentences

Remind children that a sentence tells about someone or something. Sentences also tell what is happening. Sentences tell a complete idea. A sentence begins with a capital letter and ends with a period.

Guide practice

Read this sentence aloud to children and have children repeat after you.

> **The tall man reads a book.**

Next write the sentence on the board. Read it aloud to children as you point to each word.

Now we are going to see if this is a sentence. The first thing we need to look for is someone or something that the group of words is about. Is there someone or something that the sentence is about? **(the tall man)** The next thing we need to look for is what happens in the group of words. Is anything happening? **(Possible response: The tall man is reading a book.)** Does this group of words begin with a capital letter? **(yes)** Does this group of words end with a period? **(yes)** Then we know that this group of words is a sentence! Repeat with the sentence fragment *The black cow.* and with the complete sentence *The girl plays a game.*

Connect to oral language

Have children complete these sentence frames orally. Remind them to make sure that their sentences include nouns, verbs, and adjectives.

> 1. The mouse _____.
> 2. My brother _____.
> 3. _____ inside a house.

On their own

Use *Reader's and Writer's Notebook* p. 111.

Reader's and Writer's Notebook
p. 111

Handwriting
Letter *U* and *u;*
Self-Evaluation

Model letter formation

Display upper- and lower-case letters: *Uu.* Use the stroke instructions pictured below to model proper letter formation.

D'Nealian™   Ball and Stick

Model self-evaluation

Remind children that when they write a word, they can look back at their writing and see if they did a good job. Ask yourself if your letters are the right size, if they are spaced correctly, and if you can read all the words. Write three upper-case *U*'s and three lower-case *u*'s on the board. Make one of the upper-case *U*'s too tall. Curve one of the lower-case *u*'s so it looks something like a lower-case *a.* Now, I'll look at what I wrote. My spacing is good. But this *U* is too tall. I need to write it again so it's smaller. And this *u* looks too much like an *a.* I should write that letter again, too. Checking my work helps me do my best job.

Guide practice

Write the sentence *The cub sat in the tub* on the board, and read it aloud. Make two or three obvious handwriting errors, such as writing letters too closely together or making them the wrong size.

Team Talk Have pairs talk about which letters are well-written and which could be better.

On their own

Use *Reader's and Writer's Notebook* p. 112

Reader's and Writer's Notebook
p. 112

SI **Strategic Intervention**

Distinguish Between *Uu* and *Vv* It can be difficult for some children to distinguish between *Uu* and *Vv.* You can help by emphasizing the fact that *Uu* has a rounded bottom, while *Vv* has a pointed bottom. Have children practice writing both letters with an obvious curve for *Uu* and an equally obvious point for *Vv*; do not allow children to write letters that look halfway pointed and halfway curved.

Daily Fix-It

3. zak is herE
   Zak is here.

Discuss the Daily Fix-It corrections with children. Review sentence capitalization and punctuation.

ELL

English Language Learners

Ask Questions If children do not have the vocabulary to explain what is wrong with handwriting, help them by asking questions that help provide the needed words. For instance, ask *Which letter is too tall?*, indicating height with your hand, or *Which letters are too close?*, indicating nearness with your hands as well. Children can point or use words to answer you. Encourage them to try using vocabulary such as *tall* and *close* themselves.

Objectives
- Produce a sentence.
- Write a complete sentence that contains a noun, verb, and adjective.
- Listen attentively.

Writing—Sentences

Model

Have children recall the Big Book, *First Grade, Here I Come!* Yesterday and today we heard a story about a mouse. Let's write a sentence that tells about Henry and his classroom. Write the sentence below.

> **He learns about a new corner.**

Read the sentence, and identify the noun, verb, and adjective. Point out that the sentence is a complete idea. It begins with an uppercase letter and ends with a period.

Guide practice

Write more sentences about Henry's classroom and what Henry might do there. Then read the sentences and have children identify the nouns, verbs, and adjectives.

> **Henry shuts a big window.**
>
> **A little pet runs.**
>
> **Henry reads a fun book.**

Connect to phonics

Reread the sentences with children and have them point to the words with /u/ spelled *u*.

Shared writing

Write the following sentence frame on the board: *I _____ in my _____ classroom.* Have children suggest different verbs and adjectives to complete the sentence. Tell children to think about words that describe their classroom and what they do there. Use children's suggestions to complete the sentence.

On their own

Some children may be ready to write on their own. Write the following sentence frame on the board: *The _____ was in the _____ box.* Have children think of a noun and an adjective to complete the sentence on their own. Children may also write new sentences, if they can. Have children identify the noun, verb, and adjective in each sentence. Then have them read their sentence aloud and explain how it tells a complete idea.

Listening and Speaking
Relate an Experience in Sequence

Review
sequence

Ask children to recall what they know about telling experiences in sequence. Review good listening behaviors for telling an experience in sequence.

- Decide what happened first. Tell about that part.
- Decide what happened next. Tell about those parts.
- Think about what happened last. Tell about that part at the end.

Model

Think Aloud Here's something that happened to me last weekend. First, I was walking in the park with one of my friends. Then, my friend thought she saw a beautiful red bird in the bushes. So we looked for the bird. But we couldn't find it. After that, we went home. Point out that you have told your experience in sequence. You started with what happened first and ended with what happened last.

Guide practice

Have children take turns retelling your story in order. Give them prompts such as *What happened next?* when necessary.

On their own

Have pairs of children tell each other experiences they have had. Remind children to tell the events in order and observe the listening and speaking behaviors they have learned.

Wrap Up Your Day

✔ **/u/ spelled *u*** Write the letters *U* and *u*. Have children identify the letters. Write *Up and buzz.* Point to the *U* in *Up* and the *u* in *buzz* as you say the words. Have children say them after you.

✔ **High-Frequency Words** Point to the words *where, go, here, for,* and *me* on the Word Wall. Have children read each word and use it in a sentence.

✔ **Build Concepts** Have children tell two or three events from the book in sequence. Monitor children's use of oral vocabulary as they respond. Recall the Big Book, *First Grade, Here I Come!*

Preview DAY 4

Tell children that tomorrow they will hear about Sam's father and sister and their trip to the farmers market.

Objectives
- Discuss the concept to develop oral language.
- Build oral vocabulary.
- Identify details in text.

Today at a Glance

Oral Vocabulary
cost, customer, scale

Print Awareness
Sentence Features

Phonemic Awareness
Blend and segment phonemes

Phonics
◉ Consonant Qq and *qu* /kw/

Genre
Realistic Fiction

High-Frequency Words
for, go, here, me, where

Comprehension
◉ Realism and Fantasy
◉ Background Knowledge

Writing
Sentences

Research
Library/Media Center

Handwriting
Q and *q*/Letter Size

Concept Talk

Question of the Week

 What can we see around our neighborhood?

Build concepts

To reinforce concepts and to focus children's attention, have children sing "Shopping Day" from the *Sing with Me* Big Book. What are some things you can buy in your neighborhood? (Possible responses: food, books, toys)

 Sing with Me Big Book Audio

Monitor listening comprehension

Help children recall that in the Big Book *First Grade, Here I Come!,* Henry learns a science fact from Mr. McCarthy. Explain that today you will read a selection that tells facts about a city market where food is sold. Have children listen to learn who buys food from this market. Read the selection.

Read Aloud Anthology "Market to Market to Market"

 **Produce Oral Language** Use the Day 4 instruction on ELL Poster R6 to extend and enrich language.

ELL Poster R6

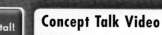

Oral Vocabulary
Amazing Words

Teach Amazing Words

Amazing Words Oral Vocabulary Routine

1. **Introduce the Word** Relate the word *customer* to the story. Some *customers* come to markets early in the morning. Supply a child-friendly definition: A *customer* is a person who wants to buy something. Have children say the word.

2. **Demonstrate** Provide examples to show meaning. A *customer* walked into the shoe store to try on shoes. That *customer* was talking about the TV she wanted to buy. The *customers* had to wait in line at the restaurant..

3. **Apply** Have children demonstrate their understanding. When are you a *customer*?

   See p. OV•3 to teach *cost* and *scale*.

Routines Flip Chart

Anchored Talk

Add to the concept map

Discuss stores and businesses that can be found in neighborhoods.

- In "Market to Market to Market," some customers buy fruits, vegetables, and fish. What kinds of places do these customers own? (restaurant and grocery stores)

- Are restaurant and grocery stores like parks, like schools, or like stores? (stores) Where should we put them in our concept map? (connected to *stores*)

Differentiated Instruction

 Strategic Intervention

Pronunciation Many children drop the final consonant in blends that end a word, such as the final *t* in *cost*. To help children master the formal pronunciation, say *cost* slowly and clearly, emphasizing the final *t*, and have children repeat.

ELL

English Language Learners

Act It Out Have children act out buying and selling in a store. Have them use words, phrases, and gestures to indicate what they want to buy. Give them play money and other items to use as props. Sum up by asking which child played the role of the customer and how much money each item cost.

Print Awareness
Sentence Features

Review
Sentence Features

Remind children that sentences begin with a capital letter and end with a period or another punctuation mark. Have children point to a capital letter somewhere in the room. Then have them use their finger to mime making a period in the air. Finally, remind children that sentences are complete ideas that contain verbs and usually contain nouns and adjectives as well.

Model

I'm going to be a sentence detective. I'll write some things on the board. Some of them might be sentences. Some of them might not be sentences. My job as a detective is to figure out which is which.

Write the following on the board:

We fill the bag with stuff   *The men run fast.*

cut the yam.   *On the sun.*

Look at the first example and read it aloud. Pretend to use a magnifying glass. Let me see if this is a sentence. It's a complete idea. I see a verb— *fill*. And I see an upper-case *W* at the beginning. But there's no period at the end. So, it isn't a sentence. To be a sentence, it needs a period. What can I do to make this one a sentence? (**add a period**)

Guide practice

Point to the next example, *The men run fast*, and read it with children. Take out your magnifying glasses, and we'll see if this is a sentence. Is it a complete thought? (**yes**) Does it have a verb? Which word is the verb? (**yes; run**) Does it begin with a capital letter? (**yes**) Have children name the last question they need to ask; then have them answer it. (**Does it end with a period? yes**) Then ask whether the example is a sentence or is not a sentence. (**it is a sentence**) Good work, detectives!

On their own

Use *Reader's and Writer's Notebook* p. 113

Reader's and Writer's Notebook p. 113

Phonemic Awareness
Segment and Blend Phonemes

Model

We just read about how fish and other foods are delivered to city markets late at night. People often use a van to make these deliveries. Listen to the sounds in *van*: /v/ /a/ /n/. Listen as I blend the sounds to say the word *van*: /v/ /a/ /n/, van. Say it with me: /v/ /a/ /n/, van. **Repeat with the word *zip*.**

Guide practice

Now we're going to blend sounds to say other words. Listen to the sounds in *yet*: /y/ /e/ /t/. Say the sounds with me: /y/ /e/ /t/. Now let's blend the sounds: /y/ /e/ /t/, *yet*. **Continue with the following words. Say the sounds in each word with the children and then blend the sounds to say the word.**

/kw/ /i/ /t/, quit	**/b/ /u/ /z/,** buzz	**/v/ /e/ /t/,** vet
/y/ /e/ /s/, yes	**/kw/ /a/ /k/,** quack	**/z/ /a/ /p/,** zap

Corrective feedback

If children make an error, model the correct response. Return to the word later in the practice.

On their own

Continue with the following words. Have children say the sounds in each word and then blend the sounds to say the word.

/h/ /e/ /n/, hen	**/f/ /i/ /z/,** fizz	**/m/ /e/ /t/,** met
/kw/ /i/ /k/, quick	**/h/ /a/ /v/,** have	**/y/ /e/ /l/,** yell

Differentiated Instruction

 Advanced

More Blending Have children work with a partner. Have them take turns mentally breaking a short word into phonemes (such as /t/ /o/ /p/ for *top*), saying the phonemes in the correct order, and challenging the partner to identify and say the word.

ELL

English Language Learners
Pronounce /kw/ The sound /kw/ may be difficult for speakers of some languages to produce. Although /kw/ appears most often at the beginning of words in English, you may find that children have an easier time producing the sound when it is preceded by a vowel. If children have difficulty saying /kw/, then, consider having them practice with words such as *aqua* and *equal* before moving on to *quick* and *queen*.

Objectives

○ Associate the letter combination *qu* with the sound /kw/.

• Write the letters *Qq*.

• Blend, read, and spell words with *qu*.

• Recognize and name the letters *Qq*.

• Demonstrate understanding that *q* is almost always followed by *u*.

Phonics
⟳ Consonants Qq and *qu* /kw/

Hear
Today you will learn how to spell the sound /kw/. Listen: /kw/, /kw/, /kw/. When you say /kw/, the back of your tongue is humped and in the back of your mouth. Then your lips make a circle. Say /kw/ and feel how your lips make a circle at the end. **Watch and listen as children produce the sound.** Say /kw/ with me: /kw/, /kw/, /kw/.

Say
Display Sound-Spelling Card 19. This is a picture of a *quilt*. Say it with me: *quilt*. The first sound in quilt is /kw/. Listen: /kw/, *quilt*. Say it with me: /kw/, *quilt*. What is the first sound in *quilt*?

See
Point to *qu*. This is *qu*. The sound /kw/ is usually spelled *qu*. The letter *q* is a special letter because the letter *u* almost always comes right after it. *Q* and *u* go together. *Quilt* begins with /kw/. *Quilt* begins with the letters *qu*. Have children say /kw/ several times as you point to *qu*.

Sound-Spelling Card 19

Read ABC Rhyme Time
Display ABC Rhyme Time, p. 22. Point to the letters *Qq* at the top of the page. The name for both of these letters is *q*. Point to Q. This is an upper-case Q. Point to q. This is a lower-case *q*. Point to each letter again and ask: What is the name of this letter?

This rhyme is called *Quiet Queen*. Read the rhyme aloud, tracking the print with your finger. Then read it again. Point to examples of upper- and lower-case *q*'s as you read each word aloud. Check with children that every *q* in the poem is followed by a *u*.

ABC Rhyme Time p. 22

Write
Now I will show you how to write upper-case Q and lower-case q. Write Q. Watch as I trace upper-case Q with my finger. Follow the stroke instructions pictured. Now you write upper-case Q. Repeat for lower-case q.

D'Nealian™   Ball and Stick

Phonics—Teach/Model
↻ Consonant *qu* /kw/

ROUTINE **Blending Strategy**

① Connect Connect *qu* to the sound /kw/. Write *qu*. This is *qu*. The sound for *qu* is /kw/. Say the sound with me: /kw/, /kw/, /kw/. When you see the letters *qu*, what sound will you say?

② Model Model how to blend *quit*. Write *qu*. What is the sound for these letters? Say the sound with me: /kw/. Write *i*. Say this sound with me: /i/. Write *t*. Say this sound with me: /t/. Listen as I blend all the sounds together: /kw/ /i/ /t/, *quit*. Blend the sounds with me: /qu/ /i/ /t/, *quit*. Now blend the sounds without me.

③ Guide Practice Continue the routine in Step 2 with the words that follow. Remember, first we say the sounds. Then we blend the sounds to read the word. Explain that qu is not a common letter combination in English.

quiz	quill	quit	zip	fizz
yen	yes	van	Von	Quin

For corrective feedback, model blending the sounds. Then have children blend the sounds and read the word with you.

④ Review What do you know about reading words that begin with the letters *qu*? (The sound for *qu* is /kw/.)

Routines Flip Chart

Spell words Now we are going to spell words with the sound /kw/ spelled *qu*. The first word we will spell is *quiz*. What are the letters for /kw/? Let's all write *qu*. What is the letter for /i/? Write *i*. What is the letter for /z/? Write *z*. Have children confirm their spellings by comparing them with what you have written. Continue practice with the words *quill* and *quit*. Ask how *quip* and *quit* are alike and how they are different.

On their own Use the *Reader's and Writer's Notebook* p. 114 for additional practice with consonant *qu* /kw/.

Reader's and Writer's Notebook p. 114

Differentiated Instruction

SI **Strategic Intervention**
Letter combination *qu* In English, most sounds are represented by just one letter. Some children may have difficulty remembering that *qu* goes together to form /kw/. They may try to blend words such as *quit* as /kw/ /u/ /i/ /t/. You can help by circling or underlining the *qu* letter pair to remind children that they are to be read as a unit.

Spelling Pattern
/kw/qu The sound /kw/ is almost always spelled *qu*.

ELL

English Language Learners
Words with *qu* /kw/ Many languages associate the letters *qu* with sounds other than /kw/. In Spanish, for instance, *qu* is always followed by the letters *e* or *i* and has the sound /k/. In French, likewise, *qu* is one way of spelling /k/, and in German, *qu* represents /kv/. If children are already familiar with the letters *qu* from another language, be sure they realize that the combination stands for a different sound in English.

Objectives

- ○ Associate letter combination *qu* with the sound /kw/.
- • Write the letters *Qq*.
- • Blend, read, and spell words with *qu, v, y, z,* and short *u*.
- • Recognize and name the letters *Qq*.

Phonics
Identify Lower-Case and Upper-Case Letters

Guide practice

Write a lower-case *q* and point to it. What letter is this? (lower-case *q*) Write an upper-case *Q* and point to it. What letter is this? (upper-case *Q*) Write a series of upper- and lower-case *q*'s. Point to each and have children identify each as upper-case *Q* or lower-case *q*.

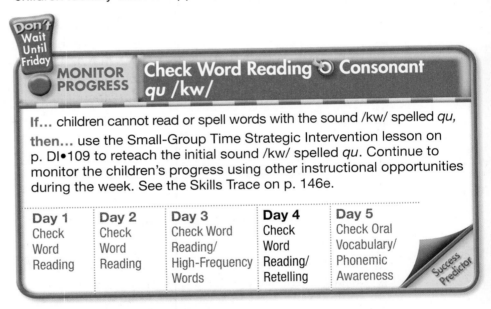

Don't Wait Until Friday

MONITOR PROGRESS

Check Word Reading ○ Consonant *qu* /kw/

If... children cannot read or spell words with the sound /kw/ spelled *qu*,

then... use the Small-Group Time Strategic Intervention lesson on p. DI•109 to reteach the initial sound /kw/ spelled *qu*. Continue to monitor the children's progress using other instructional opportunities during the week. See the Skills Trace on p. 146e.

Day 1	**Day 2**	**Day 3**	**Day 4**	**Day 5**
Check Word Reading	Check Word Reading	Check Word Reading/ High-Frequency Words	Check Word Reading/ Retelling	Check Oral Vocabulary/ Phonemic Awareness

Success Predictor

Small Group Time

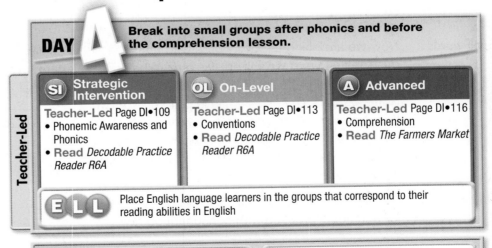

DAY 4 Break into small groups after phonics and before the comprehension lesson.

Teacher-Led

SI Strategic Intervention

Teacher-Led Page DI•109
- Phonemic Awareness and Phonics
- **Read** *Decodable Practice Reader R6A*

OL On-Level

Teacher-Led Page DI•113
- Conventions
- **Read** *Decodable Practice Reader R6A*

A Advanced

Teacher-Led Page DI•116
- Comprehension
- **Read** *The Farmers Market*

ELL Place English language learners in the groups that correspond to their reading abilities in English

Practice Stations
- Read for Meaning

Independent Activities
- Read independently/Reading log on *Reader's and Writer's Notebook* p. RR1.
- AudioText of Main Selection

Phonics—Build Fluency
Consonant *qu* /kw/ and Short *u* /u/

Model

Envision It!

Have children turn to page 146 in their Student Edition. Look at the pictures on this page. I see a picture of a *quilt* and a picture of an *umbrella*. When I say *quilt*, I begin with the sound /kw/. The /kw/ sound is spelled with the letter pair *qu*. When I say *umbrella*, I begin with the sound /u/.

Guide practice

For each word in "Words I Can Blend," ask for the sound of each letter or letter pair. Make sure that children identify the correct sound for *qu* or short *u*. Then have children blend the whole word.

Student Edition p. 146

Corrective feedback

If... children have difficulty blending a word, **then...** model blending the word, and then ask children to blend it with you.

On their own

Use *Reader's and Writer's Notebook* p. 114

Reader's and Writer's Notebook p. 114

Differentiated Instruction

A Advanced

Extend Blending Provide children who can segment and blend all the words correctly with more challenging words such as: *quilt, queens, quiet, quest,* and *quotes.*

Spelling Patterns

/kw/ Spelled *qu* The sound /kw/ is almost always spelled *qu*.

/u/ Spelled *u* The sound /u/ is usually spelled *u*.

ELL

English Language Learners

Vocabulary Building Help children build vocabulary by providing meanings for the words in the "Words I Can Blend" section. Use the words in sentences and make use of simple gestures and illustrations to help children's understanding. For *bus*, for example, say *This word is* bus. *I ride the* bus *to school*, and sketch a picture on the board. Encourage children to make up sentences of their own that use these words.

Decodable Practice Reader R6A
🔊 Consonant Qq and *qu* /kw/

Decode words in isolation

Have children turn to page 81. Have children decode each word.

Review high-frequency words

Review the previously taught words *for, a, do,* and *the.* Have children read each word as you point to it on the Word Wall.

Preview Decodable Reader

Have children read the title and preview the story. Tell them they will read words with /kw/ spelled *qu* in this story.

Decodable Practice Reader R6A

Decode words in context

Pair children for reading and listen carefully as they decode. One child begins. Children read the entire story, switching readers after each page. Partners reread the story. This time the other child begins.

Decodable Reader R6A

Corrective feedback

If... children have difficulty decoding a word, **then...** refer them to the Sound-Spelling Cards to identify the sounds in the word. Prompt them to blend the word.

- What is the new word?
- Is the new word a word you know?
- Does it make sense in the story?

Check decoding and comprehension

Have children retell the story to include characters, setting, and events. Then have children locate words with /kw/ spelled *qu* in the story. List words that children name. Children should supply *Quin, quiz,* and *quit.* Ask children how they know these words have the /*kw*/ sound. (They all have *qu*.)

Reread for Fluency

Have children reread Decodable Reader R6A to develop automaticity decoding words with the /kw/ spelled *qu* sound.

ROUTINE **Oral Rereading**

1 **Read** Have children read the entire book orally.

2 **Reread** To achieve optimal fluency, children should reread the text three or four times.

3 **Corrective Feedback** Listen as children read. Provide corrective feedback regarding their fluency and decoding.

Routines Flip Chart

English Language Learners qu /kw/

Beginning Before reading, identify Quin and Bev for children. After reading, lead children on a picture walk through *The Quiz*. Have children tell what Quin is doing in each picture, using the sentence frame: *Quin is* _____.

Intermediate After reading, have children answer the following questions with complete sentences: *What are Quin and Bev going to do? When do Quin and Bev quit? How do you know that Quin and Bev did well on the quiz?*

Advanced/Advanced High After reading, have children point to all the words with the sound /kw/ *(Quin, quit, quiz).* Ask them to make up a few sentences using those words. Monitor children's pronunciation.

Genre
Realistic Fiction

Identify features of realistic fiction

Use the story *The Farmers Market* to have children identify the features of realistic fiction.

- Later today we will read a story called *The Farmers Market*. This story is an example of realistic fiction. Let's remember what we've learned about realistic fiction. Realistic fiction is fiction, so it is made up. It isn't real. But it <u>could</u> be real. The things that happen in the story could really happen.

- One thing that happens in this story is that Pam and Dad take a bus. Is this something that could happen in real life? How do you know? **(Possible response: Yes, I've ridden on a bus.)**

- What if I told you that Pam and Dad rode the bus all the way to the stars? Is that something that could happen in real life? **(No)** How do you know? **(the stars are in space and buses don't go there).**

- When we read *The Farmers Market*, you will find that all the things that happen in the story could happen in real life. So, it is realistic fiction.

Guide practice

Explain that the class will now make two lists. Use Graphic Organizer 4. Label the first column *Could Be Real.* Label the second column *Could Not Be Real.* Read the labels aloud. Which label goes with fantasy? **(the second)** Which goes with

Could Be Real	Could Not Be Real
A girl playing basketball	a fish playing basketball

Graphic Organizer Flip Chart 4

realistic fiction? **(the first)** Let's think of some things that might happen in a story. Let's start with a girl playing basketball. Is that something that could happen in real life, or is it something that could not happen in real life? **(could happen)** That's right, it could happen, so I'll put it in the *Could Be Real* column. What if it was a fish playing basketball? **Offer several more possible events and have children determine the correct column, or have children suggest and sort events.**

On their own

Divide children into pairs. Have each pair draw pictures of things that could happen in real life on one sheet of paper, and draw some things that could not happen in real life on another sheet of paper. Have pairs share their work with another group or with the whole class.

High-Frequency Words
Build Fluency

Read words in isolation

Remind children that there are some words we learn by remembering the letters, rather than by saying the sounds. Then have them read each of the highlighted high-frequency words aloud.

Read words in context

Chorally read the I Can Read! passage along with the children. Then have them read the passage aloud to themselves. When they are finished, ask children to reread the high-frequency words.

[Team Talk] Have children choose two high-frequency words and give them time to create a sentence in which both words are used properly. Then have them share the sentence with a partner.

I Can Read!

Here is a quiz for us. Where can we go on a bus? A bus can get us to a vet. It can zip us to fun in the sun.

Yes, a bus will not quit. Get on a bus with me!

You've learned
- Consonants v, y, z, qu
- Vowel u

High-Frequency Words
where here for me go

147

Student Edition p. 147

Differentiated Instruction

A Advanced

Extend High-Frequency Words
Have pairs of children tell their own stories using this week's high-frequency words in their stories.

Objectives

- Build background about farmers markets.
- Preview and predict.
- Use structure and elements of realistic fiction to improve understanding of text.
- Set a purpose for reading text.
- Understand how background knowledge can help a reader understand texts.

Build Background

Background Building Audio

Have children listen to the CD. Tell them to listen especially for the things we can buy at a farmers market.

 Background Building Audio

Discuss farmers markets

Team Talk Have children turn to a partner and use these questions for discussion:

- What do people sell at a farmers market?
- Where do you think the fruits and vegetables come from?
- How do you think the farmers get the food to the market?

Organize information in a chart

Draw a 3-column chart or use Graphic Organizer 5. Label the columns *Fruits; Vegetables; Other*. Ask each child what kinds of things are sold at farmers markets. They may name things from their own experiences or from items listed in the audio selection. Write the items in the correct column.

Fruits	Vegetables	Other

Graphic Organizer Flip Chart 5

Connect to selection

We heard about a neighborhood farmers market and what they were selling there. Who can name some of the things they were selling? (Possible respones: fruits, vegetables, honey, flowers, cheese) We're going to read *The Farmers Market*. It is a story about what Dad and Pam do when they go to the market.

Student Edition pp. 148-149

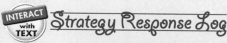
Main Selection—Let's Read
The Farmers Market

Practice the skill

 Realism and Fantasy Remind children that **realistic fiction** has made-up events that could be real. Explain that the story *The Farmers Market* is realistic fiction, and that it is about a girl and her father going to a farmers market. Ask children to look for realistic events in the story as they read.

Introduce the strategy

Background Knowledge Explain that children can use what they already know about farmers markets to help them understand the story. Have children turn to page EI•8 in their Student Edition.

Think Aloud Look at what is happening in the picture. What are the children seeing on the television screen? (somebody skiing) What do people do when they ski like this? (they go down a hill in the snow) The girl in the picture thinks that she once did something a little bit like what the skier is doing. What did she do? (went down a snowy hill on a sled) How do you know? (The picture shows that the girl is thinking about herself on a sled.) The girl knows a little bit about what skiing is like because she once went sledding. When you read, you can use what you already know to help you understand what you're reading.

Student Edition EI•8

Introduce genre

Let's Read Together Realistic fiction is a made-up story that could happen in real life. As they read *The Farmers Market,* have children look for events that indicate this story could happen in real life.

Preview and predict

Have children identify the title of the story, the author, and the illustrator. Read aloud the names of the author and illustrator and have children describe the role of each. Help children activate prior knowledge by asking them to look through the selection and use the illustrations to predict what might happen in the story.

Set a purpose

Good readers read for purpose. Setting a purpose helps us to think and understand more as we need. Have children read to find out what Pam and her father do at the farmers market.

Tell children that today they will read *The Farmers Market.* Use the Guide Comprehension notes to help children develop their comprehension of the reading selection.

Strategy Response Log

Background Knowledge
Before reading, have children use p. RR12 of their *Reader's and Writer's Notebook* to draw pictures of some items they think the characters in the story will see at the farmers market. Have children add short labels.

Differentiated Instruction

A Advanced
Draw and Label Have children write full sentences to describe the items they might find at a farmers market. Remind them to use capital letters and periods.

Academic Vocabulary

realistic fiction a made-up story that could happen in real life.

English Language Learners
Picture Walk Have children do a picture walk of the text of the book *The Farmers Market.* Ask them what they see and what they think is happening in each picture. Help them with vocabulary and sentence structure as needed.

Objectives

○ Use background knowledge to help understand text.

○ Distinguish realism from fantasy.

Student Edition pp. 148–149

Comprehension Strategy
⟳ Background Knowledge

Teach

Read the question on p. 149 aloud: *What can we see around our neighborhood?* Point out that children have already thought of a lot of people, places, and things they can see in their neighborhood. Good readers use what they know about a topic to help them make sure that what they are reading makes sense.

Model

Have children study the pictures on pages 148–149. Point out that some of the objects in the picture are small, so it isn't obvious what they are.

Think Aloud I know this story is about a farmers market, so it makes sense that the things in the picture would have to do with a farmers market. I see a person selling small red things. Maybe they are little red balls. But this is a story about a farmers market, so I think they are probably apples or another kind of fruit.

Guide practice

Have children try to identify other objects in the picture. Remind them that they should use what they already know about farmers markets.

Pam and Dad get on the <u>bus</u>.

<u>Where</u> will the <u>bus</u> <u>go</u>?

150

The <u>bus</u> will stop here.

Pam and Dad will have <u>fun</u>.

151

Student Edition pp. 150–151

Comprehension Skill
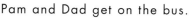 Realism and Fantasy

Teach

Remind children that they have learned about realism and fantasy during the week. Briefly review that fantasy is about things that could not possibly be true, while realism is about events that are made up but that could be real. We can look at these two pages and decide if this story is realistic or if it is fantasy. We can use both the words and the pictures to help.

Model

Think Aloud — I see that the first sentence on page 150 says *Pam and Dad get on the bus.* I know that Pam and Dad are made-up characters. They are not real. But they look like real people in the picture. And they are doing something that real people do: getting onto a bus. So, I think this story is realistic fiction.

Guide practice

Have children find other evidence that this story is realistic fiction rather than fantasy as they read pages 150–151 and beyond.

Differentiated Instruction

A Advanced

Fantasy After children identify the story as realistic fiction, have them discuss ways they could change the story so it would be fantasy—for instance, by having Dad and Pam board a space shuttle instead of a bus.

Strategic Reading

Remind children that good readers use comprehension strategies, such as using background knowledge, as they read.

English Language Learners
Future Tense This spread uses the word *will* three times. Act out the meaning by saying "I will put my hand on my head," then waiting a few seconds before actually doing it. Then say, "Now my hand is on my head." Repeat with other examples. Help children form sentences with *will*.

Farmers Market **150–151**

Look at Viv.

Viv will cut it. It is wet!

152

Look at Zak.

Zak will sell it.

153

Student Edition pp. 152–153

Comprehension Skill
Review Setting

Review

Remind children that the *setting* of a story is the time and place where it happens. We can use the words and the pictures in this story to figure out its setting.

Model

Think Aloud I know this story takes place outdoors because I can see that Pam and Dad are walking around on sidewalks. When I look at the pictures, I can see that they are at a farmers market. I know this because there are lots of people selling fruits and other things. The story did not begin at the farmers market. But these pages take place at the farmers market. So, we can say that the farmers market is the setting of this part of the story.

Guide practice

Ask children to find other details that help them tell about the setting of the story. (There are tents or booths. There are people buying the fruits, vegetables, and other items for sale.)

Dad will get it.

Dad will set it in a bag and zip it.

154

Look at Bud.

Will you get a yam for me?

155

Student Edition pp. 154–155

Phonics/High-Frequency Words
Word Reading

Model

Remind children that they have learned several new sounds and letters this week. One of the words on page 154 begins with the letter *z*. See if you can find it. That might have been a hard word to read last week. But now you know what sound goes with *z*. It's /z/. That will help me read this word: /z/ /i/ /p/, *zip*. There are words with the sounds /u/ and /y/ on these pages, too. Then remind children that some words cannot be decoded. You know some of these words, too. The last word on page 165 begins with *m*. Hmm...oh, I remember that word! That word is *me*. It's a good thing I remember what it looks like from earlier in the week!

Corrective feedback

If... children have difficulty reading these words, **then...** review the sound-letter relationships and the high-frequency words in isolation, then try again in context.

Differentiated Instruction

SI Strategic Intervention

Review Letters and Sounds
It may be hard for children to recall which new sounds go with which letters. Have children use their fingers to write the letters *v, y, z,* and *u* on sandpaper. Instruct them to say the name of the letter they are writing and then the sound. For instance, when they write *y,* they should say *y,* /y/.

E L L

English Language Learners
Flexibility with Words Instead of simply providing children with words they do not yet know, you can encourage children to "talk around" unknown words as they describe the setting of the story. For example, if they do not know the word *watermelon,* help them say *red fruit* or some other descriptive phrase. Then give them the correct vocabulary.

Dad and Pam get wet.
They will quit.

156

Dad and Pam got on the bus.
Dad and Pam had fun.

157

Student Edition pp. 156–157

Comprehension Strategy
⟳ Background Knowledge

Teach

Good readers are always thinking about what they read. They are always asking themselves if things make sense. You can use what you know about neighborhoods, farmers markets, and being outside to help you make sure you are reading the words correctly.

Model

Call children's attention to the picture on page 156. I see that Pam and Dad are under a tent, and I see that it's beginning to rain. The first sentence on this page says *Dad and Pam get...* What if I didn't know that last word? What I forgot that w goes with the sound /w/? Well, I could make a pretty good guess that this word is *wet*. I know that when it rains, people get wet if they are outside! I used what I already knew to help me read the word.

Guide practice

Have children study the picture on page 157. Have them use background information about neighborhoods and transportation to tell what they think is happening in the picture. (Possible response: They are going back home on the bus because they have finished their shopping.

Comprehension Check

Have children discuss each question with a partner. Ask several pairs to share their responses.

☑ **Realistic fiction** What are some things these characters do that real people would do? (Possible responses: take buses, go shopping.)

☑ **Background knowledge** What kinds of things did Dad and Pam buy at the market? Were you surprised that they bought those things and not cars or couches? (Possible response: They bought fruits and vegetables; not surprised, because they don't sell cars or couches at farmers markets.)

☑ **Confirm predictions** How did you use the pictures and words to confirm what happened in the story? (Possible response: I read the part that tells what Pam and Dad did at the farmers market. I used the pictures to confirm that they bought fruits and vegetables.)

☑ **Connect text to self** Suppose you visited a farmers market with someone in your family. What things would you like to buy? What would you buy if you only had a little bit of money that day? What would you buy if you had a lot of money with you? Why? (Possible response: I'd buy apples and grapes. If I had only a little bit of money I'd buy one bunch of grapes because they're my favorite. If I had lots of money I'd also buy something I never tasted before so I could see what it was like.)

Strategy Self-Check

Have children talk about any problems they encountered as they read and what they did to solve them.

Background Knowledge

• When did they use background knowledge to help them read individual words?

• When did they use background knowledge to help them understand what was happening in the story?

Remind children that good readers use many strategies as they read.

English Language Learners
Support Discussion Have children point to pictures in the story or make simple sketches to help them discuss what they might like to buy at a farmers market. Assist them in providing words as needed.

Objectives

- Retell a narrative.
- Distinguish realism from fantasy.
- Write clear, coherent sentences.

Check Retelling
SUCCESS PREDICTOR

Objectives
- Describe the problem and the solution of a story. Retell a story's beginning, middle, and end in the order in which the events happened.

Envision It! Retell

READING STREET ONLINE
STORY SORT
www.ReadingStreet.com

158

Think Critically Read Together

1. A farmers market is a place to buy fruits and vegetables. Name some other places where fruits and vegetables are sold. Text to World

2. Could this story really happen? Explain.
   Realism and Fantasy

3. **Look Back and Write**
   Look back at page 155. What can you buy at a farmers market? Write about it.
   TEST PRACTICE Extended Response

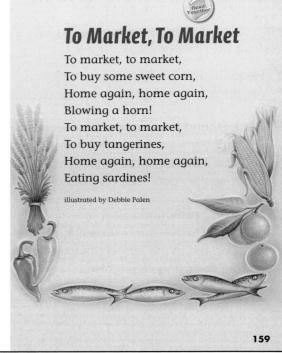

To Market, To Market

To market, to market,
To buy some sweet corn,
Home again, home again,
Blowing a horn!
To market, to market,
To buy tangerines,
Home again, home again,
Eating sardines!

illustrated by Debbie Palen

159

Student Edition pp. 158–159

Retelling

Envision It! Have children work in pairs to retell the story. Remind children to include characters, setting, and events from the story. Children should use the retelling strip in the Student Edition. Monitor children's retelling.

Scoring rubric

	Top-Score Response A top-score response makes connections beyond the text, elaborates on the author's purpose, and describes in detail the characters, setting, and plot.	

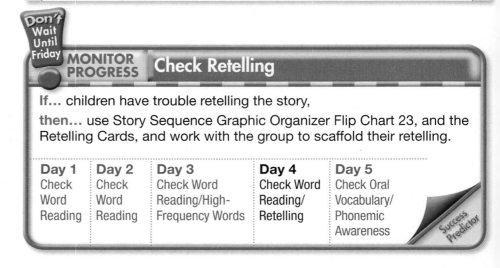

Don't Wait Until Friday

MONITOR PROGRESS Check Retelling

If... children have trouble retelling the story,

then... use Story Sequence Graphic Organizer Flip Chart 23, and the Retelling Cards, and work with the group to scaffold their retelling.

Day 1	Day 2	Day 3	Day 4	Day 5
Check Word Reading	Check Word Reading	Check Word Reading/High-Frequency Words	Check Word Reading/ Retelling	Check Oral Vocabulary/ Phonemic Awareness

Success Predictor

Think Critically

Text to World

1. Possible response: grocery stores and supermarkets.

 Realism and Fantasy

2. Yes; the events described in the story are all real-life events. People do these things every day.

 Writing on Demand

3. **Look Back and Write** To encourage writing fluency, limit children to 5 minutes of writing. As children finish, remind them to reread their responses and check for errors.

Scoring rubric

> **Top-Score Response** A top-score response uses information from the text and the pictures to describe a variety of materials sold at the farmers market. For example:
>
> You can buy fruits and vegetables and flowers at a farmers market. One kind of fruit you can buy is an apple. Another kind is a watermelon.

Read poetry

Read aloud page 159 as children follow along. Point out the rhythm of the poem as you read. Have children tap the rhythm with a pencil as you read. Ask children to identify the words that rhyme as you read the poem. Ask children:

- What things does the person in the poem buy at the market? (possible response: tangerines)

- What things would you buy at a farmers market?

Differentiated Instruction

SI Strategic Intervention

Revision Children who struggle with writing may be reluctant to revisit their work after they have finished a first draft. Some of these children are more willing to make revisions, however, if they know they won't have to do more writing. Have them tell you what they would like to change; then make the corrections on the paper as they watch.

INTERACT with TEXT

Strategy Response Log

Story Structure After reading, have children use p. RR12 of their *Reader's and Writer's Notebook* to draw a picture and write a sentence that tells about one event that happened in the story.

Plan to Assess Retelling

- ☐ Week 1: Assess Strategic Intervention children.
- ☐ Week 2: Advanced
- ☐ Week 3: Assess Strategic Intervention children
- ☐ Week 4: On-Level
- ☐ Week 5: Strategic Intervention
- ☑ This week: Assess any children you have not yet checked during this unit.

Retelling

Success Predictor

Objectives

- Identify a sentence.
- Produce a sentence.
- Write a complete sentence that contains a noun, verb, and adjective.

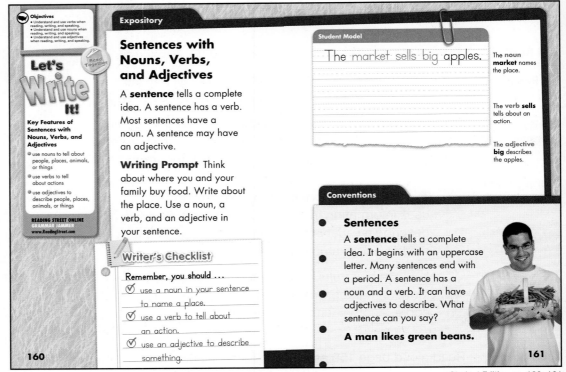

Student Edition pp. 160–161

Writing—Sentences

Teach

Look at p. 160 in the Student Edition. Read aloud the Key Features of Sentences with Nouns, Verbs, and Adjectives. Help children better understand the Writing Prompt by reading it aloud and discussing the Writer's Checklist with children.

Review the student model

Then read the Student Model on p. 161 to children. Point out that the sentence includes nouns, a verb, and an adjective to express a complete idea. Have children identify each. Ask children what the sentence starts with. (an uppercase letter) Ask them what the sentence ends with. (a period)

Guide practice

Now it is time to write your sentence. Think about where you and your family buy food. Then tell about this place. Remember, your sentence should have a noun, a verb, and an adjective. It should tell a complete idea. Guide children as they write a sentence about where they buy food. If children cannot write a complete sentence, provide them with a sentence frame, such as, *We _____ _____ _____ at the store.* Have them fill in the blanks with a verb, an adjective, and a noun that describe what they do at the store. If children are unable to write decodable words, have them orally suggest the words and model writing them in the blank. (For example: We *get red yams* at the store.)

Conventions
Sentences

Read aloud the Conventions note on p. 161 as children follow along. Have them explain what a sentence is and then read with you the example of a complete sentence. Have them identify the nouns, the verb, and the adjective in the sentence. Note that the sentence has an uppercase letter at the beginning and a period at the end. Ask children to orally provide other complete sentences.

On their own   Use *Reader's and Writer's Notebook* p. 116.

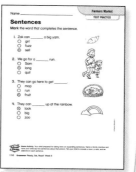

Reader's and Writer's
Notebook p. 116

Differentiated Instruction

 Strategic Intervention

Sentences Remind children that a sentence tells a complete idea. The first word in a sentence begins with an uppercase letter and the sentence often ends with a period. Write *the family goes to a big market* on the board. Model correct sentence capitalization and punctuation. Then help children identify the nouns, verb, and adjective in the sentence. Ask children to create their own short sentences and repeat the procedure above.

ELL

English Language Learners
Sentences Children who read in Spanish may recognize that a sentence begins with a capital letter and ends with a period. The Spanish word for "capital letter" is *mayúscula*, and the period is called *punto*. Write the sentence *we pet the black cat* and use the Spanish words as you model making the first letter uppercase and adding a period.

Research
Library/Media Center

Teach

Remind children of times when they have visited a library or media center. Explain that libraries are places where people can go to find facts and other information. Add that libraries have shelves with books, newspapers, and magazines, and that many libraries also have CDs, DVDs, and computers. Tell children that books and other materials at the library can often be borrowed, but that the materials must be returned so others may use them too. Explain that the people in charge of the library are called librarians, and that librarians can help people find the information they need.

Model

Display Research Transparency R6. Explain that this shows a school media center. Model how to identify different areas and functions of a media center, pointing as you describe what you see.

Guide practice

 Think Aloud I notice the girls at the desk are using a computer. They are wearing earphones. This tells me that a media center sometimes has computers. These girls must be listening to something on the computer. They are using their ears to learn something new.

Continue pointing out features on the transparency. Ask the following questions to develop children's awareness of the resources available at a library or a school media center.

Research Transparency R6

• What do you think the children on the rug are doing?
• What do you think the librarian might be doing? (The librarian is reading a story while the children listen.)
• Where in this library can you go to read the books? (to chairs or desks)
• Who will help you check out books that you want to borrow?
• Where will you go to check them out? (the librarian; to the front desk or check-out counter).

On your own

Use *Reader's and Writer's Notebook* p. 117.

Reader's and Writer's Notebook p. 117

Handwriting
Q and q/Letter Size

Model letter formation

Display upper- and lower-case letters: *Qq*. Use the stroke instructions pictured below to model proper letter formation.

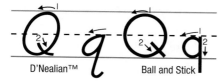

D'Nealian™   Ball and Stick

Model letter size

When I write a word, it's important to make sure I make the letters the proper size. Write the word *quit*. State whether each letter is small (u, i), tall (t), or falls below the line (q). Repeat with the same word beginning with an upper-case *Q* (*Quit*). Point out that even though the *Q* is a capital letter in this word, the *u* that follows it remains lower case.

Guide practice

Write *Quin, quill, queen, quit* on the board. Read them aloud. Explain that Quin is a name.

Team Talk Have children write one of the words. Have them share their work with a partner. Ask each child to point out the letters that are tall, that are small, and that fall below the line.

On their own

Use the *Reader's and Writer's Notebook* p. 118

Reader's and Writer's Notebook p. 118

Wrap Up Your Day

✔ **Consonant *Qu,qu* /kw/** Write the letters *qu* and have children identify them. Then have the children say the sound /kw/ as you point to *qu*.

✔ **Realism and Fantasy** How do you know if a story is realistic fiction? (Possible answer: the events could happen in real life, but the story is made up)

✔ **Background Knowledge** Good readers use what they already know to help them understand a story. Have children tell how they used background knowledge to help them understand *The Farmers Market*.

Differentiated Instruction

 Advanced

Have children work in pairs to make lists of things you would and would not find in a library/media center. Ask them to share their lists with other groups.

Academic Vocabulary

library/media center a place where books and other reference materials are kept

English Language Learners

Words to Sentences Help children expand words into sentences when they are describing details they see in the picture of the library. If a child says *books,* for example, say *A library has books,* and have children repeat. For more advanced ELL children, extend the sentence by saying *The books are on a _____* and helping children fill in the missing word *shelf.* Finally, show children how the two sentences can be combined to form *A library has books on a shelf.*

Preview DAY 5

Tell children that tomorrow they will read a made-up story called a fable. Add that fables teach lessons or have morals.

Objectives
- Review concepts: markets and neighborhoods.
- Build oral vocabulary.
- Identify details in text.

Today at a Glance

Oral Vocabulary
Review: *bargain, browse, bustling, library, fact, cost, customer, scale*

Print Awareness
Sentence Features

Phonemic Awareness
Count Phonemes

Phonics and Spelling
Review: *Vv* /v/, *Yy* /y/, *Zz* /z/, *Uu* /u/, and *Qq qu*=/kw/

High-Frequency Words
where, go, here, for, me

Comprehension
◉ Realism/Fantasy

Vocabulary
Sort Nouns for People, Animals, Places, and Things

Listening and Speaking
Relate an Experience

Handwriting
Self-Evaluation

Writing and Conventions
Sentences with Nouns, Verbs, and Adjectives

Check Oral Vocabulary
SUCCESS PREDICTOR

Concept Wrap Up

Question of the Week

What can we see around our neighborhood?

Review Concept

This week we have read and listened to stories about neighborhoods. Today you will listen to find out what buyers and sellers do at the city market. Read the story.

- What do buyers do at the market? What do sellers do at the market? (Buyers choose which fruits, fish, and vegetables to buy for the groceries and restaurants. Sellers add up the cost and write up a bill for the things the buyers want to purchase.)

"Market to Market to Market"

Review Amazing Words

Orally review the meaning of this week's Amazing Words. Then display this week's concept map.
Have children use Amazing Words such as *library*, *customer*, and *bargain*, as well as the concept map, to answer the question: "What can we see around our neighborhood?"

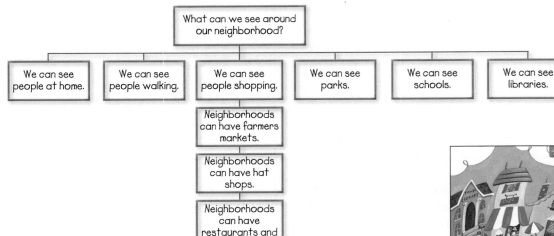

ELL Check Concepts and Language Use the Day 5 instruction on ELL Poster R6 to monitor children's understanding of the lesson concept.

ELL Poster R6

Oral Vocabulary
Amazing Ideas

Connect to the Big Question

Team Talk Pair children and have them discuss how the Question of the Week connects to this unit's Big Question, "What is all around me?" Tell children to use the concept map and what they've learned from this week's Anchored Talks and reading selections to form an Amazing Idea—a realization or "big idea" about **my world**. Then ask each pair to share their Amazing Idea with the class.

Amazing Ideas might include these key concepts:

• Customers might look for bargains at different kinds of stores in a neighborhood.

• Many neighborhoods have parks, schools, or libraries.

It's Friday

MONITOR PROGRESS **Check Oral Vocabulary**

Call on individuals to use this week's Amazing Words to talk about what people can see in their neighborhoods. Prompt discussion with the questions below. Monitor children's ability to use the Amazing Words and note which words children are unable to use.

• **Where in a neighborhood might a *customer* go to *browse* for a *bargain*?**

• **Why do you want to buy something at low *cost*?**

• **Why shouldn't a *library* be a *bustling* place in a neighborhood?**

• **What is the most interesting *fact* you have learned about neighborhoods?**

If... children have difficulty using the Amazing Words,

then... reteach the unknown words using the Oral Vocabulary Routines, pp. 141b, 144b, 146b, 146n.

Day 1	Day 2	Day 3	Day 4	Day 5
Check Word Reading	Check Word Reading	Check Word Reading/High-Frequency Words	Check Word Reading/ Retelling	Check Oral Vocabulary/ Phonemic Awareness

Success Predictor

Amazing Words

bargain	fact
browse	cost
bustling	customer
library	scale

Differentiated Instruction

SI Strategic Intervention
Review the Big Question
Before introducing the "Amazing Ideas" activity, you may find it helpful to remind children of the Big Question and how they have used it to form Amazing Ideas in previous weeks. You may also find it helpful to model how to use the concept map to form an Amazing Idea such as "People sometimes eat at restaurants in neighborhoods."

ELL

English Language Learners
Vocabulary Check Children may know the Amazing Words for the week without being able to answer questions that require explanations rather than single words. To check children's knowledge of these words, ask simpler questions, such as "Is it good to buy things at low *cost* or at high *cost*?" Encourage children to listen carefully to the explanations given by English proficient classmates.

Print Awareness
Sentence Features

Review

Briefly review the features of a sentence by singing the Old McDonald song from Day 3 with children:

Old McDonald writes a sentence, E-I-E-I-O.
The sentence is a full idea, E-I-E-I-O.
A capital's first
A period's last
Capital -- period -- capital -- period
Old McDonald writes a sentence, E-I-E-I-O.

Explain to children that sentences help readers make sense of the text they are reading, so good readers always look for the beginnings and endings of sentences as they read.

Model

Have children open their books to page 161. Explain to children that the story *Farmers Market* has lots of sentences. Call children's attention to the features of the sentences as you talk about them. Look at the first line. I see a capital *T* in the first word, which is *The*. Sentences always begin with capital letters. So this could be a sentence. The sentence ends at the end of that line, where there is a period. Sentences always end with periods or some other mark. I can guess that this is a sentence, because it begins with a capital letter and ends with a period. I also see a verb that I know in the sentence—it is the verb *stop*. It says *The bus will stop here*. That is a full idea. It begins with a capital. It ends with a period. It's a sentence.

Guide practice

Call children's attention to the first line of text on page 162 of *Farmers Market*. Have children locate the initial capital letter, the period, and the verb. Continue with the second line of text on the same page.

On their own

Use *Reader's and Writer's Notebook* p. 119.

Reader's and Writer's
Notebook p. 119

Phonological Awareness
Count Phonemes

Model

In the story *The Farmers Market*, we read about a man named *Zak*. Listen to the sounds in *Zak*: /z/ /a/ /k/. The first sound is /z/, the next sound is /a/, and the last sound is /k/. There are three sounds in the word *Zak*.

Guide practice

I will say a word, then you tell me how many sounds you hear. *Run*: /r/ /u/ /n/. How many sounds are there in *run*?

Continue this exercise using the words: *yam, fruit, bag, slip, jacket, go,* and *sell*.

Corrective feedback

If children make an error, model the correct response. Return to the word later in the practice.

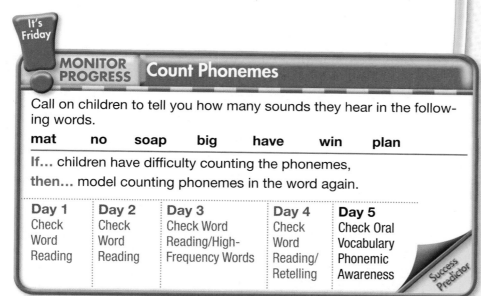

It's Friday

MONITOR PROGRESS   Count Phonemes

Call on children to tell you how many sounds they hear in the following words.

mat	no	soap	big	have	win	plan

If... children have difficulty counting the phonemes,

then... model counting phonemes in the word again.

Day 1	Day 2	Day 3	Day 4	Day 5
Check Word Reading	Check Word Reading	Check Word Reading/High-Frequency Words	Check Word Reading/ Retelling	Check Oral Vocabulary Phonemic Awareness

Success Predictor

Academic Vocabulary

sentence a group of words that forms a complete idea

phoneme smallest meaningful unit of sound in spoken language

Differentiated Instruction

 Advanced

Count Phonemes If children are easily able to determine the number of phonemes in CVC and CCVC words such as *jam* and *plug*, have them try words that begin with three consonants, such as *scrap* and *strain*, or words that end with a consonant blend, such as *held* and *mint*.

ELL

English Language Learners

Phonemes Some phonemes, such as /v/, /y/, and /r/, do not appear in some languages and may be difficult for children from those linguistic backgrounds to pronounce or distinguish. Have children repeat words such as *yam* and *have* slowly and carefully to make sure they have heard all the phonemes. You may also want to have children use mirrors to make sure they are using the correct mouth and tongue position as they speak the words.

Oral Vocabulary
Success Predictor

Objectives
- Review consonants *v* /v/, *y* /y/, *z* /z/, *qu* = /kw/, and vowel *u* /u/.
- Identify upper- and lower-case letters.
- Review high-frequency words *he, is, to, with, three; have, was, you, like, do.*

Fluent Word Reading
Spiral Review

Read words in isolation

Display these words. Tell children that they can blend some words on this list but others are Word Wall words.

Have children read the list three or four times until they can read at the rate of two to three seconds per word.

pup	like	yip	he	Gus
have	quill	you	with	vet
do	was	zip	is	Pug
three	dug	to	quit	yet

Word Reading

Corrective feedback

If... children have difficulty reading whole words,
then... have them use sound-by-sound blending for decodable words or have them say and spell high-frequency words.

If... children cannot read fluently at a rate of two to three seconds per word,
then... have pairs practice the list until they can read it fluently.

Read words in context

Display these sentences. Then randomly point to review words and have children read them. To help you monitor word reading, high-frequency words are underlined and decodable words are italicized.

<u>Three</u> *vets* <u>have</u> *dug* the *well*.

<u>Do</u> <u>you</u> <u>like</u> <u>to</u> *get wet*?

<u>He</u> <u>was</u> <u>with</u> *Quin* the *pup*.

<u>Is</u> *Gus* on the *jet yet*?

Sentence Reading

Corrective feedback

If... children are unable to read an underlined high-frequency word,
then... read the word for them and spell it, having them echo you.

If... children have difficulty reading an italicized decodable word,
then... guide them in using sound-by-sound blending.

Spell Words

Guide practice

Now we are going to spell words with the sounds and letters we learned this week. The first word we will spell is *quiz*. What sounds do you hear in *quiz*? (/kw/ /i/ /z/) What are the letters for the sound /kw/? Let's all write *qu*. What is the letter for the sound /i/? Write *i*. What is the letter for the sound /z/? Write *z*. Have children confirm their spellings by comparing them with what you've written. Continue practice with *vet, yell, buzz, yum,* and *quit* as time allows.

High-Frequency Words

Review

Point to the words *where, go, for, here,* and *me* one at a time on the Word Wall. Have children read and spell each word chorally. Have children work with a partner to use each word in a sentence. Ask several pairs to share their sentences.

Cumulative review

Point to the remaining Word Wall words one at a time. Have children read the words chorally.

On their own

Use *Reader's and Writer's Notebook* p. 100.

Reader's and Writer's Notebook p. 100

Small Group Time

DAY 5

Break into small groups after phonics and before the comprehension lesson.

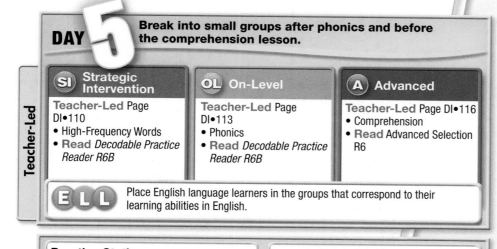

SI Strategic Intervention

Teacher-Led Page DI•110
• High-Frequency Words
• **Read** *Decodable Practice Reader R6B*

OL On-Level

Teacher-Led Page DI•113
• Phonics
• **Read** *Decodable Practice Reader R6B*

A Advanced

Teacher-Led Page DI•116
• Comprehension
• **Read** Advanced Selection R6

ELL Place English language learners in the groups that correspond to their learning abilities in English.

Practice Stations
• Get Fluent
• Let 'Write'

Independent Activities
• *Reader's and Writer's Notebook* p. RR1.
• Concept Talk Video
• AudioText of Paired Selection

These activities review
• previously taught high-frequency words *he, is, to, with, three; have, was, you, like,* and *do*
• *y* /y/; *u* /u/; *r* /r/; *w* /w/; *j* /j/; *k* /k/; *e* /e/; *l, ll* /l/; *g* /g/; *p* /p/.

Differentiated Instruction

A Advanced

Form Words Scramble words that children can spell, such as *zubz* or *tve* for *buzz* and *vet*, and write them on the board. Have children work alone or with a partner to unscramble the letters to form real words.

English Language Learners
Questions and Answers To increase familiarity with the high-frequency words, have children use these words in answering questions. For instance, ask *Where will you go?* and have children answer with the sentence frame *I will go _____.*

The Farmers Market **162f**

Objectives

- Apply knowledge of sound-spellings to decode unknown words when reading.
- Use context to confirm the word that was read.
- Practice fluency with oral rereading.
- Read high-frequency words.

Decodable Practice Reader R6B
Consonants /r/, /v/, /y/, /z/, qu=/kw/ and Short *u*.

Decodable Practice Reader R6B

Decode words in isolation

Have children turn to the first page. Have children decode each word.

Review high-frequency words

Review the previously taught words *the, with, is, they, a,* and *have.* Have children read each word as you point to it on the Word Wall.

Preview Decodable Reader

Have children read the title and preview the story. Tell them they will read words with the consonants /v/ spelled *v,* /y/ spelled *y,* /z/ spelled *z,* /kw/ spelled *qu* and /u/ spelled *u.*

Decode words in context

Pair children for reading and listen carefully as they decode. One child begins. Children read the entire story, switching readers after each page. Partners reread the story. This time the other child begins.

The sun is up.
But it is not hot!

90

Vic will zip up.
Vic will tug on a hat.

91

Roz will get a muff with fuzz on it.

92

Dad will sit.
Dad will sip. Yum!

93

Decodable Reader R6B

"Rev up the van!" they yell.
"We have a quiz!"

94

Vic will huff.
Roz will puff.
They will not quit.

95

Will they get the quiz?
Not yet!

96

Corrective feedback

If... children have difficulty decoding a word, **then...** refer them to the Sound-Spelling Cards to identify the sounds in the word. Prompt them to blend the word.

- What is the new word?
- Is the new word a word you know?
- Does it make sense in the story?

Check decoding and comprehension

Have children retell the story to include characters, setting, and events. Then have children find and locate words with /v/ spelled *v* in the story. List words that children name. Children should supply *Vic, rev,* and *van*. Ask children how they know these words have the /v/ sound. (They all have *v.*) Continue in the same way with /y/ spelled *y (yum, yell, yet)*, /z/ spelled *z* or *zz (zip, Roz, fuzz, quiz)*, /u/ spelled *u (sun, up, but, tug, muff, fuzz, huff, puff)*, and /kw/ spelled *qu (quiz, quit)*.

Reread for Fluency

Have children reread Decodable Practice Reader R6B to develop automaticity decoding words with the sounds /v/ spelled *v*, /y/ spelled *y*, /z/ spelled *z, zz,* /u/ spelled *u,* /kw/ spelled *qu*.

 ROUTINE **Oral Rereading**

1. **Read** Have children read the entire book orally.

2. **Reread** To achieve optimal fluency, children should reread the text three or four times.

3. **Corrective Feedback** Listen as children read. Provide corrective feedback regarding their fluency and decoding.

Routines Flip Chart

 E L L

English Language Learners
Review /v/ *v*, /y/ *y*, /z/ *z, zz,* /u/ *u*, /kw/ *qu*
Beginning Before reading take a picture walk through the story with children, identifying the characters and key words. Point to illustrations of the *fuzz, muff,* and *van* while saying the words. Have children repeat them after you.

Intermediate After reading, act out actions such as *huff, puff, zip, rev,* and *tug*. As you do the pantomime, say the word and ask children to repeat after you. Monitor children's pronunciation.

Advanced/Advanced High After reading the story, have children use the pictures to make up dialog for Vic, Roz, and Dad. Tell children to use words such as *sun, zip, muff, yum,* and *quiz*.

Objectives
- Predict and set purpose.
- Recognize structure and elements of a fable.
- Relate prior knowledge to new text.

Social Studies in Reading

Preview and predict

Read the title and the first sentence of the selection. Explain that *maid* is an old-fashioned word for *girl* or *young woman*. Have children look through the selection and predict what they might learn from the story. (Possible response: learn about what life was like long ago.) Ask them what clues helped them make that prediction. (Possible response: the girl's dress looks like the clothes that people used to wear.)

Genre

Fable Tell children that this story is a **fable**. Explain the key features of a fable: it is a made-up story that teaches a moral, or a lesson, and the characters in fables usually make mistakes that help them learn the lesson. Explain that fables have been told for hundreds of years, and that the people who write fables want their readers and listeners to connect the stories and the lessons in them to their own lives. Emphasize that this can be true even when the characters in the fable seem very different from the people of today.

Activate prior knowledge

Ask children to think about stories they know that remind them in some way of their own lives. Have children explain how the themes and events in the stories connect with their own experiences. (Possible response: *The Farmers Market* tells about a shopping trip; I have gone shopping with my dad, too. "A Busy Day" involves a trip to the library; our class once visited the library at school. In "Surprise!" a family throws a party; I like parties.)

Set a purpose for reading

Let's Read Together As children read, have them look for ways that the story reminds them of their own lives and experiences.

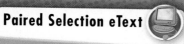

The Maid and the Milk Pail

Objectives
• Connect the meaning of a famous story or fable to your own experiences.

Social Studies in Reading

Genre
Fable
- A fable is a short story that teaches a lesson.
- Characters in fables usually learn a lesson from the mistakes they make.
- The author wants readers to connect a fable's lesson to their personal experiences.
- Read "The Maid and the Milk Pail." Think about what you've learned about fables as you read.

A girl took milk to a market. She thought, "I will sell this milk. I will buy a lovely new dress."

162

The girl let go of the pail. It fell. Now the girl could not buy a dress.

Lesson: Don't count on getting something until you actually have it.

Let's Think About...
What mistake does the girl make? **Fable**

Let's Think About...
What lesson does the girl learn? How can you connect this lesson to something that happened to you? **Fable**

Let's Think About...
Reading Across Texts When do *Farmers Market* and "The Maid and the Milk Pail" take place? Where do they take place? How do you know?

Writing Across Texts Why are Pam and Dad in *Farmers Market* going to a market? Why is the girl in "The Maid and the Milk Pail" going to a market? Write about their reasons.

163

Student Edition pp. 162–163

Guide Comprehension
Connect to Personal Experience

Guide practice

Think Aloud When I was young, I remember that I saw a great pair of gym shoes in a shoe store...I really wanted them! I told my friends I was going to get them, and I was sure they would make me run faster. But the store didn't have them in my size. That reminds me of what happens to the girl in this fable.

Let's Think About...

Fables

Possible response: The girl learns that she should wait until she has what she wants.

Reading Across Texts *Farmers Market* is in modern times, and *The Maid and the Milk Pail* is in the past.

Writing Across Texts Children should recognize that Pam and Dad will buy things, and the girl in the fable is planning to sell.

Academic Vocabulary

fable a story that teaches a moral or a lesson; usually the characters learn the lesson when they make a mistake.

Differentiated Instruction

SI Strategic Intervention

Past and Present Help children determine the time period (today or the past) by asking questions about the artwork in each story. For instance, ask if children have seen many people dressed like the girl in the fable (probably not), or if they have seen people dressed like Dad and Pam in *The Farmers Market* (probably). Then help them find other indications that *The Farmers Market* is probably set in today's world, while the fable probably is not.

ELL

English Language Learners

Act It Out To increase children's understanding of the fable, have them act out the part of the girl. Have them say the words that the girl thinks in the story, and encourage them to add comments and ideas of their own as well.

The Farmers Market **162–163**

Objectives

- ○ Relate an experience in sequence.
- • Speak clearly at an appropriate rate.
- • Listen attentively.
- • Sort nouns.
- • Use handwriting models to evaluate letter formation.

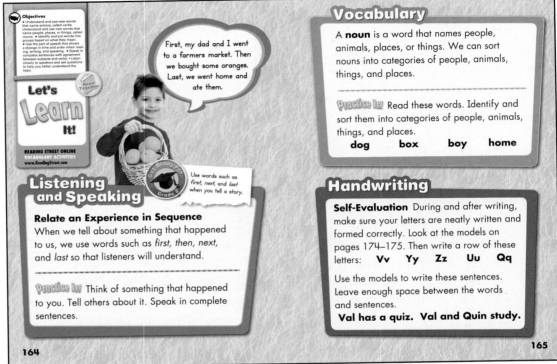

Student Edition pp. 164–165

Listening and Speaking
Relate an Experience in Sequence

Teach

Have children turn to pages 164–165 of the Student Edition. Read and discuss the boy's story together. Remind children that good speakers use sequence words to tell the order in which things happened.

Analyze model

Point out the sequence words *first, then,* and *last.* Ask children what event happened first and what event was next. (*First the boy and his dad went to the farmer's market. Then they bought some plums.*) Point out the sequence words *first* and *then.* Ask children what the boy and his dad did last. (*They went home and ate the plums.*) Point out that the sequence word *last* helps us understand the order of the story.

Introduce prompt

Read the Practice It! prompt with the class. Remind children that their story should use sequence words to tell the order of the story.

Team Talk Have pairs take turns telling something that happened to them. Tell children that good speakers speak clearly and slowly and good listeners should be able to repeat the story in sequence.

Vocabulary
Sort Nouns for People, Animals, Places, and Things

Teach

Read and discuss the Vocabulary lesson on page 165 of the Student Edition. Use the model to explain sorting nouns.

Model

Point to the photographs. What picture shows a person? (the girl) What picture shows an animal? (the cow) How about a place? (the store) And a thing? (the chair) All of these are nouns.

Guide practice

Read the instructions for the Vocabulary Practice It! Activity. Have children study the words.

The first word is *bus.* Is a bus a person, a place, an animal, or a thing? (thing) A bus is a thing. I will put the word bus into the category of things.

On their own

Have children continue with the other nouns on the page.

Corrective feedback

Circulate around the room and listen as children sort nouns into conceptual categories. Provide assistance as needed.

Handwriting
Self-Evaluation

Teach

Read and discuss the Handwriting instructions.

Write letters

Give children a moment to look at the letter models. Then have them write a row for each of these letters: *Vv, Yy, Zz, Uu, Qq, qu.* Then have children write the following sentences: *Val has a quiz today. She and Quinn will study.*

Assess
- Count phonemes.
- ⦿ Blend words with consonants *v*, *y, z, q*, and short *u*.
- Read high-frequency words.

Assessment
Monitor Progress

For a written assessment of counting phonemes, consonants *v* /v/, *y* /y/, *z* /z/, *qu* /kw/, short *u*, high-frequency words, and identifying realism and fantasy, use Weekly Test R6, pp. 31–36.

Assess words in isolation

Word reading Use the following reproducible page to assess children's ability to read words in isolation. Call on children to read the words aloud. Start over if necessary.

Assess words in context

Sentence reading Use the following reproducible page to assess children's ability to read words in context. Call on children to read two sentences aloud. Start over with sentence one if necessary.

MONITOR PROGRESS	Word and Sentence Reading

If... children have trouble reading words with consonants *v* /v/, *y* /y/, *z* /z/, *qu* /kw/, and short *u*,

then... use the Reteach Lesson in *First Stop*.

If... children cannot read all the high-frequency words,

then... mark the missed words on a high-frequency word list and have the child practice reading the words with a fluent reader.

Success Predictor

Monitor accuracy

Record scores Use the Word/Sentence Reading Chart for this unit on p. 64 of *First Stop*.

Name _____

Read the Words

van	yet
yum	for
here	go
buzz	quiz
where	me
zip	hum
yes	but

Read the Sentences

1. Here is a fun quiz.

2. But where is the van?

3. Go to the vet, Buzz.

4. Yes, Quinn will hum with me.

MONITOR PROGRESS
- Consonants v /v/, y /y/, z /z/, qu /kw/
- Short u
- High-frequency words

Objectives
- Identify a sentence.
- Produce a sentence.
- Write a complete sentence that contains a noun, verb, and adjective.
- Develop the concept: neighborhoods.

Conventions
Sentences

Review sentences

Suppose I want to draw an apple. *Apple* is a noun because it names a thing. *Red, green,* or *yellow* are adjectives that describe the noun *apple*. *Grows* is a verb that tells what the apple does: *The red apple grows.*

Guide practice

Have children think of vegetables they like. Write each on the board, and have children think of adjectives and verbs that have to do with them. Then write sentences using these words and read them aloud.

Connect to oral language

Have the class complete these sentence frames orally.

> I _____ the soft blanket.
>
> The _____ dog plays.

On their own

Put children in small groups. Have them create sentences after naming toys, adjectives that describe them, and verbs that tell what they do.

Writing—Sentences

Wrap up the weekly concept

Remind children that they have been talking about neighborhoods all week. Ask children to tell sentences about what they see around their neighborhood.

Model

I want to tell about my neighborhood. There is a store at the end of my block. I like to go to it. I will write a sentence about the store in my neighborhood. Write the following sentence and read it aloud.

> **My neighbors go to the small store.**

Guide practice

Have children name nouns, verbs, and adjectives that have to do with their own neighborhoods. Then encourage them to tell a complete sentence, using a noun, verb, and adjective. Work with children to write sentences on the board. You may suggest a sentence frame, such as *I see a _____.*

On their own

Write the following sentence frame on the board and read it aloud.

> **The _____ picked the _____ flower.**

Instruct children to complete the sentence with decodable nouns and adjectives. If children are unable to write decodable words, have them suggest the words and model writing them in the blanks.

Wrap Up Your Week!

Question of the Week

What can we see around our neighborhood?

Think Aloud This week we explored the topic of neighborhoods. In the story *The Farmers Market*, we read about how Dad and Pam went shopping at a farmers market in their neighborhood. In the story *A Busy Day*, we read all about Bonnie and Betty going to a library, a market, and a hat shop in their neighborhood. Both stories told about people, places, and things we can see in different neighborhoods. **Have children recall their Amazing Ideas about neighborhoods. Then have children use these ideas to help them demonstrate their understanding of the Question of the Week.**

E L L

English Language Learners

Poster Preview Prepare children for next week by using Unit 1 Week 1, ELL Poster 4. Read the Poster Talk-Through to introduce the concept and vocabulary. Ask children to identify and describe objects and actions in the art.

Selection Summary Send home the summary of *Sam, Come Back!* in English and the child's home language if available. Children can read the summary with family members.

Preview NEXT WEEK

Tell children that next week they will read about pets and their needs.

Unit Wrap-Up

 The Big Question

What is all around me?

Understanding By Design

*Grant Wiggins, Ed. D.
Reading Street Author*

"In short, the best questions serve not only to promote understanding of the content of a unit on a particular topic; they also spark connections and promote transfer of ideas from one setting to others. We call such questions 'essential.'"

WEEK 1

Question of the Week

What is around us at home?

Concept Knowledge

Children will understand that at home:

- our family and pets live together
- we have books, furniture, and clothes
- we have toys and games
- we have food

WEEK 2

Question of the Week

Who is in our family?

Concept Knowledge

Children will understand that family members:

- are children
- are adults
- are pets
- love each other

Discuss the Big Question

Help children relate the concept question for this unit to the selections and their own experiences. Write the question and prompt discussion with questions such as the following:

How did characters in the stories learn what was all around them? Possible answers:

- *Sam* Sam notices all of the things in his bedroom around his home.
- *Snap!* Sam and his family have a family portrait made.
- *Tip and Tam* The children clean up leaves in the yard and find Tip hiding.
- *The Big Top* The children play with their neighborhood friends and do fun things together.
- *School Day* Sam has many experiences and sees lots of things during a school day.

WEEK 3

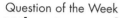

Question of the Week

What is outside our door?

Concept Knowledge

Children will understand that:

- we can see many things outside
- we can do many things outside

WEEK 4

Question of the Week

What can we do with our neighborhood friends?

Concept Knowledge

Children will understand that neighborhood friends:

- play with us
- do fun things with us
- help us out

WEEK 5

Question of the Week

What is around us at school?

Concept Knowledge

Children will understand that:

- there are many places and rooms in a school
- there are different kinds of people in school
- a classroom is filled with many things

WEEK 6

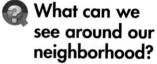

Question of the Week

What can we see around our neighborhood?

Concept Knowledge

Children will understand that in our neighborhoods we can see:

- schools, libraries, and parks
- stores, restaurants, and farmers markets
- lots of people

Where do the children in the stories find things in the world around them? Possible answers:

- *Sam* Sam has people and pets in his bedroom and house.
- *Snap!* Sam, Pam, Tam, Mom, and Dad are a family and live together in their house.
- *Tip and Tam* The neighborhood children play and learn together outside.
- *The Big Top* Children find things to do in their yard.
- *The Farmers Market* The farmers market is one place in the neighborhood to see people and exciting things.

Tell about things and people you notice in the world around you.

Responses will vary.

DAY 5 Assessment Checkpoints for the Week

Weekly Assessment

Use pp. 31–36 of *Weekly Tests* to check:

✔ 🔊 **Phonics** /v/v/, /y/y/, /z/z/, /u/u/, /qu/kw/

✔ 🔊 **Comprehension Skill** Realism and Fantasy

✔ **High-Frequency Words**
for	me
go	where
here	

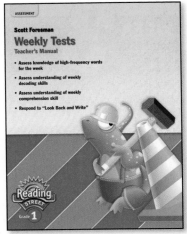

Weekly Tests

Advanced

On-Level

Strategic Intervention

Differentiated Asssessment

Use pp. 31–36 of *Fresh Reads for Fluency and Comprehension* to check:

✔ 🔊 **Comprehension Skill** Realism and Fantasy

✔ Review **Comprehension Skill** Setting

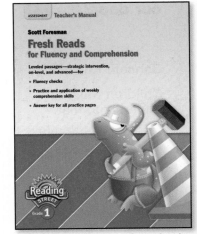

Fresh Reads for Fluency and Comprehension

Unit Assessment

Use the Unit R Benchmark Test to check progress in:

✔ **Listening Comprehension**

✔ **High-Frequency Words**

✔ **Phonics**

✔ **Writing**

Unit and End-of-Year Benchmark Tests

A Yard for Bugs and Ducks

Vin put on his tan vest. It was time to work in the yard. Vin liked his yard. "My yard is good for plants," he said.

He planted yams. He planted flowers. Some were mums. He got water. He put water on the young plants in his yard. He got mud on his hands. He got mud on his vest. Vin worked very hard. The sun was very hot.

It was time for a quick nap, so Vin rested in the sun. But a little bug landed on his chin. "A bug! I must brush it away," said Vin.

Buzz! Buzz! He saw a bee zip by his nose. "A bee! I must brush it away," he said.

Quack! Quack! A duck walked up from the pond. The duck came very close to Vin. The bug and the bee came back. Vin got up.

"They will not quit!" he said. His yard was good for bugs and ducks. It was good for yams and mums. "My yard is not good for naps!" said Vin.

Advanced Selection R6   **Vocabulary:** yams, mums

Small Group Time

Pacing Small Group Instruction

20–30 min.

5 Day Plan

DAY 1	• Phonemic Awareness/ Phonics
DAY 2	• Phonemic Awareness/ Phonics
DAY 3	• Phonemic Awareness/ Phonics • Leveled Reader
DAY 4	• Phonemic Awareness/ Phonics • Decodable Reader
DAY 5	• High-Frequency Words • Decodable Reader

3 or 4 Day Plan

DAY 1	• Phonemic Awareness/ Phonics
DAY 2	• Phonemic Awareness/ Phonics
DAY 3	• Phonemic Awareness/ Phonics • Leveled Reader
DAY 4	• Phonemic Awareness/ Phonics • Decodable Reader

3 Day Plan: Eliminate the shaded box.

Phonemic Awareness•Phonics

■ **Isolate Initial and Medial Phonemes** Reteach pp. 142–143 of the Teacher's Edition. Model isolating and matching initial and medial /v/ in these words. Then have children practice isolating and matching /v/ on their own.

vine initial /v/	**favor** medial /v/	**oven** medial /v/
shiver medial /v/	**vote** initial /v/	**vest** initial /v/

Then tell children that you are thinking of a word that begins with /v/. I'm thinking of a kind of a doctor. It's a doctor who works with animals instead of people. I'm thinking of a—. Have children fill in the word *vet* or *veterinarian*. Repeat with *vegetables* and *van*.

■ **Consonant *v* /v/** Reteach p. 143a of the Teacher's Edition. Then have children put their hands into the shape of a *v* when you say a word that begins with *v*. Have them keep their hands down if the word does not begin with *v*.

• This word is *pine*. Does it begin with the letter *v*? (No)

• This word is *very*. Does it begin with the letter *v*? (Yes)

• This word is *big*. Does it begin with the letter *v*? (No)

• This word is *valley*. Does it begin with the letter *v*? (Yes)

• This word is *vitamin*. Does it begin with the letter *v*? (Yes)

Repeat with words that include medial *v*. Use the following words: *river, juggle, over, ended, divide, moving*.

Objectives
• Isolate initial sounds in one-syllable spoken words.
• Isolate medial sounds in one-syllable spoken words.

DAY 2

More Reading
Use text at the children's instructional level.

Phonemic Awareness • Phonics

■ **Isolate Initial and Final Phonemes** Reteach p. 144d of the Teacher's Edition. Model isolating and matching initial /y/ and initial and final /z/ in these words. Then have children practice isolating and matching initial /y/ and initial and final /z/ on their own.

zip initial /z/	**young** initial /y/	**maze** final /z/
years initial /y/	**zero** initial /z/	**buzz** final /z/

Then tell children that you are thinking of a word that begins with /y/. I'm thinking of something you might do when you are tired. You open your mouth very wide and you breathe a lot of air into your lungs. When you do this, you—. Have children supply the word *yawn*. Repeat with *yell*. Then repeat with initial /z/ and the words *zebra* and *zoo*.

■ ◉ **Consonants y /y/ and z /z/** Reteach p. 144e of the Teacher's Edition. Then have children hold up a letter tile for *y* when you read a word that begins with *y*. Have them hold up a letter tile for *z* when you read a word that begins with *z*.

- This word is *zoom*. Does it begin with *y* or *z*? (z)
- This word is *yak*. Does it begin with *y* or *z*? (y)
- This word is *zigzag*. Does it begin with *y* or *z*? (z)
- This word is *your*. Does it begin with *y* or *z*? (y)
- This word is *zipper*. Does it begin with *y* or *z*? (z)
- This word is *yellow*. Does it begin with *y* or *z*? (y)

Objectives
- Isolate initial sounds in one-syllable spoken words.
- Isolate final sounds in one-syllable spoken words.

Small Group Time

Phonemic Awareness • Phonics

■ **Identify Syllables** Reteach p. 146d of the Teacher's Edition. Continue the activity with the following examples. Say each word aloud and have children clap or tap the syllables with you. Have them tell you how many syllables each word contains.

zebra (2)	**yellow** (2)	**zoo** (1)	**younger** (2)	**yesterday** (3)	**zigzag** (2)
Thanksgiving (3)	**away** (2)	**video** (3)	**watermelon** (4)	**string** (1)	**violin** (3)

■ **Short Vowel *u*** Reteach p. 146e of the Teacher's Edition. Then read the following words aloud: *sad, bug, rub, much, led, box, cut.* Have children skywrite the letter *u* if the word has short *u* in the middle. Have them keep their hands down for words with a different vowel.

Concept Literacy Leveled Reader

■ **Preview and Predict** Read the title and author's name. Ask children to look at the cover and describe what they see. Where was the picture taken? How do you know? Help children activate prior knowledge by having them look through the book and use the pictures to predict things that might take place.

■ **Set a Purpose** Remind children that setting a purpose for reading can help them better understand what they read. Guide children to pay attention to what the story tells about places in a neighborhood.

■ **Read** Provide corrective feedback as children read the story orally. Remind children that they can use the pictures to help them with unfamiliar words. During reading, ask them if they were able to confirm any of the predictions they made prior to the story.

If... children have difficulty reading the story individually,
then... read a sentence aloud as children point to each word. Then have the group reread the sentences as they continue pointing. Continue reading in this way until children read individually.

■ **Retell** Have children take turns retelling the story. Help them identify places in the neighborhood by asking, Where do you go to get books/get food/wash clothes?

■ **Text to Self** Ask children to name one place in the book that they can visit in their own neighborhoods. Then have them name a place that they visit in their neighborhood that is not mentioned in the book.

Concept Literacy

Objectives
- Isolate medial sounds in one-syllable spoken words.
- Establish purpose for reading selected texts.

SI Strategic Intervention

DAY 4

Phonemic Awareness • Phonics

■ **Blend and Segment Phonemes** Reteach p. 146p of the Teacher's Edition. Model blending and segmenting the phonemes in these words.

Continue the activity with the following examples.

Blend /kw/ /i/ /t/	Blend /v/ /e/ /t/	Segment *tug*	Segment *quiz*
Blend /y/ /u/ /m/	Blend /b/ /u/ /z/	Segment *vote*	Segment *yuck*

■ ◉ **Consonant *qu* /kw/** Reteach p. 146q of the Teacher's Edition. Then read the following words aloud: *queen, question, quill, quiet, hop, quick, when, cape, quack.* Have children hold up letter tiles for *q* and *u* for words that begin with /kw/. Have them keep their tiles down for words that start with some other letter.

Decodable Practice Reader R6A

■ **Review** Use the word lists to review short vowel *e*, consonants *v* /v/, *y* /y/, *z, zz* /z/ and *qu* /kw/, and the high-frequency words *for, a, do,* and *the*. Use the words *quiz* and *yet* to review the process of blending. Then have children read the story together, pointing to the words as they speak them.

Decodable Reader R6A

> **If...** children have difficulty reading the story individually,
> **then...** read a sentence aloud as children point to each word. Then have the group reread the sentences as they continue pointing. Continue reading in this way until children read individually.

Check comprehension by having children retell the events of the story in sequence. Next, have children locate words in the story that include short *e*. List the words children identify and write them on the board. Then have children read the words in isolation.

Words with short *e*:
Bev
pen
yet

Objectives
• Blend spoken phonemes to form one-syllable words, including consonant blends.
• Decode words in context by applying common letter-sound correspondences, including: single letters (vowels) including short e.

Small Group Time

More Reading

Use text at the children's instructional level.

SI Strategic Intervention

High-Frequency Words

■ **Review** Write *where, go, here, for, me* on the board. Model saying each word. Then have children read each word, spell each word as you point to each letter, and have them say each word again. Allow time for children to practice reading these high-frequency words using the word cards.

Decodable Practice Reader R6B

■ **Review** Use the word lists to review short vowel *e*, consonants *v* /v/, *y* /y/, *z, zz* /z/ and *qu* /kw/, and the high-frequency words *the, is, a, with, they,* and *have*. Then have children read the story chorally, pointing to the words as they speak them.

> **If...** children have difficulty reading the story individually,
> **then...** read a sentence aloud as children point to each word. Then have the group reread the sentences as they continue pointing. Continue reading in this way until children read individually.

Decodable Reader R6B

Check comprehension by having children describe the problem in the story and the way the characters try to solve the problem. Then have children locate words in the story that include consonants *v, y, z,* or *qu*. List the words children identify and help children classify the words according to the letters they contain.

v	y	z	qu
Vic	yum	zip	quiz
rev	yell	Roz	quit
van	yet	fuzz	
		quiz	

Objectives
• Decode words with common spelling patterns.
• Read at least 100 high-frequency words from a commonly used list.

DI•110   My World • Unit R • Week 6

 OL On-Level   **DAY 1**

Phonemic Awareness • Phonics

■ **Isolate Initial and Medial Phonemes** Say the words below and have children repeat them with you. Then have children generate other words that begin with the sound /v/.

vote   **very**   **village**   **vet**

Repeat with words with /v/ in the middle, such as *even, shiver,* and *oval.*

■ 🔊 **Consonant *v* /v/** Remind children that the letter v stands for the sound /v/. Have children identify whether the *v* is at the beginning or in the middle of these words: *cover, vines, leaving, vest, oven, vegetable.*

Objectives
- Isolate initial sounds in one-syllable spoken words.
- Isolate medial sounds in one-syllable spoken words.

Pacing Small Group Instruction   20–30 min.

5 Day Plan	
DAY 1	• Phonemic Awareness • Phonics
DAY 2	• Phonics • High-Frequency Words
DAY 3	• Leveled Reader
DAY 4	• Conventions • Decodable Reader
DAY 5	• Phonics • Decodable Reader

OL On-Level   **DAY 2**

Phonics • High-Frequency Words

■ 🔊 **Consonants *y* /y/ and *z, zz* /z/** Read the following words aloud. Have children identify whether the words begin with *y* or *z* by holding up the appropriate letter tile.

young   **zipper**   **zoo**   **yak**   **yours**   **zero**   **yellow**   **zoom**

Then write some of the words on the board. Have children come to the board and circle the *y* or the *z*.

■ **High-Frequency Words** Hold up this week's High-Frequency Word Cards and review proper pronunciation. Have children chorally read each word. To help children demonstrate their understanding of the words, provide them with oral sentence frames such as: The opposite of *over there* is *right* _____ . (here)

Objectives
- Isolate initial sounds in one-syllable spoken words.
- Read at least 100 high-frequency words from a commonly used list.

---

3 or 4 Day Plan	
DAY 1	• Phonemic Awareness • Phonics
DAY 2	• Phonics • High-Frequency Words
DAY 3	• Leveled Reader
DAY 4	• Conventions • Decodable Reader

3 Day Plan: Eliminate the shaded box.

  On-Level   DAY 3

Concept Literacy Leveled Reader

■ **Preview and Predict** Read the title and the author's name. Have children look at the cover and ask them to describe in detail what they see. Help children preview the story by asking them to look through the book and to use the photos to predict what might happen.

Concept Literacy

■ 🔘 **Background Knowledge** Before reading the story, have children identify a store or another place they sometimes go in their own neighborhood. Have them tell what people can do in that place. Instruct them to look for places like these as they read the story.

■ **Read** During reading, monitor children's comprehension by providing higher-order thinking questions. Ask:

- Does your neighborhood have a post office/library/farmers market?

- What other stores or businesses does your neighborhood have?

To help children gain a better understanding of the text, build upon their responses with a group discussion.

■ 🔘 **Realism and Fantasy** Review with children the differences between realism and fantasy. Have children determine whether this story is an example of realism or an example of fantasy. Ask:

- Do real people go to grocery stores, post offices, and libraries?

- Do the pictures show real people, cartoon people, or talking animals?

■ **Text to Self** Help children connect the story to their own experiences. Ask:

- If you could add one store from your own neighborhood to this book, what store would you add? Why?

Objectives
- Establish purpose for reading selected texts.
- Explain why a story is true or fantasy.

 **OL** On-Level

DAY 4

Conventions • Decodable Practice Reader

■ **Sentences** Review with children that a sentence begins with a capital letter and ends with a period or other punctuation mark. Write *we like eggs; the dog is big;* and *my cat can run* on the board. Read the sentences aloud with children and have children add capitals and periods in the appropriate places.

■ **Decodable Practice Reader R6A** Review words with short vowel *e* and the high-frequency words *for, a, do,* and *the*. Then have children blend and read these words from the story: *quiz, Bev, yet*. Have children reread the text orally. To achieve optimal fluency, children should reread the text three or four times.

Decodable Reader R6A

More Reading
Use text at the children's instructional level.

Objectives
- Use basic capitalization for the beginning of sentences.
- Use punctuation marks at the end of declarative sentences.

 **OL** On-Level

DAY 5

Phonics Review • Decodable Practice Reader

■ **Consonants *v* /v/, *y* /y/, *z, zz*/z/, *qu* /kw/ and Short Vowel /u/** Have children practice blending and reading these words:

vet	buzz	yam	zip	fuzz
van	quit	bug	quiz	yum

Have children identify the words that have the /v/, /y/, /z/, /kw/, or /u/ sounds.

■ **Decodable Practice Reader R6B** Review words with *v, y, z, qu,* and *u* and the high-frequency words *with, they,* and *have*. Have children blend and read these words from the story: *yum, tug, rev, quiz*. Have children reread the text orally. To achieve optimal fluency, children should reread the text three or four times.

Decodable Reader R6B

Objectives
- Decode words in context by applying common letter-sound correspondences, including: single letters (vowels), including short u.

Small Group Time

Pacing Small Group Instruction

20-30 min.

A Advanced **DAY 1**

Phonics

■ 🔊 **Consonant _v_ /v/** Have children practice with longer words containing consonant _v_. Read aloud the following words. Have children say _beginning_ or _middle_ to indicate where in the word the letter _v_ would go.

> **victory   universe   Oliver   villagers   uncover   videos**

Write some of the words on the board. Have children come to the board one by one to circle the letter _v_.

Objectives
- Isolate initial sounds in one-syllable spoken words.
- Isolate medial sounds in one-syllable spoken words.

A Advanced **DAY 2**

Phonics • Comprehension

A Busy Day

■ 🔊 **Consonants _y_ /y/ and _z, zz_ /z/** Have children spell the word _zap_ with letter tiles. Then have children make changes.

- Change the _z_ in _zap_ to _y_. What word did you spell? (yap)
- Change the _p_ in _yap_ to _m_. What word did you spell? (yam)
- What letter would you change to turn _yam_ into _jam_? (_y_ to _j_)
- Change the _m_ in _jam_ to _zz_. What word did you spell? (jazz)

■ **Comprehension** Reread this week's Read Aloud, "A Busy Day," with children. Remind children that some stories are realistic while others are fantasy. Review the difference with children. Then have children identify whether this story is realistic or fantasy and give two reasons for their answer.

Objectives
- Isolate initial sounds in one-syllable spoken words.
- Explain why a story is true or fantasy.

 **A** Advanced | DAY **3**

Concept Literacy Leveled Reader

■ **Activate Prior Knowledge** Read the title and the author's name. Have children describe in detail what they see on the cover. Briefly review last week's Concept Literacy Leveled Reader, *My School*. Have children predict how *Around My Neighborhood* and *My School* might be alike.

■ 🕙 **Background Knowledge** Before reading, ask children to name two places they can visit in their own neighborhoods and to tell what they do there. Explain that places like these might be mentioned in the book, and instruct children to look for similarities and differences between their neighborhood and the places in the story as they read the book.

■ **Read** During reading, monitor children's comprehension by providing higher-order thinking questions. Ask:

• Why are there post offices and libraries?

• Which of the places in the book do people need the most? Why?

Build on children's answers to help them gain a better understanding of the text.

■ 🕙 **Realism and Fantasy** Review the differences between realism and fantasy with children. Point out that this story is realistic, because it tells about real people and real places in real neighborhoods. Then ask what this book might be like if it were a fantasy instead of an example of realism. Ask the following questions to guide children's thinking.

• What kinds of places could not be in a neighborhood? How do you know?

• Would a fantasy book about neighborhoods tell about a fire station or a building as tall as the moon...about a restaurant or a zoo for talking animals?

■ **Text to Text** Help children connect the story to what they read in last week's Concept Literacy Leveled Reader, *My School*. Ask:

• How are these two stories alike? How are they different?

Concept Literacy

More Reading
Use text at the children's instructional level.

Objectives
• Locate details about stories.
• Determine whether a story is true or fantasy.

A Advanced

DAY 4

Comprehension

- **Comprehension** Have children silently read this week's main selection, *Farmers Market*. Have them retell the story to a partner describing the characters, the plot, and the setting. Then have them summarize the most important idea in the story.

  Ask children whether *Farmers Market* is fiction or nonfiction; then ask whether it qualifies as realistic fiction. (The story is realistic fiction, because it is a made-up story that could be real.)

- **Text to Self** Have children identify three items they would like to buy at a farmers market. Have them explain to a partner why they chose those three items, using full sentences with the word *because*.

Farmers Market

Objectives
- Describe characters in a story.
- Restate the main idea, heard or read.

A Advanced

DAY 5

Comprehension

- **Comprehension** After they have finished reading the selection, have children review the story by describing what Vin learns about his yard and why. Then, on the back of the selection page, have them write three sentences explaining how they could try to solve Vin's problems with bugs and ducks.

Advanced Selection R6

Objectives
- Read aloud grade-level appropriate text with fluency and comprehension.
- Write brief compositions about topics of interest to the student.

Concept Development

What can we see around our neighborhood?

Activate Prior Knowledge Write the question of the week and read it aloud. Underline the word *neighborhood* and have children say it with you. Remind children that neighborhood is the area we live in. What have you learned about your neighborhood? Have children name things they have learned about their neighborhood.

Connect to New Concept Have children turn to pages 140–141 in the Student Edition. Read the title aloud and have children track the print as you read it. Point to the pictures one at a time and use them to guide a discussion about what we can see around our neighborhood. For example, point to people shopping at the farmer's market. What are these people doing? (buying food) This is a farmer's market. People buy and sell things there. Have any of you ever been to a farmer's market? What did you see there?

Develop Concepts Display ELL Poster R6 and have children identify the setting of the poster. (neighborhood, town) What places are the people visiting? Have children point to places on the poster. (library book sale, café, produce stand, store) Use the leveled prompts below to assess understanding and build oral language. Point to pictures on the poster as you guide discussion.

Leveled Support

Beginning Ask yes/no questions, such as Are people driving cars? Are people sitting at tables?

Intermediate Ask children questions that can be answered with simple sentences. What building is on the left? What building is yellow? What is sold in the store?

Advanced/Advanced High Have children answer the Question of the Week by giving specific examples from the poster and their own neighborhoods.

Review Concepts and Connect to Writing Review children's understanding of the concept at the end of the week. Ask them to write in response to these questions: Where can you go in your neighborhood? What are some things you can do in your neighborhood? What English words did you learn this week? Encourage children to use academic language in their responses. Write and display key ideas from the discussion.

Objectives
- Internalize new basic and academic language by using and reusing it in meaningful ways in speaking and writing activities that build concept and language attainment.
- Learn new language structures, expressions, and basic and academic vocabulary heard during classroom instruction and interactions.

Content Objectives
- Describe what we can see in our neighborhood.

Language Objectives
- Share information orally.
- Use basic vocabulary for describing a neighborhood.
- Use academic language to write about neighborhoods.

Daily Planner
The ELL lessons are organized by strands. Use them to scaffold the weekly lesson curriculum or during small-group time.

Daily Lesson Planner	
DAY 1	• Concepts and Oral Vocabulary • Listening (Read Aloud) • Match Initial And Final Phonemes • Consonant *v* /v/
DAY 2	• Concepts • High-Frequency Words • Consonant *y* /y/; Consonant *z, zz* /z/
DAY 3	• Concepts • Story Words • Realism and Fantasy • Read *The Farmers Market*
DAY 4	• Concepts • Story Words • ELL/ELD Readers
DAY 5	• Concepts • Story Words • Sentences • Revising

*See the ELL Handbook for *ELL Workshops* with targeted instruction.

Support for English Language Learners

Language Objectives

- Match initial and final phonemes.

Transfer Skills

Consonant Sounds Some Asian languages have no consonant sounds that correspond to /f/ or /v/. Children from that language background may have difficulty hearing and making the distinction between the voiced /v/ and the unvoiced /f/.

ELL Teaching Routine

For more practice with consonant sounds use the Sound-by-Sound Blending Routine (*ELL Handbook*, page 496).

Phonemic Awareness: Match Initial and Final Phonemes

■ **Preteach Initial and Final Phonemes**

- Have children open to pages 142–143. Point to the van. This is a van. Emphasize the initial sound /v/. Listen as I say the sounds in *van*: /v/ /a/ /n/. What sound do you hear at the beginning? (/v/) Repeat with *vat*.

- Have children repeat with words *van* and *vat*. Ask them to say the sound at the beginning of both words.

- Say the words *yap* and *yip*. Help children identify the beginning sound /y/ in both words. Repeat with *zip* and *zap*. Review the letters *Ee, Ww, Jj,* and *Kk* and their corresponding sounds using words from previous lessons.

■ **Practice** Listen again as I say the following words. Tell me which word pairs have the same sound at the beginning. Say the following word pairs aloud to children.

cut, hop	vet, vat	year, yellow	sock, bat
very, view	cake, sink	yell, yes	zoo, zipper

Phonics: Consonant z /z/

■ **Preteach** Display Sound-Spelling Card 29. This is a zebra. What sound do you hear at the beginning of *zebra*? (/z/) Say it with me: /z/. Point to *z*. The beginning sound in *zebra* is /z/.

■ **Listen and Write** Distribute Write and Wipe Boards.

- Write the word *zebra* on the board. Copy this word. As you write *z*, say the sound to yourself. /z/. Now say the sound aloud. (/z/) Underline *z* in *zebra*. The letter *z* spells /z/ in *zebra*.

For more practice pronouncing these sounds, use the Modeled Pronunciation Audio CD Routine (*ELL Handbook*, page 501).

Objectives

- Recognize elements of the English sound system in newly acquired vocabulary such as long and short vowels, silent letters, and consonant clusters.

 *English Language Learners*

■ **Reteach and Practice**

- Have children write the letter *v* on a small piece of paper. Tell children that you will write and say a word. If the word begins with /v/, they are to say /vvvv/ and show their *v*. Use the following words: *bird, visit, cup, vet, very, vast, bake, dip.* Write these words on the board.

- Leave the words that begin with /v/ on the board, but erase the letter *v* and replace it with a blank. Have children fill in the missing *v*.

 Leveled Support

Beginning Have children read the words aloud. Monitor for accurate pronunciation. Ask them to repeat the /v/ sound orally.

Intermediate Have children read the words aloud. Monitor for accurate pronunciation. Ask them to identify and write the consonant spelled by the /v/ sound.

Advanced/Advanced High Have children read the words aloud and name another word that begins with the /v/ sound. Then have children write their word in the list on the board.

Phonics: Consonants y /y/, z /z/

■ **Preteach** Have children turn to Envision It! on page 144 of the Student Edition.

- The word for the second picture is *yo-yo.* Point to the yo-yo. What sound do you hear at the beginning of *yo-yo*? (/y/) Say it with me: /y/. The word for the third picture is *zebra.* What sound do you hear at the beginning of *zebra*? (/z/) Say it with me: /z/. Review the letters *Ee, Kk,* and *Vv* and their corresponding sounds using words from previous lessons.

■ **Practice** Distribute Letter Tiles *s, r, ck, b, i, o,* and *t* to pairs. Give each pairs two *s* Letter Tiles.

- Blend the sounds in *yam* and have pairs spell *yam* with their tiles: /y/ /a/ /m/, yam.

- Replace the *y* and *m.* Spell *van.*

- Blend the sounds in *yes.* Spell *yes.*

- Blend the sounds in *zip.* Spell *zip.*

- Blend the sounds in *jazz.* Spell *jazz.*

Language Objectives
- Associate the sounds of /v/ with its spelling.
- Associate the sounds of /y/ and /z/ with their spellings.

Catch Up
The letters *y* and *z* are the last two letters of the alphabet.

 ## Transfer Skills
Consonants Children may confuse /s/ and /z/. Both sounds are made with the teeth together and the tongue behind the teeth, but /z/ is voiced, and /s/ is unvoiced. Spanish-speaking children may associate /s/ with both *s* and *z.* Help children read *z* words correctly.

Practice Page
ELL Handbook page 255 provides additional practice for this week's skill.

Content Objectives

- Monitor and adjust oral comprehension.

Language Objectives

- Discuss oral passages.
- Use a graphic organizer to take notes.

ELL Teacher Tip

To help children identify the setting of the Read Aloud, point out that the story events happen in four different places: the library, the market, the hat shop, and the park.

ELL *English Language Learners*

Listening Comprehension

Good Friends

Bonnie Bear and Betty Bear were good friends. They planned a busy day. First, they went to the library. Bonnie liked books about the moon, stars, and planets. Betty liked books about people. "Isn't it funny that we are such good friends but we like different books?" Betty asked. "I guess so," Bonnie answered.

Next, the bears went to the market to buy fruit. Bonnie chose apples and pears. Betty chose oranges and grapes. "Isn't it funny that we are good friends, but we like different kinds of fruit?" Betty asked. "I guess," Bonnie answered.

Then, the bears went to the hat shop. Betty picked a white hat with red dots. Bonnie picked a pale blue hat with no dots. "Isn't it funny that we are good friends, but we like different hats?" Betty asked. "I guess," Bonnie answered.

The bears went to the park to eat their fruit. "I have been thinking," Bonnie said. "We may not like the same books, fruit, or hats, but we like each other. That is why we are good friends!" Betty agreed.

Prepare for the Read Aloud The modified Read Aloud above prepares children for listening to the oral reading "A Busy Day" on page 143e.

■ **First Listening: Listen to Understand**

1. Write the title of the Read Aloud on the board. This story is about two bears who are good friends. The bears do not like the same things. Why are they such good friends?

2. After reading, ask children to discuss why the bears are such good friends.

■ **Second Listening: Listen to Check Understanding** Using a Story Map graphic organizer (*ELL Handbook*, page 507), work with children to identify the characters, the setting, and what happened in the story. Review the completed maps together as a class.

Objectives

- Demonstrate listening comprehension of increasingly complex spoken English by following directions, retelling or summarizing spoken messages, responding to questions and requests, collaborating with peers, and taking notes commensurate with content and grade-level needs.

 English Language Learners

High-Frequency Words

■ **Preteach** Use the Poster Talk-Through on ELL Poster R6 to preteach this week's high-frequency words: *where, go, here, for, me.* Display the words and read each one slowly and clearly aloud as you track the print. Have children repeat each word with you. Monitor children's pronunciation. Provide daily practice using the activities on the poster.

■ **Practice** Give each pair of children two copies of the Word Cards. Then have children use these cards in a matching game. Partners should take turns turning over the cards to find pairs of matching words. Model the correct pronunciation of each word. Have children say the word aloud as they turn each card over. Guide children as they read the word.

■ **Speaking/Writing with High-Frequency Words**

• **Teach/Model** Give each child a Word Card (*ELL Handbook*, page 492). Have children hold up the Word Card as you say sentences that contain the high-frequency word. Correct any misconceptions.

• **Practice** After reteaching, have each child illustrate the word. Have children use language, appropriate to their language proficiency level.

 Leveled Support

Beginning Have children illustrate the word and describe their picture to a partner.

Intermediate Have children illustrate the word and label their picture. Then, have children describe their picture to a partner.

Advanced/Advanced High Have children illustrate the word and label their picture. Then, have children write a sentence about their drawing and share their sentence with a partner.

Language Objectives

• Understand and use basic vocabulary.

• Understand and read high-frequency words.

Objectives
• Use strategic learning techniques such as concept mapping, drawing, memorizing, comparing, contrasting, and reviewing to acquire basic and grade-level vocabulary.

Support for English Language Learners

Content Objectives
- Identify the difference between realism and fantasy.

Language Objectives
- Describe the difference between realism and fantasy.
- Use accessible language to learn essential language.

ELL English Language Learners

Guide Comprehension
Realism and Fantasy

■ **Preteach** Sometimes stories are about things and characters that are real. Sometimes they are about make-believe things and characters. A make-believe story is a fantasy.

Practice Have children turn to Envision It! on pages EI•2 and EI•3 in the Student Edition. Point to the bear family. This is a picture of a real bear family. Point to the picture on Pi•3 and explain that this bear family is make believe.

■ **Reteach** Distribute copies of the Picture It! (*ELL Handbook*, p. 96). Have children look at the images. Remind them that *fantasy* describes events that could not happen in real life, such as animals talking or a boy flying. Reality describes events that could happen in real life. Read the passage to the children as they follow along. Ask them to decide if each event is reality or fantasy. (**Answers**: Reality: You can wash socks and shirts. Fantasy: washing machines do not talk.)

Beginning Build background with the children. Ask: What are things a washing machine can do? What are things a washing machine cannot do? Read the passage to the children. Stop after each line and help the children identify if it describes an event that is reality or fantasy. Encourage them to explain how they knew. (Machines cannot talk.)

Intermediate/Advanced/Advanced High Choral read the passage with the children. Ask them to retell the story. Have them talk with a partner to find two events that are reality and one event that is fantasy. Then, share and discuss as a class.

MINI-LESSON

Academic Language
What is your favorite story? Use children's responses to explain the difference between fiction and nonfiction. Tell children that *fiction* stories are usually about something that is not real. *Nonfiction* stories are about things or people that are real.

Objectives
- Use accessible language and learn new and essential language in the process.
- Understand the general meaning, main points, and important details of spoken language ranging from situations in which topics, language, and contexts are familiar to unfamiliar.

 English Language Learners

Student Edition pp. 148–157

Reading Comprehension
Farmers Market

■ **Frontloading**

• **Background Knowledge** Read aloud the title and discuss it. Point to the market. This is a market. A market is where people go to buy and sell things. What might be something you could sell or buy at a market?

• **Preview** Guide children on a picture walk through the story, asking them to identify people, places, and actions. Reteach these words using visuals in the Student Edition: *bus stop* (p. 150), *farmers market* (p. 151), and *watermelon* (p. 152). As you preview the selection, point out the directionality of the text. Have children place their fingers on the left of the top sentence and move their fingers along the line as they choral read with you. Follow the same procedure with the second sentence. As you read with children, have them track the text as you observe to be sure children follow the directionality of the print. Focus on directionality, for example, using p. 150 of the Student Edition.

• **Predict** What do you think Pam and Dad will see at the farmers market?

Sheltered Reading Ask questions such as the following to guide children's comprehension:

• p. 150: Point to Pam and Dad. Who gets on the bus?

• p. 151: Point to the sign. Where do Pam and Dad go?

• p. 152: Point to Viv: What does Viv do?

• p. 153: Point to Pat. What does Pat do?

After Reading Help children summarize the text with the Retelling Cards. Ask questions that prompt children to summarize the important parts of the text. Use the selection to prompt discussion about formal and informal language. Turn to page 152. Work with children to role play speaking with Viv. What kind of English would they use: formal or informal? Why would you use informal language to speak to someone at the farmers market?

Content Objectives
• Monitor and adjust comprehension.
• Make and adjust predictions.
• Recognize directionality in print.

Language Objectives
• Summarize text using visual support.

Audio Support
Children can prepare for reading *Farmers Market* by using the main selection eText online or the Audio Text CD. See the Audio Text CD Routine (*ELL Handbook*, page 500) for suggestions on using these learning tools.

Objectives
• Read linguistically accommodated content area material with a decreasing need for linguistic accommodations as more English is learned.
• Adapt spoken language appropriately for formal and informal purposes.
• Recognize directionality of English reading such as left to right and top to bottom.

Support for English Language Learners

ELL English Language Learners

ELL/ELD Reader 1.R.6,

Comprehension: *At the Market*

■ **Before Reading** Distribute copies of the ELL and ELD Readers, *At the Market*, to children at their reading level.

- **Preview** Read the title aloud with children: This is a story about the things children find at a market. Activate prior knowledge. The story in our book was about a market. This is also a story about what you can find at a market. What are some things you can find at a market? Have you ever been to a market?

- **Set a Purpose for Reading** Let's read to find out what the children see at the market.

■ **During Reading** Follow this Reading Routine for both reading groups.

1. Read the entire Reader aloud slowly as children follow along and finger point.

2. Reread the Reader one sentence at a time as children echo read after you.

■ **After Reading** Use the exercises on the inside back cover of *At the Market* and invite children to share drawings and writing. In a whole-group discussion, ask children to list the things they might find at a market. Encourage children to discuss their favorite foods that can be found at a market.

ELD Reader

■ **p. 2** Point to the market. Have children describe what they see.

■ **p. 6** Point to the fruit. What kinds of fruit can you find at a market?

Writing Draw a picture of one thing you can find at a market. Label your picture. Ask children to work in pairs and then share their pictures with the whole class. Have them compare the differences in their pictures.

ELD Reader

■ **p. 3** What do you do at a market? (You shop at a market.)

■ **p. 8** What do you do before you leave the market? (You pay for the things you want.)

Study Guide Distribute copies of the ELL Reader Study Guide (*ELL Handbook*, page 64). Scaffold comprehension by reviewing the types of things that can be found at a market. Review responses together. (**Answers** See *ELL Handbook*, pp. 245–248.)

Objectives

- Understand the general meaning, main points, and important details of spoken language ranging from situations in which topics, language, and contexts are familiar to unfamiliar.

Conventions
Sentences

■ **Preteach** Write on the board *We eat fruit*. Read the sentence aloud. This is a complete sentence. Circle the capital letter and period. A complete sentence begins with a capital letter and ends with a period. Remind children that sentences have a subject and a verb. Identify the subject *We* and verb *eat* in the sentence.

■ **Practice**

Beginning/Intermediate Write the following sentence on the board: *the boy ate lunch.* Have children provide the capital letter and punctuation to make the sentence correct. Then have children read the sentence aloud.

Advanced/Advanced High Using the sentence frame *The _____ is a _____*, have children complete the sentence and draw a picture of it. Then have them read the sentence to the group.

■ **Reteach**

• Remind children that a sentence is a complete idea, and it has a capital letter and a period. Use written sentences to review. Write the following sentences on the board: *Sam sees the ball. Mom cooks dinner*. Read the sentences aloud. Have children underline the capital letters and periods in both sentences.

■ **Practice**

Beginning/Intermediate Write the following sentence frame on the board: *The _____ _____.* Have children write or dictate a noun and a verb to complete the frame. Then have children underline the capital letter and period.

Advanced/Advanced High Have children copy the sentence frame. Have them complete the sentence frame and read their sentence aloud.

Content Objectives
• Identify and use complete sentences.

Language Objectives
• Use capital letters and periods in sentences.

• Write sentences with capital letters and periods.

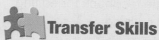 **Transfer Skills**

Capital Letters Children with literacy skills in Cantonese may need practice in starting sentences with a capital letter since these conventions exist only in alphabetic systems. Provide practice with starting sentences with capital letters.

Grammar Jammers

For more practice with sentences use the Grammar Jammers for this target skill. See the Grammar Jammers Routine (*ELL Handbook*, page 501) for suggestions on using this learning tool.

Objectives
• Speak using a variety of grammatical structures, sentence lengths, sentence types, and connecting words with increasing accuracy and ease as more English is acquired.

Support for English Language Learners

Content Objectives

- Identify sentences with nouns, verbs, and adjectives.

Language Objectives

- Write sentences with nouns, verbs, and adjectives.
- Share feedback for editing and revising.

ELL Teaching Routine

For practice spelling words related to things we see around our neighborhoods, use the Spelling Routine (*ELL Handbook*, page 499).

ELL English Language Learners

Write Sentences with Nouns, Verbs, and Adjectives

■ **Introduce Terms** Write the words *noun, verb,* and *adjective* on the board. A noun is a person, place, or thing. A verb is a word that tells an action. An adjective is a word that describes something.

■ **Introduce Sentences with Nouns, Verbs, and Adjectives** Write the following on the board: *We like red fruit.* Read the sentence aloud and have children repeat. Explain that is a complete sentence. Circle the subject. (We) Underline the verb. (like) Have a volunteer identify the adjective. (red)

■ **Model** Draw a three-column chart on the board. Label the columns *Noun, Verb,* and *Adjective*. Engage children in naming nouns, verbs, and adjectives. Write their responses in the appropriate columns of the chart.

Noun	Verb	Adjective

■ **Write** Have children copy this sentence frame: *I see the _____ _____.* Have children use words from the adjective column to fill in the first blank. Then have them think of another noun to include in the last blank. Then have partners read the completed frames together. Write the following frame on the board: *The _____ _____.*

Beginning/Intermediate Read the sentence frame to children. Have children write or dictate a noun and a verb to complete the sentence. Prompt children with suggestions from the chart.

Advanced/Advanced High Have children copy the sentence frame. Have them complete the frame with a noun and a verb. Then have them use an adjective to write a second sentence, including a noun and a verb.

Objectives

- Internalize new basic and academic language by using and reusing it in meaningful ways in speaking and writing activities that build concept and language attainment.

Customize Literacy in Your Classroom

Table of Contents
for Customize Literacy

Customize Literacy is organized into different sections, each one designed to help you organize and carry out an effective literacy program. Each section contains strategies and support for teaching comprehension skills and strategies. *Customize Literacy* also shows how to use weekly text sets of readers in your literacy program.

Weekly Text Sets
to Customize Literacy

The following readers can be used to enhance your literacy instruction.

	Decodable Readers	Concept Literacy Reader	ELD Reader	ELL Reader
Unit R WEEK 4	On Top; Hop, Pop, Dig, and Dab	My Friends	On Our Street	On Our Street
Unit R WEEK 5	We Met Meg; Get Fit!	My School	At School	At School
Unit R WEEK 6	The Quiz; Vic and Roz	Around My Neighborhood	At the Market	At the Market

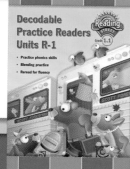

Decodable Practice Readers Units R-1
• Practice phonics skills
• Blending practice
• Reread for fluency

My Neighborho

This Land Our

Customize Literacy in Your Classroom

Instruction in comprehension skills and strategies provides readers with avenues to understanding a text. Through teacher modeling and guided, collaborative, and independent practice, students become independent thinkers who employ a variety of skills and strategies to help them make meaning as they read.

Envision It!
A Comprehension Handbook

Mini-Lessons for Comprehension Skills and Strategies

Unit R	Character, Setting, Plot, Realism, Questioning, Monitor and Clarify, Background Knowledge
Unit 1	Character, Setting, Plot, Main Idea and Details, Cause and Effect, Summarize, Important Ideas, Story Structure
Unit 2	Sequence, Cause and Effect, Author's Purpose, Compare and Contrast, Predict and Set Purpose, Inferring
Unit 3	Sequence, Compare and Contrast, Fact and Opinion, Author's Purpose, Draw Conclusions, Visualize, Text Structure
Unit 4	Draw Conclusions, Theme, Facts and Details, Cause and Effect, Important Ideas, Questioning
Unit 5	Literary Elements, Draw Conclusions, Compare and Contrast, Main Idea and Details, Sequence, Theme, Monitor and Clarify, Summarize

Envision It! Visual Skills Handbook

Author's Purpose
Categorize and Classify
Cause and Effect
Compare and Contrast
Draw Conclusions
Fact and Opinion
Generalize
Graphic Sources
Literary Elements
Main Idea and Details
Sequence

Envision It! Visual Strategies Handbook

Background Knowledge
Important Ideas
Inferring
Monitor and Clarify
Predict and Set Purpose
Questioning
Story Structure
Summarize
Text Structure
Visualize

Anchor Chart Anchor charts are provided with each strategy lesson. These charts incorporate the language of strategic thinkers. They help students make their thinking visible and permanent and provide students with a means to clarify their thinking about how and when to use each strategy. As students gain more experience with a strategy, the chart may undergo revision.

See pages 107–128 in the *First Stop on Reading Street* Teacher's Edition for additional support as you customize literacy in your classroom.

Good Readers DRA2 users will find additional resources in the *First Stop on Reading Street* Teacher's Edition on pages 110–111.

Contents

Section 1 Planning

Pacing Guide

This chart shows the instructional sequence from *Scott Foresman Reading Street* for Grade 1. You can use this pacing guide as is to ensure you are following a comprehensive scope and sequence. Or, you can adjust the sequence to match your calendar, curriculum map, or testing schedule.

Grade 1 READING — UNIT R

	Week 1	Week 2	Week 3	Week 4	Week 5	Week 6
Phonemic Awareness	Match Initial Phonemes	Match Initial Phonemes	Match Final Phonemes	Isolate Final Phonemes	Isolate Phonemes	Isolate Medial Phonemes
Phonics	/m/ spelled *m*, /s/ spelled *s*, /t/ spelled *t*, /a/ spelled *a*	/k/ spelled *c*, /p/ spelled *p*, /n/ spelled *n*	/f/ spelled *f, ff*, /b/ spelled *b*, /g/ spelled *g*, /i/ spelled *i*	/d/ spelled *d*, /l/ spelled *l*, /h/ spelled *h*, /o/ spelled *o*	/r/ spelled *r*, /w/ spelled *w*, /j/ spelled *j*, /k/ spelled *k*, /e/ spelled *e*	/v/ spelled *v*, /y/ spelled *y*, /u/ spelled *u*, /kw/ spelled *qu*
High-Frequency Words	*I, see, a, green*	*we, like, the, one*	*do, look, you, was, yellow*	*are, have, they, that, two*	*he, is, to, with, three*	*where, here, for, me, go*
Comprehension Skill	Character	Setting	Plot	Realism/Fantasy	Plot	Realism/Fantasy
Comprehension Strategy	Questioning	Predict and Set Purpose	Story Structure	Questioning	Monitor and Clarify	Background Knowledge
Fluency	Oral Rereading	Oral Rereading	Oral Rereading, Paired Reading	Oral Rereading, Paired Reading	Oral Rereading, Paired Reading	Oral Rereading, Paired Reading

UNIT 1

	Week 1	Week 2
Phonemic Awareness	Blend and Segment Phonemes	Blend and Segment Phonemes
Phonics	Short *a* Final *ck*	Short *i* Final *x*
High-Frequency Words	*on, way, in, my, come*	*take, up, she, what*
Comprehension Skill	Character and Setting	Plot
Comprehension Strategy	Monitor and Clarify	Summarize
Fluency	Accuracy	Accuracy

UNIT 3

	Week 1	Week 2	Week 3	Week 4	Week 5	Week 6
Phonemic Awareness	Segment Phonemes	Blend and Segment Words	Add Phonemes	Blend and Segment Syllables	Isolate Medial and Final Phonemes	Add Phonemes
Phonics	Vowel Sounds of *y* Long Vowels (CV)	Final *ng, nk* Compound Words	Ending *-es*, Plural *-es* r-Controlled *or, ore*	Inflected *-ed, -ing* r-Controlled *ar*	r-Controlled *er, ir, ur* Contractions *'s, 've, 're*	Comparative Endings *dge/j/*
High-Frequency Words	*always, become, day, everything, nothing, stays, things*	*any, enough, ever, every, own, sure, were*	*away, car, friends, house, our, school, very*	*afraid, again, few, how, read, soon*	*done, know, push, visit, wait*	*before, does, good-bye, oh, right, won't*
Comprehension Skill	Sequence	Compare and Contrast	Fact and Opinion	Author's Purpose	Fact and Opinion	Draw Conclusions
Comprehension Strategy	Summarize	Inferring	Monitor and Clarify	Visualize	Text Structure	Background Knowledge
Fluency	Accuracy	Phrasing	Phrasing	Expression	Expression	Expression

UNIT 4

	Week 1	Week 2
Phonemic Awareness	Substitute Initial Phonemes	Substitute Final Phonemes
Phonics	Long *a: ai, ay* Possessives	Long *e: ea* Inflected Endings
High-Frequency Words	*about, give, enjoy, would, worry, surprise(ed)*	*colors, drew, over, sign, draw, great, show*
Comprehension Skill	Draw Conclusions	Draw Conclusions
Comprehension Strategy	Monitor and Clarify	Visualize
Fluency	Expression/Intonation	Accuracy

> Are you the adventurous type? Want to use some of your own ideas and materials in your teaching? But you worry you might be leaving out some critical instruction kids need? The Customize Literacy Shop can help. **Customize Literacy** can help.

Week 3	Week 4	Week 5	Week 6
Blend and Segment Phonemes	Blend and Segment Phonemes	Blend and Segment Phonemes	Blend and Segment Phonemes
Short *o* -s Plurals	Inflected Endings -s, -ing	Short *e* Initial Blends	Short *u* Final Blends
blue, little, get, from, help, use	*eat, her, this, too, four, five*	*saw, small, tree, your*	*home, into, many, them*
Character and Setting	Main Idea and Details	Main Idea and Details	Cause and Effect
Visualize	Important Ideas	Story Structure	Text Structure
Rate	Rate	Phrasing	Phrasing

UNIT 2

Week 1	Week 2	Week 3	Week 4	Week 5	Week 6
Blend and Segment Phonemes	Blend and Segment Phonemes	Distinguish Long/Short Sounds	Distinguish Long/Short Sounds	Distinguish Long/Short Sounds	Distinguish Long/Short Sounds
Digraphs *sh, th* Vowel Sound in *ball*	Long *a* (CVCe) c/s/ and g/j/	Long *i* (CVCe) Digraphs *wh, ch, tch, ph*	Long *o* (CVCe) Contractions *n't, 'm, 'll*	Long *u*, long *e* (CVCe) Inflected Endings -ed	Long *e: e, ee* Syllables VCCV
catch, good, no, put, want, said	*be, could, horse, old, paper, of*	*live, out, people, who, work*	*down, inside, now, there, together*	*around, find, food, grow, under, water*	*also, family, new, other, some, their*
Sequence	Cause and Effect	Author's Purpose	Sequence	Author's Purpose	Compare and Contrast
Predict and Set Purpose	Monitor and Clarify	Important Ideas	Inferring	Background Knowledge	Questioning
Rate	Phrasing	Phrasing	Accuracy	Phrasing	Accuracy

Week 3	Week 4	Week 5	Week 6
Substitute Phonemes	Substitute Phonemes	Segment Syllables	Blend and Segment
Long *o: oa, ow* Three-letter Blends	Long *i: ie, igh* kn/n/ and wr/r/	Compound Words Vowels *ew, ue, ui*	Suffixes -ly, -ful Vowels in *moon*
found, once, wild, mouth, took	*above, laugh, touch, eight, moon*	*picture, room, thought, remember, stood*	*told, because, across, only, shoes, dance, opened*
Details and Facts	Details and Facts	Theme	Cause and Effect
Important Ideas	Questioning	Story Structure	Predict and Set Purpose
Expression	Accuracy/ Rate/ Expression	Phrasing	Expression

UNIT 5

Week 1	Week 2	Week 3	Week 4	Week 5	Week 6
Delete Initial Phonemes	Blend and Segment Phonemes	Add Final Phonemes	Substitute Final Phonemes	Blend and Segment Phonemes	Delete Phonemes
Diphthong *ow/ou/* Syllables C + le	Diphthong *ou/ou/* Syllables VCV	Vowels in *book* Inflected Endings	Diphthongs *oi, oy* Suffixes -er, -or	Syllable Patterns	Prefixes un-, re- Long Vowels *i, o*
along, behind, eyes, never, pulling, toward	*door, loved, should, wood*	*among, another, instead, none*	*against, goes, heavy, kinds, today*	*built, early, learn, science, through*	*answered, carry, different, poor*
Character, Setting, and Plot	Draw Conclusions	Compare and Contrast	Main Idea and Details	Sequence	Theme
Monitor and Clarify	Background Knowledge	Monitor and Clarify	Summarize	Text Structure	Inferring
Accuracy/ Rate/ Expression	Accuracy/ Rate/ Expression/ Phrasing	Expression	Phrasing	Expression	Phrasing

Pacing Guide

Grade 1

LANGUAGE ARTS — UNIT R

	Week 1	Week 2	Week 3	Week 4	Week 5	Week 6
Speaking, Listening, and Viewing	Determine the Purpose for Listening	Follow Directions	Share Information and Ideas	Share Information and Ideas	Ask Questions	Retell
Research and Study Skills	Parts of a Book	Parts of a Book	Picture Signs	Map	Calendar	Library/Media Center
Grammar	Nouns: People, Animals, and Things	Nouns: Places	Verbs	Simple Sentences	Adjectives	Sentences
Weekly Writing	Sentences	Sentences	Sentences	Sentences	Sentences	Sentences
Writing						

UNIT 1

	Week 1	Week 2
Speaking, Listening, and Viewing	Ask Questions	Share Information and Ideas
Research and Study Skills	Parts of a Book	Media Center/Library Resources
Grammar	Sentences	Subjects
Weekly Writing	Story/Voice	Fantasy Story/Conventions

UNIT 3

	Week 1	Week 2	Week 3	Week 4	Week 5	Week 6
Speaking, Listening, and Viewing	Relate an Experience	Share Information and Ideas	Give Descriptions	Present a Poem	Share Information and Ideas	Give Announcements
Research and Study Skills	Interview	Glossary	Classify and Categorize	Diagram	Technology: My Computer	Picture Graph
Grammar	Action Verbs	Verbs That Add -s	Verbs That Do Not Add -s	Verbs for Past and for Future	*Am, Is, Are, Was,* and *Were*	Contractions with *Not*
Weekly Writing	Realistic Story/Organization	Review/Voice	Expository Text/Conventions	List Sentences	Captions and Pictures	Play Scene/Sentences
Writing	Photo Writing/Expository Article					

UNIT 4

	Week 1	Week 2
Speaking, Listening, and Viewing	Give Descriptions	Share Information and Ideas
Research and Study Skills	Interview	Chart and Table
Grammar	Adjectives	Adjectives for Colors and Shapes
Weekly Writing	Letter/Organization	Invitation/Word Choice

Table 1 (Weeks 3–6)

Week 3	Week 4	Week 5	Week 6
Give Introductions	Share Information and Ideas	Give Descriptions	Give Directions
Picture Dictionary	Chart	List	Notes
Predicates	Declarative Sentences	Interrogative Sentences	Exclamatory Sentences
Short Poem/Sentences	Personal Narrative/Voice	Realistic Story/Organization	Brief Composition, Focus/Ideas

Keyboarding/Personal Narrative

UNIT 2

Week 1	Week 2	Week 3	Week 4	Week 5	Week 6
Relate an Experience	Share Information and Ideas	Give Announcements	Informal Conversation	Share Information and Ideas	Follow Directions
Parts of a Book	Interview	Map	Periodicals/Newsletters	Alphabetical Order	Picture Dictionary
Nouns	Proper Nouns	Special Titles	Days, Months, and Holidays	Singular and Plural Nouns	Nouns in Sentences
Friendly Letter/Organizations	Poster; Brief Composition/Sentences	Explanation/Conventions	Poem/Organization	Description/Voice	Expository Paragraph/Focus/Ideas

Electronic Pen Pals/Letter

Table 3 (Weeks 3–6)

Week 3	Week 4	Week 5	Week 6
Present a Poem	Purposes of Media	Purposes of Media	Purposes of Media
Bar Graph	Glossary	Technology: Using E-mail	Alphabetical Order
Adjectives for Sizes	Adjectives for What Kind	Adjectives for How Many	Adjectives That Compare
Poem; Focus/Ideas	Poster, List; Support/Voice	Thank-You Note/Conventions	Directions/Organization

Story Starters/Realistic Story

UNIT 5

Week 1	Week 2	Week 3	Week 4	Week 5	Week 6
Techniques in Media	Share Information and Ideas	Share Information and Ideas	Respond to media	Techniques in Media	Listen for a Purpose
Reference Sources/Take Notes	Dictionary	Text Features	Picture Graph	Technology: Web Page	Encyclopedia
Imperative Sentences	Pronouns	Using *I* and *Me*	Pronouns	Adverbs	Prepositions and Prepositional Phrases
Animal Fantasy/Voice	Letter/Voice	Questions/Word Choice	Persuasive Ad/Focus/Ideas	Autobiography/Sentences	Poem/Conventions

E-Newsletter/Short Report

Teaching Record Chart

This chart shows the critical comprehension skills and strategies you need to cover. Check off each one as you provide instruction.

Reading/Comprehension	DATES OF INSTRUCTION		
Confirm predictions about what will happen next in text by "reading the part that tells."			
Ask relevant questions, seek clarification, and locate facts and details about stories and other texts.			
Establish purpose for reading selected texts and monitor comprehension, making corrections and adjustments when that understanding breaks down (e.g., identifying clues, using background knowledge, generating questions, re-reading a portion aloud).			
Connect the meaning of a well-known story or fable to personal experiences.			
Explain the function of recurring phrases (e.g., "Once upon a time" or "They lived happily ever after") in traditional folk and fairy tales.			
Respond to and use rhythm, rhyme, and alliteration in poetry.			
Describe the plot (problem and solution) and retell a story's beginning, middle, and end with attention to the sequence of events.			
Describe characters in a story and the reasons for their actions and feelings.			
Determine whether a story is true or a fantasy and explain why.			
Recognize sensory details in literary text.			

Tired of using slips of paper or stickies to make sure you teach everything you need to? Need an easier way to keep track of what you have taught, and what you still need to cover? **Customize Literacy** can help. "

Reading/Comprehension	DATES OF INSTRUCTION		
Read independently for a sustained period of time.			
Identify the topic and explain the author's purpose in writing about the text.			
Restate the main idea, heard or read.			
Identify important facts or details in text, heard or read.			
Identify the details or facts that support the main idea.			
Draw conclusions from the facts presented in text and support those assertions with textual evidence.			
Retell the order of events in a text by referring to the words and/or illustrations.			
Use text features (e.g., title, table of contents, illustrations) to locate specific information in text.			
Follow written multi-step directions with picture cues to assist with understanding.			
Explain the meaning of specific signs and symbols (e.g., map features).			
Establish purposes for reading selected texts based upon desired outcome to enhance comprehension.			
Ask literal questions of text.			
Monitor and adjust comprehension (e.g., using background knowledge, creating sensory images, re-reading a portion aloud).			
Make inferences about text using textual evidence to support understanding.			
Retell or act out important events in stories in logical order.			
Make connections to own experiences, to ideas in other texts, and to the larger community and discuss textual evidence.			

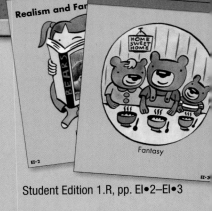

Student Edition 1.R, pp. EI•2–EI•3

Objectives:
- Children identify if a story could happen in real life or not.
- Children give evidence to support their conclusion.

Realism and Fantasy

What is it? Distinguishing realism and fantasy means to figure out whether a story could happen in real life. At Grade 1, children use clues about the characters, setting, and plot— along with their own experiences—to determine if a story is realistic or fantastic.

How Good Readers Use the Skill Identifying whether a story is realistic or fantastic requires readers to use critical thinking skills. Readers must take information from authors and illustrators and put it together with what he or she knows from personal experiences to draw conclusions about whether a story could or could not happen in real life. Understanding this difference helps readers predict story events, make inferences about story elements, and visualize the story as a whole.

Texts for Teaching

Student Edition
- *The Big Top,* 1.R, pages 96–105
- *The Farmers Market,* 1.R, pages 148–157

Leveled Readers
- See pages 24–29 for a list of Leveled Readers.

Mini-Lesson 1

Teach the Skill
Use the **Envision It!** lesson on 1.R, pages EI•2–EI•3 to visually review realism and fantasy.

Remind children that:
- **realistic stories** tell about something that could happen in real life.
- some stories tell about things that could not happen in real life. These are called **fantasies.**

Practice
Have children think about things that could happen in real life and things that could not. Ask children to answer the questions by telling whether something could really happen or could not really happen. Say:

Could a squirrel talk to you?
Could a girl score a soccer goal and win the game?
Could a boy go outside and ride a bike?
Could a monkey swing from tree to tree?
Could a kid ride a dinosaur?

Use other examples. Have volunteers ask their own questions about real and fantastic events. Have children say whether or not it could happen.

If... children have difficulty understanding the difference between realism and fantasy,
then... ask pointed questions, such as Do you know anyone who _____?

Apply
As children read, have them identify whether the story could happen or could not happen.

Writing
Children can write about something or someplace that is not real.

 **ini-Lesson 2**

Teach the Skill

Use the **Envision It!** lesson on 1.R, pages EI•2–EI•3 to visually review realism and fantasy.

Remind children that:

- **realistic stories** tell about something that could happen in real life.
- some stories tell about things that could not happen in real life. These are called **fantasies**.

Practice

Show children familiar books. Ask: Could this story happen in real life? How do you know? Create a two-column chart with the headings *Realistic Stories* and *Fantasies.* Talk about familiar stories and list them in the appropriate column. Post the list and add to it as children read more and more stories.

Realistic Stories	Fantasies
Cam Jansen	*The Three Little Pigs*

If... children have difficulty understanding the difference between realism and fantasy,
then... point to the pictures and have them talk about whether they see things that could happen or not.

Apply

As children read, have them identify whether the story could happen or could not happen.

Writing

Children can write about something or someplace that is real.

 **ini-Lesson 3**

Teach the Skill

Use the **Envision It!** lesson on 1.R, pages EI•2–EI•3 to visually review realism and fantasy.

Remind children that:

- **realistic stories** tell about something that could happen in real life.
- some stories tell about things that could not happen in real life. These are called **fantasies**.

Practice

Tell children they will write two stories. One story could happen in real life. One story could not happen in real life. Draw a story chart like the one that follows on the board for each story. List the characters, setting, and a few events for each story as suggested by children. Together write the two stories using the charts.

Who is in the story?
Where does this story happen?
What happens in this story?

If... children have difficulty understanding the difference between realism and fantasy,
then... ask pointed questions, such as Do you know anyone who _____?

Apply

As children read, have them identify whether the story could happen or could not happen.

Writing

Children can write their own stories. They can be realistic or fantastic.

Instruction

Plot

Student Edition 1.R, pp. EI•4–EI•5

Objectives:
- Children understand that a story is made up of events that happen in sequential order.
- Children identify a problem and a solution in a story.
- Children identify a story's beginning, middle, and end.
- Children can take plot events and put them in story order.

What is it? Plot refers to the events in a story. Plot, along with characters, setting, and theme, make up literary elements in stories. Identifying plot requires readers to recognize the important events in a story, which, in turn helps them understand how stories are organized. At Grade 1, children are identifying plot events and putting them in sequential order.

How Good Readers Use the Skill Understanding plot means readers have a sense of the important events in a story. This means they understand that in a story a character has a problem and the story unfolds as the character tries solve it. Good readers are alert to the relationship of characters to plot. They ask questions and make and confirm predictions as they read to understand how the story will play out.

Texts for Teaching

Student Edition
- *Tip and Tam,* 1.R, pages 70–79
- *School Day,* 1.R, pages 122–131
- *The Big Blue Ox,* 1.1, pages 74–83
- *Tippy-Toe Chick, Go!* 1.1, pages 74–83

Leveled Readers
- See pages 24–29 for a list of Leveled Readers.

Teach the Skill

Use the **Envision It!** lesson on 1.R, pages EI•4–EI•5 to visually review plot.

Remind children that:
- the **plot** is the pattern of important events in a story.
- every story has a beginning, middle, and end.

Practice
Model telling the plot of a familiar story.

The story of Peter Rabbit is all about a mischievous rabbit who sneaks into the farmer's garden to get some vegetables. Peter then gets trapped and must find a way to escape. He runs really fast when the farmer's back is turned and gets back home.

Talk with students about what parts of the story you included.
Ask: Did I tell everything that happens in the story? What parts did I leave out? Help children understand that you told only what happened in the beginning, the middle, and the end.
If... children have difficulty retelling,
then... show a story and talk only about the beginning, middle, and end.

Apply
As children read stories, have them retell what happens in the beginning, middle, and end.

Writing
Children can draw and label pictures to show beginning, middle, and end of a story.

Mini-Lesson 2

Teach the Skill

Use the **Envision It!** lesson on 1.R, pages EI•4–EI•5 to visually review plot.

Remind children that:

- the **plot** is the pattern of important events in a story.
- every story has a beginning, middle, and end.
- in a story, a character has a problem which he or she works to solve.

Practice

With children, retell a familiar story, such as "The Ugly Duckling." Then ask: What is the duckling's problem in the beginning? (Everybody laughs at him because he doesn't look like a duck.) How does the duckling solve this problem? (He goes away and grows up to become a beautiful swan.) Think aloud as you state the problem and solution. At the beginning the little duckling is sad because everyone thinks he is ugly. That's his problem. At the end he has turned into a beautiful swan and everyone admires him. Turning into a swan is the solution to the problem.

Practice stating the problem and solution of other familiar stories, such as "The Three Bears" and "The Three Little Pigs."

If… children have difficulty identifying problem,

then… ask: What does the character want? Does he or she get it?

Apply

As children read, have them think about the problem and ask: How does the character solve the problem?

Writing

Children can write sentences that tell what a character wants.

Mini-Lesson 3

Teach the Skill

Use the **Envision It!** lesson on 1.R, pages EI•4–EI•5 to visually review plot.

Remind children that:

- the **plot** is the pattern of important events in a story.
- every story has a beginning, middle, and end.
- in a story, a character has a problem which he or she works to solve.

Practice

Begin a discussion about favorite stories. Explain that children can keep track of events in a story using a story map. Model how to complete a story map. At first, just focus on what happens in the beginning, middle, and end. If children suggest lots of events for the beginning or middle, write them down and then circle the most important.

| Beginning   Character's Problem: |
| Middle |
| End   How the Problem Was Solved: |

If… children have difficulty identifying parts of the plot,

then… have children work with two events: beginning and end.

Apply

As children read, have them think about the order of events. Can they tell what happens at the beginning, the middle, and the end?

Writing

Children can draw pictures that show what happens in a story and label them *beginning*, *middle*, and *end*.

Instruction

Monitor and Clarify

Mini-Lesson

Student Edition 1.R, p. EI•11

Texts for Teaching

Student Edition
- *Sam, Come Back!* 1.1, pages 20–29
- *The Farmer in the Hat,* 1.2, pages 52–64
- *The Class Pet,* 1.3, pages 92–105
- *Mama's Birthday Present,* 1.4, pages 20–43
- *Tippy-Toe Chick, Go!* 1.5, pages 20–39
- *Dot and Jabber and the Great Acorn Mystery,* 1.5, pages 98–119

Leveled Readers
- See pages 24–29 for a list of Leveled Readers.

Understand the Strategy

Monitor and clarify means being engaged with text. A good reader knows that reading has to make sense and is aware that the text is making sense or has ceased to make sense. When understanding breaks down, good readers have strategies to use to fix the problems he or she is having with comprehension. These strategies include using background knowledge, adjusting reading rate, reading on, rereading, taking notes, and seeking help.

Teach

Use the **Envision It!** lesson on 1.R, page EI•11 to visually introduce monitor and clarify with children.

Remind children that every reader has trouble understanding what he or she is reading at times. When this happens, readers need to stop and think how to correct the situation.

Practice

Using an unfamiliar text, model some strategies children can use when comprehension breaks down. Here are some sample think-alouds.

Read On: This doesn't make sense. I thought Ruby was at the store with Max to buy *him* clothes. Why is she trying on dresses? I'm confused. I will read on to see what happens.

Reread: I read this book about weather, but I can't remember what causes clouds. I can reread to make sure I understand.

Use Text Features: I didn't know what the word *joey* meant, but the pictures helped. Here is a joey—it's a baby kangaroo.

Ask for Help: I didn't know where Little Rock was, so I went to the library and checked an atlas.

Have pairs of children read an unfamiliar text together and use some of the strategies if their comprehension breaks down. Have pairs talk about how they figured out what to do.

If... children have difficulty monitoring their own comprehension,

then... model one strategy at a time for them and have them try it out.

Apply

Ask children to think carefully as they read. Are they getting it? Do they need to stop and apply a strategy to help them understand what they are reading?

Anchor Chart

Anchor charts help children make their thinking visible. Here is a sample chart for monitor and clarify.

Monitor and Clarify

1. Look over the story before you read. Try to figure out what it might be about.

2. Read a little bit to see if it will be easy or hard to read.

3. Start reading. Ask yourself:
Does this make sense?
Do I know who the characters are?
Do I know what is happening?
Do I know what this is all about?

4. Sometimes you will be reading and you get confused. That's OK. Here are some things to try.
Make sure you know what all the words mean.
Read on to see if you can figure things out.
Reread to see if you skipped something important.
Look at the pictures. Sometimes they show you what the text says.
Ask for help!

Anchor Chart

5. Retell what you have read. Tell others what you did or did not like about what you read.

Student Edition 1.R, p. EI•8

Background Knowledge

Objectives:
- Children make connections between their own experiences, the world, and other selections they have read.
- Children use background knowledge to make predictions and draw conclusions about what they read.

Texts for Teaching

Student Edition

- *Farmers Market,* 1.R, pages 148–157
- *Life in the Forest,* 1.2, pages 146–159
- *Where Are My Animal Friends?* 1.3, pages 190–207
- *Mole and the Baby Bird,* 1.5 pages 60–77

Leveled Readers

- See pages 24–29 for a list of Leveled Readers.

Understand the Strategy

Background knowledge is what a reader knows about a given topic, gathered from reading and from personal experiences. Active readers connect what they know to text to help them comprehend it. Children who can activate their prior knowledge approach reading confidently. They engage before they begin reading because they are already thinking about what they know about the topic.

Teach

Use the **Envision It!** lesson on 1.R, page EI•8 to visually introduce background knowledge.

Remind children that thinking about what they already know about a topic before they read will help them better understand what they read. Model using a K-W-L chart that children can use to preview text, set purposes for reading, and review what they learn as they read.

KWL		
What I **K**now	What I **W**ant to Know	What I **L**earned

After children read, help them make connections by asking questions.

Text-to-Self: Does this selection remind you of something in your own life?

Text-to-World: Can you connect this selection to something you know about other people, places, or events?

Text-to-Text: What other reading—stories or articles—does this remind you of?

Practice

Provide a selection for children to read and practice the strategy with. Begin a KWL chart to preview and set purposes for reading. After children finish, record their ideas under the *What I Learned* column. Ask questions to help them make connections to the reading. Remind children that everyone's background is different and so they will bring different ideas and experiences to a reading.

If... children have difficulty activating their background knowledge,

then... provide text that has familiar information so children will build confidence and be able to make connections.

Apply

Make sure children preview text prior to reading to see what they already know about the reading. Tell them to say one thing they would like to find out as they read.

Anchor Chart

Anchor charts help children make their thinking visible. With an anchor chart, the group can clarify their thinking about how to use a strategy. Display anchor charts so readers can use refer to them as they read. Here is a sample chart for background knowledge.

Background Knowledge

1. Look over the story before you read. Ask yourself:
What do I already know about this topic?
Does this book look familiar?
Does the book seem funny? serious? hard to read?

2. Set a purpose for reading. Here are some purposes:
Read to find out what happens.
Read to learn more about something.
Read to have a good time.

3. Make a KWL chart.

4. Make connections to what you read. Ask yourself:
What does this remind me of?
What did I learn?
What else do I want to know?

5. Talk about the story with your group.
You will learn what others know!

6. Respect other people's ideas.

Anchor Chart

Instruction

Using Multiple Strategies

Good readers use multiple strategies as they read. You can encourage students to read strategically through good classroom questioning. Use questions such as these to help students apply strategies during reading.

Answer Questions

- Who or what is this question about?
- Where can you look to find the answer to this question?

Ask Questions

- What do you want to know about _____?
- What questions to do you have about the _____ in this selection? Use the words *who, what, when, where,* and *how* to ask your questions.
- Do you have any questions after reading?

Graphic Organizers

- What kind of graphic organizer could you use to help you keep track of the information in this selection?

Monitor and Fix Up

- Does the story or article make sense?
- What don't you understand about what you read?
- Do you need to reread, review, read on, or check a reference source?
- Do you need to read more slowly or more quickly?
- What is a _____? Where could you look to find out?

Predict/Confirm Predictions

- What do you think this story or article will be about? Why do you think as you do?
- What do you think you will learn from this selection?
- Do the text features help you predict what will happen?
- Based on what has happened so far, what do you think will happen next?
- Is this what you thought would happen?
- How does _____ change what you thought would happen?

Preview

- What do the photographs, illustrations, or graphic sources tell about the selection?
- What do you want to find out? What do you want to learn?

Prior Knowledge

- What do you already know about _____?

- Have you read stories or articles by this author before?

- How is this selection like others that you have read?

- What does this remind you of?

- How does your prior knowledge help you understand _____?

- Did the text match what you already knew? What new information did you learn?

Story Structure

- Who are the characters in this story? the setting?

- What is the problem in this story? How does the problem get solved?

- What is the point of this story?

Summarize

- What two or three important ideas have you read so far?

- How do the text features relate to the important ideas?

- Is there a graphic organizer that can help you organize the information before you summarize?

Text Structure

- How has the author organized the writing?

- What clues tell you that the text is structured _____?

Visualize

- When you read this, what do you picture in your mind?

- What do you hear, see, or smell?

- What do you think _____ looks like? Why do you think as you do?

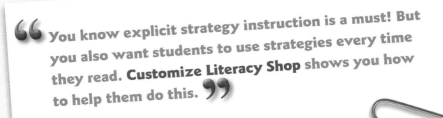

❝ You know explicit strategy instruction is a must! But you also want students to use strategies every time they read. Customize Literacy Shop shows you how to help them do this. ❞

Glossary of Literacy Terms

This glossary lists academic language terms that are related to literacy.
They are provided for your information and professional use.

A

alliteration	the repetition of a consonant sound in a group of words, especially in poetry
allusion	a word or phrase that refers to something else the reader already knows from history, experience, or reading
animal fantasy	a story about animals that talk and act like people
answer questions	a reading strategy in which readers use the text and prior knowledge to answer questions about what they are reading
antonym	a word that means the opposite of another word
ask questions	a reading strategy in which readers ask themselves questions about the text to help make sense of what they read
author's point of view	the author's opinion on the subject he or she is writing about
author's purpose	the reason the author wrote the text
autobiography	the story of a real person's life written by that person

B

background knowledge	the information and experience that a reader brings to a text
biography	the story of a real person's life written by another person

C

cause	why something happens
character	a person, animal, or personalized object in a story
chronological order	events in a selection, presented in the order in which they occurred
classify and categorize	put things, such as pictures or words, into groups
climax	the point in a story at which conflict is confronted
compare	tell how things are the same
comprehension	understanding of text being read—the ultimate goal of reading
comprehension strategy	a conscious plan used by a reader to gain understanding of text. Comprehension strategies may be used before, during, or after reading.
conclusion	a decision or opinion arrived at after thinking about facts and details and using prior knowledge
conflict	the problem or struggle in a story
context clue	the words, phrases, or sentences near an unknown word that give the reader clues to the word's meaning
contrast	tell how things are different

details small pieces of information

dialect form of a language spoken in a certain region or by a certain group of people that differs from the standard form of that language

dialogue written conversation

diary a day-to-day record of one's activities and thoughts

draw conclusions arrive at decisions or opinions after thinking about facts and details and using prior knowledge

D

effect what happens as the result of a cause

etymology an explanation of the origin and history of a word and its meaning

exaggeration a statement that makes something seem larger or greater than it actually is

expository text text that contains facts and information. Also called *informational text.*

E

fable a story, usually with animal characters, that is written to teach a moral, or lesson

fact piece of information that can be proved to be true

fairy tale a folk story with magical characters and events

fantasy a story that could not really happen

fiction writing that tells about imaginary people, things, and events

figurative language the use of language that gives words a meaning beyond their usual definitions in order to add beauty or force

flashback an interruption in the sequence of events of a narrative to include an event that happened earlier

folk tale a story that has been passed down by word of mouth

foreshadowing the use of hints or clues about what will happen later in a story

F

generalize make a broad statement or rule after examining particular facts

graphic organizer a drawing, chart, or web that illustrates concepts or shows how ideas relate to each other. Readers use graphic organizers to help them keep track of and understand important information and ideas as they read. Story maps, word webs, Venn diagrams, and KWL charts are graphic organizers.

graphic source a chart, diagram, or map within a text that adds to readers' understanding of the text

G

Instruction

H

historical fiction	realistic fiction that takes place in the past. It is an imaginary story based on historical events and characters.
humor	writing or speech that has a funny or amusing quality
hyperbole	an exaggerated statement not meant to be taken literally, such as *I'm so hungry I could eat a horse.*

I

idiom	a phrase whose meaning differs from the ordinary meaning of the words. *A stone's throw* is an idiom meaning "a short distance."
imagery	the use of language to create beautiful or forceful pictures in the reader's mind
inference	conclusion reached on the basis of evidence and reasoning
inform	give knowledge, facts, or news to someone
informational text	writing that contains facts and information. Also called *expository text.*
interview	a face-to-face conversation in which someone responds to questions
irony	a way of speaking or writing in which the ordinary meaning of the words is the opposite of what the speaker or writer is thinking; a contrast between what is expected and what actually happens

J

jargon	the language of a special group or profession

L

legend	a story coming down from the past about the great deeds of a hero. Although a legend may be based on historical people and events, it is not regarded as historically true.
literary elements	the characters, setting, plot, and theme of a narrative text

M

main idea	the big idea that tells what a paragraph or a selection is mainly about; the most important idea of a text
metacognition	an awareness of one's own thinking processes and the ability to monitor and direct them to a desired goal. Good readers use metacognition to monitor their reading and adjust their reading strategies.
metaphor	a comparison that does not use *like* or *as,* such as *a heart of stone*
meter	the pattern of beats or accents in poetry

Instruction

M

monitor and clarify	a comprehension strategy by which readers actively think about understanding their reading and know when they understand and when they do not. Readers use appropriate strategies to make sense of difficult words, ideas, or passages.
mood	the atmosphere or feeling of a written work
moral	the lesson or teaching of a fable or story
motive	the reason a character in a narrative does or says something
mystery	a story about mysterious events that are not explained until the end, so as to keep the reader in suspense
myth	a story that attempts to explain something in nature

N

narrative	a story, made up or true, that someone tells or narrates
narrator	the character in a selection who tells the story
nonfiction	writing that tells about real things, real people, and real events

O

onomatopoeia	the use of words that sound like their meanings, such as *buzz* and *hum*
opinion	someone's judgment, belief, or way of thinking
oral vocabulary	the words needed for speaking and listening
outcome	the resolution of the conflict in a story

P

paraphrase	retell the meaning of a passage in one's own words
personification	a figure of speech in which human traits are given to animals or inanimate objects, as in *The sunbeam danced on the waves.*
persuade	convince someone to do or to believe something
photo essay	a collection of photographs on one theme, accompanied by text
play	a story that is written to be acted out for an audience
plot	a series of related events at the beginning, middle, and end of a story; the action of a story
poem	an expressive, imaginative pieces of writing often arranged in lines having rhythm and rhyme. In a poem, the patterns made by the sounds of the words have special importance.
pourquoi tale	a type of folk story that explains why things in nature came to be. *Pourquoi* is a French word meaning "why."

P

predict	tell what a selection might be about or what might happen in a text. Readers use text features and information to predict. They confirm or revise their predictions as they read.
preview	look over a text before reading it
prior knowledge	the information and experience that a reader brings to a text. Readers use prior knowledge to help them understand what they read.
prop	an item, such as an object, picture, or chart, used in a performance or presentation

R

reading vocabulary	the words we recognize or use in print
realistic fiction	a story of imaginary people and events that could happen in real life
repetition	the repeated use of some aspect of language
resolution	the point in a story where the conflict is resolved
rhyme	to end in the same sound(s)
rhythm	a pattern of strong beats in speech or writing, especially poetry
rising action	the buildup of conflicts and complications in a story

S

science fiction	a story based on science that tells what life in the future might be like
semantic map	a graphic organizer, often a web, used to display words or concepts that are meaningfully related
sensory language	the use of words that help the reader understand how things look, sound, smell, taste, or feel
sequence	the order of events in a selection or the order of the steps in which something is completed
sequence words	clue words such as *first, next, then,* and *finally* that signal the order of events in a selection
setting	where and when a story takes place
simile	a comparison that uses *like* or *as,* as in *as busy as a bee*
speech	a public talk to a group of people made for a specific purpose
stanza	a group of lines in a poem
steps in a process	the order of the steps in which something is completed

S

story map	a graphic organizer used to record the literary elements and the sequence of events in a narrative text
story structure	how the characters, setting, and events of a story are organized into a plot
summarize	give the most important ideas of what was read. Readers summarize important information in the selection to keep track of what they are reading.
supporting detail	piece of information that tells about the main idea
symbolism	the use of one thing to suggest something else; often the use of something concrete to stand for an abstract idea

T

tall tale	a humorous story that uses exaggeration to describe impossible happenings
text structure	the organization of a piece of writing. Text structures of informational text include cause/effect, chronological, compare/contrast, description, problem/solution, proposition/support, and ask/answer questions.
theme	the big idea or author's message in a story
think aloud	an instructional strategy in which a teacher verbalizes his or her thinking to model the process of comprehension or the application of a skill
tone	author's attitude toward the subject or toward the reader
topic	the subject of a discussion, conversation, or piece of text

V

visualize	picture in one's mind what is happening in the text. Visualizing helps readers imagine the things they read about.

Section 3 Matching Books and Readers

Leveled Readers Skills Chart

Scott Foresman Reading Street provides more than six hundred leveled readers.
Each one is designed to:

- Practice critical skills and strategies
- Build fluency
- Build vocabulary and concepts
- Develop a lifelong love of reading

Grade 1

Title	Level*	DRA Level	Genre	Comprehension Strategy
Bix the Dog	A	1	Realistic Fiction	Summarize
Time for Dinner	A	1	Realistic Fiction	Important Ideas
Sam	B	2	Realistic Fiction	Monitor and Clarify
Mack and Zack	B	2	Realistic Fiction	Monitor and Clarify
The Sick Pets	B	2	Realistic Fiction	Summarize
On the Farm	B	2	Realistic Fiction	Visualize
At Your Vet	B	2	Realistic Fiction	Story Structure
Fun in the Sun	B	2	Expository Nonfiction	Text Structure
We Are a Family	B	2	Nonfiction	Predict and Set Purpose
Where They Live	C	3	Realistic Fiction	Visualize
Which Fox?	C	3	Realistic Fiction	Important Ideas
Which Animals Will We See?	C	3	Realistic Fiction	Text Structure
Let's Go to the Zoo	C	3	Nonfiction	Predict and Set Purpose
A Play	C	3	Realistic Fiction	Monitor and Clarify
A Class	C	3	Nonfiction	Monitor and Clarify
Here in My Neighborhood	C	3	Nonfiction	Important Ideas
Look at My Neighborhood	C	3	Realistic Fiction	Important Ideas
Look at Dinosaurs	C	3	Expository Nonfiction	Inferring
Around the Forest	C	3	Nonfiction	Background Knowledge
Learn About Worker Bees	C	3	Expository Nonfiction	Questioning
In My Room	C	3	Nonfiction	Summarize
Hank's Song	C	3	Fantasy	Inferring
Gus the Pup	C	3	Realistic Fiction	Monitor and Clarify
What Animals Can You See?	D	4	Expository Nonfiction	Text Structure
The Dinosaur Herds	D	4	Expository Nonfiction	Inferring
People Help the Forest	D	4	Expository Nonfiction	Background Knowledge
Honey	D	4	Nonfiction	Questioning
Let's Build a Park!	D	4	Fiction	Summarize
Mac Can Do It!	D	4	Fantasy	Inferring
The Seasons Change	D	4	Nonfiction	Visualize

* Suggested Guided Reading Level. Use your knowledge of students' abilities to adjust levels as needed.

The chart here and on the next few pages lists titles of Leveled Readers appropriate for students in Grade 1. Use the chart to find titles that meet your students' interest and instructional needs. The books in this list were leveled using the criteria suggested in *Matching Books to Readers: Using Leveled Books in Guided Reading, Grades K–3* by Irene C. Fountas and Gay Su Pinnell. For more on leveling, see the *Reading Street Leveled Readers Leveling Guide.*

Target Comprehension Skill	Additional Comprehension Instruction	Vocabulary
Plot	Sequence	High-Frequency Words
Main Idea and Details	Compare and Contrast	High-Frequency Words
Character and Setting	Draw Conclusions	High-Frequency Words
Character and Setting	Main Idea and Details	High-Frequency Words
Plot	Draw Conclusions	High-Frequency Words
Character and Setting	Plot	High-Frequency Words
Main Idea and Details	Theme	High-Frequency Words
Cause and Effect	Author's Purpose	High-Frequency Words
Sequence	Draw Conclusions	High-Frequency Words
Character and Setting	Theme and Plot	High-Frequency Words
Main Idea and Details	Compare and Contrast	High-Frequency Words
Cause and Effect	Setting and Plot	High-Frequency Words
Sequence	Compare and Contrast	High-Frequency Words
Cause and Effect	Main Idea and Details	High-Frequency Words
Cause and Effect	Author's Purpose	High-Frequency Words
Author's Purpose	Draw Conclusions	High-Frequency Words
Author's Purpose	Compare and Contrast	High-Frequency Words
Sequence	Cause and Effect	High-Frequency Words
Author's Purpose	Cause and Effect	High-Frequency Words
Compare and Contrast	Sequence	High-Frequency Words
Sequence	Author's Purpose	High-Frequency Words
Compare and Contrast	Realism and Fantasy	High-Frequency Words
Fact and Opinion	Cause and Effect	High-Frequency Words
Main Idea and Details	Compare and Contrast	High-Frequency Words
Sequence	Draw Conclusions	High-Frequency Words
Author's Purpose	Cause and Effect	High-Frequency Words
Compare and Contrast	Draw Conclusions	High-Frequency Words
Sequence	Author's Purpose	High-Frequency Words
Compare and Contrast	Realism and Fantasy	High-Frequency Words
Author's Purpose	Draw Conclusions	High-Frequency Words

Matching Books & Readers

Leveled Readers Skills Chart *Continued*

Grade 1

Title	Level*	DRA Level	Genre	Comprehension Strategy
Animals Change and Grow	D	4	Nonfiction	Text Structure
Ready for Winter?	D	4	Expository Nonfiction	Background Knowledge
A Party for Pedro	D	4	Realistic Fiction	Monitor and Clarify
Space Star	D	4	Realistic Fiction	Visualize
Our Leaders	D	4	Nonfiction	Important Ideas
Grandma's Farm	D	4	Realistic Fiction	Questioning
A New Baby Brother	D	4	Realistic Fiction	Story Structure
My Babysitter	D	4	Narrative Nonfiction	Predict and Set Purpose
What Brown Saw	D	4	Animal Fantasy	Monitor and Clarify
Fly Away Owl!	D	4	Realistic Fiction	Background Knowledge
What A Detective Does	D	4	Realistic Fiction	Monitor and Clarify
The Inclined Plane	D	4	Expository Nonfiction	Summarize
Using the Telephone	D	4	Expository Nonfiction	Text Structure
A Garden for All	D	4	Nonfiction	Inferring
Big Wishes and Her Baby	E	7	Realistic Fiction	Monitor and Clarify
Plans Change	E	7	Realistic Fiction	Visualize
Let's Visit a Butterfly Greenhouse	E	7	Nonfiction	Text Structure
Seasons Come and Go	E	7	Expository Nonfiction	Background Knowledge
Special Days, Special Food	E	7	Expository Nonfiction	Monitor and Clarify
The Art Show	F	10	Realistic Fiction	Visualize
Treasures of Our Country	F	10	Nonfiction	Important Ideas
A Visit to the Ranch	F	10	Realistic Fiction	Questioning
My Little Brother Drew	F	10	Realistic Fiction	Story Structure
The Story of the Kids Care Club	F	10	Expository Nonfiction	Predict and Set Purpose
Squirrel and Bear	G	12	Animal Fantasy	Monitor and Clarify
Puppy Raiser	G	12	Expository Nonfiction	Background Knowledge
A Mighty Oak Tree	G	12	Expository Nonfiction	Monitor and Clarify
Simple Machines at Work	G	12	Expository Nonfiction	Summarize
Carlos Picks a Pet	H	14	Realistic Fiction	Monitor and Clarify
That Cat Needs Help!	H	14	Realistic Fiction	Summarize

* Suggested Guided Reading Level. Use your knowledge of students' abilities to adjust levels as needed.

You know the theory behind leveled books: they let you match books with the interest and instructional levels of your students. You can find the right reader for every student with this chart.

Target Comprehension Skill	Additional Comprehension Instruction	Vocabulary
Fact and Opinion	Sequence	High-Frequency Words
Draw Conclusions	Sequence	High-Frequency Words
Draw Conclusions	Author's Purpose	High-Frequency Words
Theme	Realism and Fantasy	High-Frequency Words
Facts and Details	Cause and Effect	High-Frequency Words
Facts and Details	Plot	High-Frequency Words
Theme	Realism and Fantasy	High-Frequency Words
Cause and Effect	Main Idea	High-Frequency Words
Character, Setting, and Plot	Realism and Fantasy	High-Frequency Words
Draw Conclusions	Cause and Effect	High-Frequency Words
Compare and Contrast	Cause and Effect	High-Frequency Words
Main Idea and Details	Cause and Effect	High-Frequency Words
Sequence	Author's Purpose	High-Frequency Words
Theme	Sequence	High-Frequency Words
Fact and Opinion	Setting	High-Frequency Words
Author's Purpose	Setting	High-Frequency Words
Fact and Opinion	Author's Purpose	High-Frequency Words
Draw Conclusions	Compare and Contrast	High-Frequency Words
Draw Conclusions	Author's Purpose	High-Frequency Words
Theme	Plot	High-Frequency Words
Facts and Details	Cause and Effect	High-Frequency Words
Facts and Details	Compare and Contrast	High-Frequency Words
Theme	Realism and Fantasy	High-Frequency Words
Cause and Effect	Author's Purpose	High-Frequency Words
Character, Setting and Plot	Realism and Fantasy	High-Frequency Words
Draw Conclusions	Main Idea	High-Frequency Words
Compare and Contrast	Draw Conclusions	High-Frequency Words
Main Idea and Details	Compare and Contrast	High-Frequency Words
Character and Setting	Compare and Contrast	Amazing Words
Plot	Sequence	Amazing Words

Leveled Readers Skills Chart *Continued*

Grade 1

Title	Level*	DRA Level	Genre	Comprehension Strategy
Loni's Town	H	14	Realistic Fiction	Visualize
Baby Animals in the Rain Forest	H	14	Expository Nonfiction	Important Ideas
Cary and the The Wildlife Shelter	H	14	Realistic Fiction	Story Structure
Around the World	H	14	Narrative Nonfiction	Text Structure
The Communication Story	H	14	Expository Nonfiction	Text Structure
Marla's Good Idea	H	14	Realistic Fiction	Inferring
Rules at School	I	16	Animal Fantasy	Predict and Set Purpose
School: Then and Now	I	16	Expository Nonfiction	Monitor and Clarify
Mom the Mayor	I	16	Realistic Fiction	Important Ideas
The Dinosaur Detectives	I	16	Expository Nonfiction	Inferring
All About Food Chains	I	16	Expository Nonfiction	Background Knowledge
Bees and Beekeepers	I	16	Expository Nonfiction	Questioning
A New Library	I	16	Narrative Nonfiction	Summarize
Paul's Bed	J	18	Traditional Tales	Inferring
Britton Finds a Kitten	J	18	Realistic Fiction	Monitor and Clarify
All About the Weather	J	18	Expository Nonfiction	Visualize
Learn About Butterflies	J	18	Expository Nonfiction	Text Structure
Monarchs Migrate South	J	18	Narrative Nonfiction	Background Knowledge
Cascarones Are for Fun	J	18	Expository Nonfiction	Monitor and Clarify
Jamie's Jumble of Junk	J	18	Realistic Fiction	Visualize
America's Home	K	20	Nonfiction	Important Ideas
Go West!	K	20	Legend	Questioning
Double Trouble Twins	K	20	Realistic Fiction	Story Structure
What Makes Buildings Special?	K	20	Expository Nonfiction	Predict and Set Purpose
Grasshopper and Ant	K	20	Fable	Monitor and Clarify
Ways to be a Good Citizen	K	20	Expository Nonfiction	Background Knowledge
Great Scientists: Detectives at Work	L	24	Expository Nonfiction	Monitor and Clarify
Simple Machines in Compound Machines	L	24	Nonfiction	Summarize
Over the Years	L	24	Expository Nonfiction	Text Structure
Cody's Adventure	L	24	Realistic Fiction	Inferring

* Suggested Guided Reading Level. Use your knowledge of students' abilities to adjust levels as needed.

" You know the theory behind leveled books: they let you match books with the interest and instructional levels of your students. You can find the right reader for every student with this chart. "

Target Comprehension Skill	Additional Comprehension Instruction	Vocabulary
Character and Setting	Theme	Amazing Words
Main Idea and Details	Author's Purpose	Amazing Words
Main Idea and Details	Sequence	Amazing Words
Cause and Effect	Main Idea	Amazing Words
Sequence	Compare and Contrast	High-Frequency Words
Theme	Sequence	High-Frequency Words
Sequence	Character	Amazing Words
Cause and Effect	Draw Conclusions	Amazing Words
Author's Purpose	Cause and Effect	Amazing Words
Sequence	Draw Conclusions	Amazing Words
Author's Purpose	Cause and Effect	Amazing Words
Compare and Contrast	Main Idea	Amazing Words
Sequence	Author's Purpose	Amazing Words
Compare and Contrast	Character	Amazing Words
Fact and Opinion	Setting	Amazing Words
Author's Purpose	Plot	Amazing Words
Fact and Opinion	Cause and Effect	Amazing Words
Draw Conclusions	Author's Purpose	Amazing Words
Draw Conclusions	Sequence	Amazing Words
Theme	Character, Setting, Plot	Amazing Words
Facts and Details	Cause and Effect	Amazing Words
Facts and Details	Theme	Amazing Words
Theme	Realism and Fantasy	Amazing Words
Cause and Effect	Draw Conclusions	Amazing Words
Character, Setting and Plot	Cause and Effect	Amazing Words
Draw Conclusions	Compare and Contrast	Amazing Words
Compare and Contrast	Compare and Contrast	Amazing Words
Main Idea and Details	Cause and Effect	Amazing Words
Sequence	Draw Conclusions	Amazing Words
Theme	Sequence	Amazing Words

Matching Books & Readers

What Good Readers Do

You can use the characteristics and behaviors of good readers to help all your students read better. But what are these characteristics and behaviors? And how can you use them to foster good reading behaviors for all your students? Here are some helpful tips.

Good Readers enjoy reading! They have favorite books, authors, and genres. Good readers often have a preference about where and when they read. They talk about books and recommend their favorites.

Develop this behavior by giving students opportunities to respond in different ways to what they read. Get them talking about what they read, and why they like or dislike it.

This behavior is important because book sharing alerts you to students who are somewhat passive about reading or have limited literacy experiences. Book sharing also helps you when you select books for the class.

Good Readers read independently for longer periods of time.

Develop this behavior by taking note of the level of support students need during guided reading. Use this information to gauge independent reading time accordingly.

This behavior is important because students become better readers when they spend time reading many texts at their independent level.

Good Readers select books they can read.

Develop this behavior by providing a range of three or four texts appropriate for the student and then letting the student choose.

This behavior is important because students gain control over reading when they can choose from books they can read. This helps them become more independent in the classroom.

Good Readers use text features to help them preview and set purposes.

Develop this behavior by having students use the title and illustrations in fiction texts or the title, contents, headings, and other graphic features in nonfiction texts to make predictions about what they will be reading.

This behavior is important because previewing actually makes reading easier! Looking at features and sampling the text enables readers to predict and set expectations for reading.

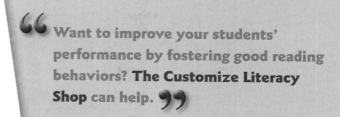

" Want to improve your students' performance by fostering good reading behaviors? **The Customize Literacy Shop** can help. "

Good Readers predict and ask questions before and while they read.

Develop this behavior by asking questions. After reading a passage, ask students what they think will happen next in a fiction text. Have them ask a question they think will be answered in a nonfiction text and read on to see if it is.

This behavior is important because when students predict and ask questions as they read, they are engaged. They have a purpose for reading and a basis for monitoring their comprehension.

Good Readers read aloud at an appropriate reading rate with a high percent of accuracy.

Develop this behavior by timing students' oral reading to calculate their reading rates. You can also record students' miscues to determine a percent of accuracy. This will help identify problems.

This behavior is important because when students read fluently texts that are "just right," they find reading more enjoyable. A fluent reader is able to focus more on constructing meaning and is more likely to develop a positive attitude toward reading.

Matching Books & Readers

Good Readers read meaningful phrases aloud with appropriate expression.

Develop this behavior by giving students lots of opportunities to read orally. As they read, note students' phrasing, intonation, and attention to punctuation and give help as needed.

This behavior is important because reading fluently in longer, meaningful phrases supports comprehension and ease in reading longer, more complex texts.

CH-
QU-
ST-

Good Readers use effective strategies and sources of information to figure out unknown words.

Develop this behavior by teaching specific strategies for figuring out unknown words, such as sounding out clusters of letters, using context, reading on, and using references.

This behavior is important because when readers have a variety of strategies to use, they are more able to decode and self-correct quickly. Readers who do these things view themselves as good readers.

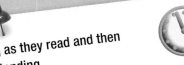

Good Readers construct meaning as they read and then share or demonstrate their understanding.

Develop this behavior by having students retell what they read or write a summary of what they read in their own words.

This behavior is important because the ability to retell or write a summary is essential for success in reading. It shows how well a student has constructed meaning.

Good Readers locate and use what is explicitly stated in a text.

Develop this behavior by asking questions that require students to go back into the text to find explicitly stated information.

This behavior is important because the ability to recall, locate, and use specific information stated in a text enables readers to respond to literal questions, as well as support opinions and justify their responses.

Good Readers make connections.

Develop this behavior by asking questions to help students make connections: *What does this remind you of? Have you ever read or experienced anything like this?*

This behavior is important because making connections helps readers understand and appreciate a text. Making connections to self, the world, and other texts supports high-level thinking.

Good Readers interpret what they read by making inferences.

Develop this behavior by asking questions to help students tell or write about what they think was implied in the text: *Why do you think that happened? What helped you come to that conclusion?*

This behavior is important because the ability to go beyond the literal meaning of a text enables readers to gain a deeper understanding. When students make inferences, they use background knowledge, their personal knowledge, and the text to grasp the meaning of what is implied by the author.

Good Readers determine importance and evaluate what they read.

Develop this behavior by always having students identify what they think is the most important message, event, or information in a text.

This behavior is important because readers must be able to sort out important from interesting information. The ability to establish and/or use criteria and providing support when making judgments is an important critical thinking skill.

Good Readers support their responses using information from a text and/or their own background knowledge.

Develop this behavior by always asking students to give the reason(s) they identified an event, message, or ideas as most important.

This behavior is important because the ability to justify one's response is important for all learners. It enables others to know the basis for a decision and provides an opening for further discussion.

CH-
QU-
ST-

Matching Books & Readers

Conversation Starters

Asking Good Questions When students read interesting and thought-provoking books, they want to share! You can encourage students to think critically about what they read. Use questions such as the following to assess comprehension as well as evoke good class/group discussions.

Author's Purpose

- Why did the author write this piece?

- How does figuring out the author's purpose help you decide how to read the text?

Cause and Effect

- Why did these events happen? How might they have been different if the causes had been different?

- Are there several causes that result in a single effect?

- Is there a single cause that has several effects?

Compare and Contrast

- What clues words show the author is comparing and/or contrasting in this article?

- How are the fictional characters and events in this story like and/or different from real people and events you know of?

Draw Conclusions

- Based on what you have read, seen, or experienced, what can you conclude about this event in the selection?

- This story seems to be a fantasy. Why might you conclude this?

- What words help you draw conclusions about the relationship between the characters?

Fact and Opinion

- What clue word or words signal that this is a statement of opinion?

- This seems to be a statement of opinion. Why is it really a statement of fact? (Alternately: This seems to be a statement of fact. Why is it really a statement of opinion?)

- Could this be a faulty opinion? How could you find out?

Generalize

- What generalization can you make about the story or the characters in it? What examples lead to that generalization?

- What details, facts, and logic does the author use to support this generalization?

- Is this a valid or a faulty generalization? Explain your ideas.

Graphic Sources

- How does the author use graphic sources (chart, maps, illustrations, time lines, and so on) to support ideas and opinions?

- This selection has many graphic sources. Which one or ones best help you understand the events or ideas in the selection? Why?

Literary Elements: Character, Setting, Plot, Theme

- Describe the main character at the beginning of the story and at the end of the story. How and why does this change take place?

- How is the setting important to the story? How might the story be different if its time or its place were different?

- What does the main character want at the beginning of the story? How does the main character go about trying to achieve this?

- A plot has a conflict, but the conflict isn't always between two characters. What is the conflict in this story? How is it resolved?

- In a few sentences, what is the plot of the story?

- What is the theme of the story? Use details from the story to support your statement.

Main Idea and Supporting Details

- What is the main idea of this paragraph or article? What are some supporting details?

- The author makes this particular statement in the article. What details does the author provide to support that statement?

Sequence

- How is the sequence of events important in the text?

- Is the order of events important in this story? Why or why not?

- Based on what has already happened, what will most likely happen next?

Connecting Science and Social Studies

Scott Foresman Reading Street Leveled Readers are perfect for covering, supporting, or enriching science and social studies content. Using these books ensures that all students can access important concepts.

Grade 1 Leveled Readers

Science

Earth and Space Science

Nonfiction Books
- *All About the Weather*
- *The Communication Story*
- *Over the Years*
- *Ready for Winter*
- *Using the Telephone*

Fiction Books
- *Cody's Adventure*
- *Marla's Good Idea*
- *What A Detective Does*

Life Science

Nonfiction Books
- *All About Food Chains*
- *Animals Change and Grow*
- *Around the Forest*
- *Around the World*
- *Baby Animals in the Rain Forest*
- *Bees and Beekeepers*
- *The Dinosaur Detectives*
- *The Dinosaur Herds*
- *Fun in the Sun*
- *Honey*
- *In My Room*
- *Learn About Butterflies*
- *Learn About Worker Bees*
- *Let's Go to the Zoo*
- *Let's Visit a Butterfly Greenhouse*
- *Look at Dinosaurs*
- *A Mighty Oak Tree*
- *Monarchs Migrate South*
- *People Help the Forest*
- *The Seasons Change*
- *Seasons Come and Go*
- *What Animals Can You See?*

Life Science

Fiction Books
- *Bix the Dog*
- *Carlos Picks a Pet*
- *Cary and the Wildlife Shelter*
- *Mac Can Do It!*
- *Mack and Zack*
- *Plans Change*
- *Sam*
- *The Sick Pets*
- *Time for Dinner*
- *What Brown Saw*
- *Which Animals Will We See?*
- *Which Fox?*

Physical Science

Nonfiction Books
- *The Inclined Plane*
- *Simple Machines at Work*
- *Simple Machines in Compound Machines*

Grade 1 Leveled Readers

Social Studies

Citizenship

Nonfiction Books

- A Class
- A Garden for All
- Great Scientists: Detectives at Work
- Here in My Neighborhood
- A New Library
- Puppy Raiser
- The Story of the Kids Care Club
- Ways to be a Good Citizen

Fiction Books

- The Art Show
- At Your Vet
- Big Wishes and Her Baby
- Double Trouble Twins
- Fly Away Owl!
- Grasshopper and Ant
- Hank's Song
- Let's Build a Park!
- Look at My Neighborhood
- My Little Brother Drew
- On the Farm
- Paul's Bed
- A Play
- Rules at School
- Space Star
- Squirrel and Bear
- That Cat Needs Help!

Culture

Nonfiction Books

- Cascarones Are for Fun
- My Babysitter
- Special Days, Special Food
- We Are a Family
- What Makes Buildings Special?

Fiction Books

- Go West!
- Grandma's Farm
- Gus the Pup
- Jamie's Jumble of Junk
- A New Baby Brother
- A Party for Pedro
- A Visit to the Ranch
- Where They Live

History

Nonfiction Books

- School: Then and Now
- Treasures of Our Country

Fiction Books

- Loni's Town

Government

Nonfiction Books

- America's Home
- Our Leaders

Fiction Books

- Mom the Mayor

Matching Books & Readers

Grade K Leveled Readers

Science

Earth and Space Science

Fiction Books
- We Can Do It!

Life Science

Nonfiction Books
- A Winter Home
- What Can You Do?
- The Trip
- Pigs
- Frog's New Home
- A Small Trip
- Safe Places for Animals

Fiction Books
- A Walk in the Forest
- Looking for Animals
- Skip and Run
- Big Cats
- My Pal Fran
- Fun with Gram
- They Will Grow
- Sad and Glad

Physical Science

Fiction Books
- Catch the Ball!
- The Best Club Hut

Grade K Leveled Readers

Social Studies

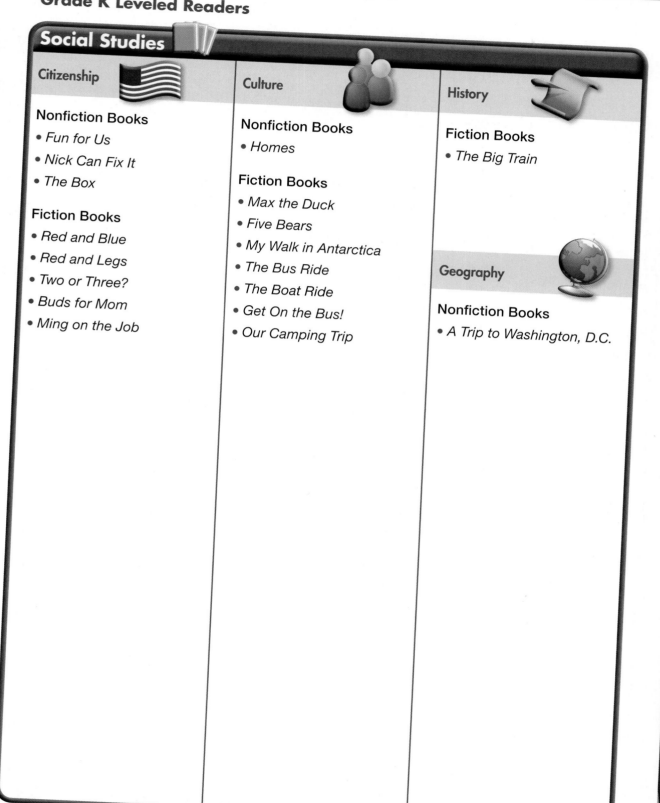

Citizenship

Nonfiction Books
- *Fun for Us*
- *Nick Can Fix It*
- *The Box*

Fiction Books
- *Red and Blue*
- *Red and Legs*
- *Two or Three?*
- *Buds for Mom*
- *Ming on the Job*

Culture

Nonfiction Books
- *Homes*

Fiction Books
- *Max the Duck*
- *Five Bears*
- *My Walk in Antarctica*
- *The Bus Ride*
- *The Boat Ride*
- *Get On the Bus!*
- *Our Camping Trip*

History

Fiction Books
- *The Big Train*

Geography

Nonfiction Books
- *A Trip to Washington, D.C.*

Grade 2 Leveled Readers

Science

Earth and Space Science

Nonfiction Books

- *All About Astronauts*
- *An Astronaut Spacewalk*
- *Desert Animals*
- *Deserts*
- *Look at Our Galaxy*

Fiction Books

- *Blizzard!*
- *Maggie's New Sidekick*
- *Rainbow Crow Brings Fire to Earth*
- *A Slice of Mud Pie*

Life Science

Nonfiction Books

- *Arachnid or Insect?*
- *Compost: Recycled Waste*
- *Farming Families*
- *How a Seed Grows*
- *How Can Animals Help?*
- *How Do Plants Grow?*
- *How to Grow Tomatoes*
- *Plants Grow Everywhere*
- *A Vet for All Animals*

Fiction Books

- *Annie Makes a Big Change*
- *Camping at Crescent Lake*
- *Growing Up*
- *Too Many Rabbit Holes*
- *Where is Fish?*

Physical Science

Nonfiction Books

- *Many Types of Energy*
- *Sink or Float?*

Fiction Books

- *The Hummingbird*
- *Our School Science Fair*

Grade 2 Leveled Readers

Social Studies

Citizenship

Nonfiction Books

- America's Birthday
- The Barn Raising
- Be Ready for an Emergency
- Everyone Can Make a Difference!
- Join an Adventure Club!
- Keeping Our Community Safe
- Protect the Earth
- Who Helps?
- Service Workers
- Special Animal Helpers
- Using a Net
- What Can You Do?
- Working Dogs

Fiction Books

- Andrew's Mistake
- Camping with Pup
- Freda the Signmaker
- Hubert and Frankie
- Let's Work Together!
- Marty's Summer Job
- Sally and the Wild Puppy
- Stripes and Silver
- Too Many Frogs!
- Training Peanut

Culture

Nonfiction Books

- Celebrations and Family Traditions
- Living in Seoul
- Showing Good Manners
- Special Chinese Birthdays
- A World of Birthdays

Fiction Books

- Ana Is Shy
- The Camping Trip
- Country Friends, City Friends
- Dotty's Art
- The First People to Fly
- Glooskap and the First Summer: An Algonquin Tale
- Happy New Year!
- The International Food Fair
- Just Like Grandpa
- Living on a Ranch
- The New Kid in Bali
- Voting Day

Economics

Nonfiction Books

- Services and Goods

Fiction Books

- Country Mouse and City Mouse
- A Quiet Place
- Snakeskin Canyon

History

Nonfiction Books

- A Few Nifty Inventions
- The Hoover Dam
- Living in a Democracy
- Making Travel Fun
- Saint Bernards and Other Working Dogs
- Starting a New Life
- Women Play Baseball

Fiction Books

- At Home in the Wilderness
- A Class Play
- A Cowboy's Life
- Down on the Ranch
- Hank's Tortilla Factory

Government

Nonfiction Books

- Communicating Then and Now
- Let's Send a Letter!

More Great Titles

Biography

- American Revolution Heroes
- Baseball Heroes Make History
- Thomas Adams: Chewing Gum Inventor
- Three Great Ballplayers

Planning Teacher Study Groups

Adventurous teachers often have good ideas for lessons. A Teacher Study Group is a great way to share ideas and get feedback on the best way to connect content and students. Working with other teachers can provide you with the support and motivation you need to implement new teaching strategies. A teacher study group offers many opportunities to collaborate, support each other's work, share insights, and get feedback.

Think About It

A weekly or monthly teacher study group can help support you in developing your expertise in the classroom. You and a group of like-minded teachers can form your own study group. What can this group accomplish?

- Read and discuss professional articles by researchers in the field of education.

- Meet to share teaching tips, collaborate on multi-grade lessons, and share resources.

- Develop lessons to try out new teaching strategies. Meet to share experiences and discuss how to further improve your teaching approach.

Let's Meet!

Forming a Study Group is easy. Just follow these four steps:

1. **Decide on the size of the group.** A small group has the advantage of making each member feel accountable, but make sure that all people can make the same commitment!

2. **Choose teachers to invite to join your group.** Think about whom you want to invite. Should they all teach the same grade? Can you invite teachers from other schools? Remember that the more diverse the group, the more it benefits from new perspectives.

3. **Set goals for the group.** In order to succeed, know what you want the group to do. Meet to set goals. Rank goals in order of importance and refer often to the goals to keep the group on track.

4. **Make logistical decisions.** This is often the most difficult. Decide where and when you will meet. Consider an online meeting place where group members can post discussion questions and replies if people are not able to meet.

What Will We Study?

Use the goals you set to help determine what your group will study. Consider what materials are needed to reach your goals, and how long you think you will need to prepare for each meeting.

How Will It Work?

Think about how you structure groups in your classroom. Then use some of the same strategies.

- **Assign a group facilitator.** This person is responsible for guiding the meeting. This person comes prepared with discussion questions and leads the meeting. This could be a rotating responsibility dependent on experience with various topics. This person might be responsible for providing the materials.

- **Assign a recorder.** Have someone take notes during the meeting and record group decisions.

- **Use the jigsaw method.** Not everyone has time to be a facilitator. In this case, divide the text and assign each portion to a different person. Each person is responsible for leading the discussion on that particular part.

Meet Again

Make a commitment to meet for a minimum number of times. After that, the group can reevaluate and decide whether or not to continue.

> " Have some great teaching tips to share? Want to exchange ideas with your colleagues? Build your own professional community of teachers. **The Customize Literacy Shop** gets you started. "

Building Community

Trial Lessons

Use your colleagues' experiences to help as you think about new ways to connect content and students. Use the following plan to create a mini-lesson. It should last twenty minutes. Get the support of your colleagues as you try something new and then reflect on what happened.

Be Creative! As you develop a plan for a mini-lesson, use these four words to guide planning: *purpose, text, resources,* and *routine.*

- **Purpose:** Decide on a skill or strategy to teach. Define your purpose for teaching the lesson.

- **Text:** Develop a list of the materials you could use. Ask your colleagues for suggestions.

- **Resources:** Make a list of the available resources, and consider how to use those resources most effectively. Consider using the Leveled Readers listed on pages 24–29 and 36–41 of the Customize Literacy Shop.

- **Routine:** Choose an instructional routine to structure your mini-lesson. See the mini-lessons in the Customize Literacy Shop for suggestions.

Try It! Try out your lesson! Consider audio- or videotaping the lesson for later review. You may wish to invite a colleague to sit in as you teach. Make notes on how the lesson went.

How Did It Go? Use the Self-Evaluation Checklist on page 45 as you reflect on your trial lesson. This provides a framework for later discussion.

Discuss, Reflect, Repeat Solicit feedback from your Teacher Study Group. Explain the lesson and share your reflections. Ask for suggestions on ways to improve the lesson. Take some time to reflect on the feedback. Modify your lesson to reflect what you have learned. Then try it again.

Checklist for Teacher Self-Evaluation

How Well Did I ...

	Very Well	Satisfactory	Not Very Well
Plan the lesson?			
Select the appropriate level of text?			
Introduce the lesson and explain its objectives?			
Review previously taught skills?			
Directly explain the new skills being taught?			
Model the new skills?			
Break the material down into small steps?			
Integrate guided practice into the lesson?			
Monitor guided practice for student understanding?			
Provide feedback on independent practice?			
Maintain an appropriate pace?			
Assess student understanding of the material?			
Stress the importance of applying the skill as they read?			
Maintain students' interest?			
Ask questions?			
Handle student questions and responses?			
Respond to the range of abilities?			

Building Community

Books for Teachers

Kids aren't the only ones who need to read to grow. Here is a brief list of books that you may find useful to fill your reading teacher basket and learn new things.

A Professional Bibliography

Adams, M. J. "Alphabetic Anxiety and Explicit, Systematic Phonics Instruction: A Cognitive Science Perspective." *Handbook of Early Literacy Research.* The Guilford Press, 2001.

Adams, M. J. *Beginning to Read: Thinking and Learning About Print.* The MIT Press, 1990.

Afflerbach, P. "The Influence of Prior Knowledge and Text Genre on Readers' Prediction Strategies." *Journal of Reading Behavior,* vol. XXII, no. 2 (1990).

Armbruster, B. B., F. Lehr, and J. Osborn. *Put Reading First: The Research Building Blocks for Teaching Children to Read.* Partnership for Reading, Washington, D.C., 2001.

Bear, D. R., M. Invernizzi, S. Templeton, and F. Johnston. *Words Their Way.* Merrill Prentice Hall, 2004.

Beck, I., M. G. McKeown, and L. Kucan. *Bringing Words to Life: Robust Vocabulary Instruction.* The Guilford Press, 2002.

Biemiller, A. "Teaching Vocabulary in the Primary Grades: Vocabulary Instruction Needed." *Vocabulary Instruction Research to Practice.* The Guilford Press, 2004.

Blachowicz, C. and P. Fisher. "Vocabulary Instruction." *Handbook of Reading Research,* vol. III. Lawrence Erlbaum Associates, 2000.

Cunningham, P. M. and J. W. Cummingham. "What We Know About How to Teach Phonics." *What Research Says About Reading Instruction,* 3rd ed. International Reading Association, 2002.

Daniels, H. *Literature Circles.* 2nd ed. Stenhouse Publishers, 2002.

Dickson, S. V., D. C. Simmons, and E. J. Kame'enui. "Text Organization: Instructional and Curricular Basics and Implications." *What Reading Research Tells Us About Children with Diverse Learning Needs: Bases and Basics.* Lawrence Erlbaum Associates, 1998.

Diller, D. *Making the Most of Small Groups: Differentiation for All.* Stenhouse Publishers, 2007.

Duke, N. K., V. S. Bennett-Armistead, and E. M. Roberts. "Bridging the Gap Between Learning to Read and Reading to Learn." *Literacy and Young Children: Research-Based Practices.* The Guilford Press, 2003.

Duke, N. K. and C. Tower. "Nonfiction Texts for Young Readers." *The Texts in Elementary Classrooms.* Lawrence Erlbaum Associates, 2004.

Ehri, L. C. and S. R. Nunes. "The Role of Phonemic Awareness in Learning to Read." *What Research Has to Say About Reading Instruction.* 3rd ed. International Reading Association, 2002.

Fountas, I. C. and G. S. Pinnell. *Guided Reading: Good First Teaching for All Children.* Heinemann, 1996.

Fountas, I. C. and G. S. Pinnell. *Matching Books to Readers: Using Leveled Books in Guided Reading,* K-3. Heinemann, 1999.

Harvey, S. and A. Goudvis. *Strategies That Work: Teaching Comprehension to Enhance Understanding.* 2nd ed. Stenhouse Publishers, 2007.

Hiebert, E. H. and L. A. Martin. "The Texts of Beginning Reading Instruction." *Handbook of Early Literacy Research.* The Guilford Press, 2001.

Indrisano, R. and J. R. Paratore. *Learning to Write, Writing to Learn. Theory and Research in Practice.* International Reading Association, 2005.

Juel, C., G. Biancarosa, D. Coker, and R. Deffes. "Walking with Rosie: A Cautionary Tale of Early Reading Instruction." *Educational Leadership* (April 2003).

National Reading Panel. *Teaching Children to Read.* National Institute of Child Health and Human Development, 1999.

Pressley, M. *Reading Instruction That Works: The Case for Balanced Teaching,* 3rd ed. The Guilford Press, 2005.

Smith, S., D. C. Simmons, and E. J. Kame'enui. "Word Recognition: Research Bases." *What Reading Research Tells Us About Children with Diverse Learning Needs: Bases and Basics.* Lawrence Erlbaum Associates, 1998.

Snow, C., S, Burns, and P. Griffin, eds. *Preventing Reading Difficulties in Young Children.* National Academy Press, 1998.

Vaughn, S., P. G. Mathes, S. Linan-Thompson, and D. J. Francis. "Teaching English Language Learners at Risk for Reading Disabilities to Read: Putting Research into Practice." *Learning Disabilities Research & Practice,* vol. 20, issue 1 (February 2006).

Building Community

The Big Top

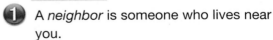
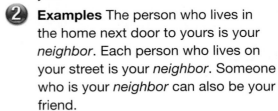
Amazing Words Routine Oral Vocabulary

DAY 1

introduce

1. To *introduce* means "to tell someone your name or someone else's name."

2. **Examples** Please *introduce* me to your brother. I will *introduce* myself to the new family that moved in next door. The teacher will *introduce* the guest speaker to the class.

3. **Apply to the instruction** Tell something you might say to *introduce* yourself to someone.

neighbor

1. A *neighbor* is someone who lives near you.

2. **Examples** The person who lives in the home next door to yours is your *neighbor*. Each person who lives on your street is your *neighbor*. Someone who is your *neighbor* can also be your friend.

3. **Apply to the instruction** What is something a good *neighbor* might do?

DAY 2

trouble

1. *Trouble* means "problems."

2. **Examples** The boy got into *trouble* for fighting with his brother. Mom was late because she had *trouble* starting the car. He stood on a ladder because he had *trouble* reaching the top shelf.

3. **Apply to the instruction** What is something you would *not* do because it would get you into *trouble?*

DAY 4

squirrel

1. A *squirrel* is a small animal with a bushy tail.

2. **Examples** A *squirrel* is an animal with red or gray fur. A *squirrel* likes to eat nuts. A *squirrel* usually lives in a tree.

3. **Apply to the instruction** Would you see a *squirrel* indoors or outdoors?

School Day

Amazing Words Routine Oral Vocabulary

DAY 1

classmate

1. A *classmate* is someone who is in your class at school.

2. **Examples** You and your *classmate* have the same teacher. Jill was not at school today, so she phoned a *classmate* to get the homework assignment. Someone who is in a different class is not your *classmate*.

3. **Apply to the instruction** Name a *classmate* who is sitting close to you.

education

1. The things you learn in school are part of your *education*.

2. **Examples** You go to school to get an *education*. Public schools provide an *education* for everyone. Someone with an *education* knows how to read, write, and speak well.

3. **Apply to the instruction** Listen to the things I name. Tell which are things you can do to help you get a good *education*: go to school everyday; sleep in class; pay attention to your teacher; do your homework.

DAY 2

recess

1. *Recess* is a short time during which classroom work stops.

2. **Examples** Our school has *recess* after lunch. In good weather, we play outside during *recess*. On rainy days, we play board games indoors during *recess*.

3. **Apply to the instruction** Tell me something you like to do during *recess*

DAY 4

applaud

1. When you *applaud*, you clap your hands to show you like something.

2. **Examples** At the end of the concert, people *applauded* to show they enjoyed it. The actors were happy to hear the audience *applaud* at the end of the play. We began to cheer and *applaud* when the batter hit a home run.

3. **Apply to the instruction** If you were performing in a show, why would you want the audience to *applaud*?

success

1. *Success* means "a good ending you planned for."

2. **Examples** The bake sale was a *success* because we sold all the baked goods. *Success* in school will come if you work hard. After many tries, I finally had *success* in learning to whistle.

3. **Apply to the instruction** Tell about something you have had *success* with. Use the word *success* when you tell about it.

The Farmers Market

Let's Learn
Amazing Words

Definitions, examples, and **applications** to use with the Oral Vocabulary in each lesson.

Amazing Words   Routine Oral Vocabulary

DAY 1

bargain

1. A *bargain* is something bought or offered for sale at a much lower price.

2. **Examples** You can usually get a *bargain* at a garage sale where things are sold for low prices. This shirt is a *bargain*; it costs only five dollars. Those books were a *bargain* because the store lowered its prices.

3. **Apply to the instruction** Stores lower the prices of some items when they run a sale. Explain why you are more likely to get a *bargain* if you shop on a sale day.

browse

1. *Browse* means "to look or read here and there."

2. **Examples** If you *browse*, you do not look carefully. If you *browse* through a book, you flip through it and read bits and pieces. If you *browse* through a store, you can get an idea of what is sold there.

3. **Apply to the instruction** Demonstrate how you would *browse* through a book and tell something you would learn about the book by doing so.

DAY 4

cost

1. The price you pay for something is the *cost*.

2. **Examples** If you pay one dollar for something, its *cost* is one dollar. If the store sells a CD for ten dollars, the *cost* of the CD is ten dollars. The bag of apples we bought at the farmers market *cost* less than two dollars.

3. **Apply to the instruction** Do you think it is a good idea to know the *cost* of something before you buy it? Explain your answer.

scale

1. A *scale* is a device used for weighing.

2. **Examples** You can weigh vegetables on a *scale*. You can weigh yourself on a *scale*. A *scale* can tell you how heavy or light something is.

3. **Apply to the instruction** Name some places in your neighborhood where you might see a *scale*.

T R

Acknowledgments

Teacher's Edition

Text

KWL Strategy: The KWL Interactive Reading Strategy was developed and is used by permission of Donna Ogle, National-Louis University, Skokie, Illinois, co-author of *Reading Today and Tomorrow,* Holt, Rinehart & Winston Publishers, 1988. (See also the *Reading Teacher,* February 1986, pp. 564–570.)

Understanding by Design quotes: Wiggins, G. & McTighe, J. (2005). *Understanding by Design.* Alexandria, VA: Association for Supervision and Curriculum Development.

Illustrations

Cover Daniel Moreton

Running Header Steven Mach

Photographs

Every effort has been made to secure permission and provide appropriate credit for photographic material. The publisher deeply regrets any omission and pledges to correct errors called to its attention in subsequent editions.

Unless otherwise acknowledged, all photographs are the property of Pearson Education, Inc.

Student Edition

Student Edition p. 176

Teacher Notes

UNIT R

Teacher Notes

Teacher Notes

Teacher Notes

Teacher Notes

Teacher Notes

Teacher Notes

Teacher Notes

Teacher Resources

Looking for Teacher Resources and other important information?

In the **First Stop**
on Reading Street

- **Dear First Grade Teacher**

- **Research into Practice**

- **Guide to Reading Street**

- **Assessment on Reading Street**

- **Customize Writing on Reading Street**

- **Differentiated Instruction on Reading Street**

- **ELL on Reading Street**

- **Customize Literacy on Reading Street**

- **Digital Products on Reading Street**

- **Teacher Resources for Grade 1**

- **Index**

Teacher Resources

Looking for Teacher Resources and other important information?

In the **First Stop**
on Reading Street